General Sir John Burnett-Stuart, G.C.B., K.B.E., C.M.G., D.S.O. (Courtesy of the Burnett-Stuart family.)

TO CHANGE AN ARMY

GENERAL SIR JOHN BURNETT-STUART AND BRITISH ARMORED DOCTRINE, 1927–1938

Harold R. Winton

Foreword by Peter Paret

UNIVERSITY PRESS OF KANSAS

Modern War Studies

Raymond A. Callahan
Jacob W. Kipp
Jay Luvaas
Theodore A. Wilson
Series Editors

© 1988 by the University Press of Kansas

Published by the University Press of Kansas (Lawrence, Kansas 66045), which was organized by the Kansas Board of Regents and is operated and funded by Emporia State University, Fort Hays State University, Kansas State University, Pittsburg State University, the University of Kansas, and Wichita State University

Library of Congress Cataloging-in-Publication Data

Winton, Harold R., 1942–
    To change an army.
    (Modern war studies)
    Bibliography: p.
    Includes index.
    1. Burnett-Stuart, John, Sir. 2. Military art and
science–Great Britain–History–20th century.
3. Tank warfare–History. I. Title. II. Series.
U43.G7W56 1988   358′.18′0924   87-25579
ISBN 0-7006-0356-5

British Library Cataloguing in Publication Data is available.

Printed in the United States of America
10 9 8 7 6 5 4 3 2 1

The paper used in this publication meets the minimum requirements of the American National Standard for Permanence of Paper for Printed Library Materials 239.48–1984.

For Barbara

We all know that our present old-fashioned divisions are suicide clubs; but it is not merely a question of reorganising them, but of remodeling the whole military machine and its responsibilities in peace so as to admit of the creation of modern war formations. We are bound to the wheel, and there is no free-wheel attachment to our wheel!

—John Burnett-Stuart to
B. H. Liddell Hart,
20 September 1932

Still it is the task of military science in an age of peace to prevent the doctrines from being too badly wrong.

—Michael Howard,
Chesney Memorial Gold Medal Lecture,
3 October 1973

FOREWORD

The strategy and operations of any war can be understood only in the light of conditions of the ten or twenty years before its beginning. Technology, organization, doctrine, training, command and staff appointments – all the essentials of action in war – are put in place and developed in peacetime. The testing experience of combat will bring about change, but prewar elements continue to affect many events throughout even the longest of conflicts. To mention three examples from just one of the belligerents in the Second World War: How can we make sense of German operations, and thus of the war as a whole, without a clear appreciation of Hitler's long-standing intentions toward Soviet Russia, the development of operational doctrine in the Reichswehr in Weimar Germany, and aircraft design and production in the 1930s?

Though obvious, the need to study the antecedents of war is inadequately reflected in the literature. Despite important exceptions, military history in general tends to be a history of wars. Even minor operations in marginal theaters are extensively and repetitively discussed, while long periods of preparation – sometimes of decisive importance and always profoundly influential – are treated far less thoroughly. In part, this imbalance is caused by the reading public's appetite, evidently shared by many writers, for the violent, which seems more interesting and certainly more dramatic than analyses of such matters as field exercises, the development of doctrine, and the intricacies of service politics. A further reason has to do with the belief, common among those who take a utilitarian view of military history, that the qualities of leadership are most clearly brought out in combat and therefore are best conveyed in accounts of combat. That this is not necessarily the case is indicated by the example of George Marshall. Finally, from the point of view of scholarship, methodological difficulties seem to justify the imbalance. Studies of military policy between wars usually require an interdisciplinary approach. Institutional and technological change, biography, politics – all these and more are involved, and they place unusually heavy demands on the range of the scholar's research and on the breadth of his interpretations.

Harold Winton has overcome these challenges, and the result is a valuable contribution to our understanding of the British Army in the interwar years and, by implication, of the Second World War. Burnett-Stuart's career, from his beginnings in 1895 as a second lieutenant in the Rifle Brigade to his retirement as a senior general in 1938, was one of exceptional interest, even if the very highest positions in the service eluded him. In 1926, after tours of duty in India, South Africa, Egypt, and on the Western Front and four years as Director of Military Operations and Intelligence in the War Office, he was put in command of the 3rd Division, an appointment that included responsibility for the Experimental Mechanized Force. From this vantage point, and in subsequent senior commands, he recognized the need for substantial innovation in the army's equipment, organization, and training; but he also understood the institutional, financial, and social realities within which modernization had to proceed. His later career therefore affords an unusually broad perspective—neither that of the radical reformer nor that of the defender of the status quo—on the difficult development of mechanization and armored warfare in the army and on the course of British military policy in general.

The author has succeeded in discovering much new information, without which a realistic, objective interpretation of Burnett-Stuart and the British Army in the interwar period would not have been possible. But his respect for the documented facts of his topic is coupled with a more general theoretical outlook, and it is this which gives his work an additional, special interest. He has written not only an enlightening analytic account of one individual and of the unique elements of his specific historical situation, but also a case study of a timeless problem of great contemporary as well as scholarly significance: How does a military organization, without losing cohesion and effectiveness, change to meet the constantly recurring challenges of the new?

Peter Paret
The Institute for Advanced Study
Princeton

CONTENTS

ILLUSTRATIONS

PREFACE

The seed for this study was sown when, as a cadet at West Point, I read the first volume of Basil Liddell Hart's book *The Tanks*. I was amazed that the concept of armored warfare, first articulated in Britain, was never fully accepted by the British Army between the world wars, and I wanted to find out why. As a graduate student at Stanford University, I thought it would be useful to make a detailed examination of the evolution of Liddell Hart's theories, with an emphasis on how they had been influenced by his experience in the Great War. My adviser, Peter Paret, pointed out that a great deal of work had already been done in the area and wisely steered me away from this approach. He suggested, however, that if I were still interested in the general subject that I should keep reading and that perhaps someone would emerge who would be worthy of further study.

As I read over a number of memoirs and other accounts of the period, the name of General Sir John Burnett-Stuart seemed to be mentioned fairly often. There was, however, little about him—a sentence here, a paragraph there, but never a comprehensive statement of what he had done or not done. I also noticed that he was something of an enigma. In some circles he was regarded as an inhibiting conservative, and in others as a dangerous revolutionary. The more I learned about him, the more fascinated I became, for it gradually became apparent that he was one of the few senior officers in the British Army between the wars who clearly foresaw the future and recognized the potential of armored warfare. At the same time it was obvious that he understood the practical limitations of British military reform and was never completely identified with the young tank advocates.

As a young officer recently returned from my second combat tour in Vietnam, I was also intrigued by how armies adapt themselves in peacetime to the demands of an uncertain future. I was convinced that my own army had not adapted itself well to the demands of fighting simultaneously a conventional war against North Vietnamese regulars and an unconventional war against South Vietnamese Communist irregulars. As a result of my original interest in the interwar British Army, my newly found fascination with Burnett-Stuart, and my desire to fathom the dynamics of the military reform process, three questions emerged that form the basis of this study. First, how did the concepts and organizations to conduct mechanized and armored warfare emerge in the British Army between the wars, and why did they develop as they did? Second, what was John Burnett-Stuart's role in this process? And finally, how does this particular case illuminate the general problem of peace-time military reform?

Many people and institutions have helped me to answer these questions. Anyone who is familiar with Peter Paret's work will immediately recognize my intellectual debt to him. His insights into the complexities of military reform in the modern state have been a constant source of enlightenment. Peter Stansky's intimate familiarity with modern Britain and his felicitous use of the English language have rescued me from many gaffes. Gordon Craig provided encouragement and sound advice in the formative stages of this project, and Michael Howard reviewed several of the early chapters. I. B. Holley of Duke University provided detailed comments on major portions of the initial draft, as did Col. A. T. P. Millen, formerly British liaison officer at the Command and General Staff College. Brian Bond has encouraged me in the labor of bringing this study to print, as has Brian Holden Reid, former editor of the R.U.S.I. journal.

The Center for Research in International Studies and the Weter Fund Committee of Stanford University provided generous financial support. Much assistance in the location of materials has been received from gracious men and women on the staffs of the Stanford Library; the Hoover Institution of War, Revolution, and Peace; the Command and General Staff College Library; the United States Military Academy Library; the Royal United Services Institute for Defence Studies; the Ministry of Defence Library (central and army); the Staff College Library; the Royal Armoured Corps Museum; the Liddell Hart Centre for Military Archives, King's College, University of London; and the Public Records Office. Particular thanks go to the Liddell Hart Centre for Military Archives, the Tank Museum, and the Burnett-Stuart family for providing illustrations.

Many retired British officers contributed their observations on Burnett-Stuart and the British Army between the wars in interviews and personal correspondence. A full list is contained in the bibliography. I would especially like to thank J. G. S. Burnett-Stuart for access to General Burnett-Stuart's papers, and Lady Kathleen Liddell Hart for access to Sir Basil Liddell Hart's papers—both collections were of inestimable value. General Donn A. Starry, U.S. Army, Retired, graciously allowed me to use "To Change an Army," the title of his 1983 *Military Review* article, as the title of this volume. The relationship between the book and the article is particularly appropriate because in many ways Starry is the Burnett-Stuart of the post-Vietnam American Army. A special debt of gratitude is owed to Brig. Gen. Thomas E. Griess, U.S. Army, Retired, formerly professor and head of the United States Military Academy Department of History, without whose support I would never have begun this study.

Above all I must thank the members of my family. My four sons have borne for too long the trials of having a constantly preoccupied and frequently unavailable father. And my wife, Barbara, has not only labored over successive drafts of the manuscript, including the final copy, she has also been a constant source of love and encouragement and has provided the necessary goads to continue working when I needed them the most.

Harold R. Winton
Fort Leavenworth, Kansas

ABBREVIATIONS

D.S.D.	director of staff duties
E.M.F.	Experimental Mechanised Force
F.S.R.	*Field Service Regulations*
G.H.Q.	General Headquarters
G.O.C.	general officer commanding
G.O.C.-in-C.	general officer commanding-in-chief
GSO1	general staff officer, 1st grade
GSO2	general staff officer, 2nd grade
GSO3	general staff officer, 3rd grade
M.G.A.	major general, administration
M.G.O.	master general of the ordnance
N.C.O.	noncommissioned officer
P.U.S.	permanent under-secretary
Q.M.G.	quartermaster general
R.A.C.	Royal Armoured Corps
R.A.F.	Royal Air Force
R.A.O.C.	Royal Army Ordnance Corps
R.A.S.C.	Royal Army Service Corps
R.T.C.	Royal Tank Corps
R.U.S.I.	Royal United Service Institution (from June 1971, Royal United Services Institute for Defence Studies)

1

INTRODUCTION

In the opening campaigns of World War II, the German Army decisively defeated the Polish, British, and French armies, each in a matter of weeks. A large portion of its success is attributable to the effective employment of a new tactical and operational doctrine, commonly referred to as *blitzkrieg*. This doctrine featured the combined use of tanks, motorized infantry, aircraft, and other supporting arms to burst through the enemy's defensive positions and to penetrate deeply into his rear areas, disrupting his command facilities and severing his lines of supply. The rapidity of these advances and the havoc they generated in the rear echelons disarticulated the defensive efforts of the opposing forces and brought about their swift collapse.[1] It is perhaps one of the greatest ironies of military history in the twentieth century that many of the basic ideas for blitzkrieg were conceived not in Germany, but in Britain, as expressed in the public writings of, among others, J. F. C. Fuller and B. H. Liddell Hart. This fact has led a number of historians to wonder why the British Army, whose members first presented concepts of blitzkrieg, or armored warfare, failed to adopt them during the interwar years.

There have been a number of answers to that question. The first, expressed most forcefully by Fuller and Liddell Hart themselves, is that the British Army was simply too wedded to old concepts and organizations and was unwilling to make the dramatic changes necessary to adapt to the new technology of war.[2] The second, held by many British soldiers as well as some recent historians, is that the army never had the money or the popular support to make significant changes in its doctrine and organization. According to this line of thought, the army was reasonably progressive between the wars, but its modernization was impeded by an indifferent Cabinet, a parsimonious Treasury, and a pacifistic electorate.[3] Another interpretation, first enunciated by Michael Howard and D. C. Watt and later convincingly documented by Brian Bond, suggests that the lack of a clear commitment to send ground forces to the Continent in the event of a future war as well as the army's responsibility for garrisoning the Empire were major factors in its not embracing the concepts of armored warfare.[4] Shelford Bidwell and Dominick Graham point the finger back at the army, criticizing not its conservatism per se, but its failure to be serious about its professional responsibilities to develop doctrine.[5]

1

In an interesting and extremely well-researched study, Robert Larson argues that none of the above was the operative reason for the British Army's rejection of armored warfare – rather it was the army's intellectual attachment to a strategy of attrition that proved the fundamental inhibitor.[6] This line of thought makes a great deal of sense, but upon examination one finds that it is, in essence, a return to the arguments of Fuller and Liddell Hart that military conservatism in the form of being wedded to old ideas was the sticking point.[7] The debate seems to have come full circle, and it is clearly the time for synthesis. Such is the primary purpose of this study – to examine the evolution of mechanization and armored warfare in the British Army between World War I and World War II to determine how they developed and why they developed as they did.

A great deal of confusion existed at the time – and some of it still persists – over the meaning of the terms *mechanization* and *armored warfare*. In the broadest sense mechanization, or "mechanicalization" as it was referred to in the early 1920s, meant the application of the gasoline engine to all forms of land warfare. To the engineers, for example, it meant gasoline-operated tools as well as gasoline-operated vehicles. For the purposes of this study, however, mechanization refers to the replacement of horses by motor vehicles as a means of locomotion. This process took place in three functional areas – the transportation of men and weapons on the battlefield, the transportation of men and weapons to the battlefield, and the transportation of supplies. In other words, it influenced tactics, operations, and logistics.[8]

Armored warfare meant the concept of employing vehicles that were not only moved by the power of gasoline engines but were also protected from the effects of weapons by some degree of armor plating. The protection inherent in armored vehicles, as well as their capability to carry large-caliber weapons themselves, meant that armored warfare would also influence tactics, operations, and logistics, but in a way that was potentially different from mere mechanization. Indeed it was the potential of transforming the tank with its associated supporting forces from a purely tactical instrument to conduct a "break-in," as it had been used in World War I, into an operational instrument that could be used to conduct a "breakthrough" and subsequent exploitation that formed in many respects the key conceptual (as opposed to mechanical) difference between mechanization and armored warfare. As was pointed out earlier, however, these distinctions were not always clear at the time, and the terms were often used interchangeably.

The development of mechanization and armored warfare in the British Army will be traced from the early writings of Fuller, Liddell Hart, and others to the trials of the Experimental Mechanised Force, later named the Experimental Armoured Force, on Salisbury Plain in 1927 and 1928; the publication of *Mechanised and Armoured Formations*, the first manual on armored warfare in 1929; the evolution of the Tank Brigade from 1931 to 1934; and the development of the Mobile Division, which eventually became the 1st Armoured Division, from 1934 to 1938. The development of tactical doctrine in the rest of the army will also be considered, as appropriate, since the evolution of armored warfare cannot be understood apart from concurrent developments in the infantry, artillery, and cavalry, as well as in the fields of supply and communications. The reform of tactical doctrine was influenced to some extent by many other practices, such as the organization for policymaking and the systems of promotion and education of officers. Efforts made to reform these areas will also be examined.

The responsibility for garrisoning the Empire, limited financial resources, and uncertainty about the strategic and technological future made developing a new doctrine extremely difficult. But doctrinal developments were influenced not only by objective factors. Individual temperaments, values, and perceptions of reality varied widely. These differences brought about a variety of responses to the problems of the day, a variety complicated by the fact that those who agreed in one area often disagreed in another. The interaction of personalities therefore played a significant, and at times decisive, role in the evolution of armored doctrine; the relationships among a variety of men, both in and out of the official policymaking apparatus, will also be studied.

A second purpose of this study will be to assess the role played in the evolution of British mechanized and armored doctrine by one person in particular—General Sir John T. Burnett-Stuart. From 1927 to 1928, as General Officer Commanding, 3d Division, Burnett-Stuart directed and assessed the trials of the Experimental Mechanised Force. From 1931 to early 1934, as General Officer Commanding, British Troops in Egypt, he conceived and supervised Britain's first large-scale mechanized operations in the desert. From mid-1934 to 1938, as General Officer Commanding-in-Chief, Southern Command, he was responsible for formulating the doctrine for the emerging Mobile Division.

In spite of his occupying these positions of responsibility, Burnett-Stuart's role has remained relatively obscure. He was not one of the original proponents of armored warfare, nor was he one of the young tank corps officers often identified with spreading the new gospel. Therefore, his work has received little notice in writings of the time or since. And because he never reached the highest position in the army, his impact, though strong in his own commands, was not as widespread as it might have been. His obscurity was also a function of his independence. Burnett-Stuart's program of doctrinal reform was based on his own estimate of what would best meet the diverse demands of the interwar army. His ideas usually differed from those of the military conservatives as well as those of the more exuberant tank enthusiasts, and he candidly pointed out the deficiencies he saw in both.

The debate over armored doctrine created intense demands for loyalty. The opponents of reform knew Burnett-Stuart was not in their camp, but the reformers themselves were never sure if he was in theirs either. Their uncertainty was manifested in Liddell Hart's reference to Burnett-Stuart as a man of "long if variable vision."[9] It was also evident in a statement by Lt. Gen. Sir Charles Broad, primary author of *Mechanised and Armoured Formations* and commander of the 1st Brigade, Royal Tank Corps, that "Burnett-Stuart was a curious character. Very puckish—I never knew if he was pro or anti!"[10] Yet it is Burnett-Stuart's independent outlook, as well as his ability to sense how the new technology would alter the conduct of land warfare and his positive accomplishments in positions of responsibility, that makes an analysis of his role so worthwhile. This analysis will consider the kind of man Burnett-Stuart was, the development of his attitudes toward mechanization and armored warfare, the actions he took to bring about doctrinal reform, and the results of these actions.

A third purpose of this study is to examine the dynamics of military reform. The objective here is to gain insight into how the reform process takes place, what factors affect the process, and how these factors operate both individually and collectively to promote or inhibit effective change in military institutions. The significance of this subject in an era of shifting national priorities, galloping technological change, rapidly diversifying threats, and fluctuating resource levels is evident in the body of literature that has sprung up in the past two decades. Drawing on the experience of Prussian military reforms in the Napoleonic era, Peter Paret pointed out the vital significance of military men being attuned to the technological and social dimensions of change as well as the controlled use of violence for the purposes of the state in developing new doctrines and employing them in war.[11] In his seminal lecture "Military Science in an Age of Peace," Michael Howard not only highlighted the fundamental intellectual challenges of military reform, he also illuminated the dynamic relationship among technological feasibility, financial capability, and operational requirements as operative forces in the process.[12]

As the U.S. Army was groping for some doctrinal verities in the wake of its extrication from a debilitating war in Indochina, I. B. Holley suggested a three-phase process of assembling objective information, formulating doctrinal generalizations, and disseminating the doctrine to the field.[13] A similar emphasis on process is contained in Timothy Lupfer's brilliant study of the evolution of German tactical doctrine during the First World War. Lupfer found that significant changes to both offensive and defensive methods were developed through a nine-step process of perception of a need for change; solicitation of ideas, especially from battlefield units; definition of the change; dissemination of the change; enforcement throughout the army; modification of organization and equipment to accommodate the change; thorough training; evaluation of effectiveness; and refinement.[14]

Recent contributions to the literature have also been made by two men who were responsible for the latest evolution in U.S. Army doctrine, known as AirLand Battle. Drawing mainly on the German experience of the interwar years, Donn Starry has identified seven generalized requirements for effecting change. These include an institution or mechanism to identify the need for change, a rigorous educational background for staff officers and commanders that produces a common cultural bias, a spokesman for change, the building of consensus, continuity among the architects of change, support at or near the top, and the conduct of field trials to test the validity of proposed changes.[15] Synthesizing a wide variety of historical experience, Huba Wass de Czege contends that the essence of successful military reform comes from developing a harmony among the three elements of soldiers, ideas, and weapons.[16]

Each of the above formulations looks at military reform, particularly doctrinal reform, from a slightly different perspective and with a slightly different emphasis on the stages of the reform process or the factors that influence the process. It is clear, however, that the process is extremely complex and highly interactive with the internal structure of the military institution and the external environment in which it takes place. Examination of the British Army's experience between the wars and Burnett-Stuart's role in that process certainly reinforces this notion. To set the stage for this examination, it will be helpful to survey the dynamics of change affecting the British Army in the half century from the Cardwell reforms of the 1870s to the first major War Office exercise utilizing mechanized formations in 1925.

NOTES

1. The most definitive explanation of blitzkrieg as well as an informed commentary on methods of defense against it remains F. O. Miksche, *Attack: A Study of Blitzkrieg Tactics* (New York, 1942). See also Larry Addington, *The Blitzkrieg Era and the German General Staff, 1865–1941* (New Brunswick, N.J., 1971), and Kenneth Macksey, *Guderian: Creator of the Blitzkrieg* (New York, 1976).

2. This argument is stated most clearly in J. F. C. Fuller, *Memoirs of an Unconventional Soldier* (London, 1936), and B. H. Liddell Hart, *The Tanks: The History of the Royal Tank Regiment and Its Predecessors Heavy Branch Machine-Gun Corps, Tank Corps and Royal Tank Corps, 1914–1945*, 2 vols. (New York, 1959).

3. None of the senior officers of the interwar years published memoirs, but this position is maintained in an unpublished memoir written by Field Marshal Lord Cavan, chief of the Imperial General Staff from 1922 to 1926, located in the Cavan papers at Churchill College, Cambridge. It is also maintained in an unpublished memoir entitled "The Autobiography of a Gunner," written by Field Marshal Archibald Montgomery-Massingberd, C.I.G.S. from 1933 to 1936, located in his papers at the LHCMA. Robin Higham also shares the view that pacifistic tendencies were largely responsible for Britain's lack of preparation for the Second World War, though he also blames the conservatism of the senior officers. See his introduction to *Armed Forces in Peacetime: Britain, 1918–1940, A Case Study* (London, 1962), p. xi.

4. Michael Howard, *The Continental Commitment: The Dilemma of British Defence Policy in the Era of the Two World Wars* (London, 1972), pp. 74–120; D. C. Watt,

Too Serious a Business: European Armed Forces and the Approach to the Second World War (Berkeley, Calif., 1975), pp. 59–84; Brian Bond, *British Military Policy between the Two World Wars* (Oxford, 1980), pp. 127–190.

5. Shelford Bidwell and Dominick Graham, *Fire-power: British Army Weapons and Theories of War, 1904–1945* (London, 1982), p. 150.

6. Robert H. Larson, *The British Army and the Theory of Armored Warfare, 1918–1940* (Newark, N.J., 1984), pp. 38, 104.

7. Larson's argument against military conservatism as the fundamental factor in the rejection of armored warfare is based on equating such conservatism with the army's attachment to the horse. Looking on it in this sense, which is actually more akin to social conservatism, he is able to demonstrate that social conservatism gradually gave way to military reality. Ibid., pp. 16–32. By arguing that the leaders of the interwar army were wedded to a strategy of attrition, Larson is essentially resurrecting the Fuller–Liddell Hart thesis.

8. For purposes of simplicity, tactics may be defined as the employment of forces on the battlefield, operations as the maneuver and support of large formations in the conduct of campaigns, and logistics as the sustainment of forces.

9. B. H. Liddell Hart, "Burnett-Stuart, Sir John Theodosius," *DNB*, 1951–1960, p. 161.

10. Lt. Gen. Sir Charles Broad to author, 15 July 1972.

11. Peter Paret, *Innovation and Reform in Warfare: The Harmon Memorial Lectures in Military History*, no. 8 (United States Air Force Academy, Colo., 1966).

12. Michael Howard, "Military Science in an Age of Peace," *JRUSI* 119 (March 1974): 3–9.

13. I. B. Holley, Jr., "The Doctrinal Process: Some Suggested Steps," *Military Review* 59 (April 1979): 2–13.

14. Timothy T. Lupfer, *The Dynamics of Doctrine: The Changes in German Tactical Doctrine during the First World War* (Fort Leavenworth, Kans., 1981), p. viii.

15. Donn A. Starry, "To Change an Army," *Military Review* 63 (March 1983): 23.

16. Huba Wass de Czege, "Preparing for War: Defining the Problem" (Fort Leavenworth, Kans., 1984).

2

PROLOGUE:
BRITISH MILITARY REFORM,
CIRCA 1870–1925

The size of the Regular Army is regulated by a system which demands an approximate equilibrium between the number of units maintained overseas and the number maintained at home. The Expeditionary Force is a by-product of this system. . . . Neither the size of the Regular Army nor that of the Expeditionary Force has any relation to the size of foreign armies. . . . the strength of the Regular Army cannot be calculated by the requirements of foreign policy, and, for purposes of a continental war, cannot be more than a pledge of our readiness to fulfil our guarantees.

—Chiefs of Staff Review of
Imperial Defence, 1926[1]

The reform of military doctrine in peacetime is never an easy task. This is true for several reasons. First, military institutions have, for good and sufficient reasons, an authoritative value system that places a high premium on obedience, even when such obedience could conceivably result in the loss of one's life. The military reformer, however, must be able to think objectively about the future, often with inadequate data upon which to base his calculations. And this objective thought frequently involves the critical examination of accepted practices in a way that calls into question the authority of those who have established them. Furthermore, projections as to what is most likely to happen in the future are always based on conjecture. Thus the reformer is not only placed in the unenviable position of frequently having to defy higher authority, he is also forced to conduct his arguments in an intellectual milieu in which all his assertions are open to challenge and difficult to verify.[2]

While these difficulties are almost universal, British military reform, both institutional and doctrinal, has been marked by a number of unique characteristics based on Britain's geographic position and social development. The peculiarities of British military reform are evident when one examines the era from roughly the Franco-Prussian War of 1870–1871 to the Great War; the early writings of J. F. C. Fuller, B. H. Liddell Hart, and others who advocated fundamental reform of the army's doctrine and organization; and the army's response to their writings in light of the particular conditions of post-war Britain.

I

Although its proximity to the European land mass has required Britain occasionally to send forces to the Continent in support of allies opposing a potentially hegemonic power, the surrounding seas have obviated the requirement for a large standing army. Therefore, the British came to regard such an army as a threat to individual liberty. As a result, military organization developed much more slowly than civil institutions. By the end of the seventeenth century, Parliament was able to define most aspects of political life, yet military administration was supervised by a loose coalition of personal advisers to the crown much as it had been for centuries. Some change took place in the eighteenth century, but during the Napoleonic wars the British Army was still administered by a confused jumble of overlapping offices including those of the Board of Ordnance, the commander-in-chief, the secretary-at-war, and the secretary of state for war and the colonies. Under the pressure of the Crimean War, the last mentioned official became simply the secretary of state for war and was made responsible to Parliament for all army administration and policy, though it was not until 1870 that he was granted control over the commander-in-chief.[3] Nevertheless, the incumbent commander-in-chief, the Duke of Cambridge, continued to exercise a restraining influence on reforming tendencies until his retirement in 1895, and the post was not abolished until the formation of the Army Council under the Esher reforms of 1904.[4] This diffuse administration, coupled with a relatively low level of public spending, ensured that the army would not be a threat to civil liberty. But it also impeded the army's adaptation to a changing environment.

The sea has not only been a barrier against Britain's enemies but also the avenue to a vast empire. This avenue stopped, however, at the opposite shore, and the acquisition, consolidation, and defense of the Empire depended as much on the army as it did on the navy. It was therefore only natural that the army's primary energies would be devoted to meeting this constant demand as opposed to the intermittent and very different demands of the Continent. Antitribal warfare and population control required small, lightly equipped units operating over large areas in relative isolation from one another. These missions exposed many men to hostile fire and helped develop bravery and individual fighting skills. They fostered, however, neither the ability to handle large formations nor development of the heavier equipment, especially artillery, needed for European warfare. These problems were exacerbated by the differences in terrain and communication networks that existed between the Empire and the Continent.

The different demands of Continental and imperial warfare were met largely on an ad hoc basis until Edward Cardwell became secretary of state for war in 1868. When he took office the army was composed entirely of long service soldiers well suited to the demands of the Empire, but who provided almost no reserve for future expansion. Spurred mainly by Prussia's use of the reserve system in its victories over Denmark, Austria, and France, Cardwell brought the number of troops overseas into balance with those at home, reduced the terms of service from twenty years to six years with the colors and six with the reserves, and reorganized the infantry regiments of the line.[5] These infantry regiments were placed on a territorial basis and reconstituted with a depot for recruiting and two "linked battalions," one to serve at home and one overseas.[6] This was in many ways an ingenious compromise, designed to meet simultaneously the actual demands of the Empire and the potential demands of the Continent. The home army, however, remained an amorphous collection of battalions suited only to finding drafts for and rotating with the units overseas, and the mounting of any protracted overseas expedition threw the system out of balance.[7] Furthermore, Cardwell's system of linked battalions dictated that the organization of the army at home mirror the organization of the army abroad.

In the wake of the army's disastrous experience in South Africa, Lord Balfour's secretary of state for war, Hugh Arnold-Forster, attempted to develop a definitive solution to the Continental/imperial dichotomy by creating a long service army for the Empire and a short service army for home defense, which could also serve as an expeditionary force in the event of war.[8] This was a logical solution, but the uncertainties of getting enough long service troops made it anathema to Edward VII and the Army Council. Although a long service option was offered on a trial basis, even this limited experiment was revoked when Sir Henry Campbell-Bannerman's Liberal government took office in 1905.[9] Viscount Richard Haldane, the next secretary of state for war, succeeded in attaining a more limited objective. He retained the essence of Cardwell's system, but organized the home battalions into an expeditionary force of six infantry divisions and one cavalry division.[10] To enhance the effectiveness of this force he transformed the militia into a special reserve to keep it up to strength and incorporated the largely defunct volunteer organization into a Territorial Force to provide additional units.[11] Haldane temporarily solved the Continental/imperial dilemma by attacking its most dangerous horn. His success, however, depended largely on a consensus among the military and political leaders concerning which horn was in fact the most dangerous. Although such a consensus existed in the prelude to the Great War, it did not continue in the aftermath of that conflict, a condition that was to affect decisively the organization of the army in the 1920s and 1930s.

Military reform in Britain has not only been influenced by geographical and social considerations, but also by the structure and values of the army itself. The most significant feature of the army's organization is the regimental system. The relative stability of British society and the value placed on continuity have led to a respect for tradition and its natural outgrowth, particularism – twin values that are enshrined in the army's separate regiments. Each cavalry and infantry regiment traces its heritage back to its origin and seeks to maintain its particular esprit. The inculcation of regimental histories, the wearing of distinctive uniforms, the formation of regimental associations, and the appointment of regimental colonels commandant made the individual feel much more a part of his regiment than the army at large. British soldiers justify this central role of the regiment by maintaining that the soldier's feeling of loyalty to his comrades makes him continue to perform effectively under conditions of stress when otherwise he might not.[12] Although this proposition is difficult to prove, its validity has been demonstrated often enough to make it worthy of consideration. Even Liddell Hart, certainly no lover of tradition, said when writing of the First Battle of Ypres:

> The little British Army had a corporate sense that was unique. To this its very smallness, as well as its conditions of service and traditions contributed. "First Ypres", on the British side, was not merely a soldiers' battle but a "family battle" – against outsiders. The family spirit was its key-note, and the key to the apparent miracle by which, when formations were broken up and regiments reduced to remnants, those remnants still held together.[13]

This "family spirit," however, is not conducive to military reform. The regimental system tends to perpetuate established procedures, narrow men's outlooks, and, most significantly, complicate organizational change. These complications arise not only from the natural resistance to disbandment that can be expected from any well-established entity, but also from the practical difficulties encountered in attempting to integrate highly particular groups into other equally particular groups.

Another salient factor in the history of British military reform, which is in some respects derivative of the army's subsidiary function in society, is the late development of a professional officer corps. The ideal of full-time military service to which one devoted the majority of one's energy developed on the Continent in the late eighteenth and early nineteenth centuries, but did not emerge in Britain until nearly a hundred years later. The founding of the Staff College in 1858 was recognition of the need for professionalism, but it was little more than an appendage to Sandhurst until 1870, and the lack of a General Staff throughout the rest of the nineteenth century vitiated its effectiveness.[14] The system of purchasing commissions also retarded professionalism, but it had several social advantages that kept it in being even after the fiasco of Crimea. From the landowners' point of view, it provided a convenient means of ensuring that their sons had a socially acceptable occupation. From Parliament's point of view, it provided an admirably inexpensive way to officer the army. Nevertheless, observation of the Franco-Prussian War and Cardwell's determined efforts to end the purchase system resulted in its abolition in 1872. But the effects of its termination were mitigated by the fact that an army officer's pay remained well below what was required to support his existence as a regimental officer and that promotion became a matter of seniority rather than merit.[15] The public school system's emphasis on classics and the humanities and general exclusion of sciences may have also retarded professionalism in an era when technical knowledge was becoming increasingly important.[16]

The aftermath of the Boer War was the next great turning point in the professionalization of the British officer corps, and in 1906 Haldane said, "A new school of officers has arisen since the South African War, a thinking school of officers who desire to see the full efficiency which comes from new organization and no surplus energy running to waste."[17] The formation of the General Staff in 1904 as a necessary adjunct to the Staff College is another indication of this process. Indeed the first chief of the General Staff, Neville Lyttleton, said in his memoirs, "I have seen or taken part in the development of our army from an occupation to a profession."[18] Professionalization continued erratically until the outbreak of the Great War, which provided yet another impetus, though many vestiges of semiprofessionalism lingered on.

Here, however, two observations must be made. First, the lack of professionalism in the army was a reflection of many other aspects of British life. The manifold social problems brought about by the industrial revolution were dealt with almost entirely on a voluntary basis throughout the nineteenth and early twentieth centuries, and even members of Parliament received no pay at all until 1911. In a society where amateurism abounded, it is perhaps unwise to castigate one element marked by this trait. Second, the effects of semiprofessionalism were not all harmful. Officers who were not immersed in military technicalities often had outside knowledge and perspectives that helped rather than hindered the performance of their duties, and the possession of private means gave them an independence that one supported totally by his army salary does not always have. Of course such results were not universal, but they occurred often enough to be noteworthy.

The inimical effects of the regimental system and semiprofessionalism of the officer corps were partially offset by institutions established for the consideration of military affairs and their subsidiaries: the military periodicals. The most well known was the United Service Institution founded in 1831, whose purposes and modus operandi were outlined in an address by the chairman given in 1857: "We propose also to continue meetings for the purpose of discussing professional and scientific questions, and to encourage inventors to exhibit and explain such inventions as have connection with the professions. . . . In the Journal of Proceedings we propose to print the lectures . . . and the discussions which take place."[19] As the institution grew, it began to sponsor annual essay contests on current military subjects. The monetary prizes and prestige of winning these contests did much to encourage contributions and helped generate informed discussion.[20] The *Journal of the Royal United Service Institution* also expanded and by the late nineteenth century included book reviews and correspondence as well as its other features. Although the readership was primarily middle- to senior-grade military and naval officers, the journal was also known in the Foreign Office and the Treasury.[21]

The next most significant military periodical was the *Army Quarterly*, founded in 1920, whose aim was "to provide a forum for the discussion, explanation, and review of all military affairs."[22] Like the R.U.S.I. journal, it sponsored essay contests and published book reviews. It was, however, published primarily for the regimental officer, particularly those in the infantry; consequently there were other differences as well. The range of articles was narrower, and the articles were generally shorter and simpler than those found in the R.U.S.I. journal. The *Army Quarterly* did not normally publish correspondence. The artillery, engineers, cavalry, and tank corps all published their own journals as did a number of infantry regiments. The quality of the journals varied widely. The *Journal of the Royal Artillery* and the *Royal Engineers' Journal* were both highly professional technical publications reflecting the long-separate development of these two branches under the Board of Ordnance. The *Cavalry Journal*, however, was a folksy, horsy collection of reminiscences. The infantry regimental journals were almost entirely newsletters of regimental activities. While it would be wrong to overestimate the effect of the military periodicals, they generally enhanced reform by giving concerned individuals the opportunity to crystallize their thoughts on contemporary military problems and by providing a medium through which a wide range of opinions could be circulated.

The wide variety of these periodicals allowed the writer to choose selectively his potential military audience and tailor his arguments accordingly, but the controversy over military reform was waged in the civil community as well. Here again the writer had a variety of publications from which to choose. Letters to or articles in the *Times*, the *Daily Telegraph*, the *Westminster Gazette*, and the *Morning Post* were frequently used to argue one side or the other; the general public could also be reached through popular periodicals such as *The Nineteenth Century and After*, the *Fortnightly Review*, the *English Review*, and the *Saturday Review*.[23] The existence of a large number of periodicals, coupled with a literary tradition in which men were accustomed to expressing new ideas in a public forum, favored the reform of the army.

On the whole, however, the prospects of meaningful reform were not great. Britain's lack of need for a large standing army, the regimental system, and lingering vestiges of semiprofessionalism acted as impediments into the early twentieth century. These impediments were overcome by Haldane chiefly because of the inadequacies revealed in the South African war and the growing certainty that the army would become involved in a Continental war. The war did come, and the British Army became involved in it in a manner and on a scale that were entirely unanticipated. One of the unanticipated developments was trench warfare. Another was a mechanical antidote thereto—the tank. The focus of British military reform thus shifted from matters of organization and administration to matters of tactical doctrine brought about by the bloody experience of the Great War.

II

The Allied victory in 1918 and the tremendous physical and psychic price paid for success led to two conflicting British Army interpretations about the Great War. The first was that it could only have been won using the methods that were actually employed. The second was that it should have been won much more economically.[24] Naturally the British debate over tactical doctrine was a large element in this controversy.[25] In the immediate postwar years, each branch of the army sought to emphasize its successes and minimize its failures in order to ensure the largest possible role for itself in the future. The prevailing opinion at the end of the war was that decisive victory had been won "by the rifle and bayonet of the infantryman."[26] Yet the machine-gun and barbed wire had effectively checked the foot soldier. And in spite of the host of supporting arms that helped restore the foot soldier's ability to advance, casualties remained high, introducing a general malaise into the British infantry.[27]

There were two positions on overcoming this problem. One was to give the infantry even more support—artillery, airplanes, and tanks—and to advance it only when this support had neutralized enemy resistance. This was, in essence, the French Army's concept immediately after the war. The other solution was to increase the infantry's mobility and to advance it using a skillful combination of fire and maneuver, a technique more in keeping with the British light infantry tradition and similar to the German tactics of March 1918. These two approaches—one emphasizing firepower, the other emphasizing mobility—also suggested the lines along which the British interwar debate would progress.

One of the most striking aspects of the Great War was the ubiquitous use of artillery.[28] The British Expeditionary Force arrived in France with just under five hundred guns. By 1918 it had over six thousand. As early as 1915 artillery became vital to tactical success, and an exposé of the shortage of shells at the front helped topple the Liberal government. In 1916 the senior artillery officers at corps and army headquarters became, in effect, deputy commanders. By November 1917, advanced survey techniques allowed the artillery to fire accurately without having to disclose their position in advance; this greatly increased the army's ability to obtain surprise. At the end of the war the gunners therefore felt confident of their future role. In the postwar years, however, they concentrated on refining those aspects of their profession that proved effective in the Great War–centralized control, survey technique, and counterbattery fire–and they often failed to consider how to provide support in a rapidly changing, fluid situation.

The machine-gun and barbed wire had stopped the mounted trooper even more effectively than they had the infantryman. The cavalry's position was therefore weak, but it justified its continued existence by the few occasions on which it had performed useful functions on the Western Front and by its key role in Viscount Edmund Allenby's Palestine campaign. During the retreat from Mons and the German offensive of March 1918, cavalry formations had helped protect the retiring British infantry, and in the final Allied advance of October–November 1918 they had made good progress against a disorganized enemy.[29] But the cavalry viewed the Western Front as an aberration and said that Palestine showed its true value. Mounted troops carried out successful raids at Magdhaba and Rafa and moved rapidly in the pursuit to Damascus. As Archibald Wavell so perceptively pointed out, however, mobility, not cavalry per se, was the key to success, and motorized formations might have performed these tasks even more effectively.[30] In the face of the contention that the horse was a relic on the battlefield, the cavalry emphasized the value of its traditional characteristics rather than attempting to adapt itself to the needs of modern warfare.

The greatest controversy raged around the past and future employment of the tank. The tank was the product of the tactical stalemate that developed in France and Belgium after the early months of the war and the invention of tracked, gasoline-powered locomotion for agricultural vehicles. The vision of the latter as the solution to the former first appeared in the mind of an imaginative British soldier, Lt. Col. E. D. Swinton.[31] Swinton's call for a motor-powered, tracked, armored vehicle that could advance under the fire of machine-guns and cross enemy earthworks resulted in the first tank being produced in 1915.[32] Tanks were committed prematurely on the Somme in 1916 and in terrain unsuited to their characteristics in Flanders in August 1917.[33] In November 1917 at Cambrai, where tanks were used en masse over suitable ground, they suffered high casualties but materially aided the infantry's advance.[34]

On 8 August 1918 the final British offensive on the Western Front was launched east of Amiens with 425 tanks in support of 13 infantry divisions.

The tanks again suffered many losses due to enemy action and maintenance problems, but they were a significant element in the British success.[35] As Douglas Haig said:

> The whole scheme of attack of the 8th August was dependent upon tanks, and ever since that date on numberless occasions the success of our infantry has been powerfully assisted or confirmed by their timely arrival. It is no disparagement of the courage of our infantry or of the skill and devotion of our artillery to say that the achievements of those essential arms would have fallen short of the full measure of success achieved by our Armies, had it not been for the very gallant and devoted work of the Tank Corps.[36]

The Tank Corps thus had every reason to be enthusiastic about its potential. From a figment of the imagination, it had become a force of 20 battalions and 12 armored car companies.[37] Despite this dramatic rise, however, its future remained uncertain.

This was due in many respects to the concept of "the cooperation of all arms," which soon became a commonplace of postwar analyses. The meaning of this phrase is revealed in Haig's final dispatch:

> Heavy artillery, trench mortars, machine guns, aeroplanes, tanks, gas, and barbed wire have in their several spheres of influence played very prominent parts in operations, and as a whole given a greater driving power to war. . . . It should never be forgotten however that weapons of this character are incapable of independent action. They do not in themselves possess the power to obtain a decision, their real function being to assist the infantry to get to grips with their opponents.[38]

This sentiment was reinforced by Maj. Gen. Archibald Montgomery (later Montgomery-Massingberd), chief of staff of the Fourth Army, who maintained that "nothing perhaps was of greater moment, or affected the issue more, than the co-operation of the various arms in battle."[39] And even Maj. Gen. Hugh Elles, commander of the Tank Corps, felt that tanks were an auxiliary to the infantry.[40] Thus the concept of the cooperation of all arms implied adjusting the speed of all supporting arms to the pace of the foot soldier and not accelerating the infantry rate of movement to that of the tank.

As long as tanks were capable of moving only 4 or 5 miles per hour and their tracks had a maximum life expectancy of 150 to 200 miles, there was little that could be said against this idea. In early 1918, however, Lt. Col. Philip Johnson developed a tank known as the "Medium C," which was smaller and lighter than the Mark IV tank used at Cambrai, but had a speed of 8 to 12 miles per hour and a track life expectancy up to 500 miles.[41] Referred to as the Whippet, it first saw action at Amiens, but it was not given an independent role. In early 1918 Col. J. F. C. Fuller, chief staff officer of the Tank Corps, requested a tank be designed with a speed of 20

A Medium D tank, the first British amphibious tank, entering the River Stour at Christchurch during flotation trials. A force of 790 of these tanks was the instrument that J. F. C. Fuller visualized using for attacking "the brain of the enemy" in his Plan 1919. (Courtesy of the Tank Museum.)

miles per hour, a radius of action of 200 miles, and a spanning power of 13 to 14 feet. Fuller's plan for the anticipated campaign in 1919 was based on the characteristics of this tank.[42]

Plan 1919 originated with the confusion caused in British front-line units when their headquarters withdrew during the German offensive of March 1918. Fuller saw that "without an active and directive brain, an army is reduced to a mob."[43] His plan envisioned a force of 790 medium tanks attacking various German headquarters to generate confusion; another force of 2,592 heavy and 390 medium tanks attacking the front lines in a series of penetrations and envelopments; and a pursuing force of 1,220 medium tanks destroying the remnant of the German Army. This plan was bandied about for several months in the War Office but was obviated by the signing of the armistice in November.[44] It became, however, the germ of Fuller's concept of armored warfare.

III

Although Fuller was a gifted tactician, an energetic organizer, and a broadly thinking theorist, he was not a man of balanced temperament. His frequently offensive personality was to play a key role in the evolution of the reform process. This personality and the precarious position of the Royal Tank Corps in the postwar army significantly influenced the subsequent development of the doctrine of armored warfare in the British Army.

Fuller was born in Chichester in 1878. At an early age he developed a love of books, an independent mind and spirit, and a self-confessed habit of blunt speaking. Although he had no particular desire for a military career, he joined the army through Sandhurst at the wish of his maternal grandfather. In his early posts he avoided the idle conversation of the officers' mess, preferring to read works of philosophy, science, and occasionally eastern metaphysics. By 1913, when he entered the Staff College, he had developed a wide knowledge of contemporary trends in many fields and a habit of thinking analytically from first premises. As such he found himself continually at odds with the directing staff. The outbreak of the war brought this unhappy relationship to a graceful close, and he was eventually posted to France. In December 1916 he was assigned as chief staff officer of the newly formed Heavy Branch Machine-Gun Corps, the forerunner of the Tank Corps.[45] This was a perfect job for Fuller in which he could fully apply his energy, inventiveness, and literary capacities. He lectured the troops, analyzed the results of each tank action, devised tactics for coming battles, and conducted a vigorous campaign to convince the High Command that the tank was the mechanical savior of the British Army.[46] Thus, at the end of the war, Fuller more than any other man, except perhaps Hugh Elles, was personally identified with the Tank Corps.

The Tank Corps had always led a tenuous existence, and after the war its future became even more uncertain. There were a number of pressures against it. Many argued that trench warfare, its original raison d'être, was unlikely to recur. More tellingly, the army was being severely reduced, and there was no prewar precedent for the Tank Corps. No one was sure if tanks could operate in India, or if they would do any good there even if they could. Fuller, then in the War Office as adviser to the director of staff duties in all matters pertaining to tanks, was well aware of these obstacles. He determined that the only way to keep the Tank Corps alive was to extend his campaign begun during the war to the public domain. As he said later: "I set forth on the quest for free speech, and with my eyes wide open. I realized that I should be proclaimed a heretic and a vulgar self-advertising fellow, and I knew also that I should create enemies; yet without a sturdy opposition it is most difficult to explode deep-rooted absurdities."[47] This apparently necessary role of intellectual agent provocateur was one Fuller clearly relished.

The opening shot in Fuller's campaign was a seminal article that won the 1919 R.U.S.I. military essay contest. The subject, "The Application of Recent Developments in Mechanics and Other Scientific Knowledge to Preparation and Training for Future War on Land," gave full scope to Fuller's imagination and eclectic outlook on war. He began by stating that war was a science "connected far more intimately than has hitherto been recognized with the progress of civilization," and that generalship was to be learned not by merely studying past campaigns, but by "appreciating what is evolving around us in the peaceful fields of the physical and moral sciences—engineering and mechanics, philosophy, industry, commerce, psychology and the general progress of mankind."[48] Fuller's review of the significant scientific developments influencing the Great War led to the statement, "Tools or weapons, if only the right ones can be invented, form 99 percent of victory . . . the rest is 1 percent." He supported this assertion with a number of hypothetical historical examples.[49]

Fuller's central argument was that the Great War had shown that specialist corps of machine-guns, tanks, and infantry "do not tend towards efficient co-operation," and that the army's main task was to "reduce the various arms to that common denominator, the tank, which more than any other arm, combines offensive and defensive power with mobility, and so best carries out the main problem of battle—'the giving of blows without receiving them.' "[50] The tank, Fuller said, could completely replace the infantry and cavalry; supplement the artillery, which would have to evolve into a type of tank anyway; enhance the value of machine-guns; and reduce the need for field engineers. Fuller then outlined a plan with a transitional New Model Divison of tanks and contemporary arms that would eventually evolve into an army of light, medium, and heavy tanks to replace the infantry, cavalry, and artillery.[51]

The chief value of Fuller's scheme was that rather than looking at the Great War and asking, "How can we better fight that type of war next time?" it asked, "Given an advancing technology, how can we fight future war more rationally?" As such it must be considered primarily as a statement of direction rather than a specific blueprint.

Fuller's concept of future warfare seems unquestionably sounder than Haig's, but it can be argued that Fuller went too far in the right direction.[52] He was right in contending that organization of the army into a plethora of separate corps had decreased its efficiency in the Great War and that the advent of the fast tank called for entirely new concepts of cooperation. He was wrong, however, in assuming that the primary land combat functions could ultimately be performed by three classes of mechanical vehicles.

His assumption was based in part on an analogy he made between sea and land warfares. Fuller felt that the cross-country capacity of the tank had liberated land combat from the constraints of fixed lines of communications. As he said in February 1920:

> If now a means can be introduced whereby the naval conditions, which are mainly dynamic, can be superimposed upon the existing land conditions, which are much

more static, an entirely new theory of war can be evolved on land which, in its progress, will completely change the whole practice of present-day land warfare. This means already exists in the Tank, or Land Ship, which, though still in an early stage of development, possesses even now many of the characteristics necessary to accomplish such a change.[53]

This analogy, while useful if properly qualified and valid in particular circumstances such as desert warfare, was stretched too far. The advent of cross-country vehicles did introduce a new fluidity to land warfare and it did call for greater emphasis on mobility in tactical concepts. Even these vehicles, however, required logistical support and they were only infrequently able to sever themselves from their lines of communication. Furthermore, they could not reduce mountains, hills, ridges, woods, swamps, and many other land features to a smooth, even, sea-like surface.[54]

Plan 1919, the R.U.S.I. Gold Medal Essay, and the sea warfare on land lecture outlined Fuller's early concept of armored warfare. The remainder of his tactical studies in the early and middle twenties reiterated his three basic themes: that the gasoline engine had revolutionized warfare, that the tank had to become the basic building block of the British Army, and that a new doctrine of swift penetration and envelopment had to replace the Great War doctrine of indecisive frontal attack.

Fuller was soon joined in his efforts to spread the armored warfare gospel by a young infantry officer, Capt. B. H. Liddell Hart. Liddell Hart was born in Paris in 1895, the son of a Methodist minister. As a young man he developed an intense interest in sports, games of all sorts, and military tactics. He read history at Cambridge and received a temporary commission in the King's Own Yorkshire Light Infantry on the outbreak of the war. He served on the Western Front until gassed in the Somme offensive of July 1916. Following his convalescence he was assigned as adjutant to a volunteer infantry battalion. These two experiences – participation in a major offensive action in which all chance of surprise was forsaken, and training a group of citizen soldiers in the fundamentals of infantry tactics – had a profound influence on his future military thought.[55] He published some of his early ideas on tactics in the military journals, and in early 1920 sent one of his articles to Lt. Gen. Sir Ivor Maxse, former inspector general of training in France.[56]

Maxse quickly recognized the value of the young captain's fertile imagination, and in 1920 chaired a R.U.S.I. lecture by Liddell Hart entitled "The 'Man-in-the-Dark' Theory of Infantry Tactics and the 'Expanding Torrent' System of Attack." The second portion of this lecture contained the most portent for future armored doctrine. Liddell Hart said the British Army had learned from bitter experience that it was folly to attack in equal strength at all points. The problem, however, was what to do when a gap was first made. If fresh troops were pushed through too quickly, they could soon be cut off; conversely if they were not brought up quickly enough, the initiative would be lost. According to Liddell Hart, the solution to this dilemma was automatically to widen the breach as the penetration was deepened. Nature provided the ideal example:

> If we watch a torrent bearing down on each successive bank or earthen dam in its path, we see that it first beats against the obstacle, feeling and testing it at all points. Eventually it finds a small crack at some point. Through this crack pour the first driblets of water and rush straight on. The pent-up water on each side is drawn toward the breach. It swirls through and around the flanks of the breach, wearing away the earth on each side and so widening the gap. Simultaneously the water behind pours straight through the breach between the side eddies which are wearing away the flanks. Directly it has passed through it expands to widen once more the onrush of the torrent.[57]

Translated into military terms this meant that each penetrating unit would continue to move forward so long as it had a reserve behind it. Units that were held up would send their reserves to the flanks to widen the gaps. The main reserves would pass through the gaps and continue forward. This system would be continued by each succeeding upper echelon, in perfect imitation of nature's method. The beauty of Liddell Hart's system of expanding torrent attack lay in its simplicity. It was easy to grasp and easy to apply, and it provided a rational basis for tactical instruction and practice. Although it did not incorporate the new mechanical technology, a combination of Fuller and Liddell Hart's concepts was within the realm of possibility.

When this combination did take place, Fuller's ideas dominated Liddell Hart's. The two men first met in June 1920 after Liddell Hart had given Fuller several of his articles for comment. In early 1922 Liddell Hart sent Fuller a copy of the article on modern infantry he was preparing for the *Encyclopaedia Britannica*, stating in his letter a suspicion that infantry was "more likely to endure because of conservatism, financial and official, than its own inherent merits."[58] Fuller's reply almost converted Liddell Hart, who responded in a subsequent letter that if he were convinced of one or two technical details, he would join the Tank Corps and "become a disciple."[59] His conversion, which took place soon after, is reflected in an article prepared for the 1922 R.U.S.I. military essay contest. Liddell Hart did not win the contest, but he later published his entry in two parts in the *Royal Engineers' Journal* and the *Army Quarterly*.[60]

Part Two, "The Development of the 'New Model' Army: Suggestions on a Progressive but Gradual Mechanicalisation," formed the basis for Liddell Hart's ideas on armored warfare for the next several years.[61] It was based on the Fullerite principle that "the replacement of muscle-power by machine-power is the cardinal fact in every department of material life."[62] Liddell Hart's mechanization program was divided into two periods. The first period had four stages calling for mechanization of divisional transport, battalion transport, artillery units, and infantry units, in that order, and culminating in the formation of a New Model division.[63] Liddell Hart's second period of mechanization strongly resembled Fuller's final period:

> Evolution will now become revolution. The tank is likely to swallow the infantry-man, the field artilleryman, the engineer and the signaller, while mechanical cav-alry will supersede the horseman. . . . The logical sequence of events points to the land, or rather overland forces being composed primarily of tanks and aircraft, with a small force of siege artillery, for the reduction and defence of the fortified tank and aircraft bases, and of mechanical-borne infantry for use as land marines.[64]

There were two main differences between Liddell Hart and Fuller's mech-anization plans. First, Liddell Hart described the transition period in far greater detail than Fuller had. He showed how each transport service could be mechanized, how much money would be required for each of the four stages, and where he felt reductions could be made to obtain these funds. These details added a note of realism to plans for reform and they point out a definite difference in temperament between the two men—Liddell Hart was somewhat more willing than Fuller to accept the constraints of the bureaucracy. Liddell Hart's prescriptions did not, however, take into account the actual workings of the Treasury system with which the War Office had to contend.[65]

The second difference was Liddell Hart's conception of the future of infan-try. The use of infantry in armored warfare has been the subject of a great deal of confused writing. The often-heard generalization—that Liddell Hart wanted infantry to accompany tanks and that Fuller did not—is true, but it requires qualification. Furthermore it tells us little about the two men's tac-tical concepts.[66] Before his conversion to Fuller's theories Liddell Hart felt that infantry would always be "the only true winner of victory," but that in order for it to retain this preeminence, a tank would have to become an integral part of each infantry platoon.[67] He also visualized the existence of the tank corps as a separate body to be used "as advanced guards, in the wider sense, and in following up and reaping the full fruits of victory."[68]

A comparison of Fuller and Liddell Hart's New Model divisions furnishes some insight into their feelings on tanks and infantry after Liddell Hart's conversion to armored warfare.[69] Fuller advocated twelve "infantry" battal-ions, each battalion having two automatic rifle companies, one tank com-pany, and one machine-gun company. Liddell Hart recommended three composite brigades, each brigade having one battalion of heavy tanks, one battalion of medium tanks, one brigade of mechanized artillery, and three transport-borne infantry battalions. Liddell Hart's New Model divisions dif-fered from Fuller's in that he saw the composite brigade as a future tactical grouping and he advocated the use of infantry in armored carriers. It is important to remember, however, that both schemes were merely transitional arrangements.

The final configurations were to be much different. Fuller had surmised that ultimately "all muscle-moving soldiers, horse and foot, will become but mere camp followers."[70] He recognized the need for infantry units but saw them employed in a strictly auxiliary role, guarding lines of communication and fixed bases. They were to have no tactical functions.[71] Liddell Hart recognized the need for auxiliary troops but felt that "a proportion of tank marines would also probably accompany each tank battalion in special armed transporter tanks. These would be used as 'landing' parties to clear land fortifications and hill defences under cover of the fire from the tank fleet."[72] Although the proportion of "tank marines" in a tank battalion was not specified, Liddell Hart seems to have had in mind at least a platoon, but no more than a company. The salient point here is that while Liddell Hart did differ with Fuller in the viability of assigning tactical missions to infantry units, the proportion of infantry he saw as necessary was as small as Fuller's. It is thus fair to conclude that in the early and mid-1920s Liddell Hart differed slightly with Fuller in functional terms, but essentially agreed with him in organizational terms.[73]

Fuller and Liddell Hart realized that in order to change the army's tactical doctrine, many other reforms were also necessary. Both desired a reorganization of the War Office. Fuller wanted to abolish the Army Council and replace it with a commander-in-chief, assisted by a chief staff officer and a single staff of five departments, each consisting of a "thinking" section, a "liaison" section, and a "routine" section.[74] Liddell Hart proposed the creation of a tactical research department to help ensure that tactics kept pace with technology.[75] The army's educational system also came under their reforming gaze. Liddell Hart suggested the amalgamation of Woolwich and Sandhurst as a move to break down the army's compartmentalization and to help prevent the loss of "mental elasticity."[76] Fuller wanted the Staff College to be replaced by a War Science College, where the potential staff officer would be grounded in the technical evolution of weapons and the application of this knowledge to future tactics.[77]

They also wanted to change the army's values. Fuller's strategy was open warfare: "Traditionalism is the dragon I am out to slay, that servile monster which breathes forth wars of bloodshed and destruction."[78] Liddell Hart's method was milder than Fuller's, but still sharply critical. Examining the army's record in the Great War, he concluded that the amateur who reflectively studies the history of war in light of contemporary developments was better qualified than the experienced but uneducated professional soldier to meet the demands of modern war.[79] Both reformers' aims were the same—more emphasis on theory as opposed to practice, a common rather than a particularistic approach to problems, and, above all, willingness to change.

Attitudes, however, are extremely difficult to alter, and neither Fuller's nor Liddell Hart's criticisms made a significant impression on the army in the immediate postwar years. To understand why this was so, it will be helpful to examine the wider context in which these ideas were put forth to include political and social attitudes toward the army, its commitments and finances, and the use of motor vehicles in society.

IV

Following a close study of the minutes and memoranda of the Committee of Imperial Defence, Michael Howard observed that "after 1918 the reader becomes conscious of a new sound: the heavy and ominous breathing of a parsimonious and pacific electorate, to the variations in which the ears of British statesmen were increasingly attuned."[80] Although out and out pacifism was not as pervasive as many military men have painted it, the casualties on the Western Front and the consequent war-weariness of the British people made the army more vulnerable than the other services to the effects of popular desire to avoid future war.[81] Until the beginning of 1927, however, the outcry against the army was generally muted. In 1923 Clement Attlee stated that "the time has come when we ought to do away with all armies, and all wars."[82] He admitted, however, that this was impossible and directed his criticisms toward the social composition and attitudes of the officer corps, not the army's existence.

In 1924 George Lansbury and other Labour pacifists tabled a motion in Parliament to reduce the army from 160,000 to 150,000 men, but the Labourites government rejected it.[83] Earlier in the debate Stephen Walsh, the Labour secretary of state for war, maintained that the requirements for manning overseas stations and providing an expeditionary force made the size and existence of the army "really a non-party question," and that there would be no further reductions in British combat units.[84] The Conservative position on the army (and defense problems in general) was that military and financial security depended on one another, i.e., that the minimum requirements should be met with the lowest possible expenditure. Although there were some differences on what constituted minimum requirements for defense, there was a general consensus among both Conservatives and Labourites that the overall amount should be low, the former for monetary concerns, the latter for reasons of ideology.[85]

Attitudes toward mechanization closely parallelled those toward the army in general. The moderate Labourites viewed the horse as a military relic and saw the cavalry as a symbol of a British upper-class society that no longer performed any useful function.[86] The extremists saw the tank as an instrument of militarism and objected to any money being spent on its development.[87] The Conservatives were also of two minds. A number, especially the ex-cavalry officers, felt that horses had performed well under certain circumstances in the Great War and that mechanical vehicles were still too unreliable to replace them.[88] Others recognized the need for mechanization, but feared that the premature purchase of equipment would bring about obsolescence and unnecessary expenditure.[89] Given this diversity of opinion, the effect of political and social attitudes is difficult to assess. The strength seemed to lie among the moderates of both parties, who favored a gradual, cautious, and economic policy of modernization. A rapid effort to reorganize the army along the lines advocated by Fuller and Liddell Hart would have probably received strong opposition on both fiscal and ideological grounds.

In the immediate postwar years, the army was involved in conflicts in Russia, Ireland, and Turkey. These outbreaks subsided, however, by the end of 1922, and the army once again turned its attention to policing the Empire. Units were stationed in Bermuda, Jamaica, Gibraltar, Malta, Egypt, Aden, India, Singapore, Hong Kong, and China.[90] Imperial policing meant mostly population control, though occasionally expeditions were required against the tribes along India's North-West Frontier, and the home army was required to reinforce any portion of the Empire threatened by outside aggression or serious internal disturbance. The geography of these areas and the mission of population control favored the use of mechanized forces but not the use of armored formations. Participation in a major European war was the only compelling justification for the development of armored forces.

The army's other major responsibility was to uphold Britain's commitments on the Continent, but as indicated in the Chiefs of Staff statement at the beginning of the chapter, this task was always regarded as being secondary. Under the terms of the Pact of Mutual Guarantee signed at Locarno in 1925, Britain was pledged to resist any effort to alter forcibly either the German-French or German-Belgian borders or to remilitarize the Rhineland. This created an obvious political commitment for a British capability to intervene militarily in the event of Continental war, but the dominant mood after Locarno was one of anticipating peace, not war.[91] Furthermore, in 1919 the Cabinet had decided that "it should be assumed for framing the revised estimates, that the British Empire will not be engaged in any great war during the next ten years, and that no expeditionary force is required for this purpose."[92] This decision was reaffirmed in 1925 and 1926. Thus at the end of 1926 the army had two major responsibilities: one actual, with a high demand for manpower but amenable to mechanization; the other vaguely potential but favoring the development of armored forces. The actual commitment was naturally given priority.

The army was also responsible for assisting the R.A.F. in the air defense of Britain. As long as no European nation had the ability to strike Britain from the air, however, this commitment was not a major factor in the allocation of the army's resources or determination of its force structure.[93] This condition, of course, changed radically in the late 1930s.

The force structuring problem was further complicated by the army's limited financial resources. In 1921 the City of London, led by Reginald McKenna, called upon the government to institute "ruthless, relentless, remorseless" measures for economy.[94] In response to these promptings, the Geddes Committee published its report recommending a total reduction of £86.75 million, the army's portion of which was initially recommended at £20 million.[95] The policy of economic retrenchment was continued by successive governments and confirmed by the return to the gold standard at prewar parity in 1925.[96] In an era of low national expenditure, the army had to compete with the demands for social services as well as the newly established R.A.F. In the event the Army Estimates decreased from £93,714,000 in 1921 to £62,300,000 in 1922 and to £42,500,000 by 1926.[97] In the face of this passion for economy, Haldane, who had been appointed lord chancellor in the first Labour government, counseled, "There is only one method to adopt, and that is to go very quietly, to cut our coat according to the cloth we have to make it with."[98] This was sound advice, but the problem was actually to apply it.

The system of Treasury control was just as important as the actual lack of money in impeding military reform between the wars.[99] Each year the War Office compiled the estimated costs of newly planned programs and those of maintaining existing forces. It then compared the total "requirements" for the following year with the money that would probably be available and then made the necessary reductions. The draft "estimates" were then sent to the Treasury Office where every entry was scrutinized and compared with the previous year's, the guiding philosophy being that each increase had to be explicitly justified. This meant that savings in one area could not be automatically credited to additional expenses in any other area. After the estimates were "approved in detail," they were printed and sent to Parliament. The estimates were almost always approved as presented, but members could, and frequently did, attempt to influence army policy by debating specific provisions. Treasury sanction was required for any expenditure not specifically provided for in the estimates, and any money left over at the end of the year reverted to the Treasury. This system had three major defects: It was overly rigid, it placed too great a premium on precedent, and it did not provide for continuity.[100]

The one factor that strongly favored mechanization in the army was the gradual incursion of motor vehicles into British society. During the war the army's requirements for lorries and ambulances and the McKenna duty of 33⅓ percent on imported automobiles greatly expanded British motor vehicle manufacturing capacity.[101] Production rose from about 35,000 in 1918 to 73,000 in 1929. Beginning in 1922 Morris and Austin introduced the assembly line techniques of Henry Ford. The Morris Minor and the Baby Austin soon transformed the private car from a luxury means of transportation into a means of weekend travel for the upper-middle-class family. The motor bus and long-distance coach displaced the tram and the passenger train, while the lorry soon substituted for the railway freight car as a cargo mover.[102] By 1927 nearly 2 million motor vehicles were in Britain.[103] Furthermore, horses were becoming scarce. In January 1916 a committee investigating the supply of military horses reported that artillery draught "has always been hard to find, but of late years, owing to the replacement of all omnibus horses and many vanners by motors, it is becoming rapidly extinct."[104] Following the war, the inspector of remounts surveyed the situation in Britain and concluded that serious difficulties would be encountered in mobilizing for any future conflict unless far-reaching steps were taken to encourage light horse breeding.[105] The separation of Ireland and the increased use of tractors on British farms further added to this problem. By 1925 the question of horse supply had become "without a doubt the biggest problem confronting the Territorial field artillery brigade commander" when preparing for annual training.[106] It would seem therefore that mechanization was a matter of course.

Unfortunately, it was not so simple. Secretary of State for War Sir Laming Worthington-Evans said in 1926 that "until . . . a satisfactory type of machine can be evolved, which also has commercial possibilities, the cost of mechanicalising large forces will certainly be prohibitive."[107] The army's thirty-hundred-weight, six-wheel, cross-country lorry had an uneconomical cost per ton-mile, and subsidies offered to civilian purchasers did little to increase its acceptance for commercial use. Since commercial vehicles could not travel off the road, the army required either more money for the purchase of vehicles or a further advance in technology.[108]

There were, then, a number of factors that influenced the army's acceptance of Fuller and Liddell Hart's concepts in the period 1919–1926. The results of the Great War cut both ways. On one hand, the large number of casualties and the demonstrated need to restore mobility to the battlefield seemed to augur well for the acceptance of a new doctrine. On the other hand, the tactical technique that had ultimately proved successful, "the cooperation of all arms," envisioned the tank as an adjunct to the infantry; the war had, after all, been won. These facts acted against the acceptance of new ideas. Further inhibiting the prospects for reform were an ambivalent attitude toward the army, the requirement to garrison the Empire, a dearth of money, and a rigid system of financial control. The mechanization of British society favored the mechanization of the army, though not armored warfare, but even mechanization was dependent upon financial consideration.

Despite these many encumbrances, the army was, in Haldane's words, responsible for cutting its coat to fit its cloth no matter how limited the cloth might be. To see how well it did so, we must examine how it actually reacted to the new concepts of armored warfare. This response may be examined in two distinct but closely related areas: the reactions of individuals, and the actual development of doctrine, organization, and equipment.

One often has the impression that unqualified support and unbridled opposition were the only two reactions to Fuller and Liddell Hart's ideas.[109] While it is true that a large measure of polarity was introduced by the passions of both sides, it is possible to identify a variety of reactions within the army. These seem to have fallen into six main groups—revolutionary, reforming, progressive, conservative, reactionary, and indifferent. Obviously, even apart from the limitations of terminology, there are great dangers in any classification of this sort; but if one remains aware of the occasional exceptions and contradictions, it can help to understand the dynamics of the reform movement.

A small group of officers, most of whom became members of the Royal Tank Corps upon its formation as a permanent element of the British Army in 1923, accepted Fuller's ideas with few, if any, modifications.[110] Their feelings are evident in the remarks of Lt. Col. W. D. Croft, whose entry placed second to Fuller's in the 1919 R.U.S.I. essay contest: "Lack of space and the writer's conviction of the overwhelming superiority of the tank over any other mechanical invention or scientific discovery, in future war on land, preclude the discussion of anything else, except in so far as it can be utilized with the tank."[111] Lt. Col. Charles Broad, Maj. Frederick Pile, and Maj. Percy Hobart were the three members of this group who had the greatest impact on armored warfare. Broad, a studious, competent gunner, became impressed with the tank when he contrasted the results of Cambrai with the Somme offensive of 1916. He transferred to the R.T.C. and in 1925 became head of the Gunnery School at Lulworth.[112] Pile, a dynamic and intense Irishman, served in the Royal Horse Artillery before the war. Fuller persuaded him to transfer to the R.T.C. while he was at the Staff College, and he soon became the army's leading exponent of light tanks.[113] Hobart, an ambitious, fiery sapper, learned the value of mobility as a brigade major in Mesopotamia. He too transferred to the R.T.C. in 1923. Although too junior to exercise any decisive influence on British armored warfare in the 1920s, he placed his imprint on it while commanding the Tank Brigade in the 1930s.[114] These men were the revolutionaries.

Others wanted to reform fundamentally the army's tactical doctrine, but neither their ends nor their means were as drastic as Fuller's. The most notable of these individuals was Col. George Lindsay. While commanding the armored car units in Mesopotamia after the war, Lindsay conducted a number of experiments with motorized desert forces. After one such trial he said:

> A true mechanical force must combine as far as possible the powers and charac-
> teristics of a force of all arms. Today it must consist of (i) Aeroplanes; (ii) Armoured
> cars; (iii) Tanks; (iv) Motor Machine Gun Units; (v) Trench Mortar Units. . . .
> Wherever obstacles exist that can be easily rendered impassable, armoured cars
> must have other troops with them, either to hold the passages over the obstacles
> open or to provide the man-power to re-open them.[115]

Lindsay also transferred to the R.T.C. in 1923, becoming first the chief of
the Central Schools and then inspector, Royal Tank Corps. In addition to
vision and tactical sense, Lindsay had an easygoing charm he used to prod
gently those less far-sighted than himself.[116]

Maj. B. C. Dening, whose entry won the *Army Quarterly's* 1924 military
essay contest, called for the creation of an integrated "close combat arm"
consisting of tank and armored carrier infantry units.[117] One significant contribution of this article was its calculation of the number of carrier units
required per tank unit based on a definition of their tactical functions. Even
more significant, however, was its description of the functions of mechanized infantry. Dening maintained that carrier units would have to hold
ground captured by tanks, mop up pockets of resistance, assault tank obstacles, defend men against tanks with antitank guns, and protect tanks against
men; to perform these functions three carrier battalions were required for
each tank battalion.

Maj. Giffard Martel was the original Heavy Branch Machine Gun Corps
operations officer; when Fuller took the position in December 1915, Martel
continued on as his assistant. After the war he remained in the Royal Engineers rather than transferring to the R.T.C. In 1925 he built a one-man tank
in his garage and later pioneered the experiments with tank bridging.[118]
Lindsay, Dening, Martel, and other reformers combined a strong desire for
basic change with a sense of tactical balance and a realization of the constraints imposed by circumstances.

Many British officers realized the inadequacies of the Great War tactics
but worked mainly for steady improvement within their own areas of expertise. The most notable progressives were the majors and lieutenant colonels,
who were old enough to learn from the war but young enough to emerge as
senior commanders twenty years later. Archibald Wavell closely observed
Allenby's Palestine campaigns and applied much of what he saw as a brigade
and division commander in the thirties.[119] Bernard Montgomery, appalled
at the loss of contact between commanders and troops on the Western Front,
worked out his own personal doctrine of command.[120] Lord Gort spent up
to four hours a day studying military matters to prepare himself for high
command. Alan Brooke, John Dill, Claude Auchinleck, Harold Alexander,
and William Slim also worked diligently to master the details of their profession between the wars.[121]

But there were also some progressive officers who were relatively senior at the end of the Great War, including Major Generals John Burnett-Stuart, Edmund Ironside, and Charles Harington.[122] The only senior commanders who could be considered progressive were Generals Henry Rawlinson, George Milne, and Philip Chetwode.[123] However, down to 1926 almost all of these officers were skeptical of the advanced claims of armored warfare and, though progressive, were not reformers. After 1926 several, most notably Burnett-Stuart, modified their views and became advocates of thoroughgoing change. Most remained at least somewhat separated from the tactical reform movement throughout the interwar years.[124]

The conservatives were opposed to armored warfare but not to mechanization. They objected to the independent use of the tank because of its vulnerability to artillery fire, lack of versatility, and threat to the existing tactical order. However, they also realized the value of tanks as infantry support weapons and felt that mechanized transport should be gradually introduced into traditional arms.[125] General Sir Alexander Godley cogently summed up the conservative position in 1926:

> The point I always put to myself when thinking about this question of the horse and the machine is whether if I were ordered to-morrow to take command of an Army on active service . . . should I like to take a force composed entirely of mounted men on horses with no machines at all? . . . Most certainly not. I should certainly want armoured cars and tanks. On the other hand, if I were asked, "Will you go to war with a mobile force composed [of] armoured cars, tanks, and such-like?" I think I should refuse to go! I should say that I would not go without a force of cavalry. I should want, and should insist on having, an ample proportion of mounted troops.[126]

The conservatives appreciated neither the limitations of the system they wished to preserve nor the potential of the new concepts. Although the rudimentary state of tank technology in the early twenties makes their anxieties partially understandable, their insistence on merely grafting the new onto the old created a number of anomalies that were to become increasingly apparent in succeeding years.

A few officers went even further and totally rejected the idea that machines could help make war more efficient. This view was clearly expressed by General Sir R. G. Eggerton:

> If we turn to the introduction of mechanical transport into the Army to replace the horse, and look into the faces of individuals who deal with the horse and the faces of the men who deal with the machine, you will see in the latter what, I might almost call a lack of intelligence! . . . I consider that the horse has a humanising effect on men, and the longer we can keep horses for artillery and for cavalry the better it will be for the Army, because thereby you keep up the high standard of intelligence in the man from his association with the horse.[127]

There were, as always, some who did not take their profession seriously at all. They looked on the army as a pleasant and socially acceptable way of passing one's time and did not care about the pros and cons of mechanization or armored warfare, or any other germane professional subject. Although probably in a minority and difficult to identify, they added dead weight and impeded reform.[128]

Although personal reactions to the new tactical ideas were important, it was the institutional response that determined army policy. From 1922 to 1926 the army was governed largely by conservatives. The chief of the Imperial General Staff, Lord Cavan, had directed the final Allied offensive in Italy and was highly regarded as a combat leader. He had, however, no experience of staff work and considered it improper for serving officers to publish books on military subjects.[129] The adjutant general, Sir Robert Whigham, and the quartermaster general, Sir Walter Campbell, had also served with distinction during the Great War, but both tended to be set in their ways.[130] The master general of the ordnance, Sir Noel Birch, was a progressive gunner, but he was outnumbered by his associates.[131] The composition of the Army Council, coupled with the effects of the imperial commitment and financial stringency, resulted in a slow evolution of doctrine and organization.

The British *Field Service Regulations* provide one indication of the army's tactical doctrine. Although practice in the field frequently differed from what was stipulated in the manuals, it is instructive to note that the regulations of the early 1920s amounted to little more than an uncritical recapitulation of Great War experience. According to *Field Service Regulations, Vol. II (Operations), 1924,* "Success in war depends more on moral than physical qualities. Neither numbers, armament, resources, nor skill can compensate for lack of courage, energy, determination, and the bold offensive spirit which springs from a national determination to conquer."[132] Infantry was defined as "the arm which in the end wins battles," whose "main object . . . to which all other operations are merely preliminaries, is to close with the enemy and destroy him by killing or capture."[133]

The capabilities of cavalry were virtually unlimited: "Armed with a lance or sword, it can attack mounted or dismounted, while its armament of machine guns, Hotchkiss rifles, and rifles enables it to act dismounted; thus it can combine fire with mounted action, and exploit either in attack or defence, the advantages inherent in its mobility."[134] No serious consideration was given to the effect of artillery, machine-guns, or man-made obstacles on mounted actions. The artillery's role was to "assist the other arms in breaking down opposition and to afford all possible support to the infantry"; its semiindependent status is evident in the additional statement that its ability "to develop an overwhelming bombardment without prior warning" gave it "a high importance in war."[135]

The same volume described the tank as

> a mechanically-propelled armoured vehicle which affords protection to its crew, armament, and machinery from ordinary rifle and machine gun fire and from shrapnel . . . it crosses trenches and surmounts obstacles; when moving through entanglements it crushes down the wire to form lanes passable by infantry in single file. The weight of the tank can be utilized to destroy hostile weapons and personnel by passing over them.[136]

This volume was not superseded until 1928. Thus at the end of 1926, the official statement of tactical doctrine was one based largely on the final campaign of the Great War and was relatively unaffected by advances in the means of warfare made since that time. However, two caveats are necessary. First, the *F.S.R.*s could not hope to keep up with these advances. Second, as mentioned above, actual tactical practice often depended more on the local commander than on the regulations.[137]

The army's organization was also reminiscent of the Great War. The five divisions forming the bulk of the home army consisted largely of infantrymen. These divisions were organized into three brigades of four battalions each. Each battalion was divided into four rifle companies and a headquarters wing with eight Vickers machine-guns. Divisional artillery included a brigade of twelve 3.7-inch pack howitzers and four field artillery brigades of 18-pdrs. and 4.5-inch howitzers; the division also had engineers and transport units.[138] This organization had two serious drawbacks. First, since the machine-guns and their ammunition were horse-drawn, it was difficult for them to be offensively employed in any but the shortest attacks. Second, the infantry battalions had no antitank capacity.

The 3.7-inch pack howitzers were the division's only weapons designated specifically for antitank defense. However, not being designed for this purpose, they were generally ineffective.[139] The 18-pdrs. in the field artillery brigades could destroy a tank if they could hit it, but their effectiveness was diminished by problems of technology, organization, and tactics. The technical problem was that without a pedestal mount the 18-pdrs. could not traverse quickly enough to hit a fast-moving tank. The organizational and tactical problem involved differing concepts of employment between the infantry and the artillery. The infantry wanted the 18-pdrs. well forward and their control decentralized so they could engage the tanks as soon as they came into view.[140] The gunners' view, which generally prevailed, was to keep them farther to the rear under centralized control providing general, indirect support to a wide section of the front.[141] This lack of an effective antitank capability was another reflection of the imperial police mission and the lack of a potential Continental enemy at that time.

The cavalry of the line was organized into twenty regiments, twelve of which were stationed at home. Of these, six were grouped into two cavalry

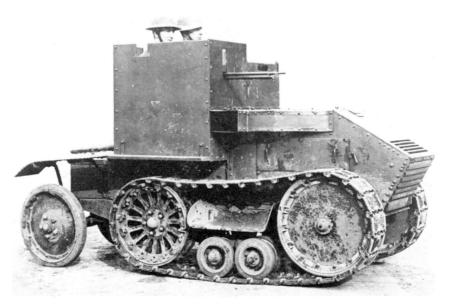

A Morris-Martel two-man prototype tankette. The first vehicle of this type was built by Maj. Giffard Martel in his garage at a cost of £400. (Courtesy of the Tank Museum.)

brigades; the other six were scattered about England at single unit stations. Each regiment had a headquarters wing with a machine-gun squadron and three line squadrons armed with rifles and either swords or lances. A reorganization scheme proposed in November 1926 recommended only minor improvements, which included mechanization of the cavalry's transport and machine-guns, the conversion of several regiments to armored car units, and design of a new lance.[142] Thus by the end of 1926, the British cavalry had taken the first tentative steps to helping it survive on the modern battlefield, but as an institution it was still wedded to the horse, the man, and cold steel.[143]

The army's four tank battalions were rather monolithic organizations consisting of a battalion headquarters with a commander's tank and four signal tanks, and three companies, each having sixteen medium tanks.[144] This meant that the battalion had to perform its reconnaissance with medium tanks or have it done by another unit. The Vickers Medium Mark II, the battalion's basic weapon, was a 12.5-ton tank powered by a 90-horsepower Armstrong Siddeley air-cooled engine, armed with a single 47-mm. 3-pdr. gun and two Vickers machine-guns and protected by 8 millimeters of armor. It had a 5-man crew, a maximum road speed of 15 miles per hour, and track with a life expectancy of roughly 1,000 miles. Although it was difficult to drive,

A Vickers Medium Mark I. This tank and its successor, the Mark II, which featured skirting plates to protect the suspension and an improved steering mechanism, served as the mainstay of the British tank fleet from its original production in 1923 until the mid-1930s. (Courtesy of the Tank Museum.)

had an unsteady gun platform, and poor ventilation, at the end of 1926 it was probably the finest medium tank in production.[145]

In September 1925 the army conducted its first large-scale peacetime maneuvers since 1914.[146] One of the purposes of these exercises was to test the new concepts of mechanized warfare. Three infantry divisions, a cavalry brigade, and a tank battalion under General Sir Philip Chetwode were pitted against one infantry division, two cavalry brigades, and a tank battalion under General Sir Alexander Godley. On the first day of the exercise Godley formed a Mobile Force with his two cavalry brigades, an infantry brigade transported on lorries, and some supporting artillery to attack an isolated portion of Chetwode's troops. According to the official report of the maneuvers, "This force was formed as an experiment in mechanicalization, and its capabilities were a matter of conjecture rather than knowledge." The action turned into a fiasco. The infantrymen, "debussed" seven to ten miles from their jumping off position, arrived too late to have any effect; their horsed transport, also moved by lorry, became hopelessly entangled with the troop carriers.[147] On the third day of the exercise, Chetwode sent his entire tank battalion on a thirty-mile flanking movement, but his infantry divisions were unable to hold Godley's units in position and the latter easily withdrew. These maneuvers showed vividly that the British Army had many of the tools needed for mechanized and armored warfare but lacked a doctrine to make them work.[148]

Given the ambiguous lessons of the Great War, the economic inhibitions facing the army, the need to garrison the Empire, and the lack of experience in moving tactical units by motor transport, the disappointing results of the 1925 maneuvers were not terribly surprising. It was, however, apparent to a number of people in the army that in order for a doctrine of armored warfare to be effectively worked out, it would be necessary to form some sort of experimental unit. Before this story can be told, however, it becomes necessary to examine the military education of John Burnett-Stuart and the course of events that led him to play a critical role in the formation of that unit.

NOTES

1. Chiefs of Staff Sub-Committee of the Committee of Imperial Defence, "A Review of Imperial Defence, 1926," Cab. 53/12.

2. Michael Howard, "Military Science in an Age of Peace," *JRUSI* 119 (March 1974): 3–9.

3. The details of War Office development can be found in a historical sketch in Great Britain, War Office, *The War Office List and Administrative Directory, 1927* (London, 1927), pp. 2–29. These sketches were included in the War Office lists at five-year intervals down to 1937. For a survey of the political developments behind these changes see Correlli Barnett, *Britain and Her Army, 1509–1970: A Military, Political and Social Survey* (New York, 1970), pp. 131–132, 166, 238–239, 246, 288–289, 309.

4. For an excellent discussion of the political intrigues behind the removal of the duke from office see Brian Bond, "The Retirement of the Duke of Cambridge," *JRUSI* 106 (November 1961): 544–553. For an assessment of the duke that brings out the quality of his testimony before parliamentary commissions and the respect he engendered see Albert V. Tucker, "Army and Society in England, 1870–1900: A Reassessment of the Cardwell Reforms," *Journal of British Studies* 2 (May 1963): 113–117.

5. For a discussion of efforts to reform the army, particularly the reserve system, between the Crimean War and Cardwell's becoming secretary of state for war, see Brian Bond, "Prelude to the Cardwell Reforms, 1856–1868," *JRUSI* 106 (May 1961): 229–236.

6. When Cardwell took office there were 141 infantry battalions of the line, 58 of which were organized into multi-battalion regiments. The other 83 were each part of single battalion regiments. Cardwell amalgamated these into 41 symbiotic, 2-regiment "brigades"; one remained independent. General Sir Robert Biddulph, *Lord Cardwell at War Office: A History of His Administration* (London, 1904), pp. 165–166. In 1881 Cardwell's successor, Hugh Childers, took the next logical, but very difficult, step of converting these brigades into supposedly homogeneous regiments. Nevertheless, the traditions of the separate elements lingered on well into the twentieth century.

7. Brian Bond reevaluates Cardwell's work in "The Effects of the Cardwell Reforms on Army Organization, 1878–1904," *JRUSI* 105 (November 1960): 515–524. He concludes that it was limited by Cardwell's lack of first-hand knowledge and the unfavorable conditions under which he worked.

8. W. S. Hamer, *The British Army: Civil-Military Relations, 1885–1905* (Oxford, 1970), p. 255.

9. General Sir Neville Lyttleton, *Eighty Years: Soldiering, Politics, Games* (London, 1927), pp. 272–273.

10. Maj. Gen. Sir Frederick Maurice, *Haldane: The Life of Viscount Haldane of Cloan*, 2 vols. (London, 1937–1939), 1:181. Haldane's maiden speech as secretary of state for war sums up his philosophy of military reform: "I have applied this test and this only. I have rejected . . . all things that do not make for fighting efficiency. Fighting efficiency is the one test to which we should submit propositions which arise at a time when we had none too much money." *H. C. Deb.*, 4th Ser., 153 (8 March 1906): 657.

11. Michael Howard, "Lord Haldane and the Territorial Army," *Studies in War and Peace* (New York, 1971), pp. 83–98. Howard emphasizes Haldane's shrewdness in blending military exigency with an awareness of British particularism.

12. The author is indebted to J. H. Leslie of the Rifle Brigade headquarters for an extended discussion of this point and also to correspondence from Maj. Gen. Douglas Wimberley, an enthusiastic and knowledgeable advocate of the regimental system. For the other side of the coin see Barnett, *Britain and Her Army*, pp. 489–490.

13. B. H. Liddell Hart, *History of the First World War* (London, 1970), pp. 177–178.

14. Brian Bond, *The Victorian Army and the Staff College, 1854–1914* (London, 1972), pp. 91–92, 109–110.

15. Evidence placed before a parliamentary committee on the pay of officers in 1903 indicated that an infantry officer receiving annual pay of £95 required an average of £150 to £200, and that a cavalry officer receiving £120 needed £600 to £700. Tucker, "Army and Society in England," *Journal of British Studies* 2 (May 1963): 128.

16. For two concise surveys of technology and tactics in the nineteenth century see the essays on armed forces in *The New Cambridge Modern History* by B. H. Liddell Hart, *The Zenith of European Power, 1830–1870*, vol. II (Cambridge, 1960), pp. 302–310, and Michael Howard, *Material Progress and World-Wide Problems, 1870–1898*, vol. 12 (Cambridge, 1962), pp. 206–210.

17. Maurice, *Haldane*, 1:177.

18. Lyttleton, *Eighty Years*, p. 309. In spite of this observation Lyttleton was castigated by Henry Wilson for not pushing the General Staff to a position of greater prominence. Bond, *The Victorian Army and the Staff College*, p. 223.

19. Col. the Honourable James Lindsay, "*Chairman's Address*," given 18 May 1857, *Journal of the Royal United Service Institution* 1 (1858): 4–5.

20. Lt. John Frederick Maurice's prize essay in a contest sponsored by the second Duke of Wellington on how to prepare the British Army for modern war netted him not only £100 but also the position as private secretary to Wolseley on the Ashanti expedition. Jay Luvaas, *The Education of an Army: British Military Thought, 1815–1940* (Chicago, 1964), pp. 175–181.

21. The percentages of new members added to R.U.S.I. in the mid-1920s were approximately: army (regular and territorial) 75 percent, navy 13 percent, air force 7 percent, marines 2 percent, other reserves 2 percent, civilians and overseas forces 1 percent. Barton C. Hacker, "The Military and the Machine: An Analysis of the Controversy over Mechanization–the British Army, 1919–1939" (Ph.D. dissertation, University of Chicago, 1967), p. 66.

22. [Maj. Gen. G. P. Dawnay], editorial in *AQ* 1 (October 1920): 2.

23. Robin Higham's *Armed Forces in Peacetime* incorporates a good deal of material from these popular reviews.

24. Field Marshal Sir William Robertson's *Soldiers and Statesmen, 1914–1918,* 2 vols. (New York, 1926), is a forceful contemporary statement of the former; Liddell Hart's *History of the First World War* is an excellent example of the latter.

25. Britain's central problem in the Great War was the deadlocked Western Front. The solutions were either to pierce it or to outflank it in other theaters. The tactical debate was over how best to accomplish the penetration; the strategic debate concerned the wisdom of the "eastern" versus the "western" areas of operations.

26. Haig's final dispatch, 21 March 1919, quoted from Lt. Col. J. H. Boraston, ed., *Sir Douglas Haig's Despatches (December 1915–April 1919),* 2 vols. (London, 1919), 2:330.

27. See Maj. Gen. H. Rowan-Robinson, *The Infantry Experiment* (London, 1934), p. 1.

28. The discussion of artillery is based primarily on Col. Charles Broad, "The Development of Artillery Tactics, 1914–1918," *JRA* 49 (1922–1923): 62–81, 127–148, and Lt. Gen. Sir Noel Birch (Haig's artillery adviser), "Artillery Development in the Great War," *AQ* 1 (October 1920): 79–89. See also Shelford Bidwell, *Gunners at War: A Tactical Study of the Royal Artillery in the Twentieth Century* (London, 1970), pp. 133–145, and Shelford Bidwell and Dominick Graham, *Fire-Power: British Army Weapons and Theories of War, 1904–1945* (London, 1982), pp. 61–146.

29. Haig, a cavalryman, emphasized his branch's few successes on the Western Front in a section of his final dispatch entitled "The Value of Cavalry in Modern War," Boraston, *Haig's Despatches,* 2:327–328.

30. Col. A. P. Wavell, *The Palestine Campaigns* (London, 1928), pp. 234–240.

31. Before the war Swinton served under Maurice Hankey in the C.I.D. Secretariat. General Horatio Kitchener sent him to France in September 1914 to act as the army's official correspondent. Maj. Gen. Sir Ernest D. Swinton, *Eyewitness: Being Personal Reminiscences of Certain Phases of the Great War, Including the Genesis of the Tank* (London, 1932), pp. 51–52, 79. Swinton's fertile imagination is evident in *The Defence of Duffer's Drift* (London, 1904), a lively little book on tactics that he wrote following the South African war.

32. Swinton, *Eyewitness,* pp. 125–157, and B. H. Liddell Hart, *The Tanks: The History of the Royal Tank Regiment and Its Predecessors, Heavy Branch Machine-Gun Corps, Tank Corps and Royal Tank Corps, 1914–1945,* 2 vols. (New York, 1959), 1:17–43.

33. Liddell Hart strongly criticizes both these decisions in *The Tanks,* 1:63–64, 110–116. Regarding the Battle of the Somme, the commander of the Tank Corps points out the difficulty of waiting until everything was ready when the efforts of thousands of men were actively engaged in the war. He also contends that it was better for the tanks to have been used at the Third Battle of Ypres under poor conditions than to have remained idle "while tremendous issues were at stake." Maj. Gen. Hugh J. Elles, Introduction to *The Tank Corps,* by Maj. Clough Williams-Ellis and A. Williams-Ellis (New York, 1919), pp. viii–ix.

34. The first day of the offensive was a great British success achieved by "predicted" artillery shooting, the massed use of tanks, and close coordination between tanks and infantry. The main factors retarding the tank's advance after the first day seem to have been crew fatigue and lack of reserves. Robert Woolcombe, *The First Tank Battle: Cambrai 1917* (London, 1967), pp. 147, 208.

35. At the end of the second day, approximately 120 of the original 415 tanks committed had been disabled by direct hits from German guns, and only 67 tanks were capable of continuing. However, on the first day alone the Australian Corps making the main attack advanced almost ten thousand yards. Liddell Hart, *The*

Tanks, 1:184. Great Britain, War Office, *Military Operations France and Belgium, 1918: 8th August–26th September, the Franco-British Offensive* (London, 1947), pp. 61, 73.

36. Haig's dispatch of 21 December 1918, Boraston, ed., *Haig's Despatches,* 2:302.

37. Liddell Hart, *The Tanks,* 1:420–421.

38. Haig's dispatch of 21 March 1919, Boraston, ed., *Haig's Despatches,* 2:329.

39. Maj. Gen. Sir Archibald Montgomery, *The Story of the Fourth Army in the Battles of the Hundred Days, August 8th to November 11th, 1918* (London, 1920), p. 263.

40. See Elles' introduction to Williams-Ellis and Williams-Ellis, *Tank Corps,* and his article "Some Notes on Tank Development during the War," *AQ* 2 (July 1921): 267–281.

41. Maj. Gen. S. C. Peck, "The Evolution of Armoured Fighting Vehicles," *JRA* 56 (July 1930): 145.

42. Maj. Gen. J. F. C. Fuller, *Watchwords* (London, 1944), p. 31.

43. J. F. C. Fuller, *Memoirs of an Unconventional Soldier* (London, 1936), p. 322.

44. Ibid., pp. 322–341.

45. Ibid., pp. 1–7, 17–18, 23–28, and Anthony J. Trythall, *"Boney" Fuller: The Intellectual General* (London, 1977), pp. 1–40.

46. Fuller, *Memoirs,* pp. 97–112. See also the illuminating sketch of Fuller at the Tank Corps headquarters written by Capt. the Honourable Evan Carter in Liddell Hart, *The Tanks,* 1:120.

47. Fuller, *Memoirs,* p. 391.

48. Col. J. F. C. Fuller, "Gold Medal (Military) Prize Essay for 1919: The Application of Recent Developments in Mechanics and Other Scientific Knowledge to Preparation and Training for Future War on Land," *JRUSI* 65 (May 1920): 240.

49. Ibid., p. 252. One such example: "Had Napoleon, at Waterloo, possessed a company of machine-guns or had his men been armed with the Minie rifle he would have beaten Wellington and Blucher combined, as completely as Lord Kitchener beat the Soudanese at Omdurman."

50. Ibid., p. 261.

51. See Appendix 5 for a schematic representation of Fuller's New Model Division.

52. Immediately following publication of the prize essay, General A. L. Lynden-Bell, Fuller's immediate supervisor as the director of staff duties, rushed into Fuller's office and exclaimed "Boney, Boney, what *have* you done?" Trythall, *Fuller,* p. 87.

53. Col. J. F. C. Fuller, R.U.S.I. lecture, 11 February 1920, "The Development of Sea Warfare on Land and Its Influence on Future Naval Operations," *JRUSI* 65 (May 1920): 283. The second half of the title is a misnomer. This lecture dealt specifically with the application of naval operational techniques to the conduct of land warfare.

54. In late 1926 Fuller slightly modified his views on this subject, stating that ground "should be divided into two categories, ground over which cross country vehicles can move freely, and ground which is unsuitable to them." J. F. C. Fuller, "The Ideal Arm of the Artillery Cycle," *On Future War* (London, 1928), pp. 368–369. (Originally published in the *JRA* in October 1926.) His definition of the former category, however, was broad and did not consider the irregularities of even generally open terrain. The second category was confined to mountain ranges and large forests.

55. B. H. Liddell Hart, *The Memoirs of Captain Liddell Hart,* 2 vols. (London, 1965), 1:4–12, 18–26, 28–33.

56. Ibid., 1:38–40. This was a crucial juncture in Liddell Hart's career as a military theorist. Maxse was favorably impressed by Liddell Hart's ideas of infantry training

and arranged for Liddell Hart to be transferred to his command. He subsequently assisted materially in getting Liddell Hart's early works not only published but also to some degree accepted in military circles.

57. Capt. B. H. Liddell Hart, R.U.S.I. lecture, 3 November 1920, "The 'Man-in-the-Dark' Theory of Infantry Tactics and the 'Expanding Torrent' System of Attack," *JRUSI* 66 (February 1921): 13.

58. Liddell Hart to Fuller, 16 January 1922, quoted from Luvaas, *The Education of an Army*, p. 382.

59. Liddell Hart to Fuller, 21 January 1922, quoted from ibid.

60. The contest was won by a more conservative officer, Maj. R. Chevenix Trench. His essay, published in the *JRUSI* in May 1923, envisioned the Tank Corps being fit distinctly into the existing tactical mold and was based mainly on the War Office's *Field Service Regulations* (London, 1920), Montgomery's *The Story of the Fourth Army*, and Foch's *Des Principes de la guerre* (Paris, 1917).

61. Capt. B. H. Liddell Hart, "The Development of the 'New Model' Army: Suggestions on a Progressive but Gradual Mechanicalisation," *AQ* 9 (October 1924): 37–50.

62. Ibid., p. 38.

63. See Appendix 6 for a schematic representation of this division.

64. Liddell Hart, "The Development of the 'New Model' Army," *AQ* 9 (October 1924): 44.

65. The influence of the Treasury on War Office finance is discussed below.

66. See Liddell Hart, *Memoirs*, 1:90; Robin Higham, *The Military Intellectuals in Britain, 1918–1939* (New Brunswick, N.J., 1966), p. 85; and Richard M. Ogorkiewicz, *Armor: A History of Mechanized Forces* (New York, 1960), p. 20.

67. Capt. B. H. Liddell Hart, "Suggestions for the Future Development of the Combat Unit: The Tank as a Weapon of Infantry," *JRUSI* 64 (November 1919): 667. This suggestion was a radical implementation of the concept of tank-infantry cooperation developed during the Great War. It was not a foreshadowing of future cooperation between tanks and mechanized infantry as suggested by Liddell Hart in *The Tanks*, 1:208n, and his *Memoirs*, 1:86.

68. Liddell Hart, "The Tank as a Weapon of Infantry," *JRUSI* 64 (November 1919): 667.

69. Compare Appendixes 5 and 6.

70. Fuller, "Gold Medal Essay for 1919," *JRUSI* 65 (May 1920): 263.

71. As Fuller's views on ground employment of infantry formations changed slightly in late 1926, so did his concept of the use of infantry. Armies were still to consist primarily of tanks, and he still viewed infantry as an encumbrance in "tank country." He proposed, however, the provision of spare tank crews to be trained as light infantry and transported in cross-country vehicles for use in "infantry country." J. F. C. Fuller, *On Future War*, pp. 369, 380–382.

72. Liddell Hart, "The Development of the 'New Model' Army," *AQ* 9 (October 1924): 45.

73. In his comments on the typescript of Correlli Barnett's *Britain and Her Army*, written in September 1967, Liddell Hart said, "what he [Fuller] did convert me to was a belief in an all-tank army, whereas–except for a short period–I argued for the inclusion of other arms, especially . . . armoured and to keep up with the tanks." Liddell Hart papers, LHCMA. Liddell Hart was still preaching the obsolescence of infantry in 1925. See his *Paris: or the Future of War* (New York, 1925), pp. 65, 68–69. His views on the subject did not begin to diverge noticeably from Fuller's until 1927.

74. Fuller, "Gold Medal Essay for 1919," *JRUSI* 65 (May 1920): 256–257.

75. Liddell Hart, "The Development of the 'New Model' Army," *AQ* 9 (October 1924): 45.

76. Ibid., p. 47.

77. Fuller, "Gold Medal Essay for 1919," *JRUSI* 65 (May 1920): 259–260.

78. J. F. C. Fuller, *The Reformation of War* (New York, 1923), p. xiv. This book was an expansion of his 1919 Gold Medal Essay designed primarily for civilian consumption.

79. B. H. Liddell Hart [Bardell], "Study and Reflection *v.* Practical Experience: A Critical Examination of the Claims of Age, the Professional and the 'Practical' Soldier to Unique Authority on War," *AQ* 6 (July 1923): 318–331. Like Fuller, Liddell Hart often overstated his case in order to get people to consider what he was saying. Unlike Fuller, however, he frequently softened his tone. In a letter to the editor of the *Army Quarterly* responding to criticisms of the above article he says that he had "recognized the soldiers executive ability, and merely pointed out that, in common with all professions, the long training to attain this skill is inimical to originality, though by no means debarring it." *AQ* 8 (April 1924): 8. Brian Bond clearly illuminates Liddell Hart's adulation of the high command during the Great War, but relates that by the early 1920s Liddell Hart had concluded that his heroes had clay feet and wooden heads. Brian Bond, *Liddell Hart: A Study of His Military Thought* (New Brunswick, N.J., 1977), pp. 18–20.

80. Michael Howard, *The Continental Commitment: The Dilemma of British Defence Policy in the Era of the Two World Wars* (London, 1972), p. 79.

81. It was primarily the political pressure generated by war-weariness that caused the government to end conscription when the army was still faced with a host of overseas commitments after the Great War. See Churchill's comments on this, *H.C. Deb.*, 5th Ser., 117 (22 March 1923): 190.

82. *H.C. Deb.*, 5th Ser., 161 (15 March 1923): 1897.

83. W. R. Tucker, *The Attitude of the British Labour Party to European and Collective Security Problems, 1920–1939* (Geneva, 1950), p. 98.

84. *H.C. Deb.*, 5th Ser., 170 (13 March 1924): 2614–2615. In pledging no further reductions, Walsh was continuing the policy established by the Conservative government in June 1923. See the statement of the Earl of Derby (secretary of state for war), *H.C. Deb.*, 5th Ser., 54 (27 June 1923): 639.

85. The general consensus is discussed in G. C. Peden, *British Rearmament and the Treasury, 1932–1939* (Edinburgh, 1979), p. 3. For a sampling of reaction in Parliament to Army Estimates reductions recommended by the Geddes Committee see *H.C. Deb.*, 5th Ser., 152 (22 March 1922): 526–553.

86. Stephen Walsh's comment was typical: "I cannot imagine that the horse can be viewed other than an anachronism. It is now a misplacement in military history. The [War] Department ought to be devoting more of its efforts towards the mechanicalisation of the Army rather than preserving that which is rapidly passing into a stage fit only for a zoological museum." *H.C. Deb.*, 5th Ser., 193 (15 March 1926): 90.

87. This view, however, was not expressed strongly until later in the 1920s.

88. See speeches in defense of cavalry, *H.C. Deb.*, 5th Ser., 193 (15 March 1926): 116–118, 173–174.

89. See, for example, the speech by James Macpherson, *H.C. Deb.*, 5th Ser., 181 (16 March 1925): 1906.

90. See Brian Bond, *British Military Policy between the Two World Wars* (Oxford, 1980), pp. 14–22, for a full discussion of the army's overseas commitments.

91. The ambiguity of Locarno for military preparedness is evident in two Foreign Office documents. Prior to the signing of the treaty, Sir James Headlam-Morley, historical adviser to the Foreign Office, wrote, "If any British Government . . . feel themselves authorised to become parties to a treaty of guarantee and to make the maintenance of this a permanent part of British policy; if this is publicly proclaimed; if in presenting the estimates for naval and military defence, the importance of providing for liabilities under this treaty is shown: then I believe that in the long run the treaty will become effective." Quoted in an undated "Memorandum on the Foreign Policy of His Majesty's Government, with a list of British Commitments in their Relative Order of Importance," under cover of a minute to Sir Austen Chamberlain, 10 April 1926, *BD,* Ser. IA, 1:849. The representatives of the parties to Locarno stated, however, their firm conviction that the agreements would "hasten on effectively the disarmament provided for in Article 8 of the Covenant of the League of Nations." "Foreign Office Memorandum respecting the Locarno Treaties," 10 February 1926, ibid., 16.

92. Quoted from Peter Silverman, "The Ten Year Rule," *JRUSI* 116 (March 1971): 42.

93. The army's role in air defense, established in December 1922, was to provide guns and searchlights, commanded by army officers but under the operational control of the Royal Air Force. This role was made public by the secretary of state for war in 1924. *H.C. Deb.,* 5th Ser., 170 (13 March 1924): 2617. At the end of 1926 this territorial army force consisted of 7 air defense batteries, 14 searchlight companies with 56 guns and 336 searchlights, augmented by a volunteer corps of air observers. Maj. Gen. E. B. Ashmore, R.U.S.I. lecture, 24 November 1926, "Anti-Aircraft Defence," *JRUSI* 72 (February 1927): 3.

94. McKenna's remarks quoted from Charles Mowat, *Britain between the Wars, 1918–1940,* Beacon Paperback ed. (Boston, 1971), p. 130.

95. Cmd. 1581, *First Interim Report of the Committee on National Expenditure,* 14 December 1921, pp. 54, 76–77.

96. Mowat, *Britain between the Wars,* p. 200.

97. Cmd. 2528, *Memorandum of the Secretary of State for War relating to the Army Estimates for 1926,* 1 March 1926, p. 2.

98. Haldane's remarks were made following an R.U.S.I. lecture on the future of the National Cadet program given on 22 November 1922, *JRUSI* 68 (February 1923): 57.

99. The description of the army's budget process is based primarily on Sir Herbert Creedy's lecture "War Office Organization–Especially with Regard to Financial Control," given at the Staff College, Camberley, on 16 January 1929. Great Britain, War Office, *Report on the Staff Conference Held at the Staff College, Camberley, 14th to 17th January 1929* (London, 1929), pp. 69–84. Creedy was permanent under-secretary of state for war from 1924 to 1939. Maj. Gen. F. E. Hotblack gave the author his personal insights into the workings of War Office finance in an interview on 24 October 1972.

100. Even G. C. Peden, who argues that Treasury control of defense expenditure in the mid to late 1930s was flexible and positive, concurs with this assessment of Treasury influence in the 1920s and early 1930s. Peden, *British Rearmament and the Treasury,* p. 7.

101. Arthur Marwick, *Britain in the Century of Total War: War, Peace and Social Change, 1900–1967* (London, 1968), p. 80.

102. Derek H. Aldcroft, *The Inter-War Economy: Britain, 1919–1939* (London,

1970), pp. 182–183; L. C. B. Seaman, "A People on Wheels," *Life in Britain between the Wars* (London, 1970), pp. 131–145.

103. *Statistical Abstract of the U.K., 1930*, p. 282. Quoted from Mowat, *Britain between the Wars*, p. 231.

104. Quoted from Lt. Col. W. D. Croft, "Second Military Prize Essay for 1919: The Application of Recent Developments in Mechanics and Other Scientific Knowledge to Preparation and Training for Future War on Land," *JRUSI* 65 (August 1920): 449.

105. Brig. T. R. F. Bate, R.U.S.I. lecture, 16 November 1921, "Horse Mobilisation," *JRUSI* 67 (February 1922): 22.

106. Capt. O. T. Firth, "Mechanical Draught and Field Artillery," *AQ* 11 (October 1925): 143.

107. *H.C. Deb.*, 5th Ser., 193 (15 March 1926): 78.

108. This problem is discussed in detail in Lt. Col. G. LeQ. Martel, "The Development of Cross-Country Transport," *In the Wake of the Tank: The First Fifteen Years of Mechanization in the British Army* (London, 1931), pp. 100–109.

109. See, for example, Robin Higham, *The Military Intellectuals*, pp. 111–112.

110. This does not mean that all members of the R.T.C. agreed with Fuller. Elles was the most obvious example of those who did not.

111. Croft, "Second Military Prize Essay," *JRUSI* 65 (August 1920): 445.

112. Broad's experience in the Great War is discussed in Bidwell, *Gunners at War*, pp. 64–65; his early career with the Tank Corps in Liddell Hart, *The Tanks*, 1:227–228. See also Kenneth Macksey, *The Tank Pioneers* (London, 1981), p. 62.

113. General Sir Frederick Pile, *Ack-Ack: Britain's Defence against Air Attack during the Second World War* (London, 1949), pp. 15–26. The author is also indebted to General Pile for recounting his entry into the Royal Tank Corps in an interview on 12 October 1972.

114. Maj. Kenneth Macksey, *Armoured Crusader: A Biography of Major-General Sir Percy Hobart* (London, 1968), pp. 51, 82. Macksey attempts to separate Hobart from the Fuller school, but the letter he cites from Hobart to Lindsay in 1925 shows Hobart's only use for infantry was to take over ground captured by tanks.

115. Lindsay was sent to Mesopotamia because the commander there was dissatisfied with the performance of the armored car units, and Fuller knew Lindsay would revive them. Fuller, *Memoirs*, p. 397. Lindsay's report quoted from Liddell Hart, *The Tanks*, 1:208. See also Macksey, *Tank Pioneers*, p. 54.

116. Liddell Hart said, "Whereas Boney Fuller, and Hobart later, were all too apt to provoke opposition among the defenders of other arms, by their caustic tone of criticism, Lindsay often managed to disarm them, or at least excite the minimum revulsion to ideas that were inherently obnoxious to conservative minds." Liddell Hart, *Memoirs*, 1:98.

117. Bvt. Maj. B. C. Dening, "Military Prize Essay, 1924," *AQ* 8 (July 1924): 236–260. The subject of the 1924 essay contest dealt with the future composition of the division and corps in light of the evils of position warfare.

118. On Martel's one-man tank see Liddell Hart, *The Tanks*, 1:237–240. For details of his bridging see Lt. Gen. Sir Giffard Martel, "The Passage of Tanks over Obstacles," *An Outspoken Soldier: His Views and Memoirs* (London, 1949), pp. 56–60.

119. The best biography of Wavell in the interwar years is John Connell, *Wavell: Scholar and Soldier* (London, 1964). A narrower treatment can be found in Maj. Gen. R. J. Collins, *Lord Wavell (1883–1941): A Military Biography* (London, 1948).

120. Bernard Montgomery, *The Memoirs of Field-Marshal the Viscount Montgomery of Alamein, K.G.* (New York, 1958), pp. 33–34, 74–83. See also Nigel Hamilton, *Monty: The Making of a General, 1887–1942* (New York, 1981), pp. 104–205.

121. On Gort between the wars see J. R. Colville, *Man of Valour: Field Marshal Lord Gort, V.C.* (London, 1972), pp. 49–83. There are no studies of either Brooke or Dill in the interwar years, but on Auchinleck, Alexander, and Slim see John Connell, *Auchinleck: A Biography of Field-Marshal Sir Claude Auchinleck* (London, 1959), pp. 51–75; W. G. F. Jackson, *Alexander of Tunis as Military Commander* (London, 1971), pp. 70–78; and Geoffrey Evans, *Slim as Military Commander* (London, 1969), pp. 24–29.

122. Burnett-Stuart's views are discussed below. For Ironside's views on mechanization see Maj. Gen. Sir George Aston, ed., *The Study of War for Statesmen and Citizens: Lectures Delivered at the University of London during the Years 1925–1926* (London, 1927). Harington was widely respected for his detailed planning of the battle of Messines and circumspect handling of the Chanak crisis. For a detailed analysis of Harington's role in the latter see David Walder, *The Chanak Affair* (New York, 1969), pp. 303–318.

123. For Rawlinson's postwar views of tanks see Sir Frederick Maurice, *The Life of General Lord Rawlinson of Trent* (London, 1928), p. 289. Rawlinson died prematurely in 1925, after having been nominated as the next chief of the Imperial General Staff. Milne was G.O.C.-in-C., Eastern Command, and became C.I.G.S. in February 1926. His views are discussed in detail below. Chetwode was G.O.C.-in-C., Aldershot Command.

124. Temperamental differences between the progressive officers and their more dynamic colleagues were the primary cause of this separation. Their gradual approach to the problems of military reform was also more in keeping with British practice; the progressives tended to advance further in the army.

125. For elaboration of the conservative position see Maj. R. Chevenix Trench, "Gold Medal (Military) Prize Essay for 1922," *JRUSI* 68 (May 1923): 207, and the discussion following Lt. Col. P. Johnson's R.U.S.I. lecture, 8 December 1920, "The Use of Tanks in Undeveloped Country," *JRUSI* 66 (May 1921): 200–204.

126. General Godley's remarks were made in closing the discussion following Maj. Gen. Sir Percy Hambro's R.U.S.I. lecture, 20 October 1926, "The Horse and the Machine in War," *JRUSI* 72 (February 1927): 100.

127. Discussion following ibid., pp. 97–98.

128. According to Michael Howard, men of this ilk "regarded the social and technical changes which were transforming the country with a mistrust and incomprehension which led them, not to study these changes to see how they could be applied to the Army but rather to regard the Army as a haven where they could escape from them." Michael Howard, "The Liddell Hart Memoirs," *JRUSI* 111 (February 1966): 61.

129. Cavan admitted that he was unsuited for the post of C.I.G.S. but felt duty bound to accept it when it was offered to him. Lord Cavan's unpublished memoir, Chapter 9, "The War Office, 1922–1926," pp. 9–14. Cavan papers, Churchill College, Cambridge. Fuller claims that in 1923 Cavan denied him permission to publish *The Foundations of the Science of War* (London, 1926). Fuller, *Memoirs,* p. 420.

130. For details of Whigham's and Campbell's careers see obituaries in the *Times,* 30 June 1950, p. 8, and 12 August 1936, p. 12.

131. F. Maurice, "Birch," *DNB*, 1931–1940, pp. 79–80.

132. Great Britain, War Office, *Field Service Regulations, Vol. II (Operations), 1924* (London, 1924), p. 12.

133. Ibid., pp. 12–13.

134. Ibid., p. 14.

135. Ibid., pp. 15–16.

136. Ibid., p. 21. The above statements were identical in the 1920 and 1924 volumes. The latter made the following additional comment: "One of the chief roles of tanks is to facilitate the forward movement of infantry when the latter are unable to continue the advance owing to the enemy's rifle and machine gun fire." Ibid., p. 22.

137. General Sir Ivor Maxse said, "The theory is that general principles embody the official doctrine and that each individual commander is expected to work out for himself his own particular method of carrying out accepted principles. The practice is to do nothing of the kind, but merely to study the whim of one's immediate superior and to endeavor to satisfy it whenever a tactical scheme has to be invented for a day's training in the field." Maxse's foreword to B. H. Liddell Hart, *A Science of Infantry Tactics Simplified*, 3d ed. (London, 1926), p. vi.

138. See Appendix 7 for a schematic representation of this division.

139. "Military Notes," *JRUSI* 68 (August 1923): 530, and Capt. G. L. Kaye, "The Evolution of Anti-Tank Defence," *JRUSI* 70 (May 1925): 327.

140. Great Britain, War Office, *Infantry Training, Vol. II (War), 1926* (London, 1926), p. 23.

141. Bidwell, *Gunners at War,* p. 80.

142. W.O. 32/2841, Cavalry Committee: Interim Report, 23 November 1926, p. 24, and W.O. 32/2842, Cavalry Committee: Final Report, 4 January 1927, p. 12.

143. The psychology of the cavalry's continuing confidence in this traditional "weapons system" is discussed with great insight in Edward L. Katzenbach, "The Horse Cavalry in the Twentieth Century: A Study in Policy Response," *Public Policy* 8 (1958): 120–149.

144. Liddell Hart, *The Tanks,* 1:247.

145. Characteristics of the Vickers Medium Mark II from S. C. Peck, "The Evolution of Armoured Fighting Vehicles," *JRA* 56 (July 1930): 145–147, and Royal Armoured Corps Tank Museum, *The Inter War Period, 1919–1939* (Bovington, Dorset, 1970), p. 35. The evaluation is the author's.

146. The description of the 1925 exercise is based on Great Britain, War Office, *Report on Army Manoeuvres, 1925* (London, 1926); B. H. Liddell Hart, "Army Manoeuvres, 1925," *JRUSI* 70 (November 1925): 647–655; and the secretary of state for war's remarks in Parliament, *H. C. Deb.,* 5th Ser., 193 (15 March 1926): 78.

147. The fear of receiving artillery fire on a large body of troops in vehicles may have influenced the placement of the dismounting point so far behind the front lines.

148. This gap between equipment and doctrine was also reflected in the exhibition of mechanized vehicles put on for the imperial prime ministers in 1926. For a description of the conducted demonstrations see Liddell Hart's article in the *Daily Telegraph,* 15 November 1926, pp. 9–10.

3

THE MILITARY EDUCATION
OF JOHN BURNETT-STUART

> How a soldier makes use of the active service that does come his way makes all the
> difference between his success or failure as a commander when he reaches the
> climax of his career. In other words, the creation of sound military judgement is
> the work of a lifetime, and depends on an officer's own efforts.[1]

John Burnett-Stuart's military career from his commissioning in 1895 through
the end of his tenure as director of military operations and intelligence in
July 1926 forms the essential background for understanding his reaction to
mechanization and armored warfare in his subsequent assignment as general
officer commanding, 3d Division.[2] This chapter examines that period and
provides a brief look at his family background and early life in order to assess
the forces and circumstances that influenced his professional development
and his reaction to them.

The Burnett-Stuart name dates back to the early eighteenth century when
in 1729 Theodosia Stuart, daughter and heiress of Capt. John Stuart of
Crichie, County Aberdeen, married John Burnett of Daleadeys, County
Kincardine, a cadet member of the Burnett family of Leys; she preserved her
family name.[3] The line of succession is unclear after this union, but in 1801
John Burnett-Stuart of Dens and Crichie, County Aberdeen, married Elizabeth
Sarah Horsfall and fathered two sons, both of whom entered the ministry.
The elder, the Reverend John Burnett-Stuart of Dens and Crichie, inherited
the estate in 1847 upon the death of his father. The younger, the Reverend
Theodosius Burnett-Stuart, married in 1838 and became vicar and lord of
the manor of Woolsey, Somerset. His eldest son, Eustace Burnett-Stuart,
was born in 1846 and was educated in Winchester. In 1865 Eustace became
an ensign in the 7th Foot (Royal Fusiliers), joining the 2d Battalion of the
regiment in May 1870, and in 1873 he inherited the Burnett-Stuart estate
when his uncle died with no direct heir.[4]

In 1873 Cardwell's territorialization plan was implemented. The 7th Foot
was brigaded at Woolwich, and Eustace Burnett-Stuart, perhaps to be associated with a regiment nearer his newly inherited estate, transferred to the
79th Foot (Queen's Own Cameron Highlanders), brigaded at Perth. In making this transfer, however, he became the junior lieutenant of the regiment,
though his army date of rank preceded that of seven other lieutenants. In

June 1874 he married Carlotta Lambert, daughter of J. Lambert of Cotting-
ham, Yorkshire; on 14 March 1875 their first of four sons, John Theodosius
Burnett-Stuart, was born in Cirencester. A month later Eustace Burnett-
Stuart retired from the army, and in 1878 he completed construction of a
new house at Crichie where he remained until his death in 1925. Whether
this decision was based primarily on the uncertainties of an army career in
the wake of transfer to a new regiment and the abolition of purchase promotion, or whether it was based on a desire to lead the more tranquil existence of a gentleman farmer is not known. Its chief importance for our
story, however, is that John Burnett-Stuart grew up with strong ties to a
particular part of the world rather than being moved from station to station
following the colors.

The fact that John Burnett-Stuart was raised in Scotland had a profound
influence on his character. The folk of northern Aberdeenshire have always
lived close to the land. The gently rolling hills, well irrigated by numerous
streams and broken occasionally by small copses, support various proportions of wheat, cattle, and sheep. John Burnett-Stuart was in many ways a
man of this country. He had a genuine affection for its people, he studied its
traditions and heraldry, he fished its streams, and he hunted its woods and
fields. Throughout his life he was referred to as "Jock," the generic nickname
of many Scotsmen. The characteristics of the men who bore this appellation
have been aptly portrayed by A. P. Wavell in his foreword to *The Black
Watch and the King's Enemies:*

> The Jock of to-day comes from the city as often as from the hills or the fields. But
> he still inherits the spirit and traditions of his Highland forebears—the clan feel-
> ing, the toughness, the fierceness in assault, the independence of character, the
> boundless self-confidence in his own powers in all circumstances and conditions.
> He has also the habit of impressing his personality on any comrades of other ori-
> gins, while retaining his own whatever his surroundings.[5]

In Burnett-Stuart's case the name fit perfectly—confidence, independence,
and force of personality became his most prominent characteristics.

There were, however, other factors that influenced his development. His
father had a substantial library that included many classics and a large selection of contemporary literature and poetry; it was perhaps an early exposure
to such works that helped produce Burnett-Stuart's wide knowledge and
keen intellect. He had planned to attend Winchester, his father's school, but
contracted scarlet fever and was unable to compete for a scholarship. When
he recovered the only scholarship examination still open was at Repton. He
successfully competed and entered on the classical side in September 1889.[6]
Although Repton was not as celebrated as Eton, Harrow, or Winchester, it
had a solid reputation for academic excellence due to the efforts of Stewart
Pears, who obtained its official recognition as a public school in 1874, and

the Reverend A. F. C. Forman, who established a modern field of studies in
1878.[7] After Burnett-Stuart's first term he was third overall in his class, and
at the end of the first year he passed into the preliminary army class in first
place.[8] He remained in this class until passing directly into Sandhurst three
years later.

Because of a lack of documentation, it is difficult to determine the extent
to which his military aptitude was developed during his two years at Sandhurst.
It is possible, however, to describe the nature of the training received there,
based on an account provided by Winston Churchill, a contemporary whose
early educational experience had been much less rewarding than Burnett-
Stuart's, but who had through the efforts of the famous "crammer," Capt.
Walter James, and his own self-determination finally achieved entry on his
third attempt.

> Tactics, Fortification, Topography (mapmaking), Military Law and Military Admin-
> istration formed the whole curriculum. In addition were Drill, Gymnastics, and
> Riding. . . . Discipline was strict and the hours of study and parade were long.
> One was very tired at the end of the day. . . . We dug trenches, constructed
> breastworks, revetted parapets with sandbags. . . . We cut railway lines with slabs
> of guncotton, and learned how to blow up masonry bridges, or make substitutes
> out of pontoons or timber. We drew contoured maps of all the hills round
> Camberley, made road reconnaissances in every direction, and set out picket lines
> and paper plans for advanced guards or rear guards, and even did some very simple
> tactical schemes.[9]

The governor and commandant, Maj. Gen. C. J. East, had little impact on
the institution; J. F. C. Fuller, who entered in 1897, said that "the cadets
saw him but twice a term—when they arrived and when they departed."[10]
Burnett-Stuart passed out of Sandhurst in February 1895. Although the
records of his exact standing have not been preserved, the fact that he received
a commission in the Rifle Brigade indicates that he did well as a cadet.[11]

The reasons for Burnett-Stuart's entering the Rifle Brigade are obscure.
His father's association with the Cameron Highlanders was quite short, and
at that time the regiment had only one battalion, which may have meant
fewer vacancies.[12] Aberdeen was Gordon Highlander country, but there was
no family connection with this regiment. The Rifle Brigade depot was located
at Winchester, and perhaps his father had retained some ties in the area after
having received his education there. Whatever the reasons, it was a decision
of great significance for the development of the younger Burnett-Stuart's
military thought. John Burnett-Stuart and another subaltern joined the 3d
Battalion at Rawalpindi in May 1895, and in Burnett-Stuart's words, "The
Regiment became at once our home, our inspiration and the starting point
for everything we did."[13] He not only learned the drill, the bugle calls, and
the manual of arms from the sergeant of the square; he also absorbed the
spirit of the regiment. It may therefore be useful to sketch this spirit.

The Rifle Brigade was formed in 1800 by Col. Coote Manningham, Lt. Col. the Honourable William Stewart commanding.[14] Originally the Experimental Corps of Riflemen, the regiment drew drafts from fourteen line regiments and augmented them with volunteers from the militia. Manningham and Stewart's purpose was to develop a new set of open, extended tactics based on the characteristics of the rifle to meet the challenge of the French revolutionary armies. They armed the corps with the Baker rifle, which was accurate to ranges of over two hundred yards; dressed the men in green uniforms with black accoutrements; and taught them to maneuver to the sound of bugles. This training "gave the Regiment an impress which it never lost – of 'the fighting, thinking soldier': a corps, not of automata acting *en masse* . . . but of alert, intelligent, adventurous individual marksmen, trained to act in separation to a common purpose."[15]

The regiment's tactical proficiency was dependent upon a humane regard for the feelings of the common soldier that is reflected in the opening paragraphs of the original regulations for the Rifle Corps:

> Whilst the Colonel directs, that obedience shall be prompt, respectful, and without a murmur, so he insists upon command being executed with steadiness, and founded upon good sense and propriety.
>
> Every inferior, whether officer or soldier, shall receive the lawful commands of his superior with deference and respect, and shall execute them to the best of his power. Every superior in his turn, whether he be an Officer, or a Non-Commissioned Officer, shall give his orders in the language of moderation, and of regard to the feelings of the individual under his command; abuse, bad language, or blows, being positively forbid in the regiment.[16]

These regulations also provided for the well-being of the soldiers' wives, the education of the soldiers and their children, recreation, rewards for exemplary service, and a judicious system of internal punishment for offenses not covered by the Articles of War, which was well ahead of its time.[17]

The Rifle Corps was designated the 95th (Rifle) Regiment in 1803, but as a result of its distinguished service during the Peninsular War it was removed from the regiments of the line in 1816 and redesignated simply the Rifle Brigade. The regiment's record of service and high standards of tactical proficiency induced in many of its officers a strong feeling of corporate confidence that gave them some advantage in their careers. But as with any elite combat unit, the attendant dangers of exclusiveness and superiority were also evident – officers of the regiment at times tended to disdain others, particularly their superiors, who were felt to be less professionally qualified. Many others outside the regiment were impressed by its accomplishments and the easy-going familiarity that existed within its ranks, but some resented the clannishness of what later came to be called the Black Mafia.[18] These tendencies – tactical proficiency, mutual respect between senior and subordi-

nate, progressive thinking, confidence, independence, and impatience with
those less able—reinforced Burnett-Stuart's already existing values and became
deeply ingrained in him.

Burnett-Stuart learned a great deal as a subaltern in India. British infantry
tactics in the late nineteenth century were relatively simple. The only weapons were the rifle, the revolver, the sword, and the bayonet; tactical exercises at times became stereotyped.[19] Burnett-Stuart was fortunate in having a
commander with a lively imagination and a habit of making his subordinates
think for themselves. On one occasion this officer took his subalterns and
section commanders into a certain street of Rawalpindi to consider some of
the problems of internal security duty.[20] He pictured the company moving
down the street during a period of rioting and shooting with himself and
some local police at the head when "suddenly a lady threw a jerry [chamber
pot] out of a top-storey window, and knocked him completely out! and the
street began to fill with excited citizens." From this rather bizarre situation
the company commander developed a series of interesting little problems:

> What was the first thing the senior subaltern ought to do? Ought he to search the
> house and arrest the lady? If so, does he do it with his own men? If the police are
> thrown out with violence, does he reinforce with his own men? If his men do it,
> do they do it with loaded rifles and fixed swords [bayonets]? Anyhow, how do
> you search a house . . . ? And what does he do with the lady when he gets her?
> And what does he do with the rest of the Company while all this is going on?—
> just let them stand there?
>
> And what does he do with his Coy. Commander's senseless body? And what
> report does he send to Bn. H.Q. if any? And how do you send a message through
> a rioting town?[21]

This type of imagination, realism, practicality, and humor became an integral part of Burnett-Stuart's own training philosophy.

Burnett-Stuart also had the opportunity to do some active campaigning in
India. In June 1897 the Madda Khel section of the Waziris attacked a unit
of Indian troops at Maizar near the Tochi Valley, and the 3d Battalion, Rifle
Brigade, was ordered to join the hastily formed Tochi Field Force.[22] The
battalion moved by rail to Kushalkgurgh and from there by foot across one
of the hottest districts in India. For the next three months the battalion
constructed fortifications, escorted convoys, posted pickets, and searched in
vain for the enemy. About the end of July a severe epidemic of dysentery
and enteric fever broke out, and by the end of October the battalion had to
be withdrawn from the field. Having begun with 20 officers and 801 other
ranks, it returned to its new station at Umballa with 12 officers and 540
other ranks, 197 of whom were immediately admitted to the hospital. Burnett-
Stuart contracted a serious case of typhoid during the campaign, and when
the battalion departed the Tochi Valley he was left at the Bannu hospital. A
grave was booked for him in the local churchyard.[23]

Despite this pessimism, he quickly recovered and soon began to demonstrate his professional competence. In early 1898 he was attached as signals officer to the Khar Mobile Brigade in the Swat Valley, having been awarded an instructor's certificate in army signaling the previous year. Signaling at this time was both simple and complex. The means were rather uncomplicated, consisting of small and large flags, the semaphore, and the heliograph; but the instructions for using these instruments were detailed to the point of pedantry.[24] Competition among the regiments in passing their signals qualification tests was remarkably intense, and possession of the signaling certificate was looked upon as one of the essential qualifications of battalion adjutants.[25] Upon his return to the battalion in the fall of 1898, Burnett-Stuart was designated acting adjutant.[26] Apparently he did well, for the report of the inspector in army signaling for 3d Battalion, Rifle Brigade, dated 4 February 1899, stated that, "The results of the inspection are most satisfactory, and the signallers all show signs of very careful training."[27] Later that year, Burnett-Stuart left India for leave at home, having absorbed the traditions of his regiment, become exposed to imaginative small-unit leadership, participated in a disastrous military campaign, and demonstrated proficiency in one of the essential technical skills of his profession. In his own words, "Behind me were my four most formative years, and I was nearly grown up."[28]

When the South African war broke out in October 1899, the British Army was, as usual, almost totally unprepared. Staffs and logistical arrangements were improvised as they had been throughout the nineteenth century. Caught up in this mêlée, Burnett-Stuart was assigned as division signal officer of the 6th Division at Aldershot in December 1899; in the wake of the "Black Week" of British defeats he left for Naauwpoort in the Cape Colony.[29] Ordered north to Modder River, the division acted as a decoy while Sir John French moved quickly into Kimberley. When the Boer general Piet Cronje evacuated Magersfontein and moved east, General Horatio Kitchener ordered French to cut him off at Koodesrand and directed the 6th Division to pursue. French accomplished his mission and the 6th Division arrived on the scene completely surrounding Cronje's force. After a week of intense fighting, the Boers surrendered with over four thousand men.

Burnett-Stuart's position allowed him to follow this important action closely and to see at first hand the tactical decisions of some of the senior British commanders.[30] Burnett-Stuart's account of the action shows him to have been a young officer with tactical sense and acute powers of observation, qualities that were to assist him immeasurably in the future. The war was profitable to Burnett-Stuart in several ways. He was awarded a D.S.O. in 1900; he was promoted to captain in 1901; and while in South Africa, he met Nina Nelson, whom he married in 1904. Following the war, he served briefly in Egypt with the 4th Battalion, Rifle Brigade, and apparently became interested in the Staff College.

He passed the Staff College entrance examination on his first attempt in August 1902, and arrived at Camberley in January 1903, a particularly propitious time.[31] Lord Roberts' testimony before the Royal Commission on the War in South Africa highlighted the need for a well-trained staff, and L. S. Amery's polemic history of that war carried the message to the public.[32] The commandant was then Maj. Gen. H. S. G. Miles, a personable man who made some limited improvements in the curriculum, but one whose concepts of staff work revolved mainly around a proper appreciation of the *King's Regulations*.[33] In December 1903, however, Miles was replaced by Brig. Gen. H. S. Rawlinson, a brilliant officer and one of the most effective column commanders in South Africa. Rawlinson had enormous drive and energy, youth (he was only forty), high social standing, and a flair for getting the most out of those under him. He substituted the title of "directing staff" for "professor," judged his students more by personal evaluation than written examinations, brought naval officers into the course, arranged for combined army-navy annual staff tours, and formed a syndicate of students to lecture weekly on the developments of the Russo-Japanese war.[34]

The greatest influence on Burnett-Stuart was most likely not that of either Miles or Rawlinson, but the chief staff duties instructor, Lt. Col. "Tommy" Capper. Capper had been appointed to the Staff College in December 1902, and in the words of Hubert Gough, a fellow member of the directing staff had

> revolutionised the teachings of staff duties. He never discussed the details of the duties of a junior staff officer in peace at Aldershot, which had been my sole study in this subject under Miles. On the contrary, he went thoroughly into the plans, orders and arrangements which might be required for the success of some definite operations in war. Moreover, he always inculcated a spirit of self-sacrifice and duty, instead of the idea of playing for safety and seeking only to avoid getting into trouble. This high-minded inspiration marked all the teaching under Rawlinson too, but it was due perhaps more to Capper than anyone else. It was like a silver thread which ran through every problem we discussed and studied.[35]

The directing staff also included Richard Haiking and John Du Cane, both of whom had practical experience in South Africa. Burnett-Stuart was fortunate to pass through the Staff College at this time of regeneration. His service in the years ahead proved he had profited from it.

When Burnett-Stuart entered the War Office in February 1905, it was in a state of flux. As a result of the Esher Report, an Army Council had been established in 1904 and a clean sweep made of the military heads of the army. Nevertheless, due to a combination of ministerial indifference, Treasury parsimony, and a good deal of resistance from the adjutant general and quartermaster general departments, a functioning General Staff was still more

Crichie House – Burnett-Stuart's birthplace and home. (Courtesy of the Burnett-Stuart family.)

vision than reality. Haldane, then secretary of state for war, effected a compromise with the older departments. In 1906 he issued an Army Order that grafted the General Staff onto the existing structure of the War Office, but also established its organization, defined its functions, and provided for the accelerated promotion of its members.[36] The General Staff at the War Office was divided into three directorates: staff duties, military training, and military operations. Burnett-Stuart was initially assigned to the "special" section of military operations with responsibility for questions concerning undersea cables, wireless telegraphy, censorship, and ciphers. At the end of two years of this rather boring duty, he was reassigned to form a section given responsibility to organize the Officer Training Corps.[37] In his new position he had the opportunity to tour the universities with Haldane as the secretary propounded the scheme to them. Burnett-Stuart found this work very satisfying, mixing as it did military training with sound education. He was appointed a general staff officer, 2d grade (GSO2), in June 1908 and left the War Office in February 1909.

These were busy years for British strategists. The month after Burnett-Stuart joined the General Staff, Kaiser Wilhelm II visited Morocco, unwittingly solidifying the newly formed Entente Cordiale; the Anglo-Russian treaty was signed in August 1907; and in July 1908 a General Staff memorandum was drafted that concluded if Germany violated Belgian neutrality, Britain's only course of action would be "to prolong the left of the French Army."[38]

Capt. John T. Burnett-Stuart in Rifle Brigade dress uniform with D.S.O. awarded for service in South Africa. (Courtesy of the Burnett-Stuart family.)

As Britain began to prepare for a possible war with Germany, the question of imperial defense also came to the fore. The self-governing Dominions were beginning to recognize their responsibility for local defense, but their forces were evolving on divergent lines and they were somewhat reluctant to commit themselves to supporting Britain in a European war. At the Imperial Conference of 1907 General Lyttleton presented a memorandum on the "Possibility of Assimilating War Organisation throughout the Empire." Haldane secured its acceptance, and preliminary instructions were issued to establish an Imperial General Staff.[39] At the next Imperial Conference in 1909, General Sir William Nicholson, the new chief of the General Staff, presented a concrete plan to form a General Staff to act as "an entity throughout the Empire" so that various imperial forces could be combined "rapidly into one homogeneous Imperial Army"; he did stipulate that full control of Dominion staffs was to be maintained by the local government, the C.G.S.' role being limited to guidance.[40] This formula was accepted by the Dominion ministers, and although no true Imperial General Staff was created, General Staffs patterned closely on the British model were soon established in Canada, Australia, and New Zealand.

In October 1910 Burnett-Stuart was sent to New Zealand as the director of military operations. Although still a captain, he was given the local rank of lieutenant colonel, commensurate with his responsibilities, which were defined as "[obtaining] information about the Dominion and neighbouring countries; preparation of plans for local defence and strategical distribution of the Forces; mapping and reconnaissance of the Dominion; war establishments and war organization; application of the principles laid down in the 'Field Service Regulation'; intelligence duties; staff tours; and plans for mobilization."[41] Under the Defence Acts of 1909 and 1910, the New Zealand Military Forces were organized into a Permanent Force and a Territorial Force. Members of the Permanent Force served for five years with the colors and eight years in a reserve, subject to recall, and were liable for service outside the borders of New Zealand. The Territorial Force was primarily for the defense of New Zealand but could volunteer for liability to outside service. Burnett-Stuart's first task was to give these units a coherent form. To do this he drafted the *Regulations (Provisional) for the Military Forces of the Dominion of New Zealand, 1911.*[42] Similar to the *King's Regulations* but simpler and adapted to local needs, these regulations provided for the organization of the forces; duties of commanders and staff officers; promotion, retirement, resignation, transfer, and discipline of personnel; training; and education. It was "the book which eventually landed the New Zealand Force in Gallipoli."[43]

Regulations, however, are often not widely read and Col. E. S. Heard, the director of staff duties and military training, soon realized that a military journal would be a useful adjunct to the development of the New Zealand Military Forces. Colonel Heard became the first editor of the *New Zealand*

Military Journal, and Burnett-Stuart wrote the lead article for the initial issue entitled "Elementary Principles of Training for Territorial Regimental Officers."[44] He began with a quotation from G. F. R. Henderson on the development of effective units, but very soon moved into his own training philosophy. He contended that lectures on strategy and grand tactics were good in their time and place, but added, "In our circumstances here, the time we can afford to give to the study of soldiering is so short, and therefore so infinitely precious, that we must devote it to qualifying ourselves to fit into our particular place in the military organization. We simply have not the time to learn anyone's job but our own."[45] He then suggested a number of specific topics he felt worthy of consideration: "Company on outpost in the New Zealand bush . . . training of isolated Territorial infantryman in the backblocks. . . . How to keep the Senior Cadet interested in his drills. . . . Small exercises for the Territorial N.C.O.'s."[46] Like many other British soldiers, Burnett-Stuart often drew analogies from sport—"We are all . . . members of an international team representing New Zealand, and if the game is worth playing at all we may as well learn to be good at it: this can only be done by practice and by sticking to the rules."[47]

After eight months of intense work, Burnett-Stuart was forced to take command of the Canterbury District, headquartered at Christchurch, after its commander suddenly died of a heart attack. He also had to continue in his staff position at Wellington since no replacement staff officers were available. The strain of both jobs and the rough passage from Christchurch finally resulted in a nervous breakdown.[48] Following a period of rest and recovery, Burnett-Stuart left New Zealand in September 1912. His brief tour was significant both for his positive contribution to the development of the New Zealand military forces and for his own professional development. It is not often that a soldier of his grade is given the opportunity to help build an army from the ground up. By doing it successfully he had proved his worth as an efficient staff officer with a wide range of knowledge. His subsequent assignments were to prove even more demanding.

In September 1913 Burnett-Stuart was appointed GSO2 on the directing staff of the Staff College and promoted temporary lieutenant colonel. Timing was again fortunate, for the commandant, Maj. Gen. W. R. "Wully" Robertson, had done much to put the Staff College on a practical footing. Robertson's methods are described in his memoirs:

> Staff tours . . . usually lasted three or four days, and I tried to conduct them in such a way as would test the students' tempers and physical powers as well as their knowledge. Information about the (imaginary) enemy would be given at all hours of the day and night and emanate from all sources—newspapers, secret agents, prisoners, inhabitants, and aeroplanes—some of the news being reliable, some doubtful, some contradictory, and it was for the students to sift and piece together the

different items, thus obtaining approximately the same amount of information as they might be expected to get in war before they could regulate the actions of their troops.[49]

From October to December 1913, Burnett-Stuart helped direct the Senior Division Annual Staff Tour, a general strategic exercise covering southern England and the Midlands; exercises in various tactical situations such as night operations, defense of river crossings, and wood fighting; and an indoor exercise that studied the opening phases of a possible war involving Great Britain, France, and Belgium with Germany.[50] He thus had the opportunity to consider a wide range of tactical and strategic problems.

One's associations at the Staff College, however, are just as important as what one learns or teaches, if not more so. The directing staff then included such notables as Frederick Maurice and W. H. Anderson with whom Burnett-Stuart got on quite well. But in January 1914 a new member of the directing staff arrived from Quetta – Lt. Col. Archibald Montgomery. Montgomery was an intelligent, efficient staff officer, but his definition of loyalty was so narrow and his emphasis on tradition for its own sake was so great that he and Burnett-Stuart were almost never able to agree on any military matters.[51] This fundamental divergence of professional and personal viewpoints had a profound effect on Burnett-Stuart's career.

Shortly after Burnett-Stuart's arrival, Robertson was replaced as commandant by Maj. Gen. L. Kiggell. According to Harold Franklyn, then a student at the Staff College, Kiggell "was a scholarly type, of a retiring nature and content to let well alone."[52] Franklyn also says that in 1914, "The main weakness of the various schemes was that no attempt was made to simulate the hustle and distractions of active service; in fact they lacked realism."[53] This was an unfortunate degeneration from the lively days of Wully Robertson. Another student in Franklyn's class, Capt. J. F. C. Fuller, had even stronger things to say about the Staff College in 1914. Fuller complained of being chastised for drafting papers showing the superiority of artillery over infantry and penetration over envelopment, both of which were contrary to the *Field Service Regulations*, and of being discouraged from attempting to codify the previously ill-defined principles of war. Fuller's view of the Staff College is summarized in his observations that "it must not be thought from this that our instructors were complete idiots; they were not. They were just parts of a machine created to produce standardised thinking."[54] Since Fuller was then a student in the Junior Division and Burnett-Stuart an instructor in the Senior Division, one cannot determine whether Fuller would have included Burnett-Stuart in this categorization. Nor is it possible to determine the extent to which Burnett-Stuart was aware of the presence of this military iconoclast in the newly entering class.

When the Great War began the Staff College was hastily disestablished, students and staff alike being ordered to various mobilization posts. Burnett-Stuart was assigned as GSO2 to the 6th Division, which was initially held in England for fear of invasion.[55] The division embarked for St. Nazaire on 8 September, and on the 16th it arrived near the front only to have its brigades parceled out as reinforcements for the first five divisions. In early October the division was reconstituted and formed the lead element of the III Corps in the "race to the sea." It attacked east of Armentières in mid-October but was forced back by strong pressure from the German 25th (Reserve) and 26th Divisions, losing nearly two thousand men on 20 October. The division did not participate in any other major actions in 1914, and Burnett-Stuart was sent home to Marlborough as GSO1 of the newly formed 15th (Scottish) Division in February 1915.

The 15th Division arrived in France in July 1915, though in hindsight it was admitted that it and the other units of the New Armies could not possibly have been ready for the field until July 1916. This unpreparedness was tragically borne out in the Battle of Loos. Douglas Haig, the First Army commander, and Wully Robertson, the chief of the General Staff of the British Expeditionary Force, both advised against a large offensive because of the insufficiency of British artillery, the strength of the German positions, and the flat, open terrain. They were overruled, however, by Kitchener, the secretary of state for war, who felt it necessary to support General Joseph Joffre's plan for a combined Anglo-French offensive in Artios and Champagne.[56] On 22 August 1915 Haig and his senior commanders witnessed an impressive demonstration of chlorine gas that led them to believe that if gas were used on a large scale, the chances for a successful offensive would be relatively good. In the event, the wind was neutral rather than favorable on the day of the attack, but there was no turning back. The gas was employed with only partial success and the divisions suffered accordingly.

The 15th Division had been given a particularly difficult portion of the line to assault that included the Lens Road and Loos Road redoubts, an objective originally scheduled for attack by two divisions. Despite heavy casualties inflicted on its forward battalion by four German machine-guns, the division finally broke through the first line of defense; but the lead elements strayed to the south of their proposed axis of advance and failed to take the second line. After the second day of fighting, the division had suffered 6,668 casualties and was removed from the line. Having a newly formed division virtually destroyed in its first combat action was undoubtedly a traumatic experience for its GSO1, Burnett-Stuart; it was probably among the factors responsible for his life-long aversion to Continental warfare.

One of the British Army's most glaring deficiencies in 1915 was the lack of suitable staff officers to guide and direct its expansion. In November of that year Burnett-Stuart was assigned to General Headquarters as the equivalent of director of staff duties, with responsibility for matters pertaining to the education and appointment of staff officers, organization, and communication—all areas in which he possessed a great deal of expertise. Shortly after Burnett-Stuart's arrival, Douglas Haig replaced Sir John French as commander of British forces in France and Robertson went home to become chief of the Imperial General Staff. Haig's new chief of staff was Major General Kiggell, who served Haig much as Berthier had served Napoleon, echoing his opinions and circulating his papers but seldom offering independent advice or criticism. Other key members of the staff suffered from the same deficiency. In the words of one of Haig's recent biographers, they were "too much in awe of Papa."[57]

There was, however, one bright spot. In December 1915, an intelligent young officer named A. P. Wavell was assigned as a GSO2 in Burnett-Stuart's section. The two men were quite different in temperament. Burnett-Stuart was gay, witty, and extroverted; Wavell was shy, diffident, and reserved. They were, however, kindred spirits. Both were reflective, but with a strong practical bent; both were dedicated to the pursuit of professional excellence; and both were lovers of poetry. Writing of this period in his "Recollections," Wavell said that Burnett-Stuart had "probably the best and quickest brain in the Army of his rank," and that he was forcible and practical, but intolerant of those over him and difficult to control. To his subordinates, however, he was kind and sympathetic. "Everyone under him always swore by him. He became a guide and friend to me at once."[58] Thus began an association that was to prove personally and professionally rewarding to both men and beneficial for the army as well.

In February 1917 Burnett-Stuart was assigned as brigadier general, General Staff of the VII Corps, commanded by Lt. Gen. Sir Thomas Snow, an accomplished commander and one of the few tactical innovators among the British senior officers. While commanding the 4th Division before the war, Snow had used camouflage extensively to deceive his opponents on maneuvers, drafted the only existing set of division standing orders, and practiced retreats as well as offensive operations. This innovative spirit helped him during the Great War.[59] In March 1917 the Germans withdrew to a fortified position known as the Hindenburg Line, leaving a wasteland facing the British Fourth and Fifth armies. Haig's plan was to use Allenby's Third Army to break through the old defenses near Arras, outflanking the Hindenburg Line. In anticipation of such a move the Germans were constructing an alternate position five miles behind the old lines covering the exposed side. Thus Allenby's main hope of success lay in achieving enough surprise to get him through both positions before German reserves could be brought up. Surprise, however, was ruled out when Haig and his artillery adviser decided that a five-day bombardment preceded by three weeks of "wire cutting" was required.[60]

The VII Corps was assigned the southernmost portion of the attacking sector, two of its four divisions facing the Hindenburg Line itself.[61] Snow's plan was to break through with his two northern divisions (56th and 30th) and merely to push forward small groups with those on the south (14th and 21st). Although Allenby instructed him to assault with all four divisions, Snow gave the 21st permission to stop short of the main defenses if the wire were insufficiently cut.

When the offensive began on 9 April, the 56th and 30th made good progress, but the 14th and 21st very little. Rather than attempting to "tidy up the line," Snow directed the 56th and 30th to continue to advance and the 14th and 21st to remain in position and support them with fire. This was one of the rare occasions in 1917 in which a senior British commander acted on the principle of reinforcing success and limiting failure. These tactics worked. For by 12 April the Germans retired from the end of the Hindenburg Line, and the 21st Division moved quickly into it. Although the first several days had been heartening, the advance had not been made quickly enough for the planned cavalry exploitation. German reserves were brought up in time, and the offensive deteriorated by the end of May. Burnett-Stuart had, however, seen at first-hand the positive effects of independence and sound tactical thinking and the folly of mindless conformity.

The effects of such thinking were soon demonstrated to him again. On 20 November General Sir Julian Byng's Third Army launched the Cambrai offensive discussed in the previous chapter. Although the VII Corps did not take a direct part in this operation, Burnett-Stuart was responsible for assembling the camouflage material for the tanks and making the preliminary reconnaissance.[62] When the British offensive bogged down near Bourlon Wood, the Germans prepared a counterattack. One of Snow's divisional commanders noticed German artillery registering their guns on new locations, their planes making detailed reconnaissance of British positions, and British planes being forced away from likely areas of German concentration.[63] On the evening of the 28th Burnett-Stuart phoned the Third Army C.G.S. telling him of these indicators and pointing out the tactical sense of a German attack at both bases of the British salient, but no action was taken in response.[64] On the 30th the Germans launched attack exactly as Snow and Burnett-Stuart had warned, inflicting heavy losses on the neighboring III Corps.[65] Soon after, Snow recommended a flank attack on the Germans; his advice was again ignored. The cavalry was instead launched directly into the German positions, stabilizing the lines but not regaining any lost ground.[66] Burnett-Stuart reportedly to have observed, "Our Generals are so stupid that even when they get opportunities they don't know how to use them."[67] On 3 December Haig instructed Byng to withdraw to a line that could be easily defended through the winter, disappointingly ending a battle begun with great promise.

During 1917 the high casualties from the abortive Passchendaele offensive, the demands of other theaters, especially Italy, the need for skilled laborers at home in the factories, and the assumption of additional portions of the French line due to the failure of the Nivelle offensive made the manpower situation one of the most crucial problems facing the British Army.[68] In August 1917 Robertson informed Kiggell that the War Office calculated a deficit of over 43,000 infantrymen and 31,000 artillerymen in France alone.[69] On 26 December Burnett-Stuart was once again assigned to G.H.Q., this time as deputy adjutant general, with primary responsibility for manpower.[70] Although he had previously served only in General Staff appointments, this assignment indicates that he had acquired a reputation for efficiency and the ability to deal effectively with difficult and important problems. It may also indicate that the General Staff wanted to get a man of their own in the adjutant general department.

Since every subordinate unit was demanding men, it was not a position in which one made friends. It may have been a source of friction with Montgomery, who in 1918 was chief of the General Staff, Fourth Army. It was certainly a source of friction with the GSO1 of the Tank Corps, Col. J. F. C. Fuller. Fuller wanted the Tank Corps doubled to support his Plan 1919, but Haig thought the existing eighteen tank battalions to be sufficient. On 2 October 1918 Fuller, Elles, and Maj. Gen. A. L. Lynden-Bell, director of staff duties at the War Office, met with Burnett-Stuart and another staff officer at G.H.Q. to discuss the problem. After several hours of haggling, it was decided that twelve thousand men from Salonika and the men of the 63d Division could be made available to the Tank Corps, but that G.H.Q. would sanction no further diversions. Thus to Fuller, Burnett-Stuart appeared as part of the obstructionist establishment, though he recognized that the decision had ultimately been Haig's.[71]

Burnett-Stuart served as deputy adjutant general for the rest of the war, remaining with the occupying force in Germany until April 1919. The Great War had not been a particularly happy experience for him. Because of his proficiency as a staff officer, he was never given the opportunity to command, which was a deep disappointment.[72] Nor did Burnett-Stuart become part of any wartime clique. Although he served at G.H.Q. for two years, he was never part of Haig's inner circle, and unlike Archibald Montgomery and Tim Harington, staff officers who became prominently identified with Lords Rawlinson and Plumer respectively, Burnett-Stuart was not attached to any particular army commander. His closest association had been with Snow, but Snow had been seriously injured in 1914 and retired quietly at the end of the war. Still in all, the four years had been put to good use. While some staff officers had become insulated in their administrative environment and proved unable to make the transition to more active duties, others had used their staff experience to observe and reflect on the problems of command.[73] Burnett-Stuart soon proved that he was among the latter.

In November 1920 Burnett-Stuart was sent to India as general officer commanding, Madras District. India was then in a state of turmoil. The Great War, the Third Afghan War, and the revolt in Waziristan had taken a heavy human and administrative toll on both the Indian Army and the British Army in India. British-Indian tensions were raised in 1919 when Brig. Gen. R. E. H. Dyer ordered his troops to fire on a large crowd at Amritsar, killing over three hundred and wounding nearly fifteen hundred. The Montague-Chelmsford reforms had placed some power into Indian hands, while retaining British sovereignty and the right of veto at the national level. But there was still a great deal of civil unrest highlighted by Gandhi's non-cooperation movement. Many military reforms had also taken place, including reorganization of the staff at Simla, reduction of Indian cavalry, regrouping Indian infantry regiments, and the establishment of four operational commands.[74] Under this reorganization scheme, Madras District, consisting of the Madras Presidency and Mysore, fell under the control of Southern Command.[75] Although Madras had been generally peaceful compared to many of the northern provinces, one subdistrict, Malabar, had a potential for violence due to the high percentage of Arab Muslims, known as Moplahs, who lived among the predominantly Hindu population.

On 20 August 1921 a Malabar magistrate arrested several Moplah leaders suspected of inciting disturbances. Shortly thereafter they were met by a large crowd, and firing ensued; the platoon of British soldiers and policemen accompanying the magistrate had to fight their way to safety.[76] A revolt soon broke out in two large sections of southern Malabar. Burnett-Stuart, having been given a free hand by the government of Madras, placed Col. Edward Humphreys of the Leinster Regiment in immediate control of the affected area, giving him an additional British infantry battalion, a section of artillery, and a squadron of cavalry. On 26 August a modified martial law ordinance was proclaimed for southern Malabar by the government of India that established summary courts, but limited the jurisdiction of these courts to cases punishable by no more than five years imprisonment. The Madras government's situation report on southern Malabar for 30 August said that "local machinery of Government has broken down. Throughout affected areas Government offices have been wrecked and looted, and records destroyed . . . ordinary business at a standstill."[77] There were also dangers of famine, and both Hindu and European refugees were fleeing the countryside. Burnett-Stuart soon requested and received two additional infantry battalions.

Burnett-Stuart had not only the Moplahs to deal with; he had the government of India as well. On 7 September the adjutant general at Simla sent a letter referring to the furor over the Amritsar affair and adding, "His Excellency the Viceroy is particularly anxious that on the present occasion in Malibar the reestablishment of order may not give rise to similar criticism and that undue severity will not be enforced by military officers under the Martial Law Ordinance."[78] Given this pressure, Burnett-Stuart could have administered martial law in Malabar personally, and indeed he was urged by Southern Command to do so. He realized, though, that this would severely limit his own freedom of action and he delegated this authority to Colonel Humphreys.[79] His instructions to Humphreys were explicit but low-key: "Petty persecution of inhabitants in places occupied by troops must be rigorously forbidden. It does no good in any case. Fortunately we are up against a fairly clear cut proposition. A Mop is a definite species; he either fights and is killed or captured; or he is wanted by the Police and arrested—otherwise he is left alone."[80]

Fortunately Rawlinson, then commander-in-chief in India, trusted Burnett-Stuart implicitly. On 21 September he wrote: "I am obliged for your letter of 13th September which tells me just what I wanted to know about your doings in Malabar. . . . You are having a great campaign all on your own down in Madras, and I am sure you will bring it off victoriously. . . . Write occasionally and keep me informed of how things are going."[81] Relations with Montgomery, Rawlinson's deputy chief of staff, were a bit strained. Montgomery was, quite rightly, concerned with press coverage of the rebellion, but he seemed unable to appreciate the difficult position of the man on the spot. Burnett-Stuart was involved in a touchy campaign and although willing to give some attention to the press, felt that Montgomery's frequent requests that he conduct press conferences and grant special interviews were unrealistic. After one exchange of correspondence on the subject, Montgomery replied, "Good luck—I always like your letters because they say exactly what you think."[82] These were words he would not so willingly repeat in the years ahead.

Throughout the month of September the situation in Malabar continued to deteriorate, and on the 26th Burnett-Stuart drafted a telegram outlining the steps he felt necessary to end the rebellion:

> I have definitely decided that the methods and powers available at present for dealing with rebellion in Malabar are not adequate. . . . The Moplah programme is framed upon plunder, guerrilla warfare, avoidance of battle, and terrorisation . . . the probable total strength of their armed fighting gangs is 10,000 and this total is tending to increase. . . . In my opinion more drastic measures are demanded owing to the new and unforeseen state of affairs which has arisen. To effect this, two additional battalions of infantry are required. . . . I should also need a pack Battery of 3.7 howitzers. . . . It is essential, furthermore, that the limited powers now enjoyed by the summary courts and special tribunals should be supplemented. . . . The death penalty, subject to final confirmation by me, should be included. . . . When application of the minimum military force is practised, attempts to handle the situation as an ordinary outbreak are liable to collapse; such efforts

have been fully exploited and failed. Widespread devastation, prolonged rebellion and famine can only be avoided by taking prompt measures as though the situation were one of actual war, which in fact it now clearly is.[83]

The government of India balked at this, but both Rawlinson and the Madras government fully supported Burnett-Stuart's position. He soon got the additional troops and the new powers for military courts, which set the stage for effective military operations.

Southern Malabar is marked by a narrow coast of sandy plain, rolling foothills covered with paddies and coconut groves, and jungle-covered mountains rising to eight thousand feet. It is difficult country for counterguerrilla operations, but by establishing close liaison with local police and by maintaining good communications among themselves, the British, Indian, and Gurkha units soon obtained accurate information concerning the location of many Moplah bands. Columns of infantry, armored cars, and pack artillery began tracking them down and defeating them. By the beginning of November, Moplah groups numbering in the hundreds began to surrender, and by the beginning of December the situation had so improved that battalions were given individual areas to control rather than being brought together for large operations. Burnett-Stuart realized that the situation had stabilized, and in the beginning of December when the chief civil servant in Madras suggested obtaining even more troops, he replied:

> Apart from the purely military difficulties of maintaining more troops and giving them the necessary degree of mobility, I would even go so far as to say that by increasing the number of troops we might defeat our own ends and produce a premature settlement. . . . If we put more troops into the area we run the risk of forcing the rebels out of it [he did not want the rebellion to spread to northern Malabar] or of producing within it a state of artificial security dependent on the actual presence of troops everywhere; a state of affairs with no enduring basis and one which it would be very difficult to depart from when the time comes for the troops to go away.[84]

During January and February 1922, troops were gradually withdrawn and increased responsibilities were turned over to the police until finally the martial law ordinance was revoked.

Burnett-Stuart's success was attributable in part to favorable circumstances—cooperation of the Madras government, Rawlinson's support, and the lack of any real identity between Moplah aspirations and those of the anti-British Indians. It was, however, a very difficult situation, and Burnett-Stuart deserves much of the credit for resolving it successfully. He skillfully controlled the tactical operations; he was sensitive to the proper use of force in civil unrest; and he picked his subordinates carefully and directed them well, without oversupervising. If his superiors trusted him, it was because he gave them cause to do so. His handling of the Moplah Rebellion proved that he was, in fact, a competent commander. It also put him in the limelight. After the Dyer affair, his firm but restrained approach was appreciated in both military and political circles.[85] In September 1922 he was selected to return to the War Office as director of military operations and intelligence, and in 1923 he was created Knight Commander of the Order of the British Empire, a distinct honor for a comparatively junior major general.[86]

Burnett-Stuart assumed his new duties in the War Office on 11 September 1922, the same day that the post of deputy chief of the Imperial General Staff, then held by Philip Chetwode, was abolished.[87] This reorganization, coupled with Lord Cavan's lack of staff experience, gave the General Staff directors a good deal of leeway, and it was commonly accepted that during Cavan's tenure Burnett-Stuart and Maj. Gen. John Gathorne-Hardy, the director of military training, played a large role in establishing General Staff policy.[88] As director of military operations and intelligence, Burnett-Stuart was responsible for the preparation of strategic plans and estimates for army forces throughout the Empire and, as a regular attendee of Committee of Imperial Defence meetings, for coordinating these plans among the other services.[89]

The first paper brought before the newly formed Chiefs of Staff Sub-Committee of the C.I.D. concerned the army's requirements for air support. The General Staff stipulated a requirement for eight permanently allotted squadrons to train with the home divisions and support the expeditionary force in the event of its being ordered abroad.[90] But Air Marshal Hugh Trenchard, the chief of the Air Staff, wanted to allocate only a few squadrons to the army on a definite basis and to provide the others as the situation demanded. Lord Salisbury, the Lord President of the Council, who had been called upon to chair the first meeting of the C.O.S., agreed with the army but said that Trenchard must be consulted in determining requirements.[91] In the event, the home army received only three squadrons, which seriously limited its capacity to conduct combined army-air training.[92] Burnett-Stuart also dealt with the defense of the Suez Canal. In order to prevent political disturbances in the army's rear while it dealt with an attack from the northeast, he felt it necessary to maintain a military hold on Cairo. He realized, however, that troops in Cairo were an affront to Egyptian nationalism and felt that a garrison at Abbasia would serve the same purpose and simultaneously protect the railroads and fresh-water canals essential to defense of the canal zone proper.[93]

In November and December 1923, Burnett-Stuart went to Baghdad for a first-hand assessment of the Middle East situation. Rather than going by rail from Alexandretta to Baghdad, he went by air from Cairo.[94] It was a rather uncertain journey, and the R.A.F. had constructed a number of small intermediate stations to establish this route. Total flying time from Cairo to Baghdad and return to Damascus was nine days, covering 2,300 miles—quite an air journey for an army officer in those days. This trip was apparently the occasion on which Burnett-Stuart began to develop his great love of flying, an affection that gave him practical knowledge of the R.A.F. as well as a great deal of personal satisfaction.

During his tenure in the War Office Burnett-Stuart also dealt with the contentious problem of army and R.A.F. control in Iraq, security of the Mosul and South Persian oil fields, establishment of a base at Singapore, and the Nationalist situation in China. Throughout this period the strategic memoranda prepared by the General Staff show a great deal of realism and an awareness of the capabilities and limitations of military power.[95] Wavell, whom Burnett-Stuart brought to his directorate in July 1923, describes his chief's work as follows: "Jock was as brilliant as ever, and as caustic, very easy to serve, difficult for his superiors to control. He had little opinion of Cavan's knowledge or intellect, and was at odds with a good deal of H.M.G.'s policy; and as usual he never concealed his views."[96]

In his memoir Burnett-Stuart intimates displeasure with each of the immediate postwar governments. In contrast to Haldane, whom Burnett-Stuart held in extremely high esteem, he said of the leaders of these governments, "The Statesmen of the Great War had tended to revert to original stock, as a rose reverts to a briar, and to become politicians again."[97] Wavell's description of Burnett-Stuart's lack of respect of Lord Cavan's intellect certainly rings true, and it is not too difficult to imagine Burnett-Stuart becoming one of the dominant personalities of the General Staff. This state of affairs was altered somewhat in February 1926 when General George Milne replaced Cavan as chief of the Imperial General Staff. On Milne's first day at the War Office, Burnett-Stuart introduced one of his remarks with the phrase, "The General Staff view is . . . ," to which Milne immediately replied, "Who is the General Staff? *I am* the General Staff."[98] Milne's assertion of his authority gained him a great deal of notoriety in his opening weeks at the War Office, but his subsequent actions were to prove that he was not so strong-willed as he initially appeared to be.

Despite the broadening aspect of his service as DMO&I, Burnett-Stuart's four years at the War Office were not really satisfying. He referred to it as a "soul-destroying institution," and despite a number of positive acquaintances he made there, he

always had the feeling, which was shared by many others of my generation, that there was something wrong with it. It was in itself too top heavy; it was constantly immersed in detail which could so easily have been dealt with by commanders . . . had reasonable powers and financial responsibility been allowed them; it was out of touch with the real Army, especially the troops overseas; the civil side in particular never even saw the soldiers or commanders with whose requirements and difficulties they were so intimately concerned; the civil staff, also, was not in cordial alignment with the military staff—as it was, for instance, in the Admiralty;

there was no close touch between the Army Council and the G.O.C. in C. of Commands, who were never brought into collaboration, or even consultation, on matters of army or defence policy; and above all, it had no real military head: the C.I.G.S. was no more than a "primus inter pares," co-equal and co-ephemeral with the other military members.[99]

In July 1926 Burnett-Stuart left this unhappy place to assume command of the 3d Division located at Salisbury Plain. Burnett-Stuart's prior service admirably prepared him for this assignment. He received a sound education in small-unit tactics during his service with the Rifle Brigade in India. He was exposed early on to divisional level operations in South Africa. He became part of the army's professional elite when he graduated from the Staff College in 1905. He developed practical knowledge in almost all areas of military organization and administration as director of military operations and intelligence in New Zealand. He served in a variety of difficult and important staff positions during the Great War. He proved himself a talented commander in Madras. And he received first-hand knowledge of the army's wide strategic responsibilities as director of military operations and intelligence at the War Office. In each of these assignments he not only performed well, he grew. He was fortunate in often being at the right place at the right time, but his success was due more to ability than to luck. In the course of thirty-one years of service he earned a reputation for exercising sound military judgment, for dealing capably with complex situations, for expressing himself with complete candor, and for frequently irritating his less-well-endowed superiors.

Burnett-Stuart's appointment as G.O.C., 3d Division, was important, however, primarily because it placed him in the official position to observe and evaluate the trials of the Experimental Mechanised Force, which was formed at Salisbury Plain in 1927. And it is to the story of the establishment of this unit that we must now turn.

NOTES

1. W.G.F. Jackson, *Alexander of Tunis as Military Commander* (London, 1971), p. 3.

2. A synopsis of Burnett-Stuart's career may be found in Appendix 1.

3. Details of Burnett-Stuart's family background are from *Burke's Landed Gentry*, 8th ed., 2 vols. (London, 1894), 2:1948, and 18th ed., 3 vols. (London, 1965–1972), 3:873–874. Details of Eustace Robertson Burnett-Stuart's military career are from Great Britain, War Office, *The Army List* (London, 1865–1875).

4. There is a slight discrepancy between the two accounts in *Burke's Landed Gentry:* The former (1894 edition) states that the Reverend John Burnett-Stuart died unmarried; the latter (1965–1972 edition) that he died without issue.

5. Field Marshal Earl Wavell's foreword to Bernard E. Fergusson, *The Black Watch and the King's Enemies* (London, 1950), p. 13.

6. John T. Burnett-Stuart, "Memoir," 2 vols., 1:3. This unpublished memoir is among Burnett-Stuart's papers.

7. F. A. M. Webster, *Our Great Public Schools: Their Traditions, Customs, and Games* (London, 1937), pp. 228–232.

8. Details of Burnett-Stuart's tenure at Repton from W. B. Downing (Repton librarian) to author, 12 October 1972.

9. Winston S. Churchill, *My Early Life: A Roving Commission* (London, 1930), pp. 57–58. Burnett-Stuart and Churchill both entered Sandhurst in September 1893.

10. J. F. C. Fuller, *Memoirs of an Unconventional Soldier* (London, 1936), p. 5.

11. J. W. Taylor (Sandhurst assistant librarian) to author, 26 July 1972, on date of Burnett-Stuart's passing out from Sandhurst. Capt. Algeron Drummond, composer of the Eton Boating Song, said that the Rifle Brigade, which he joined in 1862, "was well known as a 'crack' regiment. As the list of candidates was in the Prince Consort's hands, one had little chance of a commission unless one had passed high up in the examinations." Algeron Drummond, "Old Days in the Rifle Brigade," *The National Review* 98 (April 1932): 501.

12. Maj. Gen. Douglas Wimberley to author, 10 November 1972. Burnett-Stuart indicates in his memoirs that his name had been on the Duke of Connaught's list for the Rifle Brigade for a number of years prior to his commissioning, but he does not tell why. Burnett-Stuart, "Memoir," 1:4.

13. General Sir John T. Burnett-Stuart, "In India Sixty Years Ago," *RBC* (1954): 55.

14. Rifle Brigade origins based on Col. W. P. S. Curtis, *A Short Account of 3rd Green Jackets, the Rifle Brigade,* 3d rev. ed. (Aldershot, 1959), pp. 5–10, and an interview with J. H. Leslie, assistant secretary, Rifle Depot, Winchester, 6 November 1972.

15. Arthur Bryant, *Jackets of Green: A Study of the History, Philosophy, and Character of the Rifle Brigade* (London, 1972), p. 13.

16. *Regulations for the Rifle Corps, formed at Blatchinton Barracks, under the Command of Colonel Manningham, 25th August, 1800* (London, 1801). Quoted from *RBC* (1897): 44. Every officer of the regiment was required to be familiar with these regulations. Their full publication in the regimental journal two years after Burnett-Stuart was commissioned and the presence of this volume in his library make it highly likely that they influenced his early military thought.

17. Ibid.: 78–82, 90.

18. This phrase refers to the high proportion of Riflemen in senior army positions, particularly in the twentieth century. Resentment of the Rifle Brigade's claims to superiority over all other regiments may be evident in Field Marshal Lord Carver's reference to it as the "Piffle Brigade." See his review of Arthur Bryant's *Jackets of Green, JRUSI* 118 (March 1973): 93. There has, however, often been a tinge of envy as well, reflected in Wellington's admonition not to call the Minnie rifle a rifle "lest the whole of the infantry should clamour to be clothed in green." John W. Fortescue, *A History of the British Army,* 13 vols. (London, 1899–1930), 13:24.

19. Lt. Col. L. H. Thornton and Pamela Fraser, *The Congreves Father and Son: General Sir Walter Norris Congreve, V.C., Bt.–Major William La Touche Congreve, V.C.* (London, 1930), pp. 13–14, 18–20. Walter Congreve commanded Company C, 3d Bn., the Rifle Brigade when Burnett-Stuart was a subaltern in the unit.

20. What follows is based on an anecdote contained in the preliminary remarks on training that Burnett-Stuart made to his commanders in Egypt upon his arrival as G.O.C. in 1931.

21. Quotations are from a typescript of the above remarks among Burnett-Stuart's papers. It was published with slight textual modifications as "Address on Training Given at Cairo, October 1931," *The Fighting Forces* 9 (April 1932): 28–40.

22. Account of the Tochi Valley expedition is from the *RBC* (1897): 113–135, 220–227.

23. Burnett-Stuart, "In India Sixty Years Ago," *RBC* (1954): 58.

24. An example of this pedantry is contained in the instructions for the first movement of executing a "dash" with a large flag: "Wave the flag from the 'Ready', clear of the body, until the point of the pole is at a position 18 inches from the ground, pivoting it between the two hands, wrists rounded outwards, left elbow close to the side, left hand not to be dropped or brought across the body, head erect, eyes to look to the front, and body upright." Great Britain, War Office, *Signalling Instructions, 1896* (London, 1896), p. 32.

25. Such qualification was still felt necessary in the interwar years. See Great Britain, War Office, *Army Training Memorandum No. 4 (Collective Training Period, 1931)* (London, 1931), p. 24.

26. Burnett-Stuart, "In India Sixty Years Ago," *RBC* (1954): 59.

27. *RBC* (1899): 134. The battalion had done poorly the previous year because many of its signallers were casualties of the Tochi expedition. *RBC* (1898): 152.

28. Burnett-Stuart, "Memoir," 1:29.

29. This paragraph is based primarily on John T. Burnett-Stuart, "Modder River to Bloemfontein with the Sixth Division," *RBC* (1900): 129–142.

30. Ibid., 138.

31. The *Report on the Examination for Admission to the Staff College Held in August 1902* lists Burnett-Stuart as having passed and qualified for admission. The assistant military secretary wrote in the report that "this is the first time a paper on 'Strategy' has been included in the Staff College examination. Considering that the candidates had no previous standard to work up to, I think that on the whole the questions are well answered and show considerable reading and power of thought." K. M. White (Staff College librarian) to author, 7 March 1972.

32. For Roberts' testimony see Brian Bond, *The Victorian Army and the Staff College, 1854–1914* (London, 1972), p. 192. Amery's history was commissioned by the *Times*.

33. For divergent opinions on Miles see A. R. Godwin-Austen, *The Staff and the Staff College* (London, 1927), p. 238, and General Hubert Gough, *Soldiering On* (New York, [1957]), p. 64. Miles may have done better during his second term as commandant, which Godwin-Austen describes, than he did during his first, which is depicted by Gough, but he seems not to have been the man to attract and refine the army's best minds.

34. Discussion of Rawlinson's reforms at Staff College based on Bond, *Staff College*, pp. 196–198, Godwin-Austen, *Staff College*, pp. 241–243, and Frederick Maurice, *The Life of General Lord Rawlinson of Trent* (London, 1928), pp. 88–89.

35. Gough, *Soldiering On*, p. 93.

36. Background on the General Staff primarily from John Gooch, "The Creation of the British General Staff, 1904–1914," *JRUSI* 116 (June 1971): 50–53. For more detail see Bond, *Staff College*, pp. 212–240. For a lengthy extract of the Army Order of 1906 see Godwin-Austen, *Staff College*, pp. 243–244.

37. Details of Burnett-Stuart's assignments from Great Britain, War Office, *The War Office List and Administrative Directory* (London, 1907–1909), and Burnett-Stuart's "Memoir," 1:47.

38. Quoted from Samuel R. Williamson, *The Politics of Grand Strategy: Britain and France Prepare for War, 1904–1914* (Cambridge, Mass., 1969), p. 100.

39. W. C. B. Tunstall, "Imperial Defence, 1874–1914," *The Cambridge History of the British Empire* (Cambridge, 1959), 3:584–585, and John K. Dunlop, *The Development of the British Army, 1899–1914* (London, 1938), pp. 295–297.

40. Tunstall, "Imperial Defence, 1874–1914," *Cambridge History of the British Empire*, 3:588–589, and Dunlop, *British Army, 1899–1914,* pp. 297–298. See also D. C. Gordon, *The Dominions Partnership in Imperial Defence, 1870–1914* (Baltimore, 1965), pp. 273–277. The term "Imperial" was added to the chief of the General Staff's title by an Order in Council dated 22 November 1909.

41. New Zealand, Military Forces, *Regulations (Provisional) for the Military Forces of the Dominion of New Zealand, 1911* (Wellington, 1911), p. 17. For further discussion of these regulations see below.

42. A copy of the regulations with changes posted in Burnett-Stuart's hand is among the Burnett-Stuart papers. On the flyleaf is the notation, "With the author's compliments to himself!!"

43. Quotation on New Zealand *Regulations* from Field Marshal Sir Francis Festing et al., "The Late General Sir John Burnett-Stuart," *RBC* (1958): 67. (Hereinafter referred to as Burnett-Stuart tribute, *RBC.*)

44. According to Colonel Heard's introduction, the journal's purpose was "to provide articles of an interesting and instructive nature to all ranks of the Military Forces." Volume 1 contained ten articles, seven pages of book reviews, and a four-page listing of current periodical articles of interest. It appears to have been a most useful publication.

45. Lt. Col. John T. Burnett-Stuart, "Elementary Principles of Training for Territorial Regimental Officers," *New Zealand Military Journal* 1 (January 1912): 8–9. A copy of this article is in the Burnett-Stuart papers.

46. Ibid., p. 10.

47. Ibid. As he matured, Burnett-Stuart continued to reflect on war in terms of a game, but he became less enamored of sticking to the rules. See his correspondence with Liddell Hart in Chapter 6.

48. Burnett-Stuart, "Memoir," 1:64–66.

49. Field Marshal Sir William Robertson, *From Private to Field-Marshal* (Boston, 1921), p. 172.

50. Description of exercises in which Burnett-Stuart participated as a member of the directing staff in 1913 provided by K. M. White (Staff College librarian). The records for 1914 are no longer extant.

51. Montgomery became Montgomery-Massingberd in 1926 when his wife inherited the Massingberd estates. The genesis of the tension between him and Burnett-Stuart is difficult to determine. Sir H. Karslake, an admirer of Montgomery-Massingberd, felt that Burnett-Stuart was primarily at fault. He told Liddell Hart that during the Great War Burnett-Stuart had constantly complained that Montgomery-Massingberd was "in his way" and blocking his chances for promotion. Liddell Hart, diary note of conversation with Karslake, 20 November 1936, Liddell Hart papers, LHCMA. The author has been unable to locate any evidence that would substantiate Karslake's claim.

52. General Sir Harold Franklyn, "1914," in "Four Generations of Staff College Students," *AQ* 65 (October 1952): 47.

53. Ibid., p. 49.

54. Fuller, *Memoirs,* pp. 28–29.

55. Details on operations of the 6th Division from Great Britain, War Office, *Military Operations France and Belgium, 1914: Mons, the Retreat to the Seine, the Marne, and the Aisne August–October 1914* (London, 1922), p. 384, and *Military Operations France and Belgium, 1914: Antwerp, La Bassee, Armentières, Messines, and Ypres October–November 1914* (London, 1925), pp. 71–72, 100–102, 124, 142.

56. B. H. Liddell Hart, *History of the First World War* (London, 1970), pp. 255–259. The description of the 15th Division's participation in the Battle of Loos from Great Britain, War Office, *Military Operations France and Belgium, 1915: Battles of Aubers Ridge, Festubert, and Loos* (London, 1928), pp. 151–162, 192–194, 207, 339, and 392.

57. John Terraine, *Douglas Haig: The Educated Soldier* (London, 1963), p. 176.

58. John Connell, *Wavell: Scholar and Soldier* (London, 1964), p. 122.

59. Information on Snow from Bond, *Staff College*, p. 307, which is based on Brig. Gen. J. E. Edmonds' unpublished memoir, and on Edmonds' sketch of Snow in *DNB*, 1931–1940, pp. 821–822. Edmonds was editor of the British official history of the Great War and had been Snow's GSO1 at 4th Division.

60. Background on Arras from Liddell Hart, *First World War,* pp. 410–411. Given the capabilities of British artillery in early 1917, there is no guarantee that Allenby's proposed short bombardment would have achieved the desired results, but it may have been well worth trying. Great Britain, War Office, *Military Operations France and Belgium, 1917: The German Retreat to the Hindenburg Line and the Battle of Arras* (London, 1940), p. 541.

61. Description of the VII Corps operations at Arras from ibid., pp. 204, 214, 281–285.

62. Burnett-Stuart to Liddell Hart, 9 October 1927, Liddell Hart papers, LHCMA. Liddell Hart was gathering material for *The Real War, 1914–1918,* published in 1930, and had apparently written Burnett-Stuart on his role in the battle.

63. Liddell Hart, *First World War,* p. 447.

64. For the Third Army record of this conversation see Great Britain, War Office, *Military Operations France and Belgium, 1917: The Battle of Cambrai* (London, 1948), p. 169.

65. For an excellent discussion of the German planning and execution of this operation see Robert Woolcombe, *The First Tank Battle: Cambrai, 1917* (London, 1967), pp. 180–188.

66. Liddell Hart, *First World War,* p. 448.

67. Burnett-Stuart's remark quoted from Liddell Hart's note of a conversation with General Edmonds on Cambrai, diary note, 7 October 1927, Liddell Hart papers, LHCMA.

68. For the army's view of the manpower problem see Sir Nevil Macready, *Annals of an Active Life,* 2 vols. (New York, 1925), 1:231–300. Macready was adjutant general at G.H.Q. until February 1916, and adjutant general at the War Office for the remainder of the war.

69. Robertson to Kiggell, 13 August 1917. Kiggell papers IV/10, LHCMA. Kiggell's figures were much higher for infantrymen.

70. Burnett-Stuart's responsibilities as deputy adjutant general from an interview with Field Marshal Sir Francis Festing, 19 September 1972.

71. Fuller, *Memoirs,* pp. 354–355. Fuller correctly points out that many army commanders were asking for more tanks, but he fails to mention that they were also demanding more infantrymen and gunners. Given this and the state of tank technol-

ogy, Haig's decision is somewhat more rational than Fuller implies, though perhaps a bit too conservative.

72. Burnett-Stuart had hoped to command a brigade in the 15th Division, but his proficiency in teaching staff operations resulted in his being assigned to G.H.Q. despite his strong protestations. Burnett-Stuart,"Memoir," 1:76.

73. Burnett-Stuart spent some time closely inspecting the front and wrote a vivid account describing the monotony and tribulations of trench warfare. Unfortunately, this document is no longer extant. J. G. S. Burnett-Stuart interview, 14 September 1972. J. G. S. Burnett-Stuart to author, 11 February 1973.

74. For details of military reforms see Lt. Gen. Sir George MacMunn, *Behind the Scenes in Many Wars* (London, [1930]), pp. 319–325. MacMunn was the quarter-master general in India after the war.

75. Madras District was an administrative headquarters established to command the military units within its geographic boundaries. The government of Madras was entirely civil. Effective coordination between the headquarters and the government was dependent upon the personal efforts of the district commander and the governor rather than any hard and fast institutional arrangements.

76. The discussion of the Moplah Rebellion is based primarily on Cmd. 1552. *Telegraphic Information etc., regarding the Moplah Rebellion, 24th August to 6th December* (1921), and "The Moplah Rebellion, 1921," in Maj. Gen. Sir Charles Gwynn, *Imperial Policing,* 2d ed. (London, 1939), pp. 83–117.

77. Cmd. 1552, p. 12.

78. Lt. Gen. W. Marshall to Burnett-Stuart, 7 September 1921, Burnett-Stuart papers.

79. Burnett-Stuart to Montgomery, then Rawlinson's deputy chief of staff, 3 September 1921, Burnett-Stuart papers. Burnett-Stuart and Rawlinson often communicated privately, both directly and through Montgomery.

80. Burnett-Stuart to Colonel Humphreys, 14 September 1921, Burnett-Stuart papers.

81. Rawlinson to Burnett-Stuart, 21 September 1921, Burnett-Stuart papers.

82. Montgomery to Burnett-Stuart, 22 September 1921, Burnett-Stuart papers.

83. Cmd. 1552, pp. 20–21.

84. Burnett-Stuart to Graham, 1 December 1921, Burnett-Stuart papers.

85. Rawlinson was particularly impressed. After visiting Malabar in August 1922 he noted in his diary, "The country is much more hilly than I expected, in fact, small hills run right down to the sea. Just the country for guerrillas, and Jock Stuart and Humphreys did very well to deal with the rebellion so quickly and thoroughly." Maurice, *Rawlinson,* p. 310. The secretary of state for India noted how well the disturbance was being handled in his correspondence with the viceroy. Cmd. 1552, p. 33.

86. Of the twenty major generals on the active list in July 1923 with Burnett-Stuart's date of rank, only five had been knighted.

87. "Military Notes," *JRUSI* 67 (November 1922): 753.

88. Liddell Hart diary note of discussion with Karslake, 26 November 1936, Liddell Hart papers, LHCMA.

89. Burnett-Stuart attended twenty-six of the fifty C.I.D. meetings held during his tenure. His deputy was present at many of the others. Cab. 2, Committee of Imperial Defence Minutes, 1922–1926.

90. C.O.S. 1, "Air Requirements of the Army in Peace and War," 27 June 1923, Cab. 53/12.

91. C.O.S., 1st meeting, 17 July 1923, Cab. 53/1.

92. C.O.S. 2, 30 July 1923, Cab. 53/12.

93. C.O.S. Report 454-B, "Military Policy in Egypt and Defence of the Suez Canal," appended to C.O.S., 2d meeting, 29 September 1923, Cab. 53/1. See also Cavan's statement on Egypt, C.I.D., 180th meeting, 4 February 1924, Cab. 2/4.

94. Details of journey based on Burnett-Stuart's log of the flight in his papers.

95. See *inter alia* C.O.S. 7, "Respective Responsibilities of the Fighting Services," 25 January 1924, Cab. 53/12; C.O.S. 11, "The Military Situation vis-à-vis Turkey with Regard to the Iraq Boundary Question," 28 August 1924, Cab. 53/12; and C.O.S. 25, "Situation in China 30 June 1925," Cab. 53/12.

96. Connell, *Wavell: Scholar and Soldier,* p. 151.

97. Burnett-Stuart, "Memoir," 2:3.

98. Liddell Hart, *Memoirs,* 1:107–108.

99. Burnett-Stuart, "Memoir," 1:46, 2:23.

4

THE BIRTH OF THE MECHANISED FORCE–THE DEATH OF THE ARMOURED FORCE, 1926–1928

Here is far too potent a new wine to be put into old bottles. We must reorganize, not go on patching any more.
— *Maj. Gen. Sir John Burnett-Stuart* [1]

What I wanted, in brief, was evolution and not revolution.
— *Field Marshal Sir Archibald Montgomery-Massingberd* [2]

The world's first completely mechanized combat brigade was formed in Britain on Salisbury Plain in May 1927. This was a significant event in the evolution of British armored doctrine as well as in that of other countries, for out of the Experimental Mechanised Force grew many concepts that would profoundly influence the conduct of land warfare. In 1928 the Experimental Mechanised Force became the Experimental Armoured Force. The change in name seemed to suggest that the C.I.G.S., General Sir George Milne, was looking to the unit on Salisbury Plain to provide lessons for the conduct of armored warfare, as distinct from the mechanization of existing arms. Although the actual composition of the force changed little, this was a noteworthy indication of policy that augured well for the exercises of 1928. Unfortunately, the actual accomplishments of that year did not live up to this promise. Furthermore, at the end of the second year of trials, Milne decided to disband the Armoured Force in order to concentrate the army's efforts on the mechanization of infantry and cavalry units. Understanding of this period requires examination of the international and domestic milieus and the sequence of events leading up to the birth of the Mechanised Force, the conduct of the first year of trials and the reactions to them, the trials of the Armoured Force in 1928, and the decisions made following these exercises.

I

Internationally the Spirit of Locarno reflected in Gustav Stresemann's policy of conciliation in Germany and Aristide Briand's policy of *apaisement* in France kept the European situation relatively calm. This trend was continued with

72

the signing of the Kellogg-Briand Pact of 1928 in which the fifteen signatories, including Britain, France, Germany, and the United States, agreed to renounce war as an instrument of national policy.[3] In other areas of the world things were not so peaceful. Nationalist riots at the British concession in Hankow in January 1927 were symptomatic of general unrest throughout China, and Stanley Baldwin's Conservative government dispatched a force of twelve infantry battalions to protect British lives and interests in Shanghai.[4] The greatest area of concern was Russian activity in Central Asia. In July 1926 the secretary of state for India, Lord Birkenhead, stated his fears that Afghanistan might become a Soviet republic, and a special subcommittee of the C.I.D. was formed under his chairmanship to investigate this question.[5] This subcommittee reaffirmed previous declarations by Lords Balfour and Morley that it was in Britain's "own plain interest" to guard the independence of Afghanistan; it approved a joint plan worked out by Milne and Trenchard to advance into Afghanistan with air and mechanized forces in the event of overt Russian intervention.[6]

At home it was the era Charles Mowat has called "dead centre."[7] The general strike was over; the Labour Party was too cowed to do much, the Liberals were moving toward some unity, but were still in disarray; and, despite the forward-looking health policies of Neville Chamberlain, the Conservatives were faring badly with the problem of unemployment. Churchill's economic policy was partially to redistribute capital by selective taxation and to keep government expenditure to a minimum. In July 1928 he convinced the Committee of Imperial Defence to decree that the "ten year rule" would be revised to assume "for the purposes of framing the Estimates of the Fighting Services, that at any given date there will be no major war for ten years."[8]

In Commons an impassioned plea was made from the Labour side by Anthony Greenwood for a motion that "His Majesty's Government should, in the preparatory commission for the forthcoming Disarmament Conference, initiate proposals to secure international agreement on reductions in land forces."[9] Tanks were a particular bone of contention:

> Just as the old "wooden walls" gave way to the modern battleship, so the small tank of the Great War is to give way in course of time to a new land super-Dreadnought, and there will be the same old foolish competition between the nations, a competition in tank development on exactly similar lines to the great developments in naval armaments that took place before the War.[10]

Pacifism was also reflected in the growing spate of trench memoirs. Six were published in 1926, and fifteen in 1927; among those published in 1928 were Erich R. Remarque's *All Quiet on the Western Front*, Robert G. Graves' *Goodbye to All That,* and Siegfried S. Sassoon's *Memoirs of a Fox-Hunting Man*.[11]

Alarmed by the efforts to force reductions on the army, General Milne had drafted a comprehensive memorandum on the strength of the British Army in relation to its commitments. This memorandum pointed out the requirements for military forces generated by the Treaty of Locarno, the mandated areas (Palestine and Iraq), the Nationalist uprising in China, the growth of the Swaraj movement in India, the political ambitions of an anti-British Egypt, and "the problem of maintaining the internal security of our own country against subversive activities which are largely prompted and financed by Russia."[12] Milne was correct in his observation that compared to the situation that existed in 1914, the British Army had increased responsibilities and fewer troops with which to meet them.[13] And whereas the 1914 expeditionary force had consisted of six infantry divisions and one cavalry division capable of mobilization in one month, the 1927 force had only five infantry divisions and required, according to Milne, five months to mobilize. In short, the margin for error in simultaneously meeting the demands of the Empire and preparing for a large-scale war in Europe had become almost nonexistent. This position was recapitulated in the Chiefs of Staff annual defense review of 1928.[14] Against this background of economic stringency, popular pacifism, pressing overseas commitments, and reduced forces, the problems associated with forming and maintaining an Experimental Mechanised Force become somewhat comprehensible.

The need for an experimental force first surfaced publicly in late 1924. Following an R.U.S.I. lecture by Fuller entitled "Progress in the Mechanicalisation of Modern Armies," Liddell Hart, at Fuller's prior request, asked Fuller how he planned to test the truth of his comments without some "picked body of troops."[15] This issue was broached again in early 1925 when in the epilogue to *Sir John Moore's System of Training* Fuller concluded that a new experimental brigade was needed to test "new weapons of war . . . new tactics . . . new methods of discipline" under the guidance of "a man of character, of moral courage, integrity and foresight."[16] This pressure, combined with the results of the maneuvers of 1925, led the secretary of state for war, Sir Laming Worthington-Evans, to announce in his Army Estimates speech of 1926 that a decision had been taken to form an experimental force of all arms. However, where Fuller had mentioned the trials being used to determine new tactics and new modes of discipline as well as new weapons, Worthington-Evans dealt solely with the equipment aspects, adding that there was "no justification for uneconomic haste."[17] The period between Worthington-Evans' announcement in Commons in March 1926 and the formation of the Experimental Mechanised Force in May 1927 was marked by confusion, bureaucratic delays, and strong pressures for and against such a force both in and out of the War Office.

The army was governed by a collective body known as the Army Council, consisting of four civilian and four military members.[18] The civilian members were the secretary of state for war, the parliamentary under-secretary of state, the financial secretary, and the permanent under-secretary. The military members were the chief of the Imperial General Staff, the adjutant general, the master general of the ordnance, and the quartermaster general. Collective meetings of the council were not frequently held, but members met together informally as required to establish policy. The majority of War Office business, however, was conducted by circulating minutes on various issues among the members of the council having interest in those issues. Since each member had virtual autonomy in his own department, any matter that cut across departmental lines required consensus before implementation.

In early April 1926 Milne informed Worthington-Evans of his plans for an experimental force.[19] It was to be stationed at Tidworth and would include one tank battalion, one armored car company, a mechanized artillery brigade, an engineer field company, three infantry battalions with mechanical transport, and a special reconnaissance unit. Milne said that since no provision had been made for the vehicles these units would need in the 1926/27 estimates, they would have to wait until the 1927/28 estimates were approved; it followed that the formation could not be in full working order until 1928.[20] Worthington-Evans approved Milne's plan in principle but added two caveats: Details of cost would have to be considered, and he wanted a good deal done in 1926 to determine what changes were needed for the expeditionary force.[21]

Milne's proposal and Worthington-Evans' approval apparently caused a memorandum to be prepared by the deputy director of staff duties for organization entitled "Scheme for Experimental Work with a Mechanical Force." One paragraph in this memorandum stated, "Would it not be sound to convert a cavalry regiment into a general reconnaissance unit for our force and hand over to it the armoured cars now in the tank corps?"[22] Col. George Lindsay felt that this proposal violated the main principles of reorganization and responded that he was

> much opposed to the mere re-arming of existing units of either Infantry or Cavalry with mechanical fighting vehicles or even Machine Guns. . . . The real stumbling block in any reform or reorganization is the present regimental system by which our Army is divided into innumerable small packets each with different traditions and ideas . . . to perpetuate this in the new arms is only asking for trouble. We must face this matter now, decide generally on the form that the Army of the future is likely to take, and work towards it gradually. The formation of this first Experimental Force is definitely bound up with the future organization of our Army, and should be the model, in miniature, of that future Army.[23]

Milne was impressed by Lindsay's comments and in a minute back to the director of staff duties, Maj. Gen. A. R. Cameron, said that although he did not "propose that the Tank Corps should swallow the Army," it had the only trained personnel and had to be drawn on, and that no infantry would be required initially: "The object is *not* the creation of a light division on the French model; it should be looked upon as the embryo of a new mechanicalised fighting force."[24] Milne said that the machine-gun unit for the experimental force would be completely distinct from the proposed divisional machine-gun battalion and was to be formed at an early date. Finally, he considered "Colonel Lindsay's ideas very sound, and though at the present moment they are too ambitious, I want everything done to put them into effect as soon as this is possible."[25] Most indicative of Milne's philosophy concerning mechanization was the note on the cover page of his memorandum, "Hasten slowly, G.F.M."[26]

The original proposal envisaged replacing the 7th Infantry Brigade at Tidworth with another brigade and changing the 7th Brigade's title to H.Q. Experimental Mechanical Force. But in an 11 June reply to Milne's memorandum, Cameron recommended that the colonel commandant of the 7th Infantry Brigade be appointed to command the various units (including the three infantry battalions) for purposes of combined training, the noninfantry units to be trained in their specialities by their own arms, and the general officer commanding, 3d Division, to have general supervision over the combined training. This was intended to be a temporary measure to get the force established in 1927 in hopes that it could later be expanded. Milne accepted this proposal and on 15 June forwarded the file to the other military members of the council, saying that he wanted to establish the force as soon as possible, but that it would require moving two armored car companies into infantry barracks at Tidworth.[27] Robert Whigham, the adjutant general, saw no problems, but Noel Birch, the master general of the ordnance, pointed out that there would be no accommodation for the vehicles. The file was then forwarded to Col. A. F. Thullies, the director of fortifications and works, who asked on 30 June whether the accommodation was to be temporary or permanent. If permanent, some existing stables could be converted to sheds, but since the force was to be experimental and to last for only two or three years, it might be better to build temporary sheds of corrugated iron. He concluded, "I cannot give an estimate of the cost until the above points are answered."[28] At this moment the whole matter stopped.

Meanwhile, Burnett-Stuart was getting little guidance from the War Office on the composition of the force. In August 1926, he wrote the director of staff duties asking,

> what help are you going to give me in organizing, launching, and guiding this experiment? It is no use just handing it over to an ordinary Divisional Commander like myself. You must connect directly with it as many enthusiastic experts and visionaries as you can; it doesn't matter how wild their views are if only they have a touch of the divine fire. I will supply the commonsense of advanced middle age.[29]

The crucial question of command was still undetermined, for on 3 September Fuller, then Milne's military secretary, informed Liddell Hart, "Experimental Bde . . . will probably be [Col. G. H.] Jackson's [7th] Bde (this is confidential), Jackson will therefore have to start it off, but his time is up in Nov '27 & who will take his place I do not know."[30]

The various obstacles to the creation of the force were eventually overcome. By agreeing to form only one machine-gun battalion rather than the two he wanted—thus keeping the Cardwell system in balance—and to the construction of only temporary accommodation for the vehicles, Milne achieved the necessary consensus among the military members of the council. He informed Worthington-Evans on 1 November 1926 that plans were made to form the experimental unit at Tidworth in 1927.[31] When Fuller returned from India where he had been sent to preach the benefits of mechanization, Milne informed him that he had been selected to command the experimental force. Fuller accepted the appointment. Thus from Milne's perspective the matter was closed.

Fuller, however, had deep reservations. He wrote to Liddell Hart on 7 January 1927, "I am by no means overjoyed as it is a first day of creation show & I am not in a position to emulate the Almighty."[32] He visited Colonel Jackson's brigade in early February and discovered that he would also be required to command the Tidworth garrison. Fuller felt that these administrative responsibilities would repeat the mistakes of 1921 trials at Aldershot, which failed, he had been told, because the commander of the experimental force was constantly bothered with additional duties.[33] He therefore requested that Milne give him authority to delegate responsibility for the command of the three normal infantry battalions of the 7th Brigade to a deputy, to turn over responsibility for the Tidworth garrison to the local cavalry commander, and to obtain the services of a permanent staff captain and a shorthand typist. When Milne failed to respond to these requests, Fuller wrote Burnett-Stuart, "hoping that through his mediation, I might get the C.I.G.S. to see things a little more rationally."[34] Burnett-Stuart replied with a rather pungent letter, saying that Fuller was "not being invited to tie a wet towel round your head & evolve a new military heaven & new earth."[35] And although Burnett-Stuart was very much looking forward to having Fuller work with him, he did not think it right for Fuller to bother the C.I.G.S. with petty details. Fuller was greatly put off by this reply, and on 21 February he informed Liddell Hart that he was considering an ultimatum.[36]

On 3 March Worthington-Evans' memorandum concerning the Army Estimates was presented to Parliament.[37] It stated that arrangements had been made to assemble at Salisbury Plain "an Experimental Mechanical Force, composed of entirely mechanized units of Artillery, Engineers, Signals, Infantry, and the Tank Corps whose primary function will be to study the tactical employment and the organization of a highly mobile force."[38] After reading

Worthington-Evans' initial statement and comparing it with Burnett-Stuart's letter, Fuller asked Milne if he had considered his requests. When Milne said that he had not, Fuller walked out of Milne's office and wrote out his resignation, stating that he could not accept an appointment that was so misrepresented.

Several days after submitting his resignation, Fuller received a letter from General David Campbell, G.O.C.-in-C, Aldershot Command, requesting him to reconsider. After obtaining a commitment from Milne to continue modernizing the army, Fuller withdrew his resignation and accepted an appointment as GSO1, 2d Division at Aldershot. The intention of this appointment was to use Fuller, Campbell, and Maj. Gen. Edmund Ironside, the 2d Division commander and a close friend of Fuller's, to supervise the formation of another mechanized force within the next year.[39] It was not, as Liddell Hart and others have maintained, to banish Fuller from the War Office.[40] Few people knew of these behind-the-scenes maneuvers, however, and even Liddell Hart did not learn of Fuller's resignation until 1 April.[41]

But even after Fuller's fate had been settled, the questions of who was to command the experimental force and the exact date of its establishment had not. These issues were not influenced mainly by deliberations in the War Office, but by a bombshell in the press. In 1923 Liddell Hart had been placed on half-pay due to the gas wound he incurred at the Somme. In 1925 he was selected as military correspondent for the *Daily Telegraph* in succession to Charles Repington.[42] This position gave him not only the money he needed to make ends meet, it also provided a "platform for launching a campaign for the mechanisation for the Army."[43] Thus when the War Office announced on 21 April that Col. R. J. Collins would command the 7th Brigade but made no mention of the experimental force to which Worthington-Evans had referred in Parliament, Liddell Hart was in a perfect position to influence events.

His article "An Army Mystery—Is There a Mechanical Force?" was a masterpiece of journalistic intervention in bureaucratic affairs. After reviewing all the official pronouncements on the subject since March 1926, he asked, "Has the scheme broken down, or was the formation of such a force no more than a figure of speech? Parliament and the public . . . have a right to enlightenment, which will be awaited with some anxiety."[44] Liddell Hart's article soon achieved the desired effect. On the 27th the War Office announced the definite formation of the experimental force, and on 12 May Collins was gazetted "to command the Experimental Mechanised Force and the 7th Infantry Brigade" with priority given to the former appointment.[45]

The birth of the Mechanised Force was thus both traumatic and anticlimactic. It was traumatic because it required a shock from outside the army to make it happen. It was anticlimactic because even with this shock it produced disappointing results since Fuller would not be in command. Fuller's best course of action would have been to accept command of the 7th Brigade as it was offered and do the best he could with what he had. It certainly would have helped his own career, and it would have proved better for the army as well. Fuller's biographer calls his application to resign and concommitant refusal to accept command of the Mechanised Force the worst decision of his life. Why he acted this way is open to conjecture. Fuller worked best independently, and he detested any situation involving regimental routine.[46] Mrs. Sonia Fuller also considered the job demeaning to him and did not want the responsibilities of a commander's wife.[47] Burnett-Stuart's response to Fuller's demands may have been justified by the circumstances—many commanders would have probably reacted even more strongly. Nevertheless, one cannot help feeling that Burnett-Stuart acted in a moment of pique and that he could have put Fuller in his place with less sarcasm. His letter was definitely not in consonance with his previous statement that it did not matter "how wild their views are, if only they have a touch of the divine fire."

One can also understand the delays in the War Office. The problems of money, accommodations, troop rotation, and so forth were all very real. The War Office papers reveal that Milne continued to press for the formation of an experimental force despite the resistance of his colleagues on the Army Council. He did, however, let matters drift when the actual command arrangements were being worked out between Fuller, Godley (G.O.C.-in-C., Southern Command), and Burnett-Stuart. One can argue that in his position as C.I.G.S. Milne should not have had to bother with such details. On the other hand, if the experimental force was as important to him as his memoranda to Cameron and Worthington-Evans indicated, he should have made sure that the success of the project was not jeopardized by administrative questions. That Milne did allow events to take their own course suggests that if Liddell Hart had not acted as he did, the Experimental Mechanised Force might have been stillborn.

II

In the event, the Experimental Mechanised Force was officially formed on 1 May 1927. It consisted of a medium tank battalion, a battalion of armored cars and light tanks, a machine-gun battalion transported by six-wheeled lorries, a field artillery brigade, a light artillery battery, and a field engineer company. An R.A.F. Army Cooperation Squadron took part in most of the exercises.[48] The force was directed to test the feasibility of engaging in strategic reconnaissance in place of cavalry, of operating in conjunction with regular forces, and of conducting independent operations at a considerable distance from the main force.[49]

Col. R. J. Collins was appointed to command the force. He was a conscientious infantryman with an impressive service record, but with no experience with mechanized formations.[50] His early appointments included A.D.C. to the Sirdar in Egypt and private secretary to the commander of operations in Somaliland in 1910. During the Great War he had served as GSO1 of the 17th Division and chief instructor at the temporary Staff College established at Cambridge. After the war he was director of military training in India and was assistant director of the 1925 army maneuvers. He was not, however, another Fuller. He was abounding in energy, but this energy was directed toward collecting data on movement and administration rather than toward evolving new tactical concepts. He also had an overly developed sense of caution that seemed out of place in a position calling for imagination and daring.[51]

These characteristics were reflected in Collins' early handling of the force. Maj. Giffard Martel, commander of the engineer company, told Liddell Hart that it was being used "as a mere extra body on close flank of the infantry."[52] In June the first standing orders for the force were issued, dividing it into three groups for the regulation of marches. The Light Group consisted of the two armored car companies, the light tanks, and occasionally the light artillery; its normal speed was twenty-five miles per hour, and its normal marching distance for one day was one hundred miles. The Medium Group included the machine-gun battalion, with transport, and the engineer company; its normal speed was ten miles per hour, and its normal marching distance for one day was fifty miles. The Heavy Group contained the medium tank battalion and the field artillery brigade. Its normal rate of movement was seven miles per hour, and it was expected to cover thirty miles in a one-day march.[53] Although Collins was partially correct in ensuring that the Mechanised Force was properly organized before it began tactical experiments, this ponderous configuration, coupled with his innate caution, resulted in the circulation of a joke that the force's motto had become the banker's rule of "no advance without security."[54]

This was not, however, Burnett-Stuart's concept. In one of the early trials, Collins instructed Lt. Col. Frederick Pile, commander of the Light Group, to move forward to a certain line and consolidate his position. Not finding any enemy there, Pile decided to continue forward. He moved approximately twenty-five miles beyond Salisbury Plain before meeting the adversary, and completely stopped the maneuvers. At the critique the next day, Pile was afraid that Burnett-Stuart would chastise him for ruining the exercise. Instead, Burnett-Stuart said, "I know a lot of you will not like the tactics which you saw employed by the Light Group in these manoeuvres. You will think them risky. But I assure you that in armoured war these things will be tried, they will probably come off, there will always be people who chance their arm in this way, and you've got to be prepared to meet them when they do."[55] Burnett-Stuart's positive comments on Pile's unorthodox tactics inspired the young tank officer to continue to experiment.[56]

In September Burnett-Stuart received a letter from the War Office, apparently drafted by the director of staff duties, outlining the official concept of the Mechanised Force.[57] The force was said to consist of a headquarters, a striking group, and one or more reconnaissance groups. The medium tank battalion's role was to be "actual close combat." The artillery was to provide counter-battery fire, bombard likely antitank areas, and support attacking tanks; the machine-gun battalion's main function was to fire on enemy antitank weapons and hold ground; and the armored cars and light tanks were to gather information, though it was admitted that those on hand were not capable of adequately performing this role. Had this letter been sent the previous year, it would have represented the guidance Burnett-Stuart was then seeking. As it was, it merely confirmed what had already been worked out on the ground at Salisbury Plain.

On 8 September, Milne went to Tidworth to deliver his own thoughts on the Mechanised Force. Milne's address has been represented by Fuller and Liddell Hart as a stirring call for mechanization, and in a sense it was.[58] Quoting I Corinthians 14:8, "For if the trumpet give an uncertain sound, who shall prepare himself for the battle?" as the text for his "sermon," Milne reviewed the increased firepower of modern armies, noted the advances made possible by the gasoline engine, envisaged the eventual formation of armored divisions, and called for a complete change of mental outlook in preparing for future war. This was quite remarkable coming from the C.I.G.S., but Liddell Hart does not point out that Milne prefaced his remarks by saying that stringent finances, the dispatch of armored cars to China, and the need to test simultaneously engines, vehicles, and tactics made mechanization a necessarily slow project and that he and other senior army officers did not expect to see a great expansion during their time.[59] Reactions to Milne's lecture varied. Liddell Hart saw it as a clarion call for mechanization and, with Milne's permission, published a synopsis of it in the *Daily Telegraph*. Maj. Gen. Harry Knox, the director of military training, was horrified when he learned of it and dissuaded Milne from having it published.[60]

The culminating Southern Command exercise of 1927 pitted the Experimental Mechanised Force against Burnett-Stuart's 3d Division and a cavalry brigade.[61] The 3d Division was to advance from west of Salisbury Plain to seize the high ground near Andover; the Mechanised Force's mission was to halt their advance. On the first day Pile's Light Group moved over forty miles, seizing river crossings that permitted the rest of the force to get between the 3d Division and its cavalry screen. The division was held up and subjected to an air attack followed by a tank assault before finally reaching Tilshead. During the night, Burnett-Stuart moved the division six miles by foot to Netheravon before the Mechanised Force could react. Shortly after dawn, however, he was completely surrounded and he decided to remain at Netheravon rather than to expose his unit again to tank attack in open country. The exercise was terminated that evening. In less than forty-eight hours a brigade-sized force of tanks and armored cars had shown that, given suitable terrain, it could paralyze a unit over three times as large. It was a significant exercise in many respects, and it made a deep impression on Burnett-Stuart.[62]

The 1927 trials raised two fundamental questions. First, what were their implications for future doctrine, equipment, and organization? Second, what could reasonably be done in response to these implications in light of the many factors restraining the army's freedom of action? Given the complexity of these questions, it is not surprising that in the months following the September exercises, there was a great deal of confusion and disagreement in both areas.

On 9 November Col. Charles Broad, whom Milne had brought into the War Office as deputy director of staff duties (organization), gave a lecture at the R.U.S.I. entitled "A Mechanized Formation."[63] It was essentially an elaboration of the War Office letter sent to Burnett-Stuart on 2 September based on experience gained in subsequent exercises. Broad outlined the composition of a mechanized force and showed how it could actually be employed in an engagement from reconnaissance, to deployment, to attack, to eventual pursuit. He felt that the force would have to be completely armored and that it would need extensive wireless communications for control. Although he considered neither the need such a force would have for troops who could occasionally fight on foot nor the supply problems it would encounter, he convincingly demonstrated that armored formations could be effectively employed, especially against unarmored units.

Reactions to this lecture provide insight into the changing attitudes brought about by the 1927 trials. Col. T. N. Howard, an experienced infantry commander and the author of several works on infantry organization, suggested that tanks were assuming the role of closing with and destroying the enemy that had previously been performed by infantry; therefore, infantry regiments should be converted to tank units.[64] This was a drastic change from previous efforts by infantrymen to minimize the tank's accomplishments. Major General Ironside, then commanding the 2d Division at Aldershot, admitted that he would be very perplexed if he met the type of force Broad described. He felt it would "revolutionize warfare absolutely, even in the roughest countries in which we may have to fight."[65] Milne, however, dampened this enthusiasm by pointing out that Broad was not speaking with the authority of the Army Council, that the previous year's trials had been purely experimental, that money was scarce, and that the mechanization program would be cautious, "so as not to upset the traditions, the *esprit de corps,* and the feeling of the Army as a whole."[66]

The Annual Staff Conference held in January 1928 also reflected a wide range of views on future organization. The first item on the agenda concerned the infantry. Colonel the Viscount Gort, then GSO1, 4th Division, appealed to both operational exigencies and military tradition in presenting the case for an updated infantry capable of surviving on the modern battlefield. He maintained that any reforms should be based on the existing organization because infantry units were self-contained and capable of quick dispatch in an emergency, they were effective for internal security, and the history of British infantry was "a pearl without price and nobody would want to relegate it to a subsidiary role."[67] Fuller replied with a recapitulation of his sea warfare on land lecture. He maintained that the answer was "half an inch of steel"; that armor at sea had rendered ramming and boarding obsolete, but the army had not yet shown the same vision and scrapped the idea of assaulting with men; and that foot-soldiers were acceptable for the mountains, but only men in machines were suitable in open country.[68] Milne said that infantry should not always rely on tanks to help them, but he had no definite suggestions on mobilizing machine-guns.[69]

The last item on the agenda concerned the future organization of the infantry division. The basis of discussion was a paper prepared by Colonels Elles and C. P. Heywood that suggested adding an armored car company and a tank battalion to each division and eliminating one brigade.[70] In presenting the paper Elles concluded that Britain was not prepared for a major war, but that the financial situation would allow them to prepare for such a war slowly—over the next six years. Milne intimated that six years was not a long period at all. In the ensuing discussion Elles, Heywood, and Fuller pushed for the development of a New Model division designated specifically for a major (or European) war. General Walter Braithwaite, the new adjutant general, replied that finances would not allow the army to develop two different kinds of divisions and that "pressure all along the line was one of the fundamental points in tactics."[71] Milne agreed with Braithwaite, saying in conclusion that it was necessary to take several million off the estimates and that the Army Council preferred a gradual evolution of all divisions, with tanks being attached as necessary to the rapid development of one division with its own tanks.[72]

Worthington-Evans enunciated the official policy in his Army Estimates speech of 8 March 1928. He acknowledged the success of the 1927 trials, but cautioned that while speculations as to future organization were permissible, it was necessary to retain the forces in being until something better could be substituted:

If it were not necessary to keep expenditure in very narrow limits—I would create the new formations before I reduced or converted the existing ones, but I am not free to follow that course; I have to make continuous reductions in existing expenditure in order to find money for experiments and research and even for equipping some units with new and expensive vehicles and armaments.[73]

These estimates included £1,085,150 for vehicles and fuel, an increase of £60,000 from 1927, and £732,600 for animals and forage, an increase of £4,000 from 1927.[74]

The winds of change brought about minor modifications in cavalry organization. In July 1927 Milne informed Creedy that he was prepared to recommend the abolition of the lance.[75] During 1927 some cavalrymen finally began to see that if they did not adapt, they would soon be overtaken by events. This was reflected in Col. H. V. S. Charrington's *Where Cavalry Stands To-Day* and Major E. G. Hume's *JRUSI* article, "Mechanization from a Cavalry Point of View." The latter stated:

> Let us . . . concentrate on re-organizing our cavalry units and formations by strengthening them mechanically so as to bring them into line with modern conditions rather than try to evolve *ab initio* a mechanical reconnoitering arm under non-cavalry officers and apart from cavalry. The one may excell in mechanical skill, the other in tactical ability. Both will be needed in combination on the battlefield of the future.[76]

In November 1927 a subcommittee of the C.I.D. was appointed to investigate the strength and organization of the cavalry. The feeling that the cavalrymen were innately superb tacticians was also reflected in General Godley's testimony, which the committee's report on 3 May 1928 summarized as follows:

> If Cavalry were abolished, instead of being transformed, there would be a great danger of losing the type of officer, non-commissioned officer and man that has hitherto gone to the Cavalry, and that will be equally necessary in the new mechanized Cavalry; men who were to a great extent by birth and upbringing, and by their habits in boyhood, natural leaders with an eye for country, quickness of decision, habit of command, and all the attributes required in connection with highly mobile forces.[77]

Not surprisingly, General Godley was supported by Field Marshal Haig and General Braithwaite. The committee fully accepted the testimony of these "expert witnesses" and supported the War Office's decision merely to convert two cavalry regiments to armored car units and partially mechanize the others. These steps alone, however, involved an initial cost of £384,000, and the committee warned that all changes should be made "with due regard to financial considerations."[78] Another measure of the difficulty involved in even those gradual steps was the resistance of the army in India. Worthington-Evans had to make a personal trip to India to persuade Field Marshal Sir William Birdwood, the commander-in-chief, partially to adopt the cavalry organization of the home army.[79]

Burnett-Stuart's analysis of the implications of the 1927 experiments is outlined in a lecture he gave on 8 March 1928 at the University of London entitled "The Progress of Mechanization."[80] He said that he had prepared the lecture "in the hope that the process of tidying up my own mind might at least produce an intelligible statement of the problem even if it fails to contribute to the solution of it."[81] His conception of mechanization was that it would make war "less mechanical," and get the army out into the open spaces again. He felt, though, that constructive thought about the subject had been impeded by penny press critics who made far-fetched comparisons with the past and wild speculations about the future and did not understand the limitations placed on army policy. He then reviewed the history of the tank since the Great War, stating it had shown itself a useful subordinate of the infantry. But these developments had been radically altered by the experimental work of 1927:

> Now we have reached a point where the real significance of the armoured fighting vehicle begins to emerge. For some years past, most soldiers, I think, have been looking forward to the time when the tank would be sufficiently developed mechanically, and could be provided with the appropriate auxiliaries, to enable it to cut itself adrift from the infantry battle, and to go into business on its own as a principal, not merely an assistant. It really looks as if that time had now come, and though we are as yet only at the beginning of it, it is impossible not to be rather thrilled at the possibilities which it opens up. It marks a definite break-away—one of those developments in the business of fighting which compels us to overhaul our ideas, to bring our book of rules up to date, and to think again.[82]

The tests on Salisbury Plain had shown that the necessary mobile auxiliaries—signal, artillery, reconnaissance, bridging, and logistical units—whose absence had previously restricted the tank were at last available.

What followed was obviously the product of considerable deliberation. Burnett-Stuart maintained that mechanization was bound to come in due time, but that it would be by stages, and that financial limitations, the virtual self-determination of the army in India, and the need eventually to reorganize the territorial army made it impossible to proceed quickly. The real questions were "what is a practical programme? What degree of mechanization can we afford, and how is the introduction of it to be coordinated with the reorganization of the rest of the Army?"[83] He felt that the army could only afford a modest, partial mechanization, and his plan implementing it was twofold. First, to build up four armored brigades, one around each of the existing tank battalions with one stationed at home, one in Egypt, and two in India; or two at home, one in Egypt, and one in India. Either plan would keep the Cardwell system intact. Second, gradually modernize the rest of the regular army by partially mechanizing the cavalry, completely mechanizing the artillery and engineers, and forming three types of infantry battalions—one for direct work with the armored force, one for occasional work with armored units, and one for mountainous country. The main point, though, was the need to devise a definite plan. "However slow the progress of reorganization may be, we must at least know what we want, so that if war or the threat of war brings a sudden speeding up we shall be set on a sound course."[84]

Burnett-Stuart had been converted by the experiences of 1927 from an open-minded skeptic about mechanization to a convinced and knowledgeable advocate. Milne, who chaired the lecture, said in closing that two years before Burnett-Stuart had not in the least believed what he had just told his audience. "Today," Milne said, "the pupil has outstripped his master!"[85] The importance of this lecture, however, lies not so much in the changed attitude of an individual as in the grasp of its subject. More than any other senior British officer, Burnett-Stuart understood the full implications of mechanization and sensed how it could be used in the future. Unlike the younger, more ardent reformers, he also recognized the many real obstacles to it. His plan to form four armored brigades was probably overambitious, since India would not accept one for many years. Two was probably the largest number that could have been formed in the late 1920s – one for home and one for Egypt. Nevertheless, his was a comprehensive, rational plan for gradual expansion and it had much to commend it, not the least of which was that it put the development of armored forces ahead of the mechanization of the rest of the army.

The birth of the Mechanised Force was delayed by financial stringency, bureaucratic inertia, and some overt opposition to change in the War Office. Milne had possibly been short-sighted in failing to act on Fuller's requests for additional administrative support, but he deserves more credit than he gets from Fuller and Liddell Hart for his determination to establish a force as a vehicle for tactical experimentation. Considering the low need for a unit whose functions would be limited mainly to Continental warfare and the many obstacles that had to be overcome, Milne's determination and the fact that the force was established at all were both rather remarkable.

The conflict between Burnett-Stuart and Fuller over command arrangements for the Mechanised Force has already been commented upon. Both were partially justified in their actions, but neither emerged from the episode with a great deal of credit. Characteristically, when Worthington-Evans chastised Burnett-Stuart for obstructing the formation of the experimental unit, Burnett-Stuart took it gracefully despite the fact that the War Office, not he, had determined the command arrangements; he admitted later that he had been at fault in squelching Fuller's initiative.[86] These actions contrast vividly with Fuller's self-serving account of the incident in his memoirs.

Liddell Hart's role in the establishment of this force was dramatic and perhaps essential. The conditions in this incident, however, were particularly favorable to outside intervention – Worthington-Evans had made a public declaration that was obviously contrary to existing facts, Liddell Hart was calling for a specific action rather than a general change in policy, and he had most of the relevant facts at his disposal. Several years later when these conditions did not obtain, Liddell Hart came to grief in his attempts to influence War Office policy. In this respect, the success of 1927 may have been a stumbling block.

Reactions to Liddell Hart's article on the Mechanised Force were varied. Milne was incensed and issued orders for Liddell Hart to be physically escorted from place to place whenever he entered the War Office.[87] Montgomery-Massingberd sent him a long, patronizing letter deploring the fact that he had jeopardized his chances for success by going against the system.[88] Burnett-Stuart, who had been most directly hurt by it, spoke about the article favorably and told Martel he thought that Liddell Hart was a more intelligent commentator on military affairs than George Aston and others who, presumably, stuck too close to the party line.[89]

The 1927 trials showed a great deal of promise for armored warfare. However, a great deal of work still needed to be done before the Mechanised Force could become the flexible, powerful tool that was envisaged. The questions of how to provide infantry and artillery support for tank units were particularly important. The machine-gun unit attached to the experimental force was not adequate for infantry support, and the artillery units needed to work on rapid displacement and target location procedures that could keep pace with the rest of the unit. More small tanks were required to make Pile's Light Group effective. Although the rudiments of logistical support had been worked out, the force had a heterogeneous assortment of trucks loaded with food, ammunition, gasoline, and other supplies that limited its flexibility and increased its vulnerability.

In addition to these internal difficulties, a number of external obstacles remained that affected not only continued experimentation with the Mechanised Force but also the pace of mechanization within the rest of the army. These included financial stringency, technological uncertainty, imperial commitments, the demands of the Cardwell system, the unlikelihood that the army would fight in Europe in the near future, popular pacifism, and a strong sense of caution and traditionalism among many senior officers. The 1927 trials had given an earnest of things to come that had partially overcome these obstacles, but a central question remained concerning the Mechanised Force's future tactical doctrine and organization: What would happen in the second year of experimental work?

III

Worthington-Evans outlined the army's goals in the fields of armored warfare and mechanization in his Army Estimates speech of March 1928. The

Experimental Armoured Force was to develop experience in "the nature of the machines, in the organisation of mechanised units and in the methods of their employment"; the rest of the army was "gradually to convert existing formations . . . into formations based upon the increased mobility and fire-power given by the use of the internal-combustion engine."[90] These statements suggest movement on two fronts–the development of a specialized armored formation and the mechanization of horse-drawn infantry, cavalry, and artillery units. It also mentions three specific tasks for the Experimental Armoured Force: testing machines, determining an appropriate organization, and developing suitable tactics. The events of the next nine months were to prove that these objectives were not of equal priority.

The moderate pace of both programs was evident in General Milne's guidance to Maj. Gen. Charles Bonham-Carter, the director of staff duties. The army's policy, Milne said, was based on the views adopted by the government of the day concerning the political situation at home and abroad. Consequently, the strictest economy was essential, and since the Cabinet assumed that there would be no major war in Europe for ten years, the military leaders were to think more of the future than the present. This meant that the army's organization for modern war was not to be completed quickly, but over the next ten to fifteen years.[91]

The personalities of several key people in the War Office had a significant impact on the way in which Milne's policy was implemented and at times contested. By the spring of 1928 Major General Bonham-Carter had taken hold in his new appointment as director of staff duties and was in a crucial position to influence and interpret the tests to be conducted on Salisbury Plain. He had served under Milne during the Allied occupation of Turkey and again as Milne's brigadier general, General Staff at Eastern Command.[92] He was therefore thoroughly familiar with Milne's views on military matters and could be counted on to support fully Milne's policy. He was also a much more efficient staff officer than his predecessor and more sympathetic to the future of mechanization. Bonham-Carter's main interest, however, lay in the education of officers, and he had already been nominated as the next commandant of Sandhurst when Milne decided to bring him to the War Office instead. While Bonham-Carter was not without knowledge in matters pertaining to tactical doctrine and organization, his efforts as director of staff duties were primarily directed toward revamping the Sandhurst curriculum.[93] Col. Charles Broad, Bonham-Carter's deputy for organizational matters, provided the impetus in the development of mechanized and armored doctrine. Since Broad had technical expertise as well as an intense interest in this area, Bonham-Carter let much of what he wrote pass straight through to Milne, and Broad frequently received his instructions directly from Milne rather than through Bonham-Carter.[94] Although a relatively junior officer,

The Experimental Armoured Force in review order on Salisbury Plain, 1928.
(Courtesy of the Tank Museum.)

Broad's responsibility for drafting Milne's speeches on mechanization gave
him additional influence.

Col. George M. Lindsay, inspector, Royal Tank Corps, and his assistant,
Bt. Maj. F. E. ("Boots") Hotblack, were also involved in the development
of armored doctrine. Colonel Lindsay spent the majority of his time visiting
tank units in the field and the R.T.C. Center at Bovington and lecturing to
the officer corps at large on the future of armored warfare. He therefore did
not participate directly in the conduct or evaluation of the 1928 trials; but
he did maintain a high level of interest in them and, along with Broad,
attended most of the exercises. Major Hotblack's primary duty was fighting
the annual "battle of the estimates" for the Tank Corps.[95]

Although prospects for the development of armored warfare were enhanced
by the presence of Bonham-Carter, Broad, Lindsay, and Hotblack in the
War Office, they were somewhat inhibited by the appointment of Lt. Gen.
Sir Archibald Montgomery-Massingberd as general officer commanding-in-
chief, Southern Command, in June 1928. His predecessor, General Sir
Alexander Godley, had encouraged new ideas, but Montgomery-Massingberd
was decidedly opposed to armored warfare.[96] And whereas Godley had not
attempted to interpose his views between Burnett-Stuart and the War Office

The Experimental Armoured Force in open order on Salisbury Plain, 1928. (Courtesy of the Tank Museum.)

Vickers Medium Mark IIs passing through the Wiltshire village of Collingbourne Ducis during the 1928 maneuvers. The constricted nature of the English countryside made the openness of Salisbury Plain particularly valuable for armored exercises. (Courtesy of the Tank Museum.)

on matters concerning the Experimental Mechanised Force in 1927, Montgomery-Massingberd actively made his views known to Milne and other members of the Army Council in 1928. Furthermore, there developed a fundamental antipathy between Montgomery-Massingberd and Burnett-Stuart that was to last the rest of their mutual military careers.[97]

Burnett-Stuart's lecture on mechanization indicates that he had determined a need for the expansion of armored forces and suggests that he felt the function of the 1928 experiments was to determine the pattern upon which this expansion would be based. As usual, he was outspoken in his criticism of those above him whom he felt to be insufficiently forward looking.[98] Thus substantive differences over the future of armored organization, together with distinct differences in temperament between him and Montgomery-Massingberd, resulted in two widely divergent assessments of the 1928 trials. But Burnett-Stuart's amicable relations with his subordinates did much to put the exercises themselves on a sound, practical footing. He spoke frequently to the officers of the Armoured Force concerning its tactics, and he even knew a number of the noncommissioned officers by name.[99] He showed a lively interest in all his units, and, according to his engineer company commander, "He was incredibly quick to grasp any point one tried to make and his comments were always clear and convincing. He liked to get in personal touch with all the officers he came across and put you at ease at once. At the same time you got the message that he was just the sort of leader you would like to have in war."[100]

Burnett-Stuart's relationship with Brigadier Collins, however, was somewhat difficult. He soon recognized that Collins was not the man touched with the spark of divine fire that he had wanted to run the force, and he realized too that this was in part his own fault. Nevertheless, he appreciated Collins' energy and abilities and gave him free rein to arrange administrative and logistical details, areas in which Collins excelled. This arrangement left the major responsibility for designing exercises and testing tactical concepts to Burnett-Stuart and Wavell, whom Burnett-Stuart had brought to the 3d Division as his GSO1. Wavell was a great asset to Burnett-Stuart, and their presence on Salisbury Plain has been accurately described as "one of the most formidable concentrations of lively, original and profound military thought that had ever been put into one peace-time Headquarters."[101] The only other personnel change from 1927 was the absence of Lieutenant Colonel Pile, commander of the Light Group. Pile went to the War Office in August 1928 as assistant director of mechanization.

There was no question as to the direction the Experimental Armoured Force would take if left to Burnett-Stuart, who, after the 1927 exercises, had promised Liddell Hart "a touch of Jenghiz Khan in our game of Mechano next year."[102] This was in reference to Liddell Hart's analysis of Jenghiz Khan's armies that attributed their success to flexibility in both tactics and

A self-propelled 18-pound Birch Gun passing horse-drawn transport. A battery of four of these guns served with the 9th Field Brigade, Royal Artillery, in the Experimental Mechanised Force of 1927. (Courtesy of the Tank Museum.)

strategy obtained through rapid movement and intelligent control.[103] In order to attain such proficiency, the force developed a number of standardized "battle drills" for passing over obstacles, for laagering at night, and for identifying units on the march. It also conducted two exercises designed to determine the number of vehicles required to support the force in operations of varying duration.[104] While these drills and exercises provided some useful practice in handling the force in routine situations and determining support requirements, the overall scope of the 1928 experiments was constrained by the limited changes made in its composition after the 1928 trials—the only additions were a few trucks and six half-track carriers for the 3.7-inch howitzers. Although the new title, Experimental Armoured Force, was important as an indication of policy, it expressed, in Liddell Hart's words, "an aspiration rather than any change in reality."[105]

The greatest deficiency was the lack of suitable light tanks.[106] The eight Morris-Martel and eight Carden-Loyd two-man tanks had little armor protection, no turrets, and were armed only with Vickers machine-guns. Furthermore, the limited number did not allow for both long-range reconnaissance and local security for the medium tanks. Sir John Carden had designed and produced in prototype an Experimental Light Tank Mark I, the first light tank with a completely closed turret, but it was not available for the

1928 trials. Medium tanks were also a problem. The Vickers Medium, with its high silhouette, demanding maintenance requirements, and slow speed, was becoming obsolete. To alleviate this situation, Vickers Armstrong produced in 1928 three prototype models of a Vickers Medium Mark III. Although armed with the same 47-mm. 3-pdr. main gun, the Mark III, or "16-tonner" as it was also known, was a considerable improvement over the Mark II. It had fourteen as opposed to eight millimeters of armor, a maximum road speed of thirty versus sixteen miles per hour, and one of its three machine-guns was coaxially mounted with the main gun. It was, however, much more expensive than the Mark II and was never brought into full production.[107] The deficiencies in tanks were compounded by a lack of suitable infantry transport. The Crossley half-track and Morris six-wheel trucks were both unsuitable for moving under enemy fire and their cross-country movement was much more restricted than that of the light and medium tanks. Here again Sir John Carden had a solution in the form of a newly designed armored machine-gun carrier, but it was not available for the 1928 trials either.

The force's first major exercises were efforts in public relations.[108] On 5 July a demonstration conducted for the Staff College depicted a well-camouflaged armored force suddenly overwhelming a conventional infantry unit. This demonstration of the Armoured Force's capabilities was probably the first that many officers in the audience had seen, and it appears to have made a distinct impression on them. A week later a more elaborate show was put on for both houses of Parliament. A mock battle was staged in which the Light Group reconnoitered the objective, two companies of medium tanks conducted an attack supported by machine-gun fire and low-level air attacks, infantry units consolidated the captured position, and another company of medium tanks passed through to continue the attack. The performance was followed by a demonstration of an eight-wheeled vehicle that "writhed over obstacles like a mechanical snake," and a three-wheeled motorcycle that traveled easily across rough ground.

The Armoured Force's final exercise for 1928 was constructed quite differently from that of 1927.[109] This year Burnett-Stuart's 3d Division was given a company of tanks, a company of armored cars, a cavalry regiment, and a medium artillery brigade, which it pitted against the combined forces of the 2d Cavalry Brigade and the Armoured Force. The Armoured Force was partially dismembered, and its light tanks were placed under control of the 2d Cavalry Brigade, whose function was to locate the 3d Division for the Armoured Force to attack. Burnett-Stuart scored first when his armored car units located and destroyed the opposing air forces on the ground; but neither side was able to develop a decisive advantage, and the exercise ended in a stalemate. This is significant in itself, however, in view of the way the 3d Division had been completely routed by the Mechanised Force in 1927.

This result was due to a combination of factors: the provision of mobile units to the 3d Division; the unwieldy organization of the opposing force that deprived the Armoured Force of its mechanical scouting capability and attempted to merge horses and light tanks into a combined reconnaissance unit; and the increased confidence of the infantry in dealing with the tank threat, whose nature was no longer completely unknown.

IV

While the public relations demonstrations and the culminating exercise of 1928 were both significant, the future of armored warfare depended more on the way in which they were interpreted. The wide variety of interpretations was based on the perspective of the individual, his motivations, and his ability to extrapolate from experience.

Liddell Hart contended that the Armoured Force experiments had provided useful experience in driving and maintenance but had merely demonstrated the obvious fact that armored and unarmored vehicles could not work together effectively in one unit. The main lesson of the year, he felt, was the effectiveness of the light tanks, which, because of their low cost and high speed, could be produced in mass and distributed over a wide front. The Armoured Force of the future, he said, "should be mainly composed of light tanks, such as the new Carden-Loyd, with a proportion of 'gun-tanks' such as the new 16-ton Vickers for its extra fire support, and perhaps a sprinkling of six-wheeled armoured cars as its long-range 'feelers.' "[110]

Liddell Hart's infatuation with light tanks seems to have been based on their quick movement, which epitomized to him the dash and élan of the new mechanized warrior, as opposed to the rather cumbersome movement of the existing medium tanks.[111] Liddell Hart's feelings on infantry units in armored formations had not changed appreciably since his conversion to Fuller's views on armored warfare in 1922. He believed that a "true armoured force" could avoid most of the obstacles that would require infantry support, that an ordinary infantry battalion would be more of an encumbrance than an asset, and that a company of "land marines" specially trained in the craft of stalking and silent penetration would be sufficient for an armored brigade.[112]

Burnett-Stuart summarized his views on the 1928 trials in an eight-page memorandum attached to Brigadier Collins' report. After pointing out the many difficulties under which the force had operated, he admitted that "even when these and other disabilities have been allowed for, the major tactics of the force have not progressed as I had hoped they might."[113] The major value of the Armoured Force, he said, was its threat to an adversary when it was "at large just below the horizon."[114] Here it posed a constant threat until the opportunity came to strike. The greatest challenge facing the armored unit commander, therefore, was deciding when the threat posed by his mere presence and the risk of possible losses in an assault were outweighed by the results of a swift attack. Burnett-Stuart felt, however, that "leadership and major tactics of this kind are difficult to practice at peace training when exercises are of short duration, when ground is limited and when a sensational finale is usually expected."[115]

The second major lesson was that the Armoured Force was essentially a raiding force: "The machine is the unit, not the man, and the limitations of the force are the limitations of the machines that compose it. Unless it is followed up by other troops equally mobile (such as mechanically transported infantry or, for short distances, cavalry) it can only destroy and pass on."[116] The final major lesson was that its tactics were decisively influenced by the characteristics of the ground over which it operated. The cramped conditions on Salisbury Plain, however, had not allowed the Armoured Force adequate room to maneuver. "It will be interesting to see," he added, "whether when the force becomes accustomed to free movement on wider fronts, its preoccupation with obstacles and defiles will become less. . . . Next year I hope to get room to pass on to a more positive method of trial, when progress should be quicker."[117]

Burnett-Stuart's thoughts on the future composition of the Armoured Force indicate a keen understanding of the characteristics of armored units. He recommended that the force include a long-range reconnaissance group with an R.A.F. Army Cooperation Squadron, armored cars, and light reconnaissance cars; a group of light tanks and light self-propelled field artillery; a headquarters group containing a fighter squadron, medium artillery, a bridging train, an engineer company, an infantry battalion in armored vehicles, "and such other units as may be added according to the circumstances and the nature of the operations"; and a maintenance group.[118] There are several significant features of this organization: first, the separation of reconnaissance elements into those performing long-distance reconnaissance and those performing protective reconnaissance; second, the main body that had its own light tanks and artillery support; third, the inclusion of air reconnaissance and close air-support units; and finally, the definite inclusion of the armored transported infantry in the force itself. Burnett-Stuart's recommended armored force was a well-balanced, self-contained fighting unit capable of performing a variety of missions. Equally as significant was Burnett-Stuart's contention that although the 1928 trials had been disappointing, suitable modifications would allow the Armoured Force more nearly to realize its full tactical potential in 1929. He was clearly looking forward, rather than backward.[119]

On 12 November, three days after Southern Command had forwarded the Armoured Force report to the War Office, Milne informed Worthington-

Evans that he wished to "make certain changes for 1929/30 in our experimental formations."[120] He said that good progress had been made in vehicle design and that the Armoured Force had helped determine the probable composition of an armored brigade.[121] There were, however, several points that required further consideration, i.e., the proportion of light and medium tanks in a tank battalion and the effect of radio-telephones on tank tactics.[122] He also mentioned that senior officers did not agree whether infantry battalions should have their own tanks or the light tanks should be grouped at brigade level with each battalion equipped with machine-gun carriers.

This, according to Milne, was a very important problem, and before a decision could be reached, it would be necessary to conduct practical trials with experimental brigades comprising three infantry battalions and one light tank battalion. It was not possible, he said, "to keep the Experimental Armoured Force in being if the above experiments are to be put through in 1929/1930. I therefore propose to disperse the Experimental Armoured Force for one year. During the year 1930/31 I hope to be in a position to form the 1st Armoured Brigade as a permanent formation of the Army."[123] Milne then said that in order to conduct the infantry brigade experiments it would be necessary to order the necessary vehicles as soon as possible. He therefore requested authority to expend approximately £150,000 in anticipation of the following year's estimates.

The secretary of state's reply reflected his primary concern with economic and technical ramifications of the 1928 trials and his willingness to accept at face value Milne's analysis of their tactical implications.[124] Worthington-Evans' financial concern is not surprising. He had to present an extremely strong case to Churchill to obtain the necessary £150,000 to place the early contracts for light tanks, and this aspect of the decision naturally occupied the main part of his attention. Churchill's approval of the request, "on the understanding that this part of your programme will be given absolute priority within whatever total is fixed when Estimates come to be considered," further reinforces the impression that budgetary, as opposed to doctrinal, considerations were paramount in Worthington-Evans' deliberations on the future of the Armoured Force.[125] The secretary of state announced plans for the dispersal of the force in Commons on 27 November, saying that it had "fulfilled its purpose. Valuable experience was gained which is enabling us to extend the experiment. Two new groups of mechanized units will be formed, one in Aldershot and one in Southern Command for that purpose."[126]

It seems that Milne had reached a decision before reading the report from the field on the 1928 trials. The problem of whether to have light tanks or machine-gun carriers in infantry brigades and how these vehicles should be organized, while important, was not nearly as pressing as Milne made it out to be, and his statement that senior commanders were not agreed on it suggested that others were instrumental in persuading Milne to disperse the Armoured Force.

This conclusion is supported by a revealing passage from Montgomery-Massingberd's unpublished memoir:

> When I took over the Southern Command I found the "Armoured Force" already in existence under Brigadier R. J. Collins and doing good work as an experimental organisation. . . . After watching it at training both against and in conjunction with the other arms I came to the conclusion that, although invaluable for experimental purposes, it was definitely affecting adversely the morale and training of the Cavalry and Infantry. . . . What should have been done was to gradually mechanize the Cavalry Division and the Infantry Division and not to introduce an entirely new formation based on the medium Tank. Nor was it sound to pit the new formation, with its modern armament, against the older formations, in order to prove its superiority. What was wanted was to use the newest weapons to improve the mobility and fire power of the old formations. . . . What I wanted, in brief, was evolution and not revolution. . . .
>
> I discussed this question very fully with Lord Milne who was then C.I.G.S. and as a result the "Armoured Force" as such was abolished and a beginning was made with the mechanization of the Cavalry and Infantry Divisions.[127]

Montgomery-Massingberd's claim to have been instrumental in this decision was corroborated by Pile in a conversation with Liddell Hart on 29 November. Liddell Hart's record of their discussion reads, "The disbandment of the Armoured Force was due to Montgomery-Massingberd (G.O.C.-in-C. Southern Command) and as David Campbell (G.O.C.-in-C. Aldershot Command) tended to support him, Milne gave way to their views."[128]

Montgomery-Massingberd's opinions were based on his vision of future war. He felt that the British Army would be equipped with armored cars, tanks, and tractor-drawn artillery "to a greater extent in proportion to its size than any other army we are likely to encounter," and that "as it appears likely that, at any rate during the first six months of the next war, we shall have to fight with cavalry and infantry, it is important that we should continue to study the problem of supporting these two arms with tanks."[129] These sentiments struck a responsive cord with the adjutant general, Walter Braithwaite, who after reading the report said he could not produce anything so good as the comments of the G.O.C.-in-C., Southern Command, "whose admirable Exposition, formed as I know after close study and much thought, is worthy of the closest attention."[130]

Any attempt to assess Milne's decision must acknowledge that limited financial resources forced him to choose, at least in the short run, between the continuation of the Experimental Armoured Force and the modernization of infantry and cavalry. There were two major arguments for concentrating on the traditional branches instead of the armored force. The first was material: If Britain were to become involved in a major war, it would be better for all the branches to be equipped with proper weapons and vehicles than to have obsolete infantry and cavalry formations supplemented by a completely up-to-date armored corps. The second was psychological: The morale of the infantry and cavalry was suffering because advances had been made in armored formations without corresponding progress in their own. Both have a degree of validity, and Montgomery-Massingberd used both in his discussions with Milne, though it appears that he emphasized the second.

Against these disadvantages of not modernizing the traditional arms, Milne had to weigh the disadvantages of losing the momentum of two years of experiments in armored warfare. Since Milne did not consult with his staff in this decision, there is no record of how he weighed these considerations, or even if he defined the problem in this manner. His decision to disperse the Experimental Armoured Force appears to have resulted from three factors: first, a belief that the objectives of the tests had been reasonably well accomplished and that a one-year hiatus would not seriously jeopardize them; second, a concern for the well-being of the infantry and cavalry; and finally, an inability to stand up to the strong pressure placed on him by Montgomery-Massingberd and others.[131]

Burnett-Stuart's attitude provides an illuminating contrast. He definitely felt that the objectives of 1928 had not been adequately achieved. He agreed with Collins that a number of material improvements were required, but more significantly he felt that much additional experience was needed in the tactical handling of armored formations. He saw 1929 as a year of opportunity in which to overcome this deficiency. He also felt that, contrary to Montgomery-Massingberd's gloomy prognostications, the infantrymen were beginning to make satisfactory adjustments to the advent of armored warfare, and he did not advocate eliminating the Armoured Force merely to increase their confidence. He was also too much his own man to be easily swayed by others. Burnett-Stuart's position is also interesting in contrast to that of Colonels Lindsay and Broad. Whereas they had become dismayed by Collins' methodical approach and had more or less given up on the Armoured Force, Burnett-Stuart realized its true potential and was unwilling to sacrifice it in hopes of getting a more imaginative commander in the future.

One must, however, have some degree of sympathy with Milne's decision. His resources were limited; his commitments were legion; and he was responsible for the whole army, not just a portion of it. His minute to Worthington-Evans also makes it clear that he intended to form a permanent armored brigade in 1930 after one year of trials with the infantry and cavalry. Nevertheless, one cannot avoid the feeling that if the Armoured Force had been restructured along the lines suggested by Burnett-Stuart and that if Burnett-Stuart had been given the freedom to conduct tactical trials in 1929 in the ways intimated in his report on the 1928 exercises, a number of exciting and profitable developments might have taken place. But this is speculation. To see what the results of Milne's decision actually were we must move on to the trials of 1929 and 1930 and the subsequent years of economic depression.

NOTES

1. Maj. Gen. John T. Burnett-Stuart, University of London lecture, 8 March 1928, "The Progress of Mechanization," *AQ* 16 (April 1928): 47.

2. Field Marshal Sir Archibald Montgomery-Massingberd, "The Autobiography of a Gunner," unpublished memoir, n.d. (circa 1946), p. 53. Montgomery-Massingberd papers, LHCMA. Montgomery-Massingberd, a lieutenant general in 1928, served as general officer commanding-in-chief, Southern Command, from June 1928 to February 1931 (see below).

3. On German and French foreign policy see Erich Eyck, *A History of the Weimar Republic*, Harlow P. Hanson and Robert G. L. Waite, trans., 2 vols. (Cambridge, Mass., 1963), 2:127, and Gordon Wright, *France in Modern Times: 1760 to Present* (Chicago, 1960), pp. 427–428, 444.

4. William Louis, *British Strategy in the Far East, 1919–1939* (Oxford, 1971), p. 130, and "Army Notes," *JRUSI* 72 (February 1927): 208.

5. C.I.D., 215th meeting, 22 July 1926, Cab. 2/4.

6. C.I.D., 232d meeting, 26 January 1928, Cab. 2/5.

7. Charles Mowat, *Britain between the Wars, 1918–1940*, Beacon Paperback ed. (Boston, 1971), pp. 284–352.

8. C.I.D., 236th meeting, 5 July 1928, Cab. 2/5.

9. *H.C. Deb.*, 5th Ser., 203 (7 March 1927): 936.

10. Ibid., col. 939.

11. Correlli Barnett, *The Collapse of British Power* (New York, 1972), p. 428.

12. Memorandum under cover of minute from Milne to Worthington-Evans, 2 November 1927, W.O. 32/2823, Distribution and Strength of the British Army in Relation to Its Duties.

13. In 1914 the British Army had 157 infantry battalions; in 1927, only 136.

14. C.O.S. 141, "Third Annual Review of Imperial Defence," 27 April 1928, Cab. 53/14.

15. See comments following Col. J.F.C. Fuller, R.U.S.I. lecture, 19 November 1924, "Progress in the Mechanicalisation of Modern Armies," *JRUSI* 70 (February 1925): 86–87. Fuller asked Liddell Hart to put this question to him in a letter written several days earlier. Anthony J. Trythall, *"Boney" Fuller: The Intellectual General* (London, 1977), p. 107.

16. Col. J. F. C. Fuller, *Sir John Moore's System of Training* (London, 1925), p. 223.

17. *H.C. Deb.*, 5th Ser., 193 (15 March 1926): 78.

18. The following paragraph based on Great Britain, War Office, *The War Office List and Administrative Directory, 1927* (London, 1927), and Creedy's "War Office Organization," in *Report on the Staff Conference Held at the Staff College, Camberley, 14th to 17th January 1929* (London, 1929), pp. 69–84.

19. Milne to Worthington-Evans, 8 April 1926, W.O. 32/2821, Proposed Establishment of an Experimental Mechanical Force.

20. The financial year ran from 1 April to 31 March. Estimates were drafted in

November, sent to the Treasury in early January, and presented to Parliament in early March.

21. Worthington-Evans to Milne, 20 April 1926, W.O. 32/2821.

22. D.D.S.D.(O), "Scheme for Experimental Work with a Mechanical Force," n.d. (circa early May 1926), W.O. 32/2820, Initiation of Experimental Mechanical Force.

23. Inspector, R.T.C., comments on above dated 14 May 1926, W.O. 32/2820.

24. Milne to Cameron, 1 June 1926, W.O. 32/2820.

25. Ibid.

26. Kenneth Macksey, *The Tank Pioneers* (London, 1981), p. 69.

27. Cameron to Milne, 11 June 1926; Milne to Whigham, Campbell, and Birch, 15 June 1926, W.O. 32/2820.

28. Col. A. F. Thullies (D.F.W.) to Birch, 30 June 1926, W.O. 32/2820.

29. Burnett-Stuart's letter quoted from B. H. Liddell Hart, *The Tanks: The History of the Royal Tank Regiment and Its Predecessors Heavy Branch Machine-Gun Corps, Tank Corps and Royal Tank Corps, 1914–1945*, 2 vols. (New York, 1959), 1:244.

30. Fuller to Liddell Hart, 3 September 1926, Liddell Hart papers, LHCMA.

31. Milne to Whigham, Campbell, and Birch, 1 October 1926; their comments; and Milne to Worthington-Evans, 1 November 1926, W.O. 32/2820.

32. Fuller to Liddell Hart, 7 January 1927, Liddell Hart papers, LHCMA.

33. J. F. C. Fuller, *Memoirs of an Unconventional Soldier* (London, 1936), p. 435.

34. Ibid., pp. 435–437.

35. Burnett-Stuart to Fuller, 18 February 1927, Fuller papers, Rutgers University. The complete text of this letter is in Appendix 3.

36. Liddell Hart diary note, 21 February 1927, Liddell Hart papers, LHCMA.

37. Cmd. 2810, *Memorandum of the Secretary of State for War relating to the Army Estimates for 1927*, pp. 3, 8.

38. *H.C. Deb.*, 5th Ser., 203 (7 March 1927): 887.

39. Campbell to Fuller, 26 April 1927, Fuller papers, Rutgers University and Liddell Hart diary note of conversation with Fuller, 25 April 1927, Liddell Hart papers, LHCMA.

40. In the event, the additional mechanized force was not formed, and Fuller never did have another opportunity to work directly with mechanized forces. It was, however, Milne's intention at the time to use Fuller's special qualities in an appropriate capacity.

41. Liddell Hart diary note, 1 April 1926, Liddell Hart papers, LHCMA.

42. B. H. Liddell Hart, *The Memoirs of Captain Liddell Hart*, 2 vols. (London, 1965), 1:63, 75.

43. Liddell Hart diary note, undated, Liddell Hart papers, LHCMA. The decision to launch this campaign prompted Liddell Hart to begin keeping his now famous diary notes, which he later referred to as "Notes for History." He felt it was "important to keep a record of the effect of the case I put forward, stage by stage, as the campaign was developed."

44. B. H. Liddell Hart, "An Army Mystery—Is There a Mechanical Force?" *Daily Telegraph*, 22 April 1927, p. 9. The *Westminster Gazette* followed up with a more sensational article on the same subject several days later.

45. Liddell Hart, *Memoirs*, 1:116–117.

46. Fuller realized in 1911 that "though I had never been, in the strict meaning of the word, a 'professional' soldier, I was . . . incapable of becoming one . . . what with my freedom as an Intelligence Officer in South Africa and my freedom as a

Territorial Adjutant, I was completely spoilt professionally." Fuller, *Memoirs*, pp. 20–21.

47. This point was brought to the author's attention by Fuller's biographer, Col. A. J. Trythall. Mrs. Fuller was of Polish descent and spoke English with a heavy accent. For a humorous and revealing anecdote showing her discomfiture in public, see Brig. John Smyth, *Sandhurst* (London, 1961), p. 109.

48. Liddell Hart, *The Tanks*, 1:247. See Appendix 7 for a schematic representation of the Experimental Mechanised Force.

49. Col. R. J. Collins, Royal Artillery Institution lecture, 6 December 1927, "The Experimental Mechanised Force," *JRA* 55 (April 1928): 13.

50. Background on Collins from obituary in the *Times*, 9 March 1950, p. 9.

51. For Wavell's analysis of Collins see John Connell, *Wavell: Scholar and Soldier* (London, 1964), p. 156, and his much more generous tribute to Collins published in the *Times*, 10 March 1950.

52. Liddell Hart diary note, 4 May 1927, Liddell Hart papers, LHCMA.

53. Collins, "Mechanised Force," *JRA* 55 (April 1928): 15. Liddell Hart appropriately refers to these groups as "Fast, Medium, and Slow," *The Tanks*, 1:249.

54. Liddell Hart, *The Tanks*, 1:249.

55. General Sir Frederick Pile, "Liddell Hart and the British Army, 1919–1939," *The Theory and Practice of War*, Michael Howard, ed. (New York, 1965), p. 170.

56. Pile interview, 12 October 1972. In his memoirs, General Pile said, "I sometimes wonder whether General Patton's famous break-through in Normandy would ever have taken place if Jock Burnett-Stuart had not encouraged the British Army to try out these apparently dangerous, but actually very safe tactics." Frederick Pile, *Ack-Ack: Britain's Defence against Air Attack during the Second World War* (London, 1949), pp. 28–29.

57. War Office to G.O.C., 3d Division, 20/misc./128, 2 September 1927, Lindsay papers, LHCMA.

58. Liddell Hart, *Memoirs*, 1:128, and Fuller, *Memoirs*, p. 441. Col. Charles Broad prepared the initial draft, but Milne personally revised it.

59. Based on text of Milne's remarks in Lindsay papers, LHCMA.

60. Liddell Hart, *Memoirs*, 1:130.

61. The account of the E.M.F./3d Division exercise is based on Liddell Hart's articles in the *Daily Telegraph*, 16 September 1927, p. 7, and 17 September 1927, p. 7.

62. Burnett-Stuart gets high marks from Liddell Hart for the 3d Division's tactical dispositions and quick marching. Nevertheless, Burnett-Stuart realized that his force had been hopelessly out-maneuvered.

63. Col. Charles Broad, R.U.S.I. lecture, 9 November 1927, "A Mechanized Formation," *JRUSI* 73 (February 1928): 1–16.

64. For an expansion of Howard's views, see Col. T. N. S. M. Howard, "The Impatience of an Infantryman," *JRA* 54 (January 1928): 536–542.

65. Ironside's remarks quoted from discussion following Broad, "Mechanized Formation," *JRUSI* 73 (February 1928): 15. See also Maj. Gen. Edmund Ironside, Royal Artillery Institution lecture, 15 November 1927, "A Division in Future War and Its Problems," *JRA* 55 (April 1928): 1–11.

66. Milne's remarks quoted from discussion following Broad, "Mechanized Formation," *JRUSI* 73 (February 1928): 15.

67. Gort's remarks quoted from Great Britain, War Office, *Report on the Staff Con-*

ference Held at the Staff College, Camberley, 16th to 19th January 1928 (London, 1928), p. 24.

68. Ibid., p. 29. For a further elaboration of these points, see also Fuller's article "The Reign of the Bullet," published in *The Fighting Forces* (October 1927) and republished as Chapter 2 of Fuller's *On Future War* (London, 1928), pp. 22–37.

69. The problem here was not mobilizing the machine-gun itself, but mobilizing its entire crew of section leader, gunners, spotter, and ammunition bearers. The solution of reducing the crew to two men and mounting them in a lightly armored vehicle now seems obvious, and this is precisely what Martel had recommended at the previous year's staff conference, and what eventually took place with the development of the Bren Gun Carrier in the late 1930s. The reason that the army did not do this on a large scale in the 1920s seems to have been partially based on a belief that the machine-gun was too important a weapon to be entrusted to the private soldier and that it was impossible to have half the unit composed of noncommissioned officers.

70. Like many other officers, Elles, a wartime major general, had been reduced upon demobilization. Elles and Heywood's proposed infantry battalion was to have a machine-gun wing and a "light infantry," or scout, wing. Great Britain, War Office, *Report on the Staff Conference held at the Staff College, Camberley, 16th to 19th January 1928* (London, 1928), p. 94.

71. Ibid., p. 113.

72. Ibid., p. 114. After the formal close of the meeting, however, Milne said that he had been very impressed with the arguments of the younger officers and that efforts would be made to carry out experiments on the lines suggested.

73. *H.C. Deb.,* 5th Ser., 214 (8 March 1928): 1264–1265.

74. See Appendix 4 for a recapitulation of amounts in the Army Estimates for the purchase and maintenance of vehicles and animals from 1927 to 1938.

75. Milne to Creedy, 8 July 1927, W.O. 32/2842.

76. Maj. E. H. Hume, "Mechanization from a Cavalry Point of View," *JRUSI* 72 (November 1927): 811.

77. C.I.D., "Report of the Sub-Committee on the Strength and Organisation of Cavalry," 3 May 1928, attached to C.P. 178(28), Cab. 24/195.

78. Ibid.

79. *H.C. Deb.,* 5th Ser., 214 (8 March 1928): 1272–1273. Birdwood accepted the two-saber squadron organization, but not the mechanization of machine-gun squadrons. In 1927 India refused to accept a mechanized field artillery brigade sent from Shanghai until it was reconverted to a horse-drawn unit. Cmd. 3036, *Statement of the Secretary of State for War relating to the Army Estimates for 1928,* p. 7.

80. Burnett-Stuart, "Progress of Mechanization," *AQ* 16 (April 1928): 30–51.

81. Ibid., p. 30.

82. Ibid., p. 33.

83. Ibid., p. 43.

84. Ibid., p. 49.

85. Milne's remarks quoted from Liddell Hart's account of Burnett-Stuart's lecture, *Daily Telegraph,* 9 March 1928, p. 6.

86. Liddell Hart, *Memoirs,* 1:116.

87. Ibid., pp. 118–121. Thereafter Liddell Hart did not go to the War Office without a specific invitation, but this did not seriously retard his news gathering.

88. Montgomery-Massingberd to Liddell Hart, 9 June 1927, Liddell Hart papers, LHCMA. In the same letter Montgomery-Massingberd criticizes Liddell Hart for saying in his article on Wolfe in *Blackwood's* (subsequently published in *Great Captains*

Unveiled [London, 1927]) that Wolfe's loyalty to the weal of the army and the nation and his penchant for critical thought would have brought him into conflict with the existing rules of promotion, which made loyalty to superiors an essential require- ment. Montgomery-Massingberd says, "Both General Braithwaite and I spotted it at once (independently) and realized the harm such opinions might do in the Army amongst younger officers."

89. Liddell Hart diary note of conversation with Martel, 4 May 1927, Liddell Hart papers, LHCMA.

90. *H.C. Deb.*, 5th Ser., 214 (8 March 1925): 1265. Worthington-Evans con- cluded his remarks on mechanization with the observation that "we have determined at the earliest possible moment to utilise to the full the inventions which have been proved useful in civil life, but we have to adapt them to military uses, and we have to adapt the Army, with its ancient traditions and its historic regiments, with their invaluable *esprit de corps,* to the new conditions." Ibid., col. 1270.

91. Bonham-Carter recapitulated Milne's guidance at the 1929 staff conference. See War Office, *Report on the Staff Conference, 1929,* pp. 22–23.

92. Victor Bonham-Carter, *In a Liberal Tradition: A Social Biography, 1700–1950* (London, 1960), pp. 182–183.

93. When Bonham-Carter accepted the staff duties post, Milne promised him that he could make any changes he liked at Sandhurst. He did much to improve the curriculum and even convinced a number of headmasters that an intelligent young man would do well to consider an army career. Ibid., pp. 184, 193–194. Broad interview, 10 November 1972.

94. Broad interview, 10 November 1972. See also Liddell Hart, *The Tanks,* 1:246, 250. In his conversation with the author, General Broad tended to minimize his influence.

95. Hotblack interview, 24 October 1972.

96. John T. Burnett-Stuart, "Memoir," 2 vols., 2:43, Burnett-Stuart papers, on Godley. Although he was a gunner, Montgomery-Massingberd's close identification with the cavalry and his incremental approach to modernization were evident in his chairmanship of the War Office Cavalry Committee in 1926–27.

97. Burnett-Stuart, "Memoir," 2:43–44.

98. When Burnett-Stuart's A.D.C., Francis Festing, entered the Staff College, the commandant pointedly reminded him that he had worked for a man with a reputa- tion for criticizing his superiors and that he, Festing, should not attempt to emulate this characteristic. Festing interview, 19 September 1972.

99. See Martel's assessment of Burnett-Stuart's impact on the Armoured Force in G. LeQ. Martel, *In the Wake of the Tank: The First Fifteen Years of Mechanization in the British Army* (London, 1931), pp. 219–227.

100. Brig. W. A. F. Kerrich to author, 20 September 1972.

101. Quoted from Burnett-Stuart tribute, *RBC* (1958), p. 68.

102. Burnett-Stuart to Liddell Hart, 24 September 1927, Liddell Hart papers, LHCMA.

103. This analysis was contained in Liddell Hart's *Great Captains Unveiled* (Lon- don, 1927), a copy of which he sent to Burnett-Stuart. Burnett-Stuart said he would enjoy reading it "because I know that in your serious moments you unveil great captains with the same skill as that with which in your lighter moments you go about unveiling little ones." Burnett-Stuart to Liddell Hart, 24 September 1927, Liddell Hart papers, LHCMA.

104. Martel, *Wake of the Tank,* 2d ed. (London, 1935), pp. 165–169. One of these exercises showed that a total of 450 thirty-hundred-weight and three-ton trucks

would be required to maintain the force at a distance of 170 miles from a railhead in sustained operations. Another showed that 120 would be required to conduct a four-day operation at approximately the same distance. The organization and reduction of this unarmored logistical "tail" was one of the major problems that would have to be dealt with in the 1930s.

105. Liddell Hart, *The Tanks*, 1:259.

106. Description of the material deficiencies of the Armoured Force mainly from ibid.

107. Technical details of the Vickers Medium Mark III from the Royal Armoured Corps Tank Museum, *The Inter War Period 1919–1939* (Bovington, Dorset, 1970), pp. 10, 35.

108. This paragraph based mainly on Liddell Hart's reports on the exercises in the *Daily Telegraph*, 6 and 13 July 1928.

109. This paragraph based on Liddell Hart's reports in the *Daily Telegraph*, 19 and 20 September 1928, and his article "Armoured Forces in 1928," *JRUSI* 73 (November 1928): 720–729.

110. Liddell Hart, "Armoured Forces in 1928," *JRUSI* 73 (November 1928): 723.

111. As Kenneth Macksey has pointed out, however, Liddell Hart's emphasis on the employment of light tanks did not fully consider the vulnerability of light tanks in an encounter with tanks having heavier armor and greater fire power. Kenneth Macksey, *Tank Warfare: A History of Tanks in Battle* (New York, 1972), p. 81.

112. Liddell Hart, "Armoured Forces in 1928," *JRUSI* 73 (November 1928): 723.

113. Maj. Gen. J. T. Burnett-Stuart, "Armoured Force Training Report–1928," W.O. 32/2828, Experimental Armoured Force, 1928: Report. The War Office copy was dated simply November 1928, but Southern Command endorsed it on 9 November.

114. Ibid., p. 2.

115. Ibid.

116. Ibid., pp. 2–3.

117. Ibid., p. 3.

118. Ibid., pp. 6–7. See Appendix 8 for a schematic representation of Burnett-Stuart's proposed armored force.

119. Based on a misunderstanding of Burnett-Stuart's Armoured Force report of 1928, Larson incorrectly concludes that Burnett-Stuart was a party to the school of thought that had reacted against the tanks. Robert H. Larson, *The British Army and the Theory of Armored Warfare, 1918–1940* (Newark, N.J., 1984), p. 145. The correct interpretation of Burnett-Stuart's report would lead one to believe that he stressed the negative conditions under which the force had worked in 1928 as a strong justification for continuing the trials in 1929. His memoir contains the same implication. In fact Burnett-Stuart was, as both Milne and Liddell Hart testify, a convert to mechanization. He was also convinced of the efficacy of some, though not all, of the tenets of armored warfare. This distinction became more apparent in the mid-1930s.

120. Milne to Worthington-Evans, 12 November 1928, W.O. 32/2825, Experimental Formations for 1929.

121. The composition he listed—headquarters and signal section, a medium tank battalion, two light tank battalions, and one close support battery—was identical with that advocated by Colonel Broad in a Royal Artillery Institution lecture, 23 October 1928, "Tactics of Armoured Fighting Vehicles," *JRA* 55 (January 1929): 415–437.

122. The subject of radio control of armored units is discussed in detail in Chapter 5.

123. Milne to Worthington-Evans, 12 November 1928, W.O. 32/2825.

124. Worthington-Evans to Milne, 27 November 1928, W.O. 32/2825.

125. Quotation from Churchill to Worthington-Evans, 11 December 1928, W.O. 32/2825. Worthington-Evans had already promised that this program would be given absolute priority, but Churchill repeated the point, apparently to make it clear that it could not be used as an excuse by the War Office to obtain additional funds.

126. *H.C. Deb.*, 5th Ser., 223 (27 November 1928): 216–217. Worthington-Evans' statement was given in response to a question on the Armoured Force's future by Brigadier General Clifton-Brown. It is not clear whether the question came at Clifton-Brown's initiative or at Worthington-Evans'.

127. A. A. Montgomery-Massingberd, "The Autobiography of a Gunner," p. 53, Montgomery-Massingberd papers, LHCMA.

128. Liddell Hart diary note, 28 November 1928, Liddell Hart papers, LHCMA.

129. Lt. Gen. Sir A. A. Montgomery-Massingberd, "Armoured Force Training Report, 1928," 24 November 1928, pp. 2, 4, W.O. 32/2828.

130. Braithwaite to Milne, 18 December 1928, W.O. 32/2828. Milne had circulated the report together with all covering letters to the members of the Army Council for comment.

131. There may have also been pressure from what Arnold-Forster once referred to as "the great army of those who have left the colours and are now entrenched in the clubs of this city." Robert Blake, "Great Britain: From Crimea to the First World War," *Soldiers and Governments: Nine Studies in Civil-Military Relations*, Michael Howard, ed. (London, 1957), p. 34. When the author asked General Sir Frederick Pile why he thought Milne had dispersed the Armoured Force, he answered without hesitation that the old cavalrymen were responsible. Shortly thereafter he escorted the author into the anteroom of the Cavalry Club, pointed to the portraits on the wall, and said, "Look around you, what do you see? I'll tell you what you see – horses and Field Marshals, horses and Field Marshals!" Pile interview, 12 October 1972.

5

DOCTRINE, DEBATE, AND
THE DEPRESSION, 1929–1933

We have carried out experiments and researched on a large scale, and with such
success that we can confidently claim to lead the world not only in our equipment
of tanks but also in our ideas as to their use in War.
— *Sir Laming Worthington-Evans, February 1929*[1]

British tactical doctrine progressed somewhat unevenly during the period
from 1929 to 1933. On the one hand, the experiments with mechanized
infantry units at Aldershot and Salisbury Plain proved disappointing. On the
other hand, some of the results of the 1927 and 1928 exercises were codified
in a remarkable little manual drafted by Colonel Broad entitled *Mechanised
and Armoured Formations*. And although a tank brigade was only temporarily
brought together for trials in the early 1930s, the progress made — again by
Colonel Broad — in the command and control of armored formations was
truly remarkable. These events took place, however, in an international environment marked by progressive unease and in a domestic environment characterized by a popular revulsion to war and strict economic stringency. Appreciation of the dynamics of this period requires analysis of the significant
features of the international and domestic environment; the conduct of tactical exercises from 1929 to 1933 and the evolution of doctrine and plans for
organizations associated therewith; the debate within the officer corps accompanying these developments; the War Office report on the Great War and
the selection of a new C.I.G.S.; and the standing of Great Britain vis-à-vis
several other countries in the areas of armored doctrine, organization, and
equipment.

I

The perceptions of British defense planners in 1929 and 1930 were influenced by the relaxation of European tensions, changing conditions in the
Near and Far East, and the accession of the second Labour government
under Ramsay MacDonald in June 1929.

Regarding Europe, the chiefs of staff were obviously chafing under the
effects of the ten-year rule. They concluded their annual defense review of
1929 by stating that they felt bound to

impress on the Committee of Imperial Defence how great a responsibility this [assumption] places on those charged with the day-to-day conduct of foreign affairs to warn the Committee of Imperial Defence of the first hint of a less satisfactory state of affairs, in order that the necessary adjustments in our defensive arrangements may be considered, the requisite preparations for which would require a period of some years to bring into effective operation.[2]

And in their 1930 review noting the lack of specific measures taken to meet the provisions of Locarno, they said, "This country is in a less favourable position to fulfill the Locarno guarantees than it was, without any written guarantee, to come to the assistance of France and Belgium in 1914."[3]

The army's main concern, however, continued to be the Near and Far East. Conflicts between the Arabs and the Jews required the dispatch of two infantry battalions to Palestine in August 1929. Negotiations with Egypt over protection of the Suez Canal and the continued British presence in the interior broke down in 1930, and two battalions were still required to maintain order in the Sudan. Any hopes for reduction of the army in India were offset by the increased agitation from the Congress Party.[4] The garrison in China was substantially reduced in 1929, but troops were still required to protect the British communities in Shanghai, Tientsin, Peking, Canton, and Hankow as well as to defend the colony of Hong Kong.[5]

At home the general election of 1929 returned 288 Labourites, 260 Conservatives, and 29 Liberals. MacDonald was called upon to form a government, and Labour was again dependent upon Liberal support in the Commons. This time, however, MacDonald was much more in control of his own party, having excluded the left-wing elements from positions of responsibility.[6] MacDonald advocated moderate socialism at home, and his chancellor of the Exchequer, Philip Snowden, followed a policy of strict economic conservatism. Abroad, MacDonald pursued a course of conciliation, disarmament, and support for the League. Shortly after assuming office he directed cessation of work on the naval base at Singapore, and in April 1930 he negotiated an agreement between Great Britain, the United States, and Japan to maintain the ratio of cruisers among them at 5:5:3.[7]

The year 1931 marks a significant turning point in the history of the British Army between the wars. Before 1931 the army had existed in an environment that, in Michael Howard's words, was "at best indifferent and at worst hostile," but at least stable.[8] While the army had not prospered during this time, it had at least known what to expect. The years after 1931 were much different. Financial and political events in Britain and the world caused major shifts, which influenced both British strategic planning and doctrinal development. It is therefore not surprising that the military leaders who were unsure how best to address the difficulties of developing a new doctrine in a situation marked by financial stringency, technological uncertainty, and the dilemma posed by the conflicting requirements of imperial defense and

Continental commitment were even further confounded when these problems were exacerbated by a world financial crisis and an expansive, militaris-
tic movement in Germany.

Before 1931 the effects of the New York stock-market crash were largely
confined to the western side of the Atlantic, but beginning with the failure
of the Austrian Credit-Anstalt bank in May of that year, a series of financial
crises occurred in Germany, France, and Britain. While the causes of the
financial collapses were obscure, their effects were not. Factories were closed,
workers idled, and a profound disillusionment developed among many Euro-
peans, causing them to doubt the ability of their political leaders. With
moderate leaders discredited, political extremists of all persuasions found it
increasingly easy to mobilize support for their radical remedies.

Despite the deteriorating international situation, events in Britain were
dominated by domestic economic and political considerations. In September
1931 MacDonald's government divided over the issue of whether or not to
continue paying unemployment benefits in a time of severe financial stringency.[9] What emerged from the crisis, however, was not a Conservative government nor even a Conservative-Liberal coalition, but a National Government that included MacDonald as its titular head, Stanley Baldwin as lord
president of the council, and a leading Liberal, Sir Herbert Samuel, as home
secretary. It was not, however, a truly "National" Government. It was dominated by the Conservatives, who held 472 of its 556 seats, and MacDonald
was prime minister in name only. Division within the National Government
and the absence of any serious political threat produced a great deal of hesitation in almost all its actions, and its history has been aptly characterized
by C. L. Mowat as "one long diminuendo."[10] The National Government
relied on the traditional tools of reduced spending and increased taxation to
combat economic depression, and it attempted to deal with unemployment
by continuing the dole and reimposing the means test to keep as many people as possible from drawing unemployment benefits.[11] This policy of minimum government expenditure also created an atmosphere in which funds
for the armed forces were severely curtailed.

The tendency to reduce military spending was reinforced by a strong mood
of popular pacifism. In Commons the Labour secretary of state for war,
Thomas Shaw, was scathingly attacked by the antimilitarist members of his
party when he presented the Army Estimates in 1931.[12] In February 1933
the Oxford Union, the university debating society, voted 275 to 153 in
favor of a motion "that this House will in no circumstances fight for its King
and Country."[13] At a time when the dangers of a future war were becoming
somewhat more apparent, such sympathies placed British political leaders on
the horns of dilemma.

The effect of this popular sentiment was not to rule out rearmament, but
to make the approach to it cautious. MacDonald's defense policy was char-

acterized by a mixture of pragmatism and a desire for international conciliation. In November 1930 he intimated to the C.I.D. that he was not wedded to the ten-year rule and wanted "flexibility and not dogmas" in matters of defense.[14] Nevertheless, when Maurice Hankey, secretary to the Cabinet and the C.I.D., sent MacDonald a note suggesting a reexamination of the ten-year rule, MacDonald's private secretary replied that the prime minister did not disagree with Hankey's conclusions, but there was "scarcely any likelihood of any action being taken pending the Disarmament Conference."[15] Hankey, however, was determined to force a review, and in early 1932 he instructed the chiefs of staff to focus their annual review of imperial defense on the need to reexamine the ten-year rule.[16] The chiefs of staff concluded the resulting report with three recommendations that urged cancelling the ten-year rule, beginning the construction of bases in the Far East, and taking immediate action before the termination of the Disarmament Conference. "We cannot ignore," they said, "the Writing on the Wall."[17]

While these positions made a great deal of military sense, Neville Chamberlain, the chancellor of the Exchequer, did not think they made much economic sense. In the Treasury's view, the economic risks of increased expenditure were "far the most serious and urgent that the country has to face."[18] The Cabinet therefore compromised and on 23 March 1932 decided to cancel the ten-year rule, but with the proviso that there would be no expansion of defense spending without regard to the serious financial situation.[19]

II

In late 1928, however, it was not possible to project five years into the future. Milne's decision to disband the Armoured Force was based partly on the assumption that he would be able to reassemble it in one or two years on a permanent basis. This proved not to be the case. In order to determine what was accomplished, however, we must begin with the mechanized infantry and cavalry trials of 1929 and 1930.

The War Office tasks for the 1929 trials focused on infantry, cavalry, and tank units.[20] The experimental infantry units were instructed to test various methods of transporting machine-guns, to study the employment of the antitank machine-gun, and to determine whether or not a light tank battalion and a close support artillery unit should be included in the infantry brigade. The cavalry tasks were to determine how best to carry their machine-guns, how to employ the Austin Scout vehicles, and whether or not a 3.7-inch howitzer battery should be included in the cavalry brigade. Tank units were told to study the organization of the light tank battalion, the proportions of light and medium tanks in a mixed tank battalion, and the use of radios.

In Southern Command, which had been the focus of many of the 1929 experiments, relations between Montgomery-Massingberd and Burnett-Stuart continued to deteriorate. One incident sheds some light on relations between the two men. After driving to Salisbury in his private car to dine with Montgomery-Massingberd at his commander's invitation, Burnett-Stuart submitted a voucher to be reimbursed for travel expenses. The paymaster at Southern Command returned the voucher, stating that the trip was for pleasure rather than duty. Rather than letting the incident pass, Burnett-Stuart resubmitted the voucher with the notation, "If dining with the C.-in-C. is not a duty, God knows what it is!"[21] This story quickly got around, causing great delight among the junior officers. But from Montgomery-Massingberd's point of view, it was probably just one more example of want of respect from a troublesome subordinate.

Burnett-Stuart's pungent humor, frequently directed at his superiors, came out several other times during his tenure at 3d Division. When a senior officer giving a lecture at the R.U.S.I. emphasized the limitations of mechanized formations with the statement that horses could always keep going whereas vehicles had to stop when their carburetors ran out of gas, Burnett-Stuart made disparaging remarks about people who did not know the difference between a carburetor and a gas tank.[22] In 1929 the War Office's official Christmas card featured a picture of the military members of the Army Council arrayed in full dress uniform splendidly mounted for the king's birthday parade. Burnett-Stuart wrote on it, "Four more reasons for mechanization" and displayed it prominently on his mantle.[23] This too proved a great hit among the junior officers, but again it was probably not appreciated in higher circles.

The first War Office exercise of 1929, held on 11–12 September, pitted Maj. Gen. Thomas Cubbit's 2d Division against Burnett-Stuart's 3d Division, each of which contained one experimental infantry brigade.[24] The exercise was limited by a strict time schedule and little land on which to maneuver, but there was some room for initiative. On the 12th, Cubbit was to attack and Burnett-Stuart was to defend and then counterattack. After repulsing the 2d Division effort, Burnett-Stuart sent a company of tanks around a flank to strike at its lines of supply. He then placed his experimental infantry brigade in position and launched it toward the 2d Division's center while everyone was concentrating on the flank threat. The final outcome was not determined, for the exercise was halted before the attack could be completed.

The second exercise, conducted on the 16th and 17th, was similarly indecisive.[25] This time the 3d Division was to attack initially against the 6th Brigade, part of Cubbit's force, which was to delay back to the 2d Division's defensive position along the River Avon. Burnett-Stuart cut off the 6th Brigade with his 7th and 8th Brigades and moved his medium tanks forward in the center. Just when he was ready to deliver the *coup de grâce*, however, his attack was halted by the exercise directors. When he came to the 2d Division's main positions, he again sent his tanks to the flank, but this time in strength. They overran a number of artillery positions and were judged to have inflicted damage on 80 percent of the 2d Division's tanks. Although neither exercise produced dramatic results, Burnett-Stuart showed himself fully capable of handling armored formations and demonstrated a penchant for quick movement and surprise.

The War Office published its first analysis of the 1929 trials in a training memorandum that reflected the opinion of the major commands.[26] There was still a great deal of debate about the employment of the machine-gun. Some commands felt it should be moved forward in close support of the rifle companies. Others felt that it should be held back according to existing practice but that a special "in-fighting" unit of armored carriers should be formed to move machine-guns ahead of the infantry assault. The War Office decided to continue developing the standard employment of both the Lewis Gun and the machine-gun but also to form an experimental "in-fighting" unit in the 6th and 7th Brigades for trial in 1930.

The evaluation of cavalry experiments indicated that the Carden-Loyds were a definite improvement on wheeled vehicles for carrying machine-guns but that "across country they are not sufficiently mobile to keep up with mounted troops."[27] The commands also felt the vehicles were too small and recommended the development of a three-man, as opposed to a two-man, machine-gun carrier. Thus at the end of 1929 the cavalry had still not found a vehicle that met its demands for machine-gun carriage. This did not appear to upset the War Office, however, for no specific instructions were promulgated for the 1930 cavalry experiments, and the commands were permitted to adopt whatever organization they desired.

The tank experiments were similarly inconclusive. It was determined that the light tank battalion was not suitable for inclusion in the infantry brigade; but, as Liddell Hart had said, this was almost self-evident.[28] While the infantry units did need more offensive power, the light tank was not a suitable vehicle for their close support. In addition, to equip the 1st, 2d, and 3d Divisions alone on this scale would have required nine light tank battalions, and in 1929 there were not enough light tanks to equip even two battalions. Without such tanks, the War Office was unable to make any determination on the other two main questions—the organization of the light tank battalion itself and the proper mix of light and medium tanks in a medium tank battalion. The one bright spot was that the 1929 experiments had finally "proved the value of R/T [radio-telephone] control within the tank battalion."[29] With that question settled, it became mainly a matter of designing improved models, determining the level to which they should be installed, and perfecting the techniques for their use—assuming, of course, that the necessary funds were made available.

In summary, the 1929 trials were primarily intended to advance the mechanization of existing arms, while developments in armored warfare lay dormant. The trials were limited by a number of factors: the personalities of those overseeing them, the stereotyped tactical exercises, the lack of maneuver land, the unavailability of suitable vehicles, and to some extent the narrowness of the objectives themselves. While it can be argued that these experiments were necessary to modernize the infantry and cavalry, the paltry results seem to have justified neither the effort expended nor the dispersal of the Armoured Force in 1928.

The 1930 trials were even more limited than those of the previous year because, in addition to other factors, the final exercises of the 4th Guards Brigade, the 2d Division, and the combined Aldershot–Southern Command tests were conducted in driving rainstorms.[30] Conditions were further aggravated by the low strength of infantry units whose commanders were compelled to combine two or three companies in order to form one complete one.[31] Nevertheless, some lessons were drawn. The separate "in-fighting" unit was not deemed effective, and a need was determined for mortars in infantry battalions. No progress was reported, however, in the development of antitank weapons, which had by then become a critical deficiency. The cavalry experienced problems in the carriage of machine-guns and reached the conclusion that "a proportion of cavalry machineguns must be carried on pack."[32] Austin Scouts, however, had definitely proved themselves as reconnaissance vehicles. The cavalry units requested more from the War Office for the 1931 trials, but none were available, presumably for financial reasons. Radios in tanks were continuing to work well, and the goal of a radio in every tank was accepted in principle. But the Treasury intervened again, and for 1931 radios would be issued only down to section leaders.

Burnett-Stuart did not participate in the 1930 trials. He was promoted to lieutenant general on 18 February; as there was no vacancy for him in this grade, he was placed on half-pay in May.[33] Half-pay often meant financial hardship since it amounted to only half of the officer's basic pay, not including the allowance for quarters and other emoluments received on active duty. For Burnett-Stuart, however, it probably came as a welcome relief after the demands of the 1929 training season. Crichie and the Scottish countryside offered the joys of hunting, fly-fishing, and leisurely hours in the library reading poetry and darkening the ceiling with pipe smoke.[34] In late 1930 he was appointed general officer commanding, British troops in Egypt, a position he was to take up in early 1931.

Despite the lack of progress in equipment and organization, some significant doctrinal developments took place in 1929 and 1930. There were also two attempts in the War Office to expand the army's armored formations, both of which were unsuccessful. Shortly after the 1928 trials Milne instructed Colonel Broad to write down his thoughts on the organization and employment of armored units. Broad quickly produced a draft, which was reviewed by Colonels Lindsay and Pile. Broad revised it based on their comments and gave it to Bonham-Carter within a week of receiving Milne's directive.[35] This draft became Britain's first manual on armored warfare, *Mechanised and Armoured Formations*.[36]

According to its preface, the manual's purpose was to generate thought about mechanization and armored warfare even though the army would not be organized to fight such a war:

> For various reasons—notably financial—it is inevitable that the provision of the army's technical equipment should lag behind the corresponding stage in civil life. But this is no reason why officers should lag behind in studying its application; they must, by close study, be in a position to use profitably the numerous technical vehicles and equipments which war will at once produce.[37]

The manual was to be the basis for all staff exercises, but its provisional nature was strongly emphasized. And since equipment and therefore tactics were constantly changing, all officers were enjoined to keep "an open and flexible mind."[38] The text of the manual consisted of four brief chapters dealing with vehicles, organization, operations, and administration.

Vehicles were divided into three classes: armored fighting vehicles; armored carriers; and unarmored carriers, transport vehicles, and tractors. The reader was given a balanced survey of the capabilities and limitations of each type. A.F.V.s, for instance, were said to "enable the attacker to produce fire in movement and at the same time they give him a considerable degree of protection."[39] They were, however, "dependent on supply from a base" and "very sensitive to ground."[40] The manual stated that A.F.V.s were "less vulnerable to air and gas attack."[41] Furthermore, "the moral and material effect of the A.F.V.s on other arms is great."[42] But, it said, because guns would "always outclass armour and the accuracy of stationary guns will always be greater than that of those in movement, direct frontal assault on prepared positions will be costly unless supported by adequate covering fire."[43] The medium tank represented "the most powerful A.F.V. in service," and its main role was to "destroy the enemy by fire or shock action."[44] The analysis for other types of vehicles was similar, though not as extensive.

The chapter on organization depicted the army of the future being made up of cavalry divisions or brigades, light armored divisions or brigades, medium armored brigades, and infantry divisions augmented with armored formations. The medium armored brigades were to be the army's strongest formation. They were to take part in decisive attacks and under certain conditions support infantry and cavalry. The latter action was restricted, however, by the statement that it would "be the aim of the commander to bring about battle in such a way that his medium armoured brigades . . . act under the most favorable conditions."[45]

The chapter on operations emphasized the role of the armored brigade in the independent attack; five pages were devoted to this subject and only half a page to attacking in cooperation with infantry and cavalry. In the attack on fixed lines, however, tanks were given two roles: assisting in the initial penetration and exploiting success. For the first stage, extra measures were required to protect the tanks, including "special artillery and machine-gun fire, smoke, aeroplane co-operation and assistance from accompanying infantry."[46] The purpose of the subsequent exploitation by armored forces was to collapse the enemy's front lines and sever his lines of supply and communication. "The resultant chaos," it was hoped, would create "opportunities for decisive operations under mobile warfare conditions."[47] Broad's description of armored operations was reminiscent of Fuller's Plan 1919 and a forecast of the use of armored divisions in World War II.

The chapter on administration discussed administrative organization, supply, repair and recovery of vehicles, traffic control, and medical support. Broad recognized that the administrative requirements for armored formations were undoubtedly among their most significant liabilities. Their speed of operations restricted their foraging for food, and their requirements for ammunition, gas, and spare parts could in most cases be met only through their own supply channels.[48] In the short space available to him, however, he merely outlined the problems to be considered.

Mechanised and Armoured Formations was, in summary, a concise yet comprehensive document that described many of the essential features of armored warfare. Considering the brief time involved in its preparation and the validity of its underlying conceptions, it was a remarkable achievement.

Having launched Colonel Broad successfully in the project of codifying the extant concepts of armored warfare, Milne's next effort was to increase the proportion of armored formations in the army. Unlike doctrine, questions referred to today as "force structure" issues carry with them serious resource implications because gains for one branch almost always result in losses for another. Here Milne was not as successful. His first effort was the formation of a study group to determine the feasibility of forming four armored brigades within two or three years.[49] The study group consisted of Colonels Lindsay and Pile, Major Hotblack, and three officers not connected with the Tank Corps. They concluded that it would be possible to form only three brigades but agreed that the expansion of the Royal Tank Corps was the most feasible way to obtain them. They disagreed, however, on the rate of conversion. Lindsay and Hotblack wanted to complete the program by October 1930, while the other officers wanted to spread the program over the next four to five years.

Nevertheless, the group did recommend that three armored brigades be formed, with two stationed in Britain and one in Egypt. The unit in Egypt would have presumably replaced an infantry brigade, and was necessary to maintain the balance between overseas and home deployments essential to the proper functioning of the Cardwell system. The projected capital outlay of £454,080, mostly for light tanks, was less than the total amount contained in the 1929 estimates for all tracked vehicles. The major problem, however, was personnel. In order to raise the five tank battalions required to support the scheme, the War Office would have had to disband four infantry battalions and two armored car companies. The armored car companies were not a major problem, but there was apparently a great deal of resistance to the elimination of infantry units, for no concrete action was ever taken to implement this proposal.[50]

The second attempt occurred in March 1930 when Milne was encouraged, apparently by E. Shinwell, financial secretary to the War Office in the second Labour government, to submit "a policy on reorganization looking five years ahead."[51] Milne again directed Broad to write up his thoughts on the subject and suggested that the 5th Infantry Division and other units might be disbanded. Milne apparently did not believe that this would come to much at the time, but he hoped it might prove useful in the future. Broad was ecstatic, telling Liddell Hart that this was "the first time we have definitely been told to produce a policy."[52] Unfortunately nothing came from this effort either.

Some insights into the reasons behind the failure of these proposals can be found in Bonham-Carter's remarks following a lecture given in February 1930 on "Developments in Army Organization."[53] The director of staff duties mentioned three points that complicated the organization of the British Army for war. First, the army's main purpose was to garrison the Empire and the expeditionary force was "a sort of by-product" of the home army. Second, the army never knew where it would be committed and machines might be "quite unsuitable" for some possible theaters of war. Finally, the evolutionary progress of technology and the problems of finance made it highly unlikely that an officer on a four-year tour at the War Office would ever see both "the beginning of research and a general issue made of some new equipment." Bonham-Carter's statement presented an extremely accurate analysis of the obstacles to mechanization – and more particularly to armored warfare – facing the British Army at the beginning of the new decade.

Economic stringency and political indifference to the army impeded major changes in the army's organization and structure in the early 1930s, but doctrine was able to develop somewhat independently. *Mechanised and Armoured Formations* was updated in 1931 under the title *Modern Formations* and, as mentioned earlier, real progress was made in the radio control of armored units.

Modern Formations contained a number of changes in organizational conception. It foresaw mobile divisions as the two types of higher organizations. Mobile divisions would consist of either cavalry, infantry, and tanks, or tanks alone. The exact proportion of various troops in both mobile and infantry divisions would depend upon the terrain of the theater of war in which they would be employed.[54] Perhaps the key point in the organizational concept was that brigades would be largely homogeneous, with the mixture of various arms to occur by grouping different types of brigades together. The manual did not provide for the close integration of tanks, infantry, artillery, and aircraft within the brigade that Burnett-Stuart had recommended in his report on the 1928 experiments. This was to cause a number of problems in the late 1930s when the first armored division was formed. Nevertheless, *Modern Formations* did contain a good deal of serious thought on mechanization and armored warfare, and it was a useful attempt to make the implications of the experimental work of the years 1927 to 1930 available to the whole army.

The next major development in armored doctrine occurred during the 1931 training season when Milne authorized Colonel Broad temporarily to assemble the four existing tank battalions into a First Brigade, Royal Tank Corps, for the purpose of developing greater maneuverability in tank units.[55] The 1931 trials represented the first employment of tank units in larger than battalion strength since the maneuvers of the Experimental Armoured Force in 1928. They were significant for the future of British armored doctrine and organization in several respects: First, through the extensive use of radios and signal flags they demonstrated the ease of control and flexibility of armored formations; second, they focused the attention of the rising Royal Tank Corps officers on units made up almost entirely of tanks, rather than more balanced armored formations; and finally, their success led to the increased confidence in the Royal Tank Corps, a corresponding deterioration of morale among the infantry, and the eventual formation of a permanent Tank Brigade in 1934.

Broad did not learn of his appointment until March, and with the training season set to begin the first of April, he set to work quickly. He realized that effective control was an essential prerequisite to tactical flexibility, and one of his first acts was to get in contact with Col. A. C. Fuller at the Signals Experimental Establishment in Woolwich.[56] Colonel Fuller, not to be confused with J. F. C. Fuller, was one of the British Army's pioneers in the use of the wireless. He suggested that Broad and he test one of the new crystal-controlled frequency sets on a tank. An experimental ride along the road to Elton, during which perfect communications were maintained with a unit remaining at Woolwich, convinced Broad that radios were the solution to the problem of command.[57] There were not, however, enough radios to be distributed beyond company headquarters, so Broad devised a system of flag signals to control the movements of smaller units.[58] This system consisted of a set of two-letter codes that corresponded to various tactical maneuvers and

Brig. Charles Broad directing exercises of the provisional Tank Brigade formed at Salisbury Plain in 1931 to continue armored trials after dispersal of the Experimental Armoured Force in 1928. Broad's use of the radio and systematic battle drills were major advances in the tactical handling of armored formations. (Courtesy of the Times Newspapers Limited.)

could be conveyed by the combination of colored flags as well as by Morse code or voice radio.[59]

Broad's next task was to develop a common system of tank tactics among the different battalions. He accomplished this by visiting the various units and giving lectures to the battalion officers and N.C.O.s on tank tactics and on Jenghiz Khan's system of tactical flexibility. These lectures were followed by a series of staff exercises designed to standardize the handling of tank battalions in various tactical situations.[60] Thus by 5 September, when the brigade was assembled at Tilshead Camp on Salisbury Plain, Broad had developed the potential for concerted action. The sympathetic attitude of General Sir Cecil Romer, who had replaced General Montgomery-Massingberd as G.O.C.-in-C., Southern Command, also augured well for the success of the 1931 trials.[61]

The brigade's flexibility was demonstrated in a series of five exercises. In the first exercise, each battalion was required to move over different types of terrain, varying its formation to suit the situation. The second exercise tested deployment for battle. The third exercise featured the attack of an artillery position. The fourth exercise consisted of an attack on antitank positions with a series of quick strikes from various angles. And the final exercise involved the attack on an infantry column designed to test the brigade's ability to encircle.[62] The last exercise in particular demonstrated the moral force of the new arm as well as its flexibility, for even though the infantry column had been augmented with extra antitank guns and seemed to have been given advance warning of the Tank Brigade's direction of attack, Broad was able to detach a portion of his force to deal with the antitank screen and move the remainder of the unit to a position of attack on the infantry column's unprotected flank.[63]

The brigade's final exercise demonstrated its maneuverability to the Army Council. Broad, who was completely confident of the brigade's ability, allowed no rehearsals to be conducted for this demonstration.[64] On the day of the event, Salisbury Plain was shrouded in fog. The brigade major directed the unit across the moonlike surface of the Plain into the demonstration arena, where Broad took control by radio. Just as the fog lifted, the entire brigade appeared in front of the stands, wheeled, and came to a precise stop. The impressiveness of this exhibition made many of the onlookers feel they were victims of an elaborate hoax deliberately designed to magnify the brigade's capability. For those who knew the true situation, however, and perhaps for the less skeptical of those who did not, it was a fitting climax to a successful season.[65]

The 1931 trials had several significant implications. They demonstrated the flexibility of armored formations equipped with radios. They indicated Charles Broad's ability to translate ideas into practice. And on a broader range, they helped bring about acceptance of armored warfare in the army at large. Their success, however, caused members of the Royal Tank Corps to see the combination of light tanks, medium tanks, and close support tanks as being sufficient to solve all tactical problems. While this was perhaps true on the unbroken terrain of Salisbury Plain, it would not prove true where armored units would be required to fight over more varied ground.

At the end of the 1931 exercises, Broad was promoted to permanent brigadier and sent to Aldershot Command as the chief general staff officer.[66] This left Kenneth Laird, inspector of the Royal Tank Corps, to command the Tank Brigade when it assembled in 1932. Laird had served in the M.G.O.'s office in the directorate concerned with mechanization from 1924 to 1927, so he was familiar with the technical side of tank development, and his years as inspector of the R.T.C. had acquainted him with both the tactical and administrative sides. He also had fifty new Mark II light tanks that substantially improved the speed and maneuverability of the tank units.

The most dramatic example of these characteristics occurred in the tank-versus-tank exercises. One such exercise pitted Lt. Col. Patrick Hobart's 2d

Battalion against Lt. Col. Justice Tilly's 5th Battalion. The units began five miles apart, but within twenty minutes they were engaged at a distance of fifteen hundred yards. Hobart offset Tilly's initial advantage by maneuvering behind a ridge and coming up in another location to fire from a concealed position. Tilly then concentrated two of his companies on one of Hobart's, but Hobart won the mock battle by maneuvering his reserve around Tilly's forces and attacking them from the rear. The actual engagement was completed in another twenty minutes. This exercise not only demonstrated the new pace of armored tactics, it also confirmed Hobart as the leading tactician in the R.T.C.[67]

In one of the final exercises, the entire brigade was employed in a wide maneuver to disrupt the retreat of an enemy infantry column. For this operation Laird consolidated all the new Mark IIs into a light tank battalion to locate the opposing unit. After reporting the enemy's location and the disposition of its antitank weapons and artillery, the light battalion blocked the head of the column while the medium battalions were used to sever and disorganize it. The total time elapsed from the dispatch of the reconnaissance unit, which began eleven miles from the infantry column, to the final attack was just over one and a half hours.[68] As in 1931 the morale of the R.T.C. units was extremely high at the end of the trials. Conversely, after repeatedly suffering at the hands of the tank units, the morale among the "unprotected, foot-slogging, rifle-and-bayonet men" was beginning to deteriorate.[69]

The major impact of the 1932 trials, however, was that they finally convinced Milne of the need to establish a Tank Brigade on a permanent basis. This conviction was expressed in a memorandum to the other military members of the Army Council and the permanent under-secretary dated 15 September 1932. Citing the value of light tanks in reconnaissance duties and the mixed battalion organization proven in the 1932 trials, Milne proposed the formation of a mixed Tank Brigade of one light and three mixed battalions, one additional unbrigaded mixed tank battalion at home, and one specially composed mixed tank battalion in Egypt. Anticipating the problem of quartering, Milne proposed that the three mixed tank battalions each be assigned an extra light tank company that could be combined to form the light battalion as required. This, Milne said, would obviate the need for constructing an extra set of battalion barracks. Regarding the economic consequences, Milne pointed out that his establishment of 125 medium tanks and 178 light tanks would actually represent a savings over the 208 medium tanks called for by the existing war establishment. He concluded, "I attach considerable importance to this scheme which will, at last, place our tank units upon a sound basis, both as regards the Expeditionary Force and as regards Egypt."[70] Bowing to Milne's forcefully stated desires, the other military members of the Army Council unanimously accepted his proposal.[71] Sir Herbert

Creedy, the P.U.S., enthusiastically called it "a welcome step forward."[72] With this consensus established, Milne forwarded it to the secretary of state for war, Viscount Hailsham, who approved it on 6 October.[73]

Thus by the end of 1932, British armored doctrine and organization had taken some significant steps forward. The publication of *Modern Formations* had at least provided a coherent basis for future study; two years of limited, but successful tests in command, control, and maneuverability of armored formations had been conducted on Salisbury Plain; and official sanction had been obtained to create a permanent Tank Brigade and to moderately expand the Royal Tank Corps. There were still serious problems of materiel, particularly the age of the Vickers Mediums, and little work had been done in the area of integrated armored formations. Nevertheless, the momentum lost with the dispersal of the Armoured Force in 1928 had at last been recovered.

III

The events of 1929–1933 have thus far been studied mainly in terms of developments and perceptions in the War Office. Ultimately, however, the fate of both mechanization and armored warfare was bound up with the attitudes of the officer corps as a whole. A sampling of the literature of the period allows one to "take the pulse" of the officer corps. In so doing, one may estimate the prognosis for mechanization and armored war in the late 1920s and early 1930s and chart the directions for the future.

The two years of experimentation with the Experimental Armoured Force caused a small but distinct shift of attitudes within the officer corps toward mechanization and armored warfare. Prior to 1927 the majority of officers appeared skeptical about mechanization and opposed to armored warfare; from 1929 to 1933 most seemed convinced of the need for mechanization but still reserved concerning the practicality of armored warfare. Nevertheless, a lively debate continued, and the revolutionaries, reformers, progressives, conservatives, and reactionaries pressed their points in a number of forums.

Fuller, the most notorious revolutionary, served as GSO1 2d Division until July 1929 when he was appointed commander of the 14th Infantry Brigade in the Rhine Army.[74] He returned to England in 1930 with the withdrawal of the Allied occupation forces, and his brigade was assigned to Northern Command. Fuller's unique qualities were not properly utilized in his last years of service. He was promoted to major general in September 1930 and placed on half-pay three months later. He remained without employment until he retired in 1933. Nevertheless, Fuller continued to think about mechanization, and in 1929 and 1930 he published several articles on the subject. The most notable were two articles in the *Army Quarterly* entitled "One Hundred Problems on Mechanization."[75] These articles reflected further modifications of Fuller's concepts, foreshadowed in 1927, and they provided an outline for his future works, *Lectures on F.S.R. II* (1931) and *Lectures on F.S.R. III* (1932).

Fuller's comparison of land and sea warfare had changed somewhat since the early postwar years. Whereas he had previously made an almost direct analogy between the two, in 1929 he stated that "Future [land] warfare would appear to approximate more closely to sea warfare *in an ocean full of islands and shallows* [emphasis added]."[76] These "islands and shallows" referred to so-called tank-proof areas and obstacles that inhibited the free movement of mechanized forces on land. They demanded the continued existence of nonmechanized forces, especially infantry, which would "have to revert to the old light infantry idea and . . . move rapidly over difficult country, stalking the enemy rather than attacking him."[77] Fuller also recognized the existence of areas that contained both open and broken ground. Here, he said, infantry and tanks would have to work in close cooperation.

He had also broadened his concepts of how armored forces should be composed. In the early 1920s he felt that self-propelled artillery and antitank weapons were unnecessary since tanks could do both their jobs better. In 1929 he described the functions and organization of an armored force as follows: "finding being carried out by armoured cars and aeroplanes; protection by self-propelled artillery and anti-tank weapons; holding and hitting by anti-tank weapons and light and medium tanks; and smashing by highly mobile armoured machines of which, today, no type exists."[78] Except for the exclusion of an infantry battalion in armored carriers and a squadron of fighter aircraft, this description almost exactly parallels Burnett-Stuart's recommended armored force of 1928. In terms of tactical concepts—and not temperament—Fuller was beginning to sound somewhat less like a revolutionary and somewhat more like a reformer. This change seems to have been based first on an awareness that, despite mechanization, there were still significant differences between naval and land warfare, and second on appreciation for the different characteristics of tanks, artillery, and antitank guns, which could not be lumped together in a single weapon.

The clearest statement of the reformers' position came from an articulate sapper who twice won the *Army Quarterly's* military essay contest—Maj. B. C. Dening. In *The Future of the British Army: The Problems of Its Duties, Cost, and Composition* (1928), Dening presented a complete plan for the reequipment of each of the major arms, the redistribution of British forces throughout the Empire, and the reorganization of the territorial army.[79] These plans were supported by detailed appendixes explaining their financial implications. Dening's future army was to be based around medium and light tanks, armored cars, infantry in armored carriers, and mechanized artillery all working in cooperation with large air contingents. To implement this scheme while retaining the Cardwell system, he identified specific areas of the Empire where old-style units would remain due to local conditions and other areas where he felt new-style units could operate. Because of declining strengths and the need for an immediate reserve, Dening recommended reducing the territorial army from fourteen to ten divisions, concentrating the newest weapons in one or two of these divisions, and amalgamating the fourteen yeomanry regiments into a Mechanised Mobile Division. Dening's scheme was one of the most comprehensive military reform proposals published between the wars.

There were also a number of articles in the military journals calling for fundamental reform short of an all-tank "revolution." "The Future of Mechanization," by Capt. D. A. L. Wade, Royal Corps of Signals, advocated the formation of an armored division for European war that closely paralleled the German *Panzergrenadier* division developed in the late 1930s. Like the other reformers, Wade felt that the Armoured Force experiments of 1927 and 1928 had shown that medium tanks would work on the battlefield, but that they had to be supplemented by light tanks, artillery, machine-guns, and "troops of occupation" carried in armored vehicles.[80] Captain Wade's article was significant in several respects. It presented a judicious balance of all arms and services. It pointed to the division as the best level at which to group these units. And since it was written by an officer not prominently associated with the experimental units, it reflected an increasing acceptance of the ideas of mechanization and armored warfare throughout the army.

There were also many who recognized the need for change but wanted it to take place more deliberately than did the reformers. These progressive officers were primarily concerned with the improvement of their own branches rather than the army as a whole. But there were exceptions, the most notable being Brig. A. P. Wavell.

Wavell, who was given command of the 6th (Experimental) Infantry Brigade in July 1930, stated the progressive case clearly in a *JRUSI* article, "The Army and the Prophets." Wavell first reviewed the development of armored forces since the end of the war. He then concluded that "in the gradual process of mechanization a time will come" when war would be fought primarily from machines; that these machines would have to rely on speed rather than on armor; that a proportion of highly trained foot-soldiers would have to accompany them; and that long-term professional armies were best suited to fight such wars.[81] He also felt that the brigade rather than the division would become the basic combined arms unit of the future. He felt that air forces should provide reconnaissance, artillery observation, air superiority, attacks on enemy troops, and supply. These were rather comprehensive observations, but two elements differentiate Wavell's thoughts from those of the reformers. First, he did not offer any detailed proposals as to how these changes should be brought about. Second, he seemed content with what he described as the natural, evolutionary process of change. Wavell clearly recognized the demands of future war, but he did not wish to accelerate the army's adaptation to these demands.

The conservatives also had some convincing arguments. There were, however, no really articulate spokesmen for the conservative position, which was put forward in print by a number of officers who can at best be considered minor military thinkers. Maj. Gen. C. P. Deedes, editor of the 1929 *Field Service Regulations,* was such an officer. He felt that the nature of terrain was the dominant consideration in land warfare and therefore believed that armored vehicles would be of limited utility to the British Army.[82] He also felt that vehicles, being completely dependent upon gasoline for propulsion, would be much more closely tied to their lines of supply than horses, which could continue to move on half rations. He recognized, however, that mechanical transport could cross most types of terrain.

Similar arguments were advanced by that perennial conservative, Lt. Col. A. G. Baird Smith in his critique of Liddell Hart's analysis of the 1929 exercises. Baird Smith said that a strategic thrust against the enemy's lines of supply by a wholly armored force "might inflict nothing more than a deep wound on the body of its adversary."[83] While Liddell Hart's statements concerning the effectiveness of such operations were somewhat hyperbolic, Baird Smith's criticism neglected the possibility that a number of such "deep wounds" could eventually prove fatal. It also neglected the psychological effect that a wound produced from an unexpected direction could have on an opponent.

There remained some sentiment in the officer corps that the substitution of firepower and mobility for horsepower or manpower in almost any form was fallacious. These feelings emerged in General Sir George Barrow's comments following General Deedes' lecture cited above. Barrow stated that mechanized forces would never have achieved what Allenby's mounted troops had accomplished at Megiddo in 1918, because the mechanized forces could have been stopped by simply mining the roads and employing machine-guns against them.[84] Cavalry, he said, could have easily moved off the roads and outflanked the machine-guns. Similar sentiments were evident in Maj. G.W. Redway's assertion that the substitution of machine-guns for infantrymen seriously risked defeat in war. As he saw it, "the mechanicians who hold the British Army in a firm grip to-day . . . having abolished the horse, are now trying to abolish the foot soldier."[85] Similar thoughts were expressed by V. W. Germains, who in a 1930 *JRUSI* article quoted Haig's dictum that "only by the rifle and bayonet of the infantryman can the decisive victory be won."[86] While such views could have been considered conservative as late as 1926, the potential shown in the Mechanised and Armoured Force experiments of 1927 and 1928 and the subsequent advances made in infantry organization made them seem almost reactionary in 1929 and 1930.

Within this general context of differing opinions of the merits of mechanization and armored warfare, there was specific disagreement over the usefulness of tanks and mechanical vehicles in India and the need for reform of the Cardwell system. The greatest obstacle to mechanization had always been the British Army in India. As Fuller said, "If mechanised arms cannot operate in this possible theatre of war, the reorganisation of the army at Home will either be seriously delayed, or two armies will have to be maintained, one for European warfare and the other for Oriental."[87]

There was, however, little that could be directly done to influence the composition of that army.[88] The army in India was not paid for out of the Army Estimates, but by the government of India, and it purchased its equipment directly from the manufacturers without reference to the War Office. The commander-in-chief of the army in India was responsible to the viceroy and through him to the secretary of state for India; he was not subject to the authority of the Army Council. The chief of the Imperial General Staff's position vis-à-vis the army in India was therefore somewhat anomalous. As military adviser to the Cabinet, he was well acquainted with India's defense problems, but as the first military member of the Army Council, he had no authority to direct the army in India's policy. This meant that the War Office had to negotiate with the army in India on the extent of its mechanization, and these negotiations were complicated by the feeling in India that Indians were paying for imperial defense rather than their own.

Since mechanization in India looked tenuous at best, some thought was given to modifying the Cardwell system of home/overseas rotation. The most common proposal was for the creation of two separate active armies: one of long service, roughly twenty years, for colonial duty, and one of shorter service for Continental duty in the event of a major war.[89] The Indian government strenuously opposed this scheme since it doubted that enough recruits could be found for the long-service army. A variation suggested partial elimination of the infantry regimental system by bringing various regiments together on a regional basis, establishing one large depot for each region, and providing overseas replacements by individuals rather than by unit.[90] This proposal, however, was actively resisted by the infantry regiments, and some senior officers felt that the Cardwell system was virtually sacrosanct.[91] With no consensus to change the mechanism for manning the army, its senior leaders remained firmly on the horns of the Continental/imperial defense dilemma.

The major doctrinal accomplishments of the period from 1931 to 1933 were the publication of *Modern Formations* and the experimental work with the provisional Tank Brigade by Colonels Broad and Laird. The area of unofficial doctrine and debate showed some similarities as well as some contrasts to that of the evolution of War Office policy. In the area of armored warfare, Fuller's *Lectures on F.S.R. III,* published in 1932, represented the codification of this thinking and paralleled Broad's concept of homogeneous armored units. A great deal of attention was also given to the logistics of mechanized warfare, to wider questions of strategy and national defense, and to the problem of developing open-minded attitudes toward military issues.

The organizational concepts in *F.S.R. III* were similar to those expressed in Fuller's "One Hundred Problems on Mechanization" discussed above. The thrust of his work, however, was the tactical flexibility inherent in mechanized forces and the need for adaptability in employing them on the battlefield.[92] Fuller envisioned that in future warfare mechanized armies would maneuver in large, open areas using their antitank forces for the protection of mobile base areas from which the tank forces would sally forth to sever the opposing army from its bases or to destroy the bases themselves.[93] The publication of *F.S.R. III* also marked the beginning of the divergence in theories of armored warfare between Fuller and Liddell Hart, who wrote after reading the book that it contained "rather too much emphasis on the mechanism of tactics, and not on the art, or on strategy."[94] The purpose of *F.S.R. III,* however, was to "jog the minds of thinking soldiers," and in this regard it attained a certain degree of success.[95]

The success was evident in a gradual shift toward acceptance of both mechanization and armored warfare during the early 1930s, which was reflected in both the reviews of works on mechanization and in the thoughts of officers outside the Tank Corps. The *JRUSI* review of *F.S.R. III* stated that "notwithstanding his partisanship for the armoured vehicle, General Fuller's book deserves serious study in the absence of any official pronouncements on this whole subject of future warfare."[96] And the *Army Quarterly* review of Martel's less futuristic work, *In the Wake of the Tank,* which traced the history of British armored vehicles and formations down to 1931, said, "It is . . . remarkable to note how many of what may seem the wilder dreams of the enthusiasts have a basis in past practice; and the progress made in the short fifteen years since 1916 has been so great and far-reaching that he would be a rash man who would attempt to set its bounds for the future."[97]

There were still articles in military literature that argued against the utility of the tank on the basis of pseudo-scientific calculations of engine efficiency and against mechanization on the basis of the difficulties of supplying large numbers of mechanical vehicles.[98] These articles, however, were increasingly strident in tone and seem to represent a minority determined to oppose mechanization and armored warfare at any cost rather than the honestly skeptical majority that had voiced similar concerns in the 1920s. In the early 1930s, in fact, a good deal of serious thought was being devoted to the problems of sustaining mechanized forces in the field. This thought dealt

with two main subjects: the supply of mechanized forces, which was primarily a question of transportation, and the maintenance of mechanized forces,
which was primarily a question of workshop organization.[99]

A number of questions were still left unanswered by these articles, including exact numbers of men and vehicles in each unit, the precise supplies or
repair parts that would be carried by each, and, most significantly, the way
in which supply and maintenance would be conducted within the combat
units.[100] These questions, however, could not be answered without a great
deal of practical experience, and the articles represented an excellent attempt
to deal with a complex and significant problem that was too often neglected.

The infantry's lack of suitability for modern war also received attention. In
early 1932 General Sir Cecil Romer, G.O.C.-in-C., Southern Command,
invited Liddell Hart to present a series of lectures to his officers on "The
Future of Infantry," which were subsequently published in a book of the
same title.[101] Liddell Hart argued that the true role of infantry was not to
act as the decisive force, but as the fixing force that allowed mobile arms to
defeat the enemy. Even the best light infantry, he said, "cannot replace the
need for a modernized cavalry *because they cannot strike quick enough or follow
through soon enough* for decisiveness in battle."[102] Liddell Hart argued that
infantry of the future would be of two types: heavy infantry for occupation
and protection duties, and light infantry for cooperation with mobile forces
in combat. He suggested that a light infantry battalion of the future consist
of a light-car reconnaissance company, a mechanized support company, and
one or two motorized rifle companies. While he felt that the ultimate solution to the problem of tactical mobility for the rifle companies would be to
mount them in armored carriers, he said that the cost of these forces would
postpone such a development for many years.[103] He felt that the tactics of
such a force would be those of the expanding torrent that he had outlined in
1922, and that light infantry should be trained to become "*tria juncta in
uno*—stalker, athlete, and marksman."[104]

It was in the early 1930s, however, that Liddell Hart began shifting his
thinking from questions of tactics to those of strategy. In January 1931 he
gave a lecture at the R.U.S.I. entitled "Economic Pressure or Continental
Victories," which offered one of the first comprehensive examinations of
British strategy between the wars and articulated the concepts behind the
policy of "limited liability." Examining the conduct of war from Elizabethan
times through the wars against Napoleon, Liddell Hart concluded that Britain's
success "was based on economic pressure exercised through sea-power," and
that British military expeditions to the Continent were only part of a traditional grand strategy of indirect approach.[105] The war of 1914–1918, he
said, marked a radical departure from this strategy in which "in the swamps
of Passchendaele . . . we spent the strength of England, pouring it out with
whole-hearted abandon on the soil of our allies."[106] Blaming a misguided

fixation on Clausewitz's conception of mass for this disastrous mistake, he advocated a return to a policy of minimum involvement on the Continent in the event of a future war.[107] These ideas were to become increasingly significant during the remainder of the decade.

Regarding the immediate problem of military reform, Liddell Hart and Fuller agreed that orthodoxy was the root cause of the British Army's failure to adapt. They mounted a sustained attack against rigid thinking. Citing the works of Spenser Wilkinson, Charles Repington, and various Continental critics Liddell Hart suggested that independent military critics were more frequently correct about the future of war than were military hierarchies.[108] In his biting little book *Generalship: Its Diseases and Their Cure,* Fuller stated that the army's emphasis on conformity created a group of "knock-kneed persuasive tact-ticians who gut an army not with a knife but with a honeyed word."[109] Shortly after the publication of this work, Fuller declined the offer to command a "second-class" district in India and was retired in 1933.[110]

In his review essay of Ernest Swinton's book *Eyewitness,* which described the resistance to the tank in the early years of World War I, Liddell Hart identified the lack of detached, objective thinking as the main cause of military orthodoxy. The soldier, he said, "has never been taught to approach his problem in a scientific spirit of inquiry. His early training is directed, above all, to the cultivation of loyalties. . . . The attitude of uncritical loyalty may be essential towards the winning of a war, but it is a fatally blind attitude in which to prepare for a war."[111] To remedy this deficiency he called for a "change of attitude towards criticism and independence of thought" and a "new humility" that would end complacency with existing levels of knowledge.[112] Here Liddell Hart penetrated to a key element of the reform movement: Until a widespread feeling of discontent with things as they were was created and the psychic energies of the officer corps were aroused and tapped, really meaningful changes would remain improbable if not impossible.

IV

Certainly one ingredient in creating a dissatisfaction with things as they were would have been an analysis of the Great War experience which suggested either that the army's performance had been found wanting or that the potentialities of military science since the end of the war dictated that fundamental changes be made. In fact, no analysis at all of the army's Great War experience had been conducted throughout the 1920s. To remedy this deficiency, Milne formed a high-level committee in early 1932 to "study the lessons of the late war, as shown in the various official accounts, and to report whether these lessons are being correctly and adequately applied in our manuals and in our training generally."[113]

To head the committee, Milne selected Lt. Gen. Sir Walter Kirke, a progressive officer who had headed Britain's military mission to Finland in 1924
and 1925 and who was later to gain distinction as commander-in-chief of the
Home Forces from 1939 to 1940.[114] Another prominent member of the
committee was Maj. Gen. Sir Bertie Fisher, former commandant of the Senior
Officers School at Sheerness whose 1929 R.U.S.I. lecture on the training of
regimental officers had demonstrated a clear realization of the need to adapt
to changing conditions.[115] The other senior members of the committee,
Major Generals A. E. McNamara and J. Kennedy and Brig. Gen. C. C.
Armitage, seem to have shared Kirke and Fisher's progressivism and to have
offset what may have been the more conservative tendencies of Brig. R. G. H.
Howard-Vyse, inspector of cavalry and commandant of the Equitation School.
    The committee's final report was highly critical of the British conduct of
World War I and made a number of recommendations for the future. The
impact of the committee's study is indicated in the section on the Western
Front drafted by Major General McNamara:

> In looking back at the war and all its lessons we must not overlook the most
> important lesson of all, viz., all wars produce new methods and fresh problems.
> The last war was full of surprises—the next one is likely to be no less prolific in
> unexpected developments. Hence we must study the past in the light of the prob-
> abilities of the future, which is what really matters.[116]

In their report on Mesopotamia, Generals Fisher and Armitage emphasized the importance of achieving surprise by moving on wide fronts or
under the cloak of darkness.[117] They also recognized the need for converting
a "break-in" into a "break-through," advocating a more flexible system of
command the rapid employment of reserves to achieve this objective.[118]
    Regarding future organization, the committee accepted Milne's statement
in the 1932 training memorandum concerning the lack of definition of the
potential adversary, but it cautioned that "it looks as if the holders of all the
trophies might in due course be called upon to defend their titles. . . . Should
we again have to intervene on the Continent we must be prepared for mobile
warfare supported by every possible mechanical contrivance, on or over the
ground."[119] This implied a definite increase in the proportion of tanks and a
probable increase in the proportion of artillery, which would require some
reduction of infantry forces.[120] The committee made no firm recommendation as to whether the increase in armored vehicles should come about through
the expansion of the Royal Tank Corps or the creation of special infantry
battalions, but it did note significantly that "one objection put forward, that
expansion [of armored forces] should be post-poned until war is imminent
owing to constant improvement in design does not appear to us to be an

adequate reason for delay."[121] This statement was in almost direct opposition to existing policy.

The Kirke Committee did not provide the specific decisions required for organizational reform. The report it produced did, however, articulate a number of principles upon which such reform could be based and was also a useful document for the education of the officer corps. To understand why this potentially valuable document was used neither for reform nor for education, we must now turn to the selection of Milne's successor as C.I.G.S.

As the time for the C.I.G.S. selection drew near, Maurice Hankey approached Liddell Hart for suggestions on likely candidates. While lunching with Hankey at the United Service Club on 8 November 1932, Liddell Hart mentioned Generals Harington, Romer, Chetwode, and Montgomery-Massingberd as well as Lieutenant Generals Burnett-Stuart, Ironside, and Charles.[122] Liddell Hart apparently refrained from commenting on the relative qualifications of these officers, but it is significant that he included in his list three lieutenant generals, one of whose selection over the heads of his superiors could be interpreted as a desire by the War Office for more pronounced reform.[123]

Realistically, however, the field was most likely limited to the four full generals. Of these, Romer had only recently been promoted, and Chetwode was in India. This left Montgomery-Massingberd and Harington, who was at this time G.O.C.-in-C., Aldershot Command. Harington was the senior and the more widely known, both for his role as Plumer's chief of staff in planning the Battle of Messines, one of the few successes on the Western Front, and for his moderation during the Chanak crisis of 1922. Montgomery-Massingberd, however, had established a reputation as an effective administrator, and he had found favor with the more conservative elements of the army through his service on the Cavalry Committee in 1926 and his role in the dispersal of the Experimental Armoured Force in 1928. In his capacity as adjutant general he was familiar with a wide range of the army's problems and visible to the politicians. In the event, he was selected as Milne's successor.[124]

The implications of Montgomery-Massingberd's selection concerning future appointments in the army were quickly apparent to Liddell Hart and Ironside. On 2 December Liddell Hart wrote Hankey:

> I shall be pleasantly surprised if Fuller is not squeezed out of the Army without further employment. . . . I shall be surprised too if the prospects of Burnett-Stuart and Ironside are not impaired. On the other hand I anticipate that Gen. Knox, who is well known throughout the Army as the most obstinate opponent of change, will receive an enlarged opportunity for resisting it.[125]

And in July 1933, Ironside, speculating on who might be selected as C.I.G.S. in 1937 wrote Liddell Hart, "I don't suppose M-M [Montgomery-

Massingberd] would put in much of a good word for Jock Stuart, though he would be the most capable of them all, I think."[126] This was a prophetic observation.

The announcement of Montgomery-Massingberd's selection as C.I.G.S. was followed by several assessments of Milne's seven-year tenure. Hailsham stated that Milne had increased the army's efficiency, maintained its strength, and advanced the progress of mechanization despite the fact that the estimates were £4.5 million less in 1933 than they had been when Milne had taken office in 1926.[127] In an essay entitled "Seven Years: The Regime of Field-Marshal Lord Milne," published in the *English Review* of April 1933, Liddell Hart presented a much more critical evaluation.[128] "For practical purposes," he contended, " 'mechanization' is still a catchword rather than a reality."[129] He pointed out that there had been no major changes in the army's structure, that the army still had only four tank battalions, and that only four of its twenty-eight artillery brigades had been mechanized. Although recognizing the many constraints under which Milne had worked, Liddell Hart felt that the true explanation for this "huge gulf between promise and performance" lay in Milne's character and the effect of age on his urge to make changes.[130]

There is a great deal of truth in Liddell Hart's analysis of the state of the British Army in early 1933 and of Milne's response to the problems of modernization. Taken as a whole, however, it appears somewhat unbalanced. In light of the material conditions that obtained from 1926 to 1933, all of which Liddell Hart mentioned, it seems in retrospect that Milne accomplished almost all that one could have reasonably expected. While he was too quick to placate the demands of the more conservative commanders and hesitated to make fundamental reforms, he searched for new solutions to tactical and strategic problems, he provided for a moderate expansion of the Tank Corps, and most significantly, he encouraged the army to *think* about the future so that when money did become available it would be able to expand along proper lines. This was Milne's greatest contribution to the British Army from 1926 to 1933, and it has been insufficiently recognized by Liddell Hart and by the historians whose view of Milne he influenced.[131]

The contrast in outlook between Milne and his successor is evident in Montgomery-Massingberd's handling of the Kirke Committee report. When the final draft was prepared in mid-October 1932, Milne directed that five hundred copies be produced, a sufficient number to distribute it throughout the army.[132] Montgomery-Massingberd, however, decided to circulate the full report only to senior officers and to have a shortened version prepared for distribution to junior officers.[133] A comparison of the condensed version with the full report reveals a number of omissions and changes that significantly altered the committee's intent concerning the questions of future doctrine, equipment, and organization.[134] The statement in the full report that objected to postponing the expansion of tanks in the army until war became evident was deleted. More significantly, the section on training that mentioned the increasing probability of Continental war was changed to read, "The variety of our possible war problems prevents us from concentrating on any one to the exclusion of others."[135] While a condensation of the full report was not itself improper, these alterations constitute a significant distortion. This distortion was especially regrettable since the junior officers, who would provide the army's leadership in World War II, appear to have accepted the shorter report at face value.[136]

The 1933 training program reflected Montgomery-Massingberd's policy that preparation for imperial policing would be the prime training activity. At the end of the 1933 training season, however, two developments took place that were to have a pronounced influence on future British doctrine. The first was the announcement of the permanent formation of the Tank Brigade under Colonel Hobart, who also retained his new duties as inspector of the Royal Tank Corps. The second was the establishment of liaison between Hobart and Brig. George Lindsay, then commanding the experimental 7th Infantry Brigade, concerning the possible conduct of joint exercises in 1934 to test the feasibility of a Mobile Division.[137] These events will be discussed in detail in Chapter 7. At this point it is appropriate to examine briefly the evolution of mechanization and armored warfare in other armies in order to establish a frame of reference for the British Army's relative position in the early 1930s.

V

French doctrine in the 1920s reflected France's tremendous losses of life in World War I and was even more conservative than the British.[138] The dominant idea was to develop an overwhelming mass of firepower, principally through the use of artillery and machine-guns, propelling the infantry forward with as few casualties as possible. This concept was reflected in the *Instruction provisoire sur l'emploi tactique des grandes unités,* which stated that tanks were designed to "augment the offensive power of the infantry by facilitating its progress in combat."[139] Tanks, therefore, were part of the infantry, with one tank regiment being included for each group of three infantry battalions. In the early 1920s, General Jean-B. Estienne among others published a number of articles arguing for more dynamic use of the tank. These articles, however, made little impact on Henri Philippe Pétain and Maxime Weygand, who continued to be concerned with using machines to achieve a quantitative rather than qualitative advantage on the battlefield.[140]

French tank design, therefore, made little headway in the first postwar decade. The principal tank throughout the period was the Renault F. T., which had been developed during World War I. The Renault had a 37-mm. gun, which was respectable for a light tank, but its speed was only five miles per hour. And although the French Army had nearly three thousand on hand, they were not really suitable vehicles. By 1930 the army had a new medium tank, the D-l, roughly equivalent to the prototype British sixteen-tonner. As usual for an army enmeshed in domestic politics, French doctrinal development was complicated by hierarchical command structure developed as a result of competing political and military interests.[141]

Because of their late entry into World War I, American postwar tactical doctrine reflected both the French and British experiences.[142] The National Defense Act of 1920 established the tank service as a part of the infantry, and the U.S. Army's principal tank was the French Renault. The Americans also had a smaller number of Mark VIII heavy tanks, which had been produced in a joint effort with Britain in 1918. Toward the end of 1927 the secretary of war, Dwight Davis, directed the establishment of an Experimental Mechanized Force patterned on the British model. The force's equipment was obsolete and in ill repair, and the unit itself was dispersed after several months of trials.[143] The newly formed Mechanization Board, however, recommended that it be permanently reestablished. Although there were strong objections from the chief of infantry, who did not want to lose control of the tanks, the experimental force was reformed in November 1930.

Germany's long-term professional army and the need to restructure completely its armed forces provided some compensation for the prohibition of tank production imposed by the Treaty of Versailles.[144] The commander-in-chief, General Hans von Seeckt, while not an advocate of armored warfare, was determined to develop a compact, mobile, and modern army. He therefore established contacts with the Russians that resulted in the production of German prototype tanks and the establishment of a school for tank officers at Kazan on the Volga. During the late 1920s several experimental tanks designed by Krupp, Daimler-Benz, and MAN were tested at Kazan. These kept the design capacity alive but did not produce any great results.

The most important developments were the insights of Col. Heinz Guderian, who closely followed the tank developments in Britain and France and conducted a number of tactical exercises with mock tanks. He concluded that "tanks would never be able to produce their full effect until the other weapons on whose support they must inevitably rely were brought up to their standard of speed and of cross-country performance. In such a formation of all arms, the tank must play the primary role, the other weapons being subordinated to be requirements of the armour."[145] The German Army thus did not have the physical means to conduct armored warfare, but it did have the embryo of a sound tactical and operational doctrine.

The greatest handicap to the development of Soviet armored doctrine was the U.S.S.R.'s technological backwardness.[146] Imperial Russia had produced some armored cars during World War I, but the only tanks available to the revolutionary army had been approximately one hundred Renault F.T.s and British Mark Vs, which had been captured from the counterrevolutionary forces in the Civil War. The Red Army, however, had several advantages to offset this deficiency. As a new organization, it had few traditional obstacles to overcome in developing new concepts. And it had gained experience in open, mobile conflict during the Civil War. A countervailing disadvantage was the antithesis between military professionalism and political control by the Communist Party. This tension plagued the army throughout the 1920s, until the initiation of the first Five-Year Plan in 1928 brought together the professional interest in modernization and the political desire for expansion of the industrial base.

In order to produce anything worthwhile, the Soviets had to import Western technology. The German prototypes brought into Kazan helped somewhat, but they were not of the best quality. The Soviets therefore imported tanks from Italy and Czechoslovakia as well as the British Carden-Loyd Mark VI and the Vickers-Armstrong six-ton tank, which became the basis for the Soviet T-23. By 1930 the U.S.S.R. had some relatively modern models upon which to base production, but industrial weakness was still a problem and no armored doctrine had been developed.

It appears from this brief survey that Worthington-Evans' claim that Britain led the world in both tank design and doctrine in February 1929 was still true in the early 1930s. The prognosis, however, was somewhat less certain. The next stage in the evolution of armored doctrine and organization was the development of an armored division. A division is the first level of organization that combines all arms and is self-sufficient in combat. It was in the transition from brigade-level organization to division-level armored formations that the British Army not only lost its lead but fell seriously behind other nations, most notably the German Army. Before this story is told, however, we should follow Burnett-Stuart to Egypt where his application of mechanized concepts to desert conditions and his imaginative training schemes had a profound impact on a generation of British officers that would eventually practice the art of armored warfare in the desert in World War II.

NOTES

1. Quoted from Worthington-Evans' Army Estimates speech, *H.C. Deb.*, 225 (28 February 1929): 2214–2215.
2. C.O.S., "Imperial Defence Policy," June 1929, Cab. 53/17.
3. C.O.S., "Imperial Defence Policy," July 1930, Cab. 53/21.
4. Sir John Simon's report recommending an enlarged electorate and responsible government for the Indian provinces was published in June 1930 and quickly "over-

taken by events" when Gandhi began his campaign of mass civil disobedience. Charles Mowat, *Britain between the Wars, 1918–1940,* Beacon Paperback ed. (Boston, 1971), pp. 377–378. For a comprehensive analysis of the military implications of Indian sovereignty see T. A. Bisson, "The Military Problem in India," *Foreign Policy Reports* 7 (October 1931): 299–308.

5. C.O.S., "Imperial Defence Policy," July 1930, Cab. 53/21.

6. Specifically excluded were John Weatley and F. W. Jowwett, staunch advocates of the Independent Labour Party's "Socialism Now" program. G. D. H. Cole, *A History of the Labour Party from 1914* (New York, 1969), p. 227.

7. France and Italy did not sign this treaty as they had the 1922 Washington agreement. Japan seems to have gained the most from the 1930 accord since it had to scrap only one capital ship, whereas Britain and the United States destroyed five and three respectively. S. W. Kirby, *Singapore: The Chain of Disaster* (London, 1971), p. 17. MacDonald felt that the accord was a legitimate "risk for peace."

8. Michael Howard, "Military Science in an Age of Peace," *JRUSI* 119 (March 1974): 4. In using this phrase, Howard is referring generally to the social environment in which armies in "ages of peace" usually find themselves. It is clear from the context of his lecture that he thinks interwar Britain created such an environment.

9. The account of the fall of the second Labour government and formation of the National government of 1931 is based primarily on Mowat, *Britain between the Wars,* pp. 379–413. A more detailed account can be found in Robert Skidelsky, *Politicians and the Slump: The Labour Government of 1929–1931* (London, 1967), pp. 334–383. See also Cole, *History of the Labour Party, pp. 224–267.*

10. Mowat, *Britain between the Wars,* p. 413.

11. Ibid., pp. 455–458, 470–473. See also A. J. P. Taylor, *English History, 1914–1945,* Oxford Paperback ed. (New York, 1970), pp. 336–338. Taylor points out that whereas the budgets of 1932 and 1933 were not in accordance with strict financial orthodoxy, they "helped create a psychology of economy, not of spending." Ibid., p. 338.

12. Shaw's estimates speeches were generally supported by Conservatives and moderate Labourites, but the pacifist Labourites bitterly attacked him as a hypocritical traitor to the cause of peace. See especially the speech by Brendan Bracken, which characterized Shaw as "a great whale floundering in crocodile tears." *H. C. Deb.,* 5th Ser., 249 (10 March 1931): 1131.

13. Mowat, *Britain between the Wars,* p. 422. There has been a great deal of controversy concerning the significance of the Oxford Union resolution. Taylor's position is summed up in his observation that there is "no documentary evidence that foreign governments noticed it or drew from it the moral that Great Britain had ceased to count in the world." Taylor, *English History,* p. 362n.

14. MacDonald's statement quoted from minutes of 251st meeting of C.I.D., 28 November 1930, in C.O.S. 295, "Imperial Defence Policy, Annual Review for 1932," 23 February 1932, Cab. 53/22.

15. Stephen W. Roskill, *Hankey: Man of Secrets,* 3 vols. (London, 1970–1974), 2:535.

16. As a civil servant, Hankey had no official authority to issue instructions to the service chiefs in his own right. There seems to be little doubt, however, that he was the moving spirit behind the review of the ten-year rule in 1932. See Roskill, *Hankey,* 2:535–539.

17. C.O.S. 295, "Imperial Defence Policy, Annual Review for 1932," 23 February 1932, Cab. 53/22.

18. Treasury comments on C.O.S. 1932 Review, 11 March 1932, quoted from Michael Howard, *The Continental Commitment: The Dilemma of British Defence Policy in the Era of the Two World Wars* (London, 1972), p. 98.

19. Cabinet meeting, 23 March 1932, quoted from Howard, *Continental Commitment*, p. 98. Stephen Roskill argues that the ten-year rule was not actually cancelled in March 1932 because the Cabinet stated its conclusion as "not dissenting from," rather than "approving," the C.I.D.'s acceptance of the C.O.S. recommendation to cancel the rule. He supports this by citing a letter from Hankey to MacDonald in January 1933 that "at present no-one quite knows whether the rule stands or not." See Roskill, *Hankey*, 2:537. While Hankey may have been pressuring MacDonald to clear up the ambiguities of the Cabinet's decision, it is clear from the C.O.S. subsequent review in October 1933 that, contrary to Roskill's assertion, they regarded the rule as having been cancelled by the Cabinet in response to their 1932 review. See C.O.S. 310, "Imperial Defence Policy, Annual Review (1933)," 12 October 1933, Cab. 53/23.

20. An extract of the letter containing these instructions is in Great Britain, War Office, *Supplementary Memorandum on Army Training (Collective Training Period, 1928)* (London, 1929), p. 46.

21. Burnett-Stuart's remark quoted from Liddell Hart's diary note of a conversation with Maj. J. W. Jordan, 9 October 1933, Liddell Hart papers, LHCMA. The incident is also mentioned in Giffard Martel, *An Outspoken Soldier: His Views and Memoirs* (London, 1949), pp. 54–55.

22. Festing interview, 19 September 1972.

23. Ibid. The author is also indebted to Lt. Gen. Sir Charles Broad for showing him a copy of the 1929 Christmas card.

24. The discussion of the first exercise is based on Liddell Hart's reports in the *Daily Telegraph*, 11, 12, and 13 September 1929.

25. The discussion of the second exercise is based on Liddell Hart's reports in the *Daily Telegraph,* 17 and 18 September 1929.

26. The following three paragraphs are based on Great Britain, War Office, *Supplementary Memorandum on Army Training (Collective Training Period, 1929)* (London, 1930).

27. Ibid., p. 10.

28. B. H. Liddell Hart, "Army Exercises in 1929," *JRUSI* 74 (November 1929): 790–791.

29. War Office, *Supplementary Training Memorandum, 1929,* p. 29. For a detailed discussion of the radios available for use in a tank battalion see Maj. Gen. R. F. H. Nalder, *The Royal Corps of Signals: A History of Its Antecedents and Development (circa 1800–1955)* (London, 1958), pp. 250–253.

30. B. H. Liddell Hart, "The Army Exercises of 1930," *JRUSI* 75 (November 1930): 681.

31. Great Britain, War Office, *Army Training Memorandum No. 1 (Collective Training Period, 1930)* (London, 1930), p. 23.

32. Great Britain, War Office, *Army Training Memorandum No. 2 (Collective Training Period, 1930, Supplementary)* (London, 1931), p. 7.

33. Great Britain, War Office, *The Army List, July 1933* (London, 1933), p. 19.

34. The author is indebted to J. G. S. Burnett-Stuart for pointing out the black marks on the ceiling of the den at Crichie over the spot where General Burnett-Stuart kept his chair.

35. Broad interview, 10 November 1972, and letter from Lt. Gen. Sir Charles Broad to librarian, LHCMA, 12 August 1968. This letter was written explaining

General Broad's participation in the development of armored doctrine since General Broad destroyed his papers in 1940 to prevent the possibility of their capture by the Germans. With characteristic modesty Broad stresses Lindsay and Pile's work, "throughout the 4 years I was at the W.O. we three worked as a team."

36. The full title was *Mechanised and Armoured Formations (Instructions for Guidance when Considering Their Action), 1929 (Provisional)* (London, 1929). It was familiarly known as the Purple Primer because of the color of its covers.

37. Ibid., p. 7.

38. Ibid., p. 8.

39. Ibid., p. 9.

40. Ibid., pp. 9–10.

41. Ibid., p. 10.

42. Ibid.

43. Ibid., p. 11.

44. Ibid.

45. Ibid., p. 18.

46. Ibid., p. 32.

47. Ibid.

48. Ibid., pp. 37–47.

49. Milne's proposal appears to have been triggered by Burnett-Stuart's suggestion in his March 1929 mechanization lecture to establish four armored brigades. The details of this scheme are based primarily on a memorandum from Broad to Bonham-Carter dated July 1929, a copy of which is among the Lindsay papers, LHCMA. See also B. H. Liddell Hart's account in *The Tanks: The History of the Royal Tank Regiment and Its Predecessors Heavy Branch Machine-Gun Corps, Tank Corps and Royal Tank Corps, 1914–1945*, 2 vols. (New York, 1959), 1:274–275.

50. General Broad said that when this plan was presented, "everyone was horrified and it never came off." Broad to librarian, LHCMA, 12 August 1968.

51. Liddell Hart, *The Tanks*, 1:276.

52. Ibid.

53. Bonham-Carter's remarks following Lt. Col. P. G. Scarlett, R.U.S.I. lecture, 26 February 1930, "Developments in Army Organization," *JRUSI* 75 (August 1930): 514–515.

54. Great Britain, War Office, *Modern Formations, 1931 (Provisional)* (London, 1931), pp. 23–24.

55. Great Britain, War Office, *Army Training Memorandum No. 4 (Collective Training Period, 1931)* (London, 1931), pp. 24–25; Liddell Hart, *The Tanks*, 1:290.

56. Broad interview, 10 November 1972; Liddell Hart, *The Tanks*, 1:290.

57. Broad interview, 10 November 1972. An appendix to *Modern Formations* contains a detailed list of the types of radios available in 1931 and their characteristics. The set Broad was apparently using had a voice range of 10 to 20 miles. A smaller model for light tanks had a voice range of 3 to 5 miles. Great Britain, War Office, *Modern Formations, 1931 (Provisional)* (London, 1931), pp. 66–67. See also Kenneth Macksey, *Tank Warfare: A History of Tanks in Battle* (New York, 1972), p. 87, for the importance of radios and crystal-controlled frequencies.

58. Broad to librarian, LHCMA, 12 August 1968.

59. B. H. Liddell Hart, "Contrasts of 1931: Mobility or Stagnation?" *AQ* 23 (January 1932): 241–242.

60. Liddell Hart, *The Tanks*, 1:290–291. The reference to Jenghiz Khan is contained in a letter from Broad to Lindsay describing his preparations for the upcoming exercises.

61. Liddell Hart, *The Tanks, 1:290.*

62. Ibid., p. 292.

63. B. H. Liddell Hart, "Contrasts of 1931," *AQ* 23 (January 1932): 245–247.

64. Broad's prohibition of rehearsals is a remarkable testament to his capacity as a commander and his faith in his unit.

65. Account of the final exercise based on Kenneth Macksey, *Armoured Crusader: A Biography of Major-General Sir Percy Hobart* (London, 1968), p. 104. See also Macksey, *The Tank Pioneers* (London, 1981), p. 87.

66. Broad's assignment to Aldershot demonstrates the anomalous position of R.T.C. officers in the 1930s. They were clearly able and were frequently promoted; but with no large tank units in existence, it was impossible to give them a command of units in their branch.

67. This account based on Liddell Hart's description of the exercise in *The Tanks,* 1:300. The judgment of its impact on Hobart's fortunes is the author's. Macksey's biography does not discuss Hobart's role in the 1932 trials.

68. Based on B. H. Liddell Hart, "Mind and Machine: Part II–Tank Brigade Training, 1932," *AQ* 26 (April 1933): 51–58.

69. The description of British infantrymen of the time from ibid., p. 51.

70. Untitled minute from C.I.G.S. to the A.G., Q.M.G., M.G.O., and P.U.S., 15 September 1932, W.O. 32/2852, General Situation of Tank Units at Home and in Egypt: Resulting Reorganization.

71. The only reservation was the M.G.O. General James Charles' notation that there were not, in fact, yet enough light tanks in production to support the scheme. Milne, however, was aware of this fact and had stipulated that Carden-Loyd machine-gun carriers could be used in the interim.

72. P.U.S. to C.I.G.S., 23 September 1932, W.O. 32/2852.

73. Secretary of state to C.I.G.S., 6 October 1932, W.O. 32/2852.

74. Details of Fuller's assignments from Great Britain, War Office, *The Army List, July 1933* (London, 1933), p. 61, and the stationing list in *AQ* 20 (April 1930): 195.

75. Brig. J. F. C. Fuller, "One Hundred Problems on Mechanization," *AQ* 19 (October 1929): 14–25, and *AQ* 19 (January 1930): 256–269.

76. Ibid., p. 15.

77. Ibid., p. 18.

78. Ibid. There is an interesting similarity between Fuller's functions of finding, protecting, holding, hitting, and smashing, and the functions of security, reconnaissance, fixing, decisive maneuver, and exploitation mentioned by Liddell Hart in his 1920 lecture of the "man-in-the-dark" theory of infantry tactics.

79. Maj. B. C. Dening, *The Future of the British Army: The Problems of Its Duties, Cost and Composition* (London, 1928).

80. Capt. D. A. L. Wade, "The Future of Mechanization," *JRUSI* 74 (November 1929): 696–698.

81. A. P. Wavell, "The Army and the Prophets," *JRUSI* 75 (November 1930): 671.

82. Maj. Gen. C. P. Deedes, R.U.S.I. lecture, 14 November 1928, "The Influence of Ground on Modern Military Operations," *JRUSI* 74 (February 1929): 38–48.

83. Lt. Col. A. G. Baird Smith, "The Theory and Practice of Mechanization," *JRUSI* 75 (May 1930): 307.

84. General Barrow's remarks were made following Major General Deedes' lecture "The Influence of Ground on Modern Military Operations," *JRUSI* 74 (February 1929): 45.

85. Maj. G. W. Redway, "The Elimination of Infantry," *JRUSI* 74 (February 1929): 147.

86. Victor Wallace Germains, "The Limitations of the Tank," *JRUSI* 75 (February 1930): 129. A contrasting view was expressed in a letter to the editor by "A Thinking Bayonet," *JRUSI* 74 (May 1929): 398–401, which said, "it is fire and mobility, not bayonets, that wins battles. Fire, because it enables infantry or other arms ultimately to assault and hold positions, and mobility because it is conducive to surprise and manoeuvre."

87. J. F. C. Fuller, *On Future War* (London, 1928), p. 262. The essay from which this quotation is taken was written in 1927 following Fuller's tour of the North-West Frontier of India.

88. What follows is based primarily on a memorandum Milne wrote for Worthington-Evans in 1929 explaining why he did not feel it appropriate to testify before the Simon Committee on the defense of India. Although Milne's points are valid in a strict constitutional sense, they also seem to reflect an unwillingness to become involved in the affairs of India.

89. See, for example, Capt. J. Keith Edwards, "Second (Military) Prize Essay for 1927," *JRUSI* 73 (August 1928): 458–473.

90. Capt. G. L. Appleton, "The Cardwell System: A Criticism," *JRUSI* 72 (August 1927): 591–599.

91. See, for example, Lt. Gen. A. E. Altham, "The Cardwell System," *JRUSI* 73 (February 1928): 108–114.

92. See especially Chapter 3, "Strategic Preliminaries to Joining Battle," and Chapter 4, "Battle," in J. F. C. Fuller, *Lectures on F.S.R. III (Operations between Mechanized Forces)* (London, 1932), p. 15.

93. Ibid., pp. 29–30.

94. B. H. Liddell Hart, diary note, 1932, Liddell Hart papers, LHCMA.

95. Fuller, *F.S.R. III*, p. ix.

96. Review of Fuller's *Lectures on F.S.R. III, JRUSI* 77 (August 1932): 682.

97. Review of G. LeQ. Martel's *In the Wake of the Tank: The First Fifteen Years of Mechanization in the British Army* (London, 1931), *AQ* 23 (October 1931): 189. The reviewer carefully distinguished between Martel and Fuller, whom he regarded as a "tank merchant."

98. See, for example, Bvt. Maj. G. MacLeod Ross, "The Utility of the Tank," *JRUSI* 76 (November 1931): 786–794, and Maj. L. A. W. B. Lachlan, "Mechanized-Mindedness," *JRUSI* 78 (August 1933): 554–558.

99. See, for example, Capt. D. W. Boileau, "Gold Medal Essay (Military), 1930," *JRUSI* 76 (May 1931): 335–354, and Lt. Col. C. A. H. Montanaro, "The Mechanized Unit in the Field," *JRA* 57 (October 1931): 302–321.

100. A detailed description of the existing system of supply and maintenance can be found in Col. W. G. Lindsell, *Military Organization and Administration,* 12th ed. (Aldershot, 1932). Maj. Gen. J. C. Harding-Newman's *Modern Military Administration, Organization and Transportation* (Aldershot, 1933) is a forward-looking critique of that system. Maj. G. C. Shaw, "Spares and Repairs," *AQ* 24 (July 1932): 349–357, discusses the difficulty and importance of gathering consumption figures for spare parts in order to establish stockage lists.

101. B. H. Liddell Hart, *The Future of Infantry* (London, 1933).

102. Ibid., p. 34.

103. Ibid., p. 45. Liddell Hart also felt that troops mounted in armored vehicles would be more analogous to dragoons than to infantry.

104. Ibid., p. 63.

105. B. H. Liddell Hart, R.U.S.I. lecture, 28 January 1931, "Economic Pressure or Continental Victories," *JRUSI* 76 (August 1931): 500. This lecture was later published as Chapter 1, "The Historic Strategy of Britain," in *The British Way in Warfare* (London, 1932) and *When Britain Goes to War* (London, 1935).

106. B. H. Liddell Hart, "Economic Pressure or Continental Victories," *JRUSI* 76 (August 1931): 488.

107. Liddell Hart qualified his criticism of Clausewitz by saying that Clausewitz's concepts were often "exaggerated in transfer" and carried to an "extreme pitch" by British and French leaders of World War I. Ibid., p. 489. However, his analysis of Clausewitz as "the Mahdi of Mass" in *The Ghost of Napoleon* (London, 1933) reveals a lack of discrimination in distinguishing between what Clausewitz said about the theoretical as opposed to the actual nature of war and the way in which he was subsequently interpreted. For a detailed discussion of this point see Peter Paret, "Clausewitz and the Nineteenth Century," *The Theory and Practice of War*, Michael Howard, ed. (New York, 1965), pp. 21–41.

108. B. H. Liddell Hart, "Military Critics and the Military Hierarchy: A Historical Examination as to whether Superior Rank and Number Promise Superior Wisdom," *AQ* 22 (April 1931): 41–56.

109. J. F. C. Fuller, *Generalship: Its Diseases and Their Cure* (Harrisburg, Pa., 1936), p. 88.

110. J. F. C. Fuller, *Memoirs of an Unconventional Soldier* (London, 1936), pp. 447–450. Fuller turned down the appointment because he felt that it would not offer adequate scope to his mechanization talents. Given his own temperament and the attitudes toward him in the upper echelons of the army, he was probably right to have done so. But it should be pointed out that his problem was no different from that of Broad and Lindsay, both of whom did accept appointments in India when they reached the rank of major general.

111. B. H. Liddell Hart, "The Tale of the Tank," review of *Eyewitness*, by Ernest Swinton, *The Nineteenth Century and After* (November 1932): 606. Admiral Sir Herbert Richmond identified a similar problem in the Royal Navy. See Herbert W. Richmond, "The Service Mind," *The Nineteenth Century and After* (January 1933): 90–97.

112. Liddell Hart, "Tale of the Tank," *The Nineteenth Century and After* (November 1932): 606–607.

113. Untitled minute C.I.G.S. to P.U.S., 16 March 1932, W.O. 32/3115, Lessons of the 1914–1918 War. Milne appears to have been prompted in this by reading Liddell Hart's review of the official history of the Somme offensive. Liddell Hart, *Memoirs*, 2:111.

114. Information on Kirke from *Who Was Who*, 1941–1950, pp. 644–645.

115. B. D. Fisher, R.U.S.I. lecture, 23 January 1929, "The Training of the Regimental Officer," *JRUSI* 74 (May 1929): 241–261.

116. W.O. 33/1297, Report of the Committee on Certain Lessons of the Great War. The final report was based on studies done on the various fronts by individual members of the committee, and in certain places it quoted directly from them.

117. Ibid. These concepts paralleled those submitted to Fisher by Liddell Hart. Liddell Hart, *Memoirs*, 1:211–213. Fisher and Armitage added, however, that "preponderating fire, powerful enough to produce the effect of surprise," was an acceptable alternative.

118. W.O. 33/1297, Report of the Committee on Certain Lessons of the Great War. These recommendations parallel Liddell Hart's concept of the expanding torrent attack, but they appear to have been derived independently.

119. Ibid.

120. Ibid.

121. Ibid.

122. Liddell Hart, diary note, 9 November 1932.

123. In a letter to Hankey after the selection had been made Liddell Hart stated that he had not wanted to mention any personal characteristics of the candidates for fear of prejudicing their chances. He had, however, previously stated that Montgomery-Massingberd was "set in his mind." Liddell Hart to Hankey, 2 December 1932, Liddell Hart papers, LHCMA.

124. Another explanation for Montgomery-Massingberd's selection may be the difference in attitude toward advancement between him and Harington. His publication of *The Story of the Fourth Army in the Battles of the Hundred Days, August 8th to November 11th, 1918* (London, 1920), his chairmanship of the War Office Cavalry Committee in 1926, and his frequent battlefield tours depict a man who was determined to thrust himself forward in the army bureaucracy. Harington, on the other hand, seems to have been self-effacing and comparatively unconcerned with professional position. In his memoirs he states, "In the summer of 1933, I was offered the Governorship of Gibraltar, which I accepted. I had been passed over for C.I.G.S., and I thought it was best to get out of the way, so I was glad to go to Gibraltar, and I have never regretted it." General Sir Charles Harington, *Tim Harington Looks Back* (London, 1940), p. 184. The same humility is evident in his biography of Plumer (General Sir Charles Harington, *Plumer of Messines* [London, 1935]).

125. Liddell Hart to Hankey, 2 December 1932, Liddell Hart papers, LHCMA.

126. Extract of letter from Ironside to Liddell Hart of 10 July 1933 contained in Liddell Hart's diary notes, Liddell Hart papers, LHCMA.

127. "Extracts from the Memorandum of the Secretary of State for War relating to the Army Estimates for 1933," *JRUSI* 78 (May 1933): 425.

128. B. H. Liddell Hart, "Seven Years: The Regime of Field-Marshal Lord Milne," *English Review* 56 (April 1933): 376–386. A similar assessment is contained in the article "Field-Marshal Lord Milne," *Daily Telegraph,* 20 February 1933.

129. Liddell Hart, "Lord Milne," *English Review* 56 (April 1933): 381.

130. Ibid., p. 382.

131. Liddell Hart's pervasive influence on subsequent historians' views of Milne is evident in Jay Luvaas, "The Captain Who Teaches Generals: Captain B. H. Liddell Hart," *The Education of an Army: British Military Thought, 1815–1940* (Chicago, 1964), pp. 390–391, and Robin Higham, *Armed Forces in Peacetime: Britain, 1918–1940, A Case Study* (London, 1962), p. 96. Perhaps the most unfair attack on Milne is Bidwell and Graham's reference to him as, "with the Duke of Cambridge as his only rival, the greatest reactionary in its [the British Army's] history." Shelford Bidwell and Dominick Graham, *Fire-Power: British Army Weapons and Theories of War, 1904–1945* (London, 1982), p. 155. At the other end of the spectrum is Macksey's inclusion of "Uncle George" with the other reformers. Macksey, *Tank Pioneers,* pp. 66–78.

132. Milne's comments contained in a minute dated 14 October 1932, W.O. 32/3115, Lessons of the 1914–1918 War.

133. Liddell Hart, *Memoirs*, 1:213.

134. What follows is based on a comparison of W.O. 33/1297, Report of the Committee on Certain Lessons of the Great War, with W.O. 33/1305, Notes on Certain Lessons of the Great War.

135. W.O. 33/1305, Notes on Certain Lessons of the Great War, p. 24.

136. Maj. Gen. E. K. G. Sixsmith, who was a junior officer in the 1930s, refers to the short report as "an excellent, abridged edition." *British Generalship in the Twenti-*

eth Century (London, 1970), p. 176. This statement does not appear to have been based on a comparison with the full Kirke Committee Report.

137. Liddell Hart, *The Tanks*, 1:328–331.

138. This paragraph is based primarily on Richard Ogorkiewicz, *Armor: A History of Mechanized Forces* (New York, 1960), pp. 64–65, 169–174; Judith Hughes, *To the Maginot Line: The Politics of French Military Preparation in the 1920s* (Cambridge, Mass., 1971), pp. 68–75; and Jean Psomades, *The Military Organization of France and Formation of the French Army, and Modern French-English Military Terms* (Paris, 1926), pp. 1–25.

139. France, Ministère de la Guerre, Etat-Major de l'Armée, *Instruction provisoire sur l'emploi tactique des grandes unitées* (Paris, 1922), p. 24.

140. Insight into French thinking on the importance of materiel in the 1920s from an anonymous article in *Revue des Deux Mondes* (November 1926), translated and summarized as "The Army France Requires," *JRUSI* 72 (May 1927): 284–294; the report of remarks by Marshal Foch on the mechanization of war prepared by Lord Onslow in July 1927, Great Britain, War Office, W.O. 32/2824, Disarmament: Views of Marshal Foch on Mechanization; and André Beaufre, "Liddell Hart and the French Army, 1919–1939," Howard, ed., *Theory and Practice of War*, pp. 129–141.

141. Robert A. Doughty, *The Seeds of Disaster: The Development of French Army Doctrine, 1919–1939* (Hamden, Conn., 1985), p. 122.

142. The description of American armored doctrine is based on Timothy K. Nenninger, "The Development of American Armor, 1917–1940," M.A. thesis, University of Wisconsin, 1968, pp. 83–106; General Service Schools, *The Employment of Tanks in Combat* (Fort Leavenworth, Kans., 1925), pp. 7–14; Duncan Crow, ed., *Armoured Fighting Vehicles of the World*, vol. 1: *AFVs of World War One* (Windsor, 1970), pp. 119–131; and Duncan Crow, ed., *AFVs in Profile*, vol. 4: *American AFVs of World War II (New York, 1972)*, Part 2, "United States Armored Organization (1917–1947)," pp. 8–12.

143. Nenninger contends that the American Experimental Mechanized Force was originally intended to be dissolved. Although he does not give a specific citation to support this assertion, his reliable study is based on extensive research in the National Archives.

144. The description of German doctrine is based primarily on B. H. Liddell Hart, *The Other Side of the Hill*, rev. ed. (London, 1951), pp. 26–32; Hans von Seeckt, *Thoughts of a Soldier*, Gilbert Waterhouse, trans. (London, 1930), pp. 59–63; George W. Hallgarten, "General Hans von Seeckt and Russia, 1920–1922," *Journal of Modern History* 21 (March 1949): 28–34; and Brian T. White, *German Tanks and Armored Vehicles* (New York, 1968), pp. 48–49.

145. Guderian quoted from Kenneth Macksey, *Panzer Division* (New York, 1968), p. 10.

146. The description of Soviet armored doctrine is based on Garrett Underhill, "The Story of Soviet Armor," *Armored-Cavalry Journal* 53 (January–February 1949): 22–30; Raymond Kolkowicz, *The Soviet Army and the Communist Party: Institutions in Conflict* (Santa Monica, Calif., 1966), pp. 57–79; and Richard Ogorkiewicz, "Soviet Tanks," *The Red Army*, B. H. Liddell Hart, ed. (Gloucester, Mass., 1968), pp. 295–297.

6

BURNETT-STUART AND MECHANIZATION IN EGYPT, 1931–1934

All is well–I think Egypt should suit both my arthritis and my independent spirit. . . . Collect as many A.F.V.'s as you can for us to play with–I think we will have some fun.

—Burnett-Stuart to Col. George Lindsay, November 1930[1]

In contrast to the bleak conditions of peacetime training in the home army, the Egyptian command provided an arena in which training could be made both exciting and realistic. The freedom of action Burnett-Stuart enjoyed in Egypt gave him full scope to utilize his tactical understanding and common sense and to demonstrate the practicality of employing mechanized forces in the desert. In Egypt he confirmed his capacity for higher command and made a significant contribution to the British Army's understanding of modern desert warfare. The extensive correspondence carried on with Liddell Hart during his tenure there reveals that Burnett-Stuart also devoted a great deal of thought to the larger problems of reforming the army; it also illuminates a striking contrast in perspective between an internal military reformer and an external military critic.

I

In November 1930, six months after having been placed on half-pay, Burnett-Stuart wrote his old friend George Lindsay, then GSO1 of British Troops in Egypt, to inform him of his impending appointment as commander of those troops. His letter shows a tinge of sadness at having to leave Crichie, but the overall tone is positive: "I confess I rather regret exchanging my kilt for khaki again–& often wonder if it is worth it. But I shall look to you to see me through. . . . Collect as many A.F.V.'s as you can for us to play with– I think we will have some fun."[2] In his reply Lindsay expressed delight at Burnett-Stuart's appointment but informed him that the armored vehicles in Egypt consisted of only sixteen Vickers Medium Mark IIs and the Rolls Royce armored cars belonging to the recently mechanized 12th Lancers. He also told Burnett-Stuart that he had received a letter from Colonel Pile, assistant director of mechanization, stating Pile's intention to send to Egypt for experimental work two light tanks, a Carden-Loyd machine-gun carrier, a two-ton tractor, and a Crossley armored car. This and correspondence from Bonham-Carter, the director of staff duties, had encouraged Lindsay about the War Office's attitude, and he urged Burnett-Stuart to lobby for even more. "It is needless for me to tell you," he said, "that, if they really wished to try out the possibilities of mechanical warfare over long distances in undeveloped country, we here are in the ideal position to do it."[3]

Burnett-Stuart's appointment to Egypt was briefly called into question by the vacancy created at Aldershot when General Sir Warren Anderson unexpectedly died in December 1930.[4] Milne filled the position, however, by bringing General Harington home from India, and Burnett-Stuart informed Lindsay that he was "immensely relieved that there has been no alteration as far as I am concerned."[5] This is an interesting commentary on Burnett-Stuart's character, for Aldershot was considered the most prestigious of the home commands and one that augured well for advancement to C.I.G.S. It was characterized, though, by an artificial environment; the training areas were limited and much emphasis was placed on ceremony. Furthermore, the proximity to London invited frequent visits from royalty, politicians, and senior officials at the War Office. The command environment of Aldershot was, in short, the exact opposite of Egypt. Burnett-Stuart was well out of it, and he knew it.[6]

The visionary presence of George Lindsay as the chief staff officer in Egypt was another asset of that command. Since Lindsay's arrival in October 1929, he had continually advocated using the Egyptian forces to experiment with armored vehicles in the desert. He stayed abreast of the latest mechanical developments in England; he formed the 3d and 5th Armoured Car Companies into the R.T.C. Group, Egypt, which he hoped would be the embryo of a future tank battalion; and he established a local mechanical warfare experimental section.[7] These actions were taken on Lindsay's initiative, even though the War Office would not sanction them. In a letter of 5 June 1931 Kenneth Laird, inspector of the R.T.C., informed Lindsay that not only would the tank group not be recognized, but that it was "still considered necessary to lie low about the existence of the 5th Armoured Car Coy."[8]

Resistance to the expansion of the Tank Corps in Egypt apparently stemmed from three sources—an unwillingness to make the reductions in the cavalry contingent that would be required to obtain additional barracks and garage space, financial restrictions, and the uncertain political situation. In the original proposal for formation of a tank battalion in Egypt in 1929, Burnett-Stuart's predecessor, Lt. Gen. Sir Peter Strickland, said, "The C.I.G.S. told me that he was not keen on Cavalry being given up as it might affect their future existence. So if there are objections to reducing Cavalry here, then this Scheme must fall to the ground, as I do not see any other way in which

I can make a beginning."[9] The 5th Armored Car Company had been scheduled for disbandment upon mechanization of a cavalry regiment in 1930.
Despite the somewhat pointed inquiries of the Financial Section of the War
Office, it was kept in existence throughout the early 1930s by Milne's insistence that it was required to train cavalrymen in mechanized war and by
outright evasiveness when such justifications were no longer acceptable. Hence
Laird's instructions to Lindsay to "lie low."[10] The Anglo-Egyptian negotiations concerning the future of British forces in Egypt were in a delicate stage.
Britain had offered to remove all troops from the Egyptian interior to the
Canal Zone, but the Egyptians insisted on full control of the Sudan, a condition unacceptable to the British. Talks were broken off in 1930, but it was
obvious that they would have to be continued; in this highly charged atmosphere the Foreign Office objected to any efforts that appeared to increase the
strength of the British garrison in Egypt.[11]

   Burnett-Stuart's instructions from the Army Council made him responsible for the defense of the Suez Canal, for the protection of British citizens
and property in Egypt, and for the administration of British forces in Palestine, the Sudan, and Cyprus.[12] They did not contain any directives concerning either the training of his command or the use of mechanized forces. But
it was in these areas that Burnett-Stuart, like Lindsay, exercised the greatest
amount of initiative and made the most significant contributions.

   The British garrison, apart from the unofficial tank group, consisted of
three cavalry regiments, one of which was mounted in armored cars; six
infantry battalions; three batteries of Royal Horse Artillery; and three light
artillery batteries. These units were organized into a cavalry brigade stationed
in Cairo and two infantry brigades, one in Cairo and one in the Canal
Zone.[13] There was also one Army Cooperation Squadron that was under
Burnett-Stuart's direction for purposes of training, as well as two bomber
squadrons and assorted transport units that could be made available to him
in operational emergencies.[14] This conventional infantry-cavalry-artillery force
was a far cry from the Experimental Armoured Force on Salisbury Plain, and
it seemed to offer little potential for experiments in mechanized warfare. But
Burnett-Stuart's fresh outlook and lively imagination soon transformed it
into one of the most exciting units in the British Army.

                                    II

Shortly before his departure for Egypt, Burnett-Stuart wrote Lindsay: "I do
not yet know when your training season begins or what training you do in
the summer. But I shall know what I want when I come. I've had a good
deal of experience of the value of regimental & coy. exercises in internal
security work, and shall want a good deal of that—we neglect that."[15] On

the eve of this first training season, which Lindsay had informed him ran from October to March, Burnett-Stuart presented an address on training that demonstrated that he did, in fact, know what he wanted to accomplish in Egypt.[16] This address was subsequently published throughout the command and served as the basis of all training conducted in Egypt during his tenure.[17]

Burnett-Stuart's address discussed the characteristics of armored warfare, the use of supporting arms, and the training of infantry and cavalry. Throughout it, one is struck by his realistic understanding of the capabilities and limitations of a wide range of military units; his appreciation for the impact that new weapons, particularly the tank and the airplane, had on the conduct of war; and his insistence that successful fighting in war demanded quick thinking that in peacetime could be developed only in realistic, imaginative, and lively exercises.

He told his commanders that his purpose was not to lay down rules and instructions but to "give you an atmosphere, so that you can know what my particular beliefs and methods are without having to waste your time in finding out."[18] Recalling his experience on Salisbury Plain, he said, "We learned a lot about A.F.V.'s and their possibilities and thought a great deal more—the results are embodied in the 'Purple Primer.' But I discovered, too, what a lot the older arm[s] had to learn if they were to be fit to compete in the more scientific and brisker atmosphere which the advent of the A.F.V. has created."[19] He then noted that on Salisbury Plain the 3d Division and 2d Cavalry Brigade had first registered a "detached interest and even amusement in the Armoured Force, as if it were a travelling circus," followed by the development of a "definite inferiority complex," but that they finally realized that "unless they learned to change some of their methods, and to think quicker and act quicker and move quicker, they would have to take a very back place" and were in the end "thankful for the fresh impetus and interest which the advent of this new arm was giving to their trade."[20]

This description probably characterizes Burnett-Stuart's own response to tanks more than it does that of many of his colleagues, but it also represents a definite attempt to get his new command to think positively rather than negatively about armored warfare. He realized that there were not enough tanks in Egypt to employ them properly in large, homogeneous formations but that the chief value of the tanks they did have was as a means of conducting mechanical experiments and "as a reminder of the revised standard of training which their existence demands from the rest of the troops."[21]

Among his most interesting remarks are those dealing with training regulations:

Be guided by the Training Regulations—but don't think that the Regulations contain all there is to be known about soldiering. They don't. Remember what the

Regulations are; they are a potted extract of past experience, and like other potted extracts they are best taken in a diluted form—and sometimes with a grain of salt. They are full of nourishment—of sound sense, and wise warnings; and of useful proformas and aide-memories [*sic*] for use where such mechanical aids apply. They abound too in dangerous catch-words . . . so use them properly and conscientiously—see that the principles, and warnings, and facts that they contain are understood. That is your foundation. But build up on it as great a variety of schemes as you can; and the more original and interesting and even outré your schemes are, the better, so long as they teach a definite lesson and represent what might be *real* situations.[22]

Burnett-Stuart's main concern was to make training as much like actual war as possible. To this end he told his commanders to "never stop an exercise in the field because things are getting mixed up; far the best training you can have is getting out of a mess"; to extend exercises beyond their normal point of termination—"it is in that extra bit that you will find out which are your best men"; and to make their schemes "human and crisp and simple and alive."[23] "There is no reason," he said, "to imagine the whole world at war in order to attack a pill box with a platoon; all you want is the pill box and a platoon!"[24] He then recounted the time in India he had been caught up in the exercise involving a company commander placed *hors de combat* by a chamber pot thrown out a window and the value of a vivid imagination in training small units in internal security duties.[25]

The object of these exercises was for his commanders to develop their own mental processes and help develop the minds of their subordinates. To this end he wanted those engaged in training to be "thinking what they are going to do next right up to the end."[26] He wanted "plenty of time for conferences" at the end of each exercise, with junior officers given an opportunity to say their piece and hold their own conferences.[27] He wanted his subordinates to create an atmosphere for training in their units, but to then guide the training of their subordinates without interfering with it—"people are often led into doing stupid things because of being constantly checked."[28] He also suggested allowing noncommissioned officers to take charge of at least one battalion exercise a year in order to increase their prestige in the eyes of their men and to get them deeply involved in the training process.

He concluded by warning his commanders of the dangers of dogmatism:

Finally, I should like to remind you how unwise it is to be too dogmatic about training. Directly you lay down a tactical rule, the first example of its application that turns up is almost sure to be an exception! In tactics there are many answers to every problem, all of which are right. What we want to find, and as commanders, to pronounce upon, is a really good answer in each separate case. So often we are inconsistent—we preach the development of initiative and then proceed to cramp initiative & hopelessly by laying down rigid rules, and rigid restrictions, by giving rigid judgements. Let us avoid that.[29]

This address was an earnest of an exciting and realistic training program.

III

Burnett-Stuart's capacity to translate into practice the ideas contained in his inaugural training address is demonstrated in the training exercises and mechanical warfare experiments conducted in Egypt during his tenure and in his rapid response to civil disturbances in Cyprus and Iraq. Burnett-Stuart's arrival in Egypt brought about a distinct improvement in morale. His predecessor, Lieutenant General Strickland, was a competent soldier who had been employed with the Egyptian Army from 1896 to 1903 and had successively commanded divisions in France, the Rhineland, Ireland, and England.[30] Lindsay felt that "his opinion on Egypt and affairs here is about as good as you can get" and told Burnett-Stuart that Strickland and his wife had "both been kindness itself to me."[31] The junior officers in Strickland's command, however, felt that he pushed too hard and lacked a sense of humor. Lt. Col. Rory Baynes, who was second in command of a battalion of the Cameronians in Egypt under both Strickland and Burnett-Stuart, said that "under Jock Stuart morale soared because everyone felt that they were part of a team and everyone was working together rather than being pushed into it. It was a totally different atmosphere than under General Strickland."[32]

Burnett-Stuart created this new atmosphere by making the training itself interesting and by ensuring that his men had ample opportunities to enjoy themselves. He trained them hard but also required every soldier in the command to take two weeks leave each year, which could be spent in any of the major Egyptian cities, or merely sleeping at the barracks absolved from all responsibilities.[33] While it was standard policy for officers to be granted liberal leaves, Burnett-Stuart appears to have been one of the few senior officers to insist that private soldiers took leave as well.

Shortly after his arrival Burnett-Stuart requested that Colonel Pile, who had shown great dash as commander of the Light Group on Salisbury Plain, be assigned to command the Canal Brigade. Although this position was usually given to an infantryman and Pile was a tanker and a former gunner to boot, Burnett-Stuart knew that he was perfectly suited to implement his policies.[34] The combination of these two men's efforts made a significant contribution to the training of the British Army in desert operations between the wars. Burnett-Stuart provided the general atmosphere that encouraged innovation and suggested new ways of doing things. Pile took these suggestions, added ideas of his own, and developed the detailed programs required to put them into practice. The exercises carried out under the Burnett-Stuart–Pile regime emphasized mechanization, the use of aircraft, night operations, and, above all, the education of subordinate commanders.

Although the small number of available tanks made it almost impossible to conduct experiments in armored warfare, Burnett-Stuart was able to inject ideas of mechanized warfare into his exercises by giving Royal Army Service Corps vehicles to the infantry units for training.[35] The effect that this had upon the men in Egypt is evident in the account of 1932 training written by the journalist of the West Yorkshire Regiment:

> From the training point of view, this winter promises to be even more interesting than last. We refer to the fact that the watchword for this year's training is "mechanization." A large proportion of the Platoon and Company Training is being carried out with the aid of motor-transport specially sent down here [Moascar] from Cairo and the results are, so far, entirely satisfactory from everyone's point of view. The painful trudging over loose sand, which was an outstanding feature of last year's training season, is now reduced to a minimum, with the result that, fatigue being reduced, the interest taken in the actual work done is increased considerably, while training area – the whole of the desert is brought practically to our doors – is almost indefinitely enlarged, and the repetition of the same scheme over and over again . . . is relegated to the limbo of things that are best forgotten.[36]

Burnett-Stuart also appreciated the value of aircraft in modern war. Although he did not work out a Guderian-like concept of close air support from low-level bombing, he extensively used the air assets available to him and encouraged his subordinates to do likewise. He frequently traveled by air himself and often landed in the desert to confer with his brigadiers during field exercises.[37] On some occasions his subordinate commanders used aircraft administratively, merely to move troops between their permanent stations and remote training areas. The West Yorkshire Regiment, for example, shuttled units by air from Moascar to the southern end of the Great Bitter Lake to conduct company training.[38] On other occasions, however, they were used tactically. In one major exercise, Burnett-Stuart gave Lt. Col. Harold Franklyn, then commanding a battalion of the West Yorkshires, a large number of aircraft and told him to use them in any way he liked. Although neither Franklyn nor Pile was terribly enthusiastic about having the planes foisted on them, Franklyn used them to move his entire battalion behind an opposing unit to attack it from the rear. Although the modern concept of vertical envelopment by helicopter makes this type of exercise seem commonplace, Franklyn's actions represented a distinct departure from the norm in the early 1930s. Characteristically, Burnett-Stuart spoke favorably of them in his summing-up conference.[39]

Operations at night are always difficult, but particularly so in the desert where the absence of prominent features complicates the problems of navigation and hence the control of forces. Despite these difficulties, Burnett-Stuart felt that his units had to be able to fight at night, so Pile instituted a training plan to give the Canal Brigade this capability. The system included the progressive development of "night sense," the ability to conduct night reconnaissance, and finally the capacity to conduct night attacks. At the culmination of this phase of training, platoons were tested on their ability to cross thirteen miles of desert and attack an enemy position during the hours of darkness, with marks being given on silence, speed, and the ability to maintain direction.[40] After the basic individual and small-unit skills had been mastered, companies and battalions were practiced in night operations. Under some pressure from Pile, Lt. Col. Bernard Montgomery, who commanded a battalion of the Warwickshires in Egypt and was initially quite skeptical of the value of night operations, made a long night march across the desert and completely surprised a battalion of Foot Guards in another brigade.[41]

When Pile arrived in Egypt Burnett-Stuart told him that the way to learn tactics, which applied from himself down to the lowest subaltern, was to get out of the barracks into the desert and to do things—to make mistakes if necessary, but to learn from what one did.[42] At the lowest level this principle was applied in Franklyn's battalion with a series of "section marches," in which sections were taken into the desert by truck and left at a distant point to find their way back. Upon their return they were required to report on what they had observed and the condition of their unit. This type of training developed the leadership abilities of the N.C.O.s and inspired a great deal of confidence among the men.[43]

In his efforts to educate his subordinates, Pile regularly turned the brigade over to one of the battalion commanders for the conduct of special exercises. He also allowed other officers to assume the role of brigade major. This allowed the battalion-level officers to gain experience in handling larger formations, and it gave Pile the opportunity to evaluate their potential for higher command. One such operation, in which Lieutenant Colonel Montgomery was the acting brigadier, and Maj. Francis De Guingand the acting brigade major, established a relationship that eventually resulted in De Guingand's serving as Montgomery's chief of staff of both the Eighth Army (1942–1943) and the 21st Army Group (1944–1945).[44]

On another occasion, Major Baynes, whose battalion commander was on leave, was acting brigade commander for a river crossing exercise. When Burnett-Stuart visited the headquarters, Baynes outlined his appreciation of the situation, mission, various courses of action available, and his decision on how to conduct the operation. Burnett-Stuart replied, "That's all right, but if you have a spark of genius make your plan first, then use your appreciation to test it. This will save you a lot of time and produce better results."[45] Baynes was nonplussed. He had never heard a senior officer say anything so unorthodox. He adopted the practice, however, and found that it did, in fact, work for him. This is an excellent example of the effect that Burnett-Stuart's unconventional but realistic attitude toward training had on the development of his subordinates.[46]

Lindsay also did a great deal to assist Burnett-Stuart in the education of officers in Egypt. His culminating effort in this area was the development of a large staff exercise conducted during the 1931–1932 training season. The exercise was based upon Allenby's third battle of Gaza, and its purpose was to study "the employment of an Army in a stage of evolution between that of the Great War and that of the future."[47] Lindsay envisioned using forces mentioned in *Modern Formations* that included one cavalry division, four infantry divisions, four army tank battalions, one tank brigade, one armored car regiment, and supporting artillery. His plan was to crush an imaginary Turkish center with a combined infantry-artillery-tank attack and then to exploit the success with tanks, mechanized artillery, and aircraft moving through the gap in the Turkish lines. Lindsay's composition of the forces and the realization of the need for a set-piece battle to breach prepared positions as well as a fluid battle to capitalize upon the breakthrough demonstrated a remarkable vision of the future.

In the postexercise conference, Lindsay's plan was questioned by Brig. William Dobbie, who suggested sending the mobile forces around the flank. Burnett-Stuart replied that while he was not wedded to Lindsay's solution, he felt that a flanking force would not have been able to receive adequate logistical support and that Lindsay's plan, by dealing an initially severe blow to a less-well-armed enemy, would have had a better chance of success.[48] Burnett-Stuart's main point, however, was not the merits of a particular tactical solution, but the need for new concepts of time in the employment of mechanized and armored units:

This exercise was not designed as a war game, but as a study of the handling and the capabilities of the modern mechanized formations, to the provision and use of which we are told to look forward. It brings out the extent to which we must modify our ideas of time and pace. The tank formations with which we will, in future, have to deal move with very great speed, and have a great radius of action; in dealing with them we must accustom ourselves to think big, and think quickly, and other arms working with them on the same battlefield will have to move quickly too.[49]

Although staff exercises such as Lindsay's were extremely valuable, Burnett-Stuart's main tools for training his subordinates were the annual command exercises held at the end of each training season. They involved nearly every unit in Egypt and were designed to bring out some particular lessons concerning the capabilities and limitations of mechanized and armored forces. One brigade, usually Pile's, was given a majority of the vehicles available to the command, while the other was confined to movement by foot and horse. For the 1934 exercise, however, Burnett-Stuart reversed the roles. All the tanks and armored cars were given to the Cairo Brigade, and Pile was left with only some cavalry and lorried infantry. He was soon surrounded, but he emplaced his unit behind a series of water obstacles and destroyed all the bridges. This brought a virtual stalemate, and after two days of little action, Burnett-Stuart ordered Pile to break out to an oasis fifty miles away. Pile was soon surrounded again. He then elected to stand and fight and was inevitably defeated. He felt he had made the best of a bad situation, but at the summing-up conference Burnett-Stuart criticized him for not attempting to break out again, to save at least his motorized infantry. Burnett-Stuart's implicit dictum was that one should never fight a battle at a disadvantage unless absolutely necessary. This was a revelation to Pile, but after reflecting on it he felt that it was correct.[50]

Perhaps the major fact that comes out of all the exercises conducted under Burnett-Stuart's command was that the results were not nearly as significant as what was learned from them. The learning came primarily from the reflections of the participants, but the reflections were to be refined and sharpened at the postexercise conference. According to De Guingand, Burnett-Stuart excelled at this technique: "At the end of a Big [sic] exercise his summing up & criticism was a real pleasure to hear. He never minced his words & parceled out criticism & praise without fear or favor."[51] This was much different from the artificial atmosphere in the home army where criticism at an exercise was often considered detrimental to one's career. News of Burnett-Stuart's command exercises went far beyond Egypt, and in early 1934 Brig. Bertie Fisher informed Liddell Hart that Burnett-Stuart's maneuvers in Egypt were the best known at the War Office.[52]

While Burnett-Stuart praised or criticized his infantry commanders to encourage them to innovate or force them to examine their tactical assumptions, his attitude toward the cavalry was almost implacably hostile. The *Cavalry Journal* in the early 1930s reveals an infatuation with horsemanship and the glories of cavalry traditions, with little attention given to serious professional development.[53] Removed from the experimental work going on in England, the cavalry units in Egypt were particularly deficient, their major concern often being polo games at the Gezira sports stadium in Cairo.[54] Burnett-Stuart was particularly incensed by this attitude. After one exercise he expressed the feeling that he was "dealing with professional polo players and amateur soldiers."[55] After another he said that while wars of the past may have been won on the playing fields of Eton, wars of the future would not be won on

the polo grounds of Gezira.[56] In a report to the War Office on cavalry training in Egypt, he wrote, "This exercise confirmed my previous conviction
that the Cavalry are still behind the other arms in their conception of war, in
professional leadership, and in the thoroughness of their training. They are
inclined to forget that the Cavalry spirit requires very careful professional
technique as their medium of expression."[57]

Burnett-Stuart's feelings were different from those of Montgomery-
Massingberd, who felt that the cavalry could be salvaged if it learned to act
in conjunction with armored cars and tanks. In 1930 Montgomery-
Massingberd wrote to Brig. Geoffrey Brooke, commander of the Cavalry Brigade in Egypt, suggesting that he and Lindsay "ought to be able to work out
some very good *co-operation between mechanised vehicles and cavalry* [emphasis in
original]."[58] This line of thinking led Brooke to inform Lindsay of his belief
that cooperation between cavalry and A.F.V.s "will produce results in war,
and inculcate a spirit . . . between the two—never to let the other down."[59]
He suggested that cavalry might occasionally be able to protect the advance
of armored units; to support tanks in the withdrawal by "holding ground,
covering the withdrawal of injured machines and personnel"; and to assist in
the attack by coming from the flank to destroy antitank guns "when all eyes
are fixed on the tanks."[60] Although there might have been some ways in
which cavalry could have assisted armored formations with close-in reconnaissance in wooded areas or other specialized situations, Brooke's notion
that cavalry formations could work intimately with armored units on a modern battlefield suggests that wishful thinking had colored his judgment. It is
little wonder that Burnett-Stuart was exasperated.

In late 1931 Burnett-Stuart decided to press the War Office again for the
authority to form an embryonic tank battalion in Egypt. He told Lindsay
that he wanted

> a letter drafted to Vesey [Bonham-Carter's replacement as director of staff duties]
> suggesting that the Egypt group which you propose [be formed]. But the question
> of accommodation must be gone into at once and concrete proposals put forward
> or suggestions made. I am quite prepared to give up one cavalry regt.—in fact I
> should be quite glad to get rid of it—but that will mean a reorganisation of the
> Cav. Bde. command.[61]

The resulting message recommended the formation of an R.T.C. Group,
Egypt, consisting of a headquarters wing equipped with one medium and
one light tank, a medium wing equipped with nine medium tanks and six
close-support tanks, and a light wing equipped with sixteen light tanks.
Burnett-Stuart strongly recommended that accommodation be made available for this force by not replacing the 17th/21st Lancers when they departed
in the subsequent troop rotation. He was

War Office experimental convoy in Cairo, January 1932. This convoy, actively sponsored by Burnett-Stuart and his chief staff officer, Col. George Lindsay, traveled over 5,600 miles through Egypt and the Sudan. (Courtesy of the Burnett-Stuart family.)

Light tanks of the 6th Battalion, Royal Tank Corps, at a desert camp in Egypt. This mixed heavy/light battalion was formed at Burnett-Stuart's insistence on the value of having a tank unit in Egypt to test armored formations in desert conditions. (Courtesy of the Tank Museum.)

of the opinion that this change in the garrison of Egypt would add greatly to the fighting strength of the force under my Command. It also would enable more realistic training to be carried out, which would be to the benefit both of the A.F.V.'s and the other troops. In addition, much useful experiment could be done under conditions which, for such purpose, are probably superior to that available in any other command.[62]

In January 1932 Laird informed Lindsay that the proposal had been favorably received, but in February he wrote that there would be a long delay in getting the light tanks required because the twenty-two being procured in the 1931/32 financial year were earmarked for the mixed battalions at home, and the nine that were "squeezed into the Estimates" for 1932/33 would be needed by the tank school and experimental warfare establishment.[63] By March, however, he promised to send the required tanks out after Tank Brigade training in September.[64] Sanction was subsequently obtained for the official creation of the 6th Battalion, Royal Tank Corps, in Egypt.[65] It is difficult to determine why the War Office's response to this request was so much more favorable in 1931 than it had been in 1929. The Anglo-Egyptian negotiations were not in as delicate a stage as they had been earlier, but the financial situation was much worse. It is also not clear what arrangements were made for accommodations since the Cavalry Brigade was not, in fact, reduced. It seems likely, however, that Burnett-Stuart's firm insistence on the value of a tank unit in Egypt supplied a key ingredient that was absent in Strickland's previous request.

Although Lindsay was unable to establish an official branch of the Mechanical Warfare Experimental Establishment in Egypt, he was able, with the help of the M.G.O., Lt. Gen. Webb Gillman, to obtain a small group to assist with the experiments of mechanized vehicles in the desert. This was an important step because vehicles could not be adequately tested in England, where the heat, dust, and rough terrain of the Empire were not present. It was also more expedient to test vehicles in Egypt than in India since it was not only closer to home but also under the control of the War Office.[66] Perhaps the most significant mechanical experiments conducted in Egypt were the cross-country convoys sent out in 1932 and 1933. The first convoy, composed of four vehicles, traversed approximately 5,600 miles over various types of desert in Egypt and the Sudan. The second, composed of six vehicles, covered over 3,500 miles. The vehicles used on these journeys demonstrated excellent mechanical reliability; a good deal of data was gathered on the consumption of water, gasoline, oil, and spare parts.[67] Burnett-Stuart often participated in this exercise himself. He traveled with Lindsay on one 2,000-mile trip from Cairo to Palestine, Transjordania, and Akaba, and on another fifteen-day outing in the western desert. During these trips he traveled in his six-wheeled Morris Saloon staff car, and whenever spare parts were needed that were not on hand, they were flown out from Cairo in response to a radio request.[68]

Burnett-Stuart's response to internal disturbances in Cyprus and Iraq demonstrated that the principles of decisiveness and sound judgment that characterized his tactical exercises were equally evident in political-military emergencies. In October 1931 a large number of Cypriots who desired the transfer of Cyprus to Greek control rioted in Nicosia and burned the Government House. The British garrison, consisting of only one company, was unable to deal with the situation, and the governor wired Burnett-Stuart for reinforcements. Sensing that any delay could be dangerous, Burnett-Stuart immediately dispatched one company by air without waiting for approval from London. The reinforcing company arrived just in time to help provide security that the original garrison was unprepared to provide during a large funeral procession. Although it took several weeks to return conditions to normal, the immediate danger was averted, due in large part to Burnett-Stuart's prompt, decisive action.[69]

In June 1932 a group of Assyrians who helped maintain internal stability in Iraq announced their intention to terminate their services. This created a great deal of apprehension among the British citizens. Burnett-Stuart quickly dispatched a battalion of the North Hamptonshire Regiment to Iraq by air, moving over five hundred men eight hundred miles in less than six days. Again, the timely arrival of British troops stabilized the political situation. Although this type of move is common today, in the early 1930s it was a new and demanding venture, with airplanes frequently having to land in the desert, cramped conditions in the planes themselves, and no standard interservice doctrine established for troop transport.[70] In a letter to Liddell Hart, Burnett-Stuart referred to it as "a useful demonstration of our capacity to reinforce quickly at a distance" and observed that "all my soldiers are trained to emplane and embus—and they like it."[71]

It is difficult precisely to assess Burnett-Stuart's long-term influence in Egypt. On the one hand, it was not institutionally permanent. His successor, Lt. Gen. Sir George Weir, was a former commandant of the Equitation School. He felt that armored cars were no use in the desert and once said to Pile that while he could at times see the value of light tanks, "give me cavalry on the battlefield."[72] Pile attempted to retain Burnett-Stuart's training policies in his command, but there was not much he could do to offset the new atmosphere.[73] There is also evidence that the British Army was not properly trained for its opening campaigns in the desert in World War II. In 1942 Auchinleck, then commanding British forces in the Middle East, bluntly declared, "Our armoured forces are tactically incapable of meeting the enemy in the open, even when superior to him in number."[74]

On the other hand, Burnett-Stuart exposed a large number of junior officers who later rose to positions of prominence to the realities of mechanized desert warfare and sensitized them to the concepts of armored desert warfare. De Guingand, adjutant to the West Yorkshire Regiment, later became Montgomery's chief of staff in Egypt. Maj. Alexander Galloway, who served as a GSO3 on Burnett-Stuart's staff and as Pile's brigade major, was instrumental in the planning of Lt. Gen. Sir Richard O'Connor's successful advance on Sidi Barrani in 1940 and served as chief of staff, Eighth Army, in late 1941.[75] Maj. James Steele, Pile's training officer after Burnett-Stuart's departure, was the chief of staff, Middle East, from 1942 to 1943.[76]

Perhaps the most notable example of Burnett-Stuart's influence is Bernard Law Montgomery. Montgomery arrived in Egypt in 1931 as a proficient but conventional infantry commander. He had instructed at the Staff College and had a large hand in rewriting *Infantry Training* in 1930.[77] He had not, however, considered either the value of night operations or the use of armored and mechanized forces.[78] Although his memoirs are silent on the subject, the frequency of his night attacks in World War II and his self-described belief in the "ubiquitous use of armor" seem to have stemmed at least in part from his exposure to Burnett-Stuart and Pile.[79] After the war he wrote Pile that his campaigns in the western desert had definitely been influenced by his earlier training in Egypt.[80]

Burnett-Stuart's main influence on Montgomery, however, was not in modifying his tactical principles, but in rescuing his military career. Montgomery always had a difficult time dealing with people, and in his opening months as a battalion commander he made a number of serious errors in judgment. On one occasion he demanded that every man in the unit purchase a regimental magazine and jailed several men for refusing to do so. On another he apparently established a regimental brothel as a measure for controlling venereal disease.[81] Pile, his immediate commander, considered Montgomery a "darned nuisance" and wanted to relieve him, a step that could have seriously inhibited his chances for higher advancement.[82] Burnett-Stuart, however, counseled patience, and in the end Montgomery's conduct as a battalion commander improved considerably and his qualities as a trainer, which neither Pile nor Burnett-Stuart doubted, earned him a great deal of credit.[83]

Almost everyone who served in Egypt in the early 1930s recognized Burnett-Stuart's unique qualities as a trainer and tactician. De Guingand said, "He was quite outstanding and had far more ability & imagination than his contemporaries."[84] Galloway said, "Jock Burnett-Stuart knew perfectly well . . . that there would be a war . . . and that armor was going to play a much bigger thing than it could do at the time he was working on it."[85] Pile wrote in his memoirs that "Jock Burnett-Stuart had a great reputation as a tactician. He was a most wise and far-sighted man. Any scheme which was propounded to him he was prepared to see tried out, and I think his time in Egypt had greater effect on British tactics in the late war than any other factor."[86] And Montgomery, who practically never praised anyone, particularly his superiors, referred to him as "the most brilliant general in the Army" and felt that he rather than Montgomery-Massingberd should have been selected for C.I.G.S. in 1933.[87] These testimonies leave little doubt that despite the fact that Burnett-Stuart's training policies were not continued, his tenure as commander of British Troops in Egypt from 1931 to 1934 was a success. This was true both in his efforts to improve the overall morale and quality of training in the command and in his efforts to advance the concepts of mechanized warfare in the desert. It was particularly true in his education of subordinates.

IV

During Burnett-Stuart's tenure in Egypt, he also engaged in an extensive correspondence with Liddell Hart. This exchange of views between two articulate and informed individuals offers a revealing insight into the problems of modernizing the British Army. It also illuminates two distinct perspectives in dealing with these problems. Burnett-Stuart and Liddell Hart were of one mind concerning the army's condition, but their different positions and experiences led to disagreements concerning the root causes of this condition and, therefore, the appropriate means to improve it. One man argued from the point of view of the concerned military professional. The other from the point of view of the outside military critic.

The correspondence began in earnest when Liddell Hart sent Burnett-Stuart a copy of *The British Way in Warfare,* which argued that Britain should return to its historic naval and economic strategy and criticized the army for the slowness of its mechanization program. Burnett-Stuart's comments were written from Crichie during a leave from Egypt.

Sep. 14th '32.

My dear Liddell Hart,
    Yes, I owe you a letter. But when I come home I get into my kilt and try and forget all about soldiering. I read your "British Way in Warfare" on the boat, and have just read it again. Most of it I like very much, but why do you try to make capital out of running down the higher Command . . . ? This modern complex of running down everything British always gets a rise out of me! The criterion by which I wanted to judge your clever book was this:—Does it help us to get what we know we ought to have? I don't think it does. It is deliberately calculated to destroy confidence in the higher Command, and unless there is confidence in the management nothing will ever be done.
    I was moved to look up the lecture which I gave at London University in

March 1928 . . . just to see if I, for one, was such an ass as you make out. And I
was comforted to find that, even by your standards, I was not!

It is not the Higher Command that want educating—it is the public, the press,
and above all the Cabinet and Parliament. We know what we want quite well, but
every financial and political obstacle is put in the way of getting it. Also with a tiny
Army so dispersed as ours is, and always on duty, the practical difficulties of conversion are immense. Could you not couch a lance in support of the General Staff
instead of telling them what to do (which they know already) and then abusing
them for not doing it?

. . . .

Yours very sincerely,
J. Burnett-Stuart[88]

Liddell Hart's quick response discussed his different experience with the
military bureaucracy and his role as a seeker after truth as he saw it.

                                                              17.9.32.
My dear General,

The qualities that have long made me an admirer of yours have been not only
the keen insight which singled you out from the mass of senior officers I have met
but the sense of humour which made you take the rough with the smooth in such
good part. I'm going to rely on those qualities in making a very frank answer to
your most welcome letter.

. . . .

. . . I am utterly baffled as to where you can find this "running down of everything British." In reality, I go about with an eager eye for any achievement where
I can give praise for those responsible, and soften down my criticisms as much as
my idea of the truth allows. . . . [89]

But I must try to be true to what I believe to be the truth, even though I'm
sufficiently aware of human fallibility to realize the possibility that my view of the
truth may not be the right one. One can only follow one's light. But one must
follow it. The future of the British Empire is more important than any particular
higher command, and truth more important still.

Experience is the best guide. You say "unless there is confidence in the management nothing will ever be done." Now the whole of human history shows that
practically every step of progress has been achieved in spite of "the management."
And the history of the British Army shows that nothing has ever been done unless
the management was almost driven to do it.

From within my personal experience I have seen this fact proved over and over
again—seen one intelligent proposal after another swamped under the dead weight
of complacent or tired authority. So must you—for some of your ideas have been
among them! And it has only been sometimes, and then only by ceaseless prod-
ding, that such proposals have been translated into reality.

. . . .

Incidentally, for you to deprecate my critical attitude seems to me not merely a
case of the kettle calling the pot black, but of the pungent critic upbraiding the
gentle critic for his violence! Your justified criticisms have set many of the die-
hards against you. And you are the sort of forward-thinking soldier for whom I'm
trying to clear the path a bit, by rooting up weeds and rocks.

. . . .

So many of mankind's troubles have come from pure misunderstanding, among those who have similar intentions. It is to save one more of such misunderstandings that I write at this length.

Yours very sincerely,

B. H. Liddell Hart

P.S.

. . . .

. . . as regards the question of modernising the Army, it is certainly the responsibility of the Government if this is not large enough, but surely the responsibility of the General Staff if it is not efficient for its size? . . . Do you seriously contend that if the G.S. [General Staff] said that our divisions must be reorganised the Government would interfere?

Burnett-Stuart's reply called upon Liddell Hart to look at the army's condition from the point of view of the responsible head of the service who had to take into account a number of practical obstacles to reform.

20.9.32.

My dear Liddell Hart,

I am delighted at the length of sincerity of your letter – and being stuck indoors with a cold, am going to answer it, though I don't expect you to waste any more valuable copy on me in return. . . .

You proclaim yourself the faithful servant of reality and truth – Bon! So do I. Unfortunately truth is not an absolute, and no one knows what it is – except Einstein, who knows for certain that it doesn't exist at all. Let us try "sweet reasonableness" instead.

I see that you are beginning to suspect me of an inceptive thickening of the blood-flow, but I am quite all right, really, and I can offer you a brand of criticism, (if you want it) rather different from that which you get from junior G.S. officers or professional reviewers or the outside public.

Imagine yourself the responsible head of the Army and read your book from that stand-point. Wouldn't you rather resent your own accusations of incompetence and rather contemptuous assumption of superiority? And wouldn't all sorts of difficulties confront you, which as a critic you make no allowance for? Here are some of them:

(i) Your army is supposed to act as a police force in peace, and as a thunderbolt in war. The two functions are incompatible. I, for instance, in the Near East must have men. I cannot with machines occupy and control large cities, protect scattered communities, deal with civil unrest, or occupy and pacify areas. Partial mechanisation simplifies my task, but total mechanisation would make my task impossible. The same considerations apply to India, and to every other over-seas garrison. Meanwhile, the army at home is a mere skeleton and feeder for the overseas garrisons. No doubt, if you could reduce your garrisons abroad (which you cannot do as they are far below the safety mark already), you could reduce the feeding establishments at home also, and save so much money with which to form a small ultra-modern striking force. Though as a matter of fact if you dared to show a possible saving on minimum peace requirements, the army vote would be cut down at once, and you would be worse off than before!

(ii) All progress towards increased military efficiency in peace time, especially if new appliances are involved, is at once branded an *offensive* militarism, and our own so-called statesmen at once rush to Geneva to have such aggressiveness stopped. . . .

(iii) All the army's work is done in an atmosphere that is not only unsympathetic, but definitely antagonistic. Neither the Cabinet nor Parliament nor the public nor the Civil Service (including the W.O. [War Office] civil staff) care two hoots about the army. Finance is a constant nightmare. . . . Finally all press criticism of the Army Command is either contemptuous or hostile, and incredibly ill-informed. The result of all this is that the energies of the Higher command are exhausted in efforts to keep what they have, in living from hand to mouth, and in making bricks without straw – hardly the atmosphere in which to fashion the Army of a Dream.

I could go on a long time in this strain, but I only want to make the point that you, in common with most critics and students however erudite, do not make enough allowance for the practical difficulties of those who have the responsibility for keeping the army going at all.

. . . .

. . . We all know that our present old-fashioned divisions are suicide clubs; but it is not merely a question of reorganising them, but of remodeling our whole military machine and its responsibilities in peace so as to admit of the creation of modern war formations. We are bound to the wheel, and there is no free-wheel attachment to our wheel!

However, I must stop. Don't think I am a defeatist. Far from it. Things might be much worse and are getting better. And don't think I am registering resentment. I have no use for anyone who doesn't say what they think (so long as they think intelligently!), and if I wasn't genuinely interested in your views I wouldn't have inflicted this letter on you.

Yrs. very sincerely,
J. B-S.

Liddell Hart replied that while truth was not absolute, it could best be approached through a spirit of detached, scientific inquiry, which most soldiers seemed to lack, and that the army was more to blame than the public and politicians for the atmosphere of social antipathy.

7.10.32.

My dear General,

I was equally delighted at the length and frankness of your further letter. . . . For it is a satisfaction to have a verbal spar with someone whom one knows will take a thrust with a smile. . . .

Now for your points – I was amused at the masterly way you evade mine.

1. Truth may not be absolute, but for practical purposes it is. And in any case the way of approach to truth is absolute. For we are certainly likely to come nearest the truth if we search for it in a spirit of scientific enquiry and analyze the facts with complete detachment from all loyalties save the one to truth itself.

Now here the soldier is up against a fundamental difficulty. His whole training is towards the cultivation of loyalties – multiple loyalties – to king, country, service, regiment and superiors. To strengthen him for this function, and for the tremendous trials which this entails, the development of this intense spirit of loyalty is a splendid thing. But, obviously and inevitably, it becomes an obstacle when the man so brought up turns to investigate the facts of warfare. Only a superhuman philosopher could adapt himself equally well to both roles. I know the difficulty myself, for even my early training in historical work could not prevent me writing loyalty-inspired eulogies of our direction in the war that now, as an historian, I read with a sense of shame. . . . I realise that it was the best attitude to do one's little bit towards the winning of the war, but I can see equally clearly that it is the worst attitude in which to prepare for another war.

. . . .

3. The argument . . . that our army cannot be modernised because of its "police" functions would only be legitimate if the G.S. had candidly told the Government that the army was unfit for war. . . . It is surely for the Government rather than for the G.S. to decide that the army is only a body of policemen. . . .

4. Most of those who commanded companies and battalions in the war now know that the present division [sic] are suicide clubs—and are saying so as loudly as they dare. It is more rare, if refreshing, to find an officer of your seniority admit this truth. I know plenty of generals who don't and won't admit it.[90] I only wish I could share your belief that I am pushing an open door, but I have too much personal experience to the contrary!

. . . .

7. From my own personal knowledge I cannot agree with you as to the politician being the stumbling block. . . . The root trouble is that the G.S. always hanker after more money instead of reapportioning what they have. It is a dim hope that they will ever get more money, but it is a delusion that they will be frustrated in using what they have to the best value.

8. If the political, public and press atmosphere is unsympathetic to the army, the fault lies mainly with its own heads. In their patent unwillingness to admit past errors that no amount of varnish will cover up. Frank confession would create sympathy just as a reasoned plan of reorganisation would inspire confidence that they are turning over a new leaf.

. . . .

Yours ever,
B. H. Liddell Hart

Burnett-Stuart's reply, written from Egypt, restated his confidence in the army's senior officers, described the dangers he saw in the international and domestic situation, and called upon Liddell Hart to shift his focus to higher defense matters.

22.10.32

My dear Liddell Hart,
    Very many thanks for your letter of the 7th which followed me out here. I was really sorry not to have had a talk with you.
    I see there are some things on which we shall never agree:
    I cannot see that to abuse and discredit the senior officers of the army is any more justifiable or sensible than to condemn those at the top of any other calling or profession, simply because they *are* at the top.

. . . .

    I am *not* convinced, from my own experience, that young regimental and staff officers are wiser and more capable than their seniors.
    And I do not believe that any of the above, or similar, lines of attack, will advance the cause which we both have at heart.

The reformer and the critic. J. T. Burnett-Stuart, date unknown (above), and B. H. Liddell Hart, 1932 (below). (Courtesy of the Liddell Hart Centre for Military Archives.)

. . . I think you are unfair to the G.S. (and to the C.I.G.S. [then Milne]) when you say they have failed to inform the responsible ministers of the true state of the army. I know that I told Hailsham the other day, when he asked after the army in Egypt, that they were totally unorganised and unequipped for modern war, so much so that I did not feel justified in training them for it. And he showed no surprise.[91]

My few days in London were enough to give me the wind up badly at the grim possibilities of the international situation, especially when I realised that the state of all three defence services was worse than I believed. . . .

But I could detect no public interest in these matters, and no interest in defence except as an obstacle to complete disarmament. . . . If there is another great war soon, as seems inevitable if things go on as they are going now, we shall not only be unable to play any part or exert any influence in it, but, far worse, we shall not even be strong enough to keep out of it. What are you going to do about it? . . . You have studied war, you write about it with knowledge and vision, and you have great influence as a critic of war. You have presented us with your army of a dream, but you have left the gap between what we are and what you (and we) wish us to be unbridged.

Could you not now change your battlefield, and instead of following the manoeuvres of tanks and platoons at training, follow the manoeuvres of the Committee of Imp. Defence and its sub-committees, of the Govt. Depts. concerned with C.I.D. decisions, and of the Cabinet? It will be difficult because the fetish of Secrecy is still devotedly worshipped. But I am sure you could do it (Charles Reppington [*sic*] did) and you would find it a much more productive field. Go on showing up the helpless state we are in as much as you like – that is all to the good, but get down to basic causes, and from them to basic remedies. You could do great work.

No doubt I am indiscreet in writing to you like this and I hope you don't mind it. If I was not a believer in your ability and honesty I wouldn't bother to do it.

Yours ever,
J. Burnett-Stuart

Liddell Hart replied that he was not attacking individuals in the army but the diseases of an institution, and that while he was attempting to deal with larger questions of defense, they did not lend themselves to newspaper treatment.

5th December, 1932.

My dear General,

I began this letter exactly a month ago today but had to lay it aside, owing to the necessity of fulfilling an urgent job. . . . Forgive me for being so long in answering.

. . . .

. . . If you charge me with attacking individual generals in any way that might impair their power of service, I reply – can you quote me any instance in the book? If you charge me with pointing out the diseases of an institution, the symptoms of which are palpable to anyone who examines history, I admit the charge – and reply that to refrain would be a crime against the country. . . .

In exploring the history and documents of the war I have frequently come on suggestions to the effect–"we had better gloss over this" or "it's no good raking up what is past and done with." That sort of attitude is responsible for the trouble that overtakes each fresh generation. It induces nausea in anyone who has the least historical sense and is only to be excused by ignorance of history.

For history is a catalogue of the troubles caused by inadaptability–the failure to change in time with the need. And armies, which because of their role should be the most adaptable of institutions, have been the most rigid. . . .

. . . .

With your later suggestions about tackling the broader questions of Imperial Defence I thoroughly agree–and welcome them. But I think you have missed some of the things I have written already on this line. . . .[92] There is also the fact that these broader issues often do not lend themselves to newspaper treatment. It has been in speeches and conversations, perhaps more than in writing that one has sought to call attention to the urgent problems of defence. But your remarks spur one on to pursue the effort.[93]

With all good wishes,
    Yours ever,
    B. H. Liddell Hart
    P.S. I am sorry that the latest appt. [of Montgomery-Massingberd as C.I.G.S.] has not gone your way. It looked like doing so just before, and the Army would have welcomed it, but as far as I can gather the final decision was rather hurried, with so many other matters on hand.[94]

In September 1933 Burnett-Stuart asked Pile, who was home on leave, to extend Liddell Hart a personal invitation to attend the Egyptian command exercises the following year.[95] When Pile returned to Egypt, he reiterated the offer: "Brigade training starts 10th Feb and winds up with a 4 days continuous war 1–5 March. The latter should be fun as here our wars are real. Nothing is neutral till the cease fire blows."[96]

Several letters are missing from Liddell Hart's Burnett-Stuart correspondence file, but in a letter of 2 November 1933 Burnett-Stuart discussed his views on principles of war and renewed an offer apparently made earlier to allow Liddell Hart not only to visit the command exercises, but to command a desert column during them.[97]

2 November, 1933

My dear Liddell Hart,
    I did not mean to inflict another letter on you–but something you said in your last letter rather interested me. You say that your lance (or pen) is couched against the soldiers "who in spite of years of practice go on making the same mistakes"– To my mind it is just years of make-believe, peace-time practice, or rather the "lessons" & "regulations" produced by an unimaginative "control" during those years, that cramp the style of commanders in war, & produce the state of mind which produces the mistakes. Your eternal "rules" & "principles" of war (which always, like volcanic clay, harden when exposed to the air) have the same effect– I am coming in my old age to the belief that the only rule worth bothering about

in war is the off-side rule – get off-side, keep off-side, & take no notice of the whistle.[98]

And the best peace-time training is that which is based on a knowledge of the rules and principles of war not with the idea of following them but with the fixed intention of getting the better of them.

All this is an exaggeration of course, but there is a lot in it – You say that the lack of practice would make my offer to give you command of a column (a fantastic offer, of course!) an unfair experiment. Why? You have spent years . . . in analysing & criticising the performances of commanders great & small; so surely you should be able to put up a performance yourself which should be proof against your own criticism, & therefore, if your published judgements are correct, well-nigh perfect? Don't destroy my faith in you – And come out here in the spring –

Yrs. ever,

J. B-S.

Liddell Hart replied somewhat condescendingly that Burnett-Stuart's recognition of the "off-side" rule coincided with his own conclusion that adaptability was the supreme quality in warfare and somewhat evasively that the military critic was not required to prove the validity of his criticisms in his own practice.

21st December, 1933.

My dear General,

I know hardly anyone else who can lure me into an argument as you can – that is a tribute to your strategic gifts even on paper. . . .

You say that you are coming to the belief that the only rule worth bothering about in war is the "off-side" rule. That is only another name for "the unexpected". May I congratulate you on a conclusion which is the beginning of military wisdom. It is interesting in studying history to see how many of the greatest leaders tend to shed the text-book rules they have learnt before and become more and more essentially opportunists. Yet I think that this view, of the supreme importance of doing the unexpected, is really a starting point for the scientific study of war. One must first unlearn, shake oneself free of traditional fetters, and mere technicalities, grasp the basic truth, and then, having acquired this practical wisdom, one can begin building on it. . . .

The argument of your letter really coincides with the conclusion reached in "The Ghost of Napoleon" that *adaptability* is the supreme requirement.

Your belief in the "off-side" rule is, however, so strong that you even carry it into argument, as I observe in the later part of your letter! For the ability to criticise truly has no relation to the power of executing successfully. I have sufficient confidence in myself to believe that I could handle a desert column successfully, especially if the test were not governed merely by Staff College rules but by the existence of a real opponent whom one had a chance to outwit under war conditions. . . . Even so, commonsense tells me that I might not do as well at 38 as at 28. . . . It would be commonsense also to demand a short interval to familiarise myself with local conditions and the particular technicalities of desert warfare – one of my strongest articles of faith is an objection to people taking on jobs without preparation. . . .

But whether I succeeded or failed as commander would be little or no gauge on my value as a critic. . . .

. . . .

I am still very hopeful of coming to see you in the Spring–if there is one magnet that attracts me it is the prospect of renewing our arguments across the table.

Yours ever,

B.H. Liddell Hart

In the event Liddell Hart did not get to Egypt. In his memoirs he states that "more pressing developments at home" forced him to postpone his trip.[99] Despite this disclaimer, one gets the definite impression from his letter to Burnett-Stuart that he was less than eager to face the possible embarrassment of being shown up in a war game. Burnett-Stuart's final letter from Egypt indicates a feeling of satisfaction from his nearly three years in Egypt and some apprehension concerning his ability to readjust to the artificial conditions in England in his new capacity as G.O.C.-in-C., Southern Command.

1.3.34.

My dear Liddell Hart,

Very many thanks for your letter. I was really sorry you could not come out here. I finished my command manoeuvres yesterday and am now leaving it to my staff to collect the troops from all over the western desert! It was a good variety entertainment and would have amused you.

I am now for home and shall hope to see you on Salisbury Plain before long. I shall miss the independence of this Command and the variety of responsibilities and interests outside the mere soldiering. . . .

I'll find it hard to revert to home conditions of training.

Yrs. ever,

J. B-S.

Taken as a whole, one gets the distinct impression that Burnett-Stuart got the better of this extended exchange. Liddell Hart not only hesitated to take up the offer to command a desert force, which was really rather understandable, he also failed to reply seriously to Burnett-Stuart's major point that the army had too many varied responsibilities and too few resources to undergo a fundamental transformation. There is also a difference in the type of conviction between the two. Burnett-Stuart seemed to be honestly attempting to inform Liddell Hart of the difficulties of military reform, in order to help bring about beneficial change. Liddell Hart, while obviously sincere, seemed more concerned with maintaining his intellectual purity than with effecting solutions to the army's problems. Although it could be debated that he felt intellectual purity was the best tool for solving these problems, his high level of ego involvement tended to detract from the force of his arguments.[100] The contrast between Burnett-Stuart's statement of the "off-side" rule, based upon many years of personal observation and reflection, with Liddell Hart's conclusions about "adaptability," based primarily upon vicarious study, is equally striking. Clearly Burnett-Stuart was the superior practical soldier, and although Liddell Hart was a serious military critic, at times one wonders at Burnett-Stuart's patience in continuing the correspondence. Nevertheless, Liddell Hart must be given his due. His study of history and his observation of the War Office in the fourteen years since the end of the Great War had resulted in some brilliant insights into the reasons that armies fail to change, and it was undoubtedly helpful for the army to have the well-intentioned and searching questioning that only Liddell Hart could provide.

Burnett-Stuart's correspondence with Liddell Hart shows him to have been a serious soldier with a strong desire for reform who nevertheless understood the practical difficulties of modernization. His insistence on the formation of an armored unit in Egypt demonstrates that he advocated as much positive change as could be made within the existing constraints. The most interesting aspects of his tenure in Egypt, however, were the articulation of a set of sound, realistic guidelines for the conduct of tactical training and the conduct of both small- and large-scale tactical exercises that put these ideas into practice. And despite the fact that his policies were not continued in his absence, his exercises sensitized many middle-grade officers who subsequently served in the North African campaign during World War II. This was a significant contribution.

Although Burnett-Stuart's appointment as G.O.C.-in-C., Southern Command, represented a professional advancement, the atmosphere in the home army was very different from that of Egypt, in which he had been able to set the tone for the whole command and design his exercises for the sole purpose of educating himself and his subordinates. His 1 March letter to Liddell Hart indicates that he was returning home with a sense of accomplishment for what he had done, but also a sense of uneasiness for what might be ahead.

NOTES

1. Burnett-Stuart to Lindsay, 17 November 1930, Lindsay papers, LHCMA.
2. Ibid. Although Lindsay had worked with the Machine Gun Corps in World War I and transferred to the Royal Tank Corps in 1923, he was originally commissioned in the Rifle Brigade, and he and Burnett-Stuart had a common outlook on matters pertaining to mechanization.
3. Lindsay to Burnett-Stuart, 13 December 1930, Lindsay papers, LHCMA.
4. The feeling that Burnett-Stuart might go to Aldershot is found in Lindsay to Burnett-Stuart, 13 December 1930, Lindsay papers, LHCMA, and Ironside to Fuller, 16 December 1930, Fuller papers, Rutgers University. Ironside felt that Burnett-Stuart "would hardly be persona grata" with either Harington or Montgomery-

Massingberd, whom he saw then as the most likely prospects to succeed Milne as C.I.G.S.

5. Burnett-Stuart to Lindsay, 16 January 1931, Lindsay papers, LHCMA.

6. Burnett-Stuart's memoir indicates that he clearly preferred command in Egypt to any command at home.

7. As soon as Lindsay learned that a Morris Saloon six-wheeled car was being produced in England as a staff car for the army, he asked Burnett-Stuart to get it for trips to the Sinai, Palestine, and Transjordan. Lindsay to Burnett-Stuart, 27 April 1931, Lindsay papers, LHCMA; Lindsay to Laird, 20 December 1930, Lindsay papers, LHCMA; Lindsay to Laird, 15 January 1931, Lindsay papers, LHCMA.

8. Laird to Lindsay, 5 June 1931, Lindsay papers, LHCMA.

9. B. H. Liddell Hart, *The Tanks: The History of the Royal Tank Regiment and Its Predecessors Heavy Branch Machine-Gun Corps, Tank Corps and Royal Tank Corps, 1914–1945*, 2 vols. (New York, 1959), 1:280.

10. Ibid., pp. 279–280.

11. Ibid., p. 290. Details of the political situation in Egypt and Anglo-Egyptian negotiations can be found in D. H. Cole, *Imperial Military Geography*, 7th ed. (London, 1934), pp. 289–290; Maj. E. W. Polson Newman, "The Defence of the Suez Canal," *JRUSI* 75 (February 1930): 159–162; and the editorial in *AQ* 21 (January 1931): 239–240.

12. Army Council Instructions for the General Officer Commanding, British Troops in Egypt, 9 June 1931, W.O. 32/3548.

13. Cole, *Imperial Military Geography*, 7th ed., p. 298.

14. Ibid., and Army Council Instructions, 9 June 1931, W.O. 32/3548.

15. Burnett-Stuart to Lindsay, 19 April 1931, Lindsay papers, LHCMA.

16. Lindsay to Burnett-Stuart, 30 April 1931, Lindsay papers, LHCMA.

17. "Training" brochure for Canal Brigade, n.d. (circa October 1934), attached to letter from Pile to Liddell Hart, 1 November 1934, Liddell Hart papers, LHCMA.

18. "Training: Preliminary Remarks by G.O.C.," typescript in Burnett-Stuart's papers annotated "1931," p. 1. A slightly edited version can be found in *The Fighting Forces* 9 (April 1932): 28–40. The author is indebted to Kenneth White and the staff of the Staff College Library, Camberley, for locating the published version. All quotations are from Burnett-Stuart's typescript.

19. Ibid.

20. Ibid., p. 2.

21. Ibid.

22. Ibid., p. 3.

23. Ibid., pp. 4–5.

24. Ibid., p. 5.

25. Ibid., pp. 5–6.

26. Ibid., p. 4.

27. Ibid.

28. Ibid., p. 7.

29. Ibid.

30. Information on Strickland from Great Britain, War Office, *The Army List, July 1927* (London, 1927), p. 20.

31. Lindsay to Burnett-Stuart, 13 December 1930, Lindsay papers, LHCMA.

32. Interview with Lt. Col. Sir Rory Baynes, Bt., 11 November 1972. Lieutenant Colonel Baynes also related a revealing anecdote. The Cameronians had previously

served under Strickland in England. Once when inspecting the battalion in Egypt, Strickland asked a subaltern, "Were you with me at Aldershot?" When the officer replied that he had been, Strickland asked, "Was I ever rude to you?" "Yes sir, very often," the lieutenant replied. The author is extremely grateful to Lieutenant Colonel Baynes, who was nearly sightless at the time but whose memory was still clear and precise, for granting this interview, and to his son, Lt. Col. J. C. M. Baynes, for helping to arrange it.

33. This leave policy is favorably commented upon in *Ca Ira: The Journal of the West Yorkshire Regiment* 5 (September 1932): 5–6.

34. Pile had originally been selected to be the commander, Royal Artillery at Aldershot, one of the best artillery brigadier's positions in the army. But the M.G.O., General Gillman, told Milne that this appointment would not be well received by other gunners since Pile had left the artillery to join the Tank Corps. Burnett-Stuart's request for Pile to come to Egypt thus got Pile out of a difficult position. Frederick Pile, *Ack-Ack: Britain's Defence against Air Attack during the Second World War* (London, 1949), p. 30. Burnett-Stuart recounts that he moved the previous commander of the Canal Brigade out quickly in order to get Pile in. John T. Burnett-Stuart, "Memoir," 2 vols., 2:57.

35. Interview with Brig. G. Taylor, 3 October 1972. Brigadier Taylor served as a junior officer in the West Yorkshire Regiment in Egypt under Burnett-Stuart's command.

36. *Ca Ira: The Journal of the West Yorkshire Regiment* 5 (December 1932): 64.

37. Pile interview, 12 October 1972.

38. *Ca Ira* (December 1932): 64.

39. Details of this exercise taken from Taylor interview, 3 October 1972, and Pile interview, 12 October 1972. Lieutenant Colonel Franklyn later became General Sir Harold Franklyn and commanded the Home Forces in Britain during World War II.

40. Diary note on Pile's night training in Egypt, 16 August 1934, Liddell Hart papers, LHCMA. Further information is found in an undated note concerning implementation of the Kirke Committee's recommendations on night operations in the "Night Attack" file, Liddell Hart papers, LHCMA. See also B. H. Liddell Hart, *The Memoirs of Captain Liddell Hart,* 2 vols. (London, 1965), 1:214.

41. Liddell Hart, *Memoirs,* 1:214. On another occasion, Pile strongly chastised both Franklyn and Montgomery for prematurely terminating a night operation because they felt the situation had become too confused. This was a distinct breach of Burnett-Stuart and Pile's guidance to play out each exercise no matter how confusing it became. Pile, *Ack-Ack*, pp. 33–34.

42. Pile interview, 12 October 1972.

43. This account of Franklyn's training program is based upon comments in *Ca Ira* 5 (December 1932): 64, and Taylor interview, 3 October 1972.

44. A full account of the incident is contained in Francis De Guingand's memoirs, *Operation Victory* (London, 1947), pp. 168–169.

45. Baynes interview, 11 November 1972.

46. Baynes said that he learned two main things from Burnett-Stuart: first, to create a spirit of teamwork in which men worked hard because they wanted to rather than because they felt compelled to; and second, to always try to think at least two moves ahead. Ibid.

47. "Gaza Staff Exercise," Lindsay papers, Royal Armoured Corps Museum, Bovington Camp, Dorset, file 214.11.

48. Notes from the final conference on the Gaza Staff Exercise, Lindsay papers, Royal Armoured Corps Museum, Bovington Camp, Dorset, file 214.11.

49. Ibid.

50. The general format for Burnett-Stuart's command exercises from Brig. A. C. Stanley-Clarke, who commanded a battalion of the Royal Scots Fusiliers in Egypt, to author, 3 September 1972. The description of this particular exercise is based mainly upon Frederick Pile's account in "Liddell Hart and the British Army, 1919–1939," *The Theory and Practice of War,* Michael Howard, ed. (New York, 1965), p. 181. Burnett-Stuart's comments and Pile's reactions to them are from Pile interview, 12 October 1972.

51. Maj. Gen. Sir Francis De Guingand to author, 3 October 1972.

52. Diary note of Liddell Hart conversation with Fisher, 22 March 1932, Liddell Hart papers, LHCMA.

53. Prominent articles included "Exploits of the Eighth Hussars," "My Horse (An Equestrian Odyssey)," and "Cavalry Battle Honours," *Cavalry Journal* 22 (January, 1932): 1–8; 46–66; 95–105.

54. This impression of cavalry training in Egypt is primarily based on interview with Lt. Gen. Sir Alexander Galloway, Pile's brigade major in Egypt.

55. Brush interview, 17 September 1972.

56. Lt. Gen. Sir John Evetts to author, 5 October 1972, and Maj. Gen. Sir Francis De Guingand to author, 3 October 1972. Evetts, then a lieutenant colonel, commanded a battalion of the Ulster Rifles in Egypt. Burnett-Stuart's statement was also cited in the Galloway interview, 15 September 1972.

57. "Extract from Report on Cavalry Brigade Training," n.d. (circa 1932), Lindsay papers, Royal Armoured Corps Museum, Bovington Camp, Dorset. The War Office did not retain the annual reports on training from the various commands, and this fragment in Lindsay's papers is the only example of Burnett-Stuart's official written analysis of training in Egypt that has been located. The author is indebted, however, to Brig. H. B. C. Watkins of the army's training directorate for making detailed but unfortunately fruitless inquiries at the War Office and Public Records Office concerning the original reports.

58. Montgomery-Massingberd to Brooke, 2 October 1930, Lindsay papers, LHCMA.

59. Brooke to Lindsay, 3 November 1930, Lindsay papers, LHCMA.

60. Ibid.

61. Undated note from Burnett-Stuart to Lindsay (circa November 1931), Lindsay papers, LHCMA.

62. Burnett-Stuart to D.S.D., War Office, 8 December 1931, Lindsay papers, LHCMA.

63. Laird to Lindsay, 8 January 1932 and February 1932, Lindsay papers, LHCMA.

64. Laird to Lindsay, 16 March 1932, Lindsay papers, LHCMA.

65. There is some doubt about the exact date of the battalion's formation. Liddell Hart gives it as 1932 in *The Tanks,* 1:285. It was announced in the "Army Notes" section of the *JRUSI* in August 1933.

66. Based on Lindsay to Peck, 27 May 1929, and Gillman to Strickland, 27 January 1931, Lindsay papers, LHCMA. See also Liddell Hart, *The Tanks,* 1: 284–285.

67. Information on the 1932 convoy is in "Army Notes," *JRUSI* 77 (February 1932): 198, and *JRUSI* 77 (May 1932): 429, as well as the 1933 Army Estimates speech, *H. C. Deb.,* 5th Ser., 275 (9 March 1933): 1372. A complete report of the

1933 convoy is contained in H. P. Drayson, "The War Office Experimental Convoy, 1933," *Royal Engineers' Journal* 48 (March 1934): 60–72.

68. Lindsay to Laird, 21 May 1932, Lindsay papers, LHCMA. Pile indicates that Burnett-Stuart was obsessed with the desert and traveled across it frequently. Pile interview, 12 October 1972. Burnett-Stuart's memoirs mention frequent cross-desert trips lasting up to several weeks.

69. A detailed account of the incident is contained in Charles Gwynn, *Imperial Policing*, 2d ed. (London, 1939), pp. 331–336.

70. Based primarily on accounts of the operation contained in the *Journal of the Northamptonshire Regiment* 4 (October 1932).

71. Burnett-Stuart to Liddell Hart, 9 July 1932, Liddell Hart papers, LHCMA.

72. Diary note of Liddell Hart conversation with Pile, 16 August 1934, Liddell Hart papers, LHCMA.

73. In Pile's training brochure written after Burnett-Stuart's departure he said that the report of Burnett-Stuart's original training conference would "repay continual re-reading, and I hope Battalion and Company Commanders will give it their deep consideration before preparing their schemes for collective training this year." Pile, "Training" brochure, n.d. (circa October 1934), Pile correspondence file, Liddell Hart papers, LHCMA.

74. Auchinleck to Smith, his chief of staff, 30 January 1942, quoted in John Connell, *Auchinleck: A Biography of Field-Marshal Sir Claude Auchinleck* (London, 1959), pp. 445–446.

75. Information on Galloway from Correlli Barnett, *The Desert Generals* (New York, 1972), pp. 10, 16.

76. Steele to author, 15 July 1972; *Who's Who*, 1971, p. 2994.

77. Alan Morehead, *Montgomery: A Biography* (London, 1946), pp. 72–73.

78. Liddell Hart, *Memoirs*, 1:214. Liddell Hart also felt that Montgomery's infantry manual gave insufficient attention to exploitation of victories, a deficiency in Montgomery's make-up that he saw later manifested in his hesitancy to pursue after the battle of El Alamein. Ibid., pp. 55–56.

79. Montgomery's statement on armor comes from his postwar lecture "21st (British) Army Group in the Campaign in North-West Europe, 1944–1945," *JRUSI* 90 (November 1945): 448.

80. Pile interview, 12 October 1972; Frederick Pile, "Liddell Hart and the British Army, 1919–1939," Howard, ed., *Theory and Practice of War*, pp. 180–181.

81. The first incident is described fully in Morehead, *Montgomery*, pp. 77–78. The second is alluded to both by Morehead and by Montgomery's brother, who says, "He was particularly concerned at the incidence of venereal disease and he adopted preventive measures on the lines of those which, when repeated eight years later in Europe . . . got him into serious trouble." Brian Montgomery, *A Field-Marshal in the Family* (London, 1973), p. 215. Liddell Hart's commentary on Morehead's biography states, "This glides lightly over the episode of Monty's to run a regimental brothel, which nearly landed him in serious trouble." "Alan Morehead's 'Montgomery': Some Queries," appended to Liddell Hart to Morehead, 23 January 1947, Liddell Hart papers, LHCMA. Neither incident is mentioned in Nigel Hamilton's *Monty: The Making of a General, 1887–1942* (New York, 1981).

82. Pile interview, 12 October 1972.

83. Burnett-Stuart and Pile's reports on Montgomery as a battalion commander both emphasized his professional competence and capacity for higher command, but

also pointed to a need for greater tact and judgment. They are quoted in Morehead, *Montgomery*, p. 83.

84. De Guingand to author, 3 October 1972.

85. Galloway interview, 15 September 1972.

86. Pile, *Ack-Ack*, p. 30.

87. Bernard Montgomery, *The Memoirs of Field-Marshal the Viscount Montgomery of Alamein, K. G.* (New York, 1958), p. 37. Montgomery's feelings about the 1933 C.I.G.S. selection reflect some optimism as to the realities of Burnett-Stuart's chances at that early date, but they do indicate the high esteem in which Montgomery held him.

88. This letter and those that follow are contained in the Burnett-Stuart correspondence file, Liddell Hart papers, LHCMA. All except two are contained in a consolidated, typed record.

89. Although Liddell Hart's reports on many of the army's exercises in the 1920s and 1930s indicate that he did soften his criticism of particular commanders, statements in *The British Way in Warfare* (London, 1932) such as "a hasty and haphazard fusion of such mechanized units as were available . . . was characteristically British" (p. 185) and "our national want of logic" (p. 203) tend to support Burnett-Stuart's point.

90. In a subsequent article entitled "The Grave Deficiencies of the Army," Liddell Hart indirectly quoted Burnett-Stuart's analysis: "There is scarcely a thoughtful soldier to-day . . . who does not privately confess that our existing divisions are hardly better than 'suicide clubs.'" *English Review* 56 (February 1933): 147.

91. It is not known whether Burnett-Stuart was familiar with the C.O.S. review for 1932 that catalogued the major deficiencies of the three services, but he was correct in his contention that the soldiers had informed the politicians of the state of the army. Hailsham's lack of surprise over Egypt may have reflected his awareness of the C.O.S. review. Liddell Hart's statement in his previous letter reflected his lack of knowledge about the internal debates over defense and demonstrates the difficulty the outside critic has in making meaningful contributions to defense policy.

92. Liddell Hart may have been referring to his lecture "Economic Pressure or Continental Victories," *JRUSI* 76 (August 1931), mentioned in Chapter 5.

93. Two years later Liddell Hart was appointed military correspondent of the *Times*, where he had a considerably wider charter than he did on the *Daily Telegraph*.

94. Liddell Hart followed the military appointments quite closely and often wrote notes of condolence if his correspondents were not selected for significant positions. In 1930 Ironside informed Fuller, "I was actually the recipient of sympathy from Liddell Hart for not being made M.G.O." Ironside to Fuller, 16 December 1930, Fuller papers, Rutgers University.

95. Liddell Hart diary entry, 17 September 1933, Liddell Hart papers, LHCMA.

96. Pile to Liddell Hart, 27 October 1933, Liddell Hart papers, LHCMA.

97. Between the typed record of Liddell Hart to Burnett-Stuart of 5 December 1932 and Burnett-Stuart to Liddell Hart of 1 March 1934, there is a penciled notation in Liddell Hart's hand, "See also B.St. to LH 2/11/33 LH. to B.St. 21/12/33." Although originals of these letters were in the files, other letters apparently written in the interval were not.

98. Burnett-Stuart's sentiments are somewhat similar to those later expressed by Lt. Gen. Sir Montagu Stopford, who congratulated one of his division commanders for shooting "a goal when the referee wasn't looking" when he unexpectedly crossed the Irrawaddy and attacked Shwebo to take advantage of a favorable change in the

enemy situation. Field Marshal Sir William Slim, *Defeat into Victory,* 2d ed. (London, 1956), p. 52.

99. Liddell Hart, *Memoirs,* 1:215. This is a contrast to his statement made in 1920 that he felt he could command a brigade with distinction. Brian Bond, *Liddell Hart: A Study of His Military Thought* (New Brunswick, N.J., 1977), p. 32.

100. Brian Bond has also noted that in argument Liddell Hart was "unashamedly egocentric" and always liked to win points. Bond, *Liddell Hart,* p. 3.

7

THE QUEST FOR A MOBILE
DIVISION, 1934–1938

We are now proposing to spend very large sums on modern equipment and armament with the object of producing a small but efficient Field Force for warfare in any theatre under modern conditions. So long as the organization of the Army at home remains dependent upon that of the Army overseas, we can do little more than superimpose modern armament on an organization that is not designed for that specific purpose.

— General Sir Cyril Deverell [1]

Burnett-Stuart's return to England in 1934 found the British Army at a significant transformation point. The Tank Brigade had become a permanent formation, and the next logical step in the evolution of mobile formations was the development of a divisional organization. There was, however, a great deal of debate over the form that organization should take. Although there were a number of variations, there were two polar positions. The first held that the division should be an armored formation, composed mostly of tanks, capable of conducting penetrations deep into the enemy's rear in a Continental war. The second advocated a motorized, or perhaps lightly armored, cavalry division, capable of performing reconnaissance and screening missions for motorized infantry just as the horse cavalry division had for foot-mobile infantry, but not designed specifically for a European war. This debate was never conclusively resolved.

Analysis of this debate requires first a brief description of the domestic and international environment of the mid-to-late 1930s that conditioned the evolution of mechanized and armored doctrine; an examination of the Mobile Force exercise of September 1934 that Burnett-Stuart directed in his capacity as G.O.C.-in-C., Southern Command; an analysis of subsequent mechanization policy under the aegis of General Montgomery-Massingberd as C.I.G.S. and Alfred Duff Cooper as secretary of state for war; a continued study of that policy in the era of the Hore-Belisha/Liddell Hart partnership; and finally an assessment of the efficacy of British military reform in the late 1930s in light of progress in mechanization and armored warfare in other armies.

I

The violent, unpredictable mood of the mid-to-late 1930s was most clearly evident in Nazi Germany. The internal assassination of Ernst Roehm and other leaders of the S.A. foreshadowed the external use of intimidation that came to characterize Adolf Hitler's foreign policy; his amalgamation of the presidency and the chancellorship and his imposition of an oath of loyalty on the officer corps created the domestic conditions required to put that policy into effect.[2] The French were plagued by chronic instability. The resignation of Edouard Daladier's Radical government and the outbreak of wildcat strikes that heralded the ascension of Léon Blum's Popular Front pointed to an increasing dissolution of the French body politic.[3]

Internationally, Hitler moved cautiously to restore German security prior to expansion. In 1935 he announced German abrogation of the military clauses of the Treaty of Versailles, and in 1936 he directed the remilitarization of the Rhineland. Feeling more secure by 1938, he began Germany's expansion with the Austrian *Anschluss*. Benito Mussolini, meanwhile, launched an Italian invasion of Abyssinia, which divided Britain and France; and Francisco Franco precipitated a civil war in Spain, which heightened ideological cleavages in both countries.[4]

In Great Britain, domestic politics, economic developments, and a set of popular attitudes that looked with disfavor upon the use of military force as an instrument of national policy conditioned the response to this changing international situation. Ramsay MacDonald resigned as prime minister in May 1935 in favor of Stanley Baldwin, the Conservative leader whose party dominated the National government.[5] Baldwin called for a general election and ran on an ambiguous platform, which alluded to Britain's declining security but promised "no great armaments."[6]

Although the natural forces of economic demand worked to bring Britain out of the depression in the mid-1930s, pockets of outdated industry in northeast England, south Wales, and industrial Scotland were not as fortunate. Total unemployment fell from 2.4 million in 1934 to 2.13 million in 1936, and the industrial production index rose from 104 to 118 (1929=100) in the same period.[7] In the "special areas," however, unemployment varied from 35 to 65 percent, breeding hunger, want, apathy, and despair.[8]

The pacifist mood–reflected in the Oxford Union resolution not to fight for king and country and in the East Fulham by-election of 1933, which appeared to indicate strong popular support for disarmament–became more widespread over the next several years. In his book *Peace with Honour* (1934), A. A. Milne advanced the idea that war was "something of man's own fostering, and if all mankind renounces it, then it is no longer there."[9] The Peace Pledge Union obtained 100,000 members and included among its supporters a number of prominent political and literary figures such as George

Lansbury, Bernard Shaw, and Virginia Woolf.[10] Despite these sentiments, the National government adopted a policy of cautious, gradual rearmament.

It was, however, the form of rearmament rather than the pace that was decisive for army doctrine. This question hinged on the outcome between two conflicting strategic concepts. The concept of Continental intervention called, in the event of a European war, for the immediate dispatch of a modern expeditionary force backed by a well-equipped territorial army. Alfred Duff Cooper, who became secretary of state for war in November 1935, successive chiefs of the Imperial General Staff, and the majority of army officers in the War Office and Cabinet Secretariat supported this view.[11] The opposing concept was one of "limited liability," which called for Britain to contribute air and naval forces to a future Continental war but to avoid a major ground contribution on the scale of the Great War. Chamberlain, Liddell Hart, and Burnett-Stuart argued this view in the Cabinet, the press, and private military circles respectively.

The key question for the army in this debate was whether its primary mission was to fight in Europe or to safeguard the Empire. One of the most significant facts influencing the army's doctrine was that the question was still not resolved at the end of 1938, after five years of protracted study and debate. The Defence Requirements Committee, which had been commissioned in late 1933 to survey the worst of Britain's arms needs, reported in early 1934 that the protection of Belgium and the security of Great Britain from air attack demanded the immediate dispatch of an expeditionary force. Chamberlain replied, however, that "our experience in the last war indicated that we ought to put our major resources in our Navy and our Air Force . . . the Army must be maintained, so that it can be used in other parts of the world."[12] In October 1935 the D.R.C. put up a new statement on requirements that called for a field force of four infantry divisions and one mobile division of the regular army to be dispatched to the Continent immediately, followed by twelve territorial divisions in four-division increments at intervals of four, six, and eight months.[13]

A ministerial group known as the Defence Policy and Requirements Committee reviewed this report and recommended to the Cabinet that the equipping of the territorial army be postponed for three years due to the limits of industrial capacity and the priority of reequipping the regular army and the air force.[14] The Cabinet accepted this recommendation and further insisted that in describing the army's raison d'être, the words "assistance abroad" be substituted for "assistance to Continental allies."[15] This ambivalence was also reflected in the Defence White Paper of 1936, which stated that the army's three main roles were "to maintain garrisons overseas in various parts of the Empire, to provide the military share in Home Defence, including antiaircraft defence, coast defence, and internal security, and, lastly in time of emergency or war to provide a properly equipped force ready to proceed overseas wherever it may be wanted."[16]

Chamberlain's ascension to the prime ministership in May 1937 augured well for limited liability. In December of that year he was able to force a decision in the Cabinet to make the Continental commitment the army's last priority, behind air defense of Great Britain, protection of trade routes, and defense of the Empire.[17] Hitler's occupation of Austria in March 1938, however, raised again the latent Continental tendencies in the General Staff and the Chiefs of Staff Committee. Although the tendencies were not strong enough to reverse the Cabinet's decision, they were sufficiently persuasive to cast doubt on its validity. This extended, unresolved debate over the role of the army left the army uncertain of its purpose. Lack of direction from the political leadership was a major factor in the army's doctrinal drift. Without a clear concept of where or why they were to be prepared to fight, it became extremely difficult, if not impossible, for the professional heads of the army to determine how they would fight.

II

While the strategic debate was going on in the Cabinet, the press, and the War Office, another debate was coming to the surface in the Royal Tank Corps between two different concepts of armored warfare. One concept was the Mobile Division Idea advocated by George Lindsay, who had left Egypt in 1932 to assume command of the experimental, mechanized 7th Infantry Brigade. Lindsay visualized a balanced force of all arms and services that would be capable of executing a variety of tactical and operational missions, the most important of which was to make penetrations deep into the enemy's rear area to disrupt his command and supply network. The other concept was the Tank Brigade Idea advanced by Brig. P. C. S. Hobart, inspector of the R.T.C. and commander of the recently formed Tank Brigade. Hobart agreed with Lindsay that the primary function of the Tank Corps was to make deep strategic penetrations, but he viewed other arms, particularly the infantry, as encumbrances and felt that tank brigades with a modicum of attached units were capable of executing such missions independently.

In November 1933 Hobart wrote Lindsay suggesting that they meet to discuss cooperation between the Tank Brigade and the 7th Infantry Brigade in 1934. In articulating the vision of future war that lay behind this proposal, Hobart said that large concentrations of troops would be impossible and that "only forces that can work dispersed and be controlled whilst dispersed will have much effect."[18] In an attached paper entitled "Use of Armoured and Mechanised Forces in the Early Stages of a European War," he stated his belief that when the enemy was off balance a deep thrust by tanks would be vital. A key point, however, was the need to protect tanks. He saw the main body of tanks being guarded by aircraft, armored cars, and light tanks.[19] The supply echelon, however, required another body of troops for security; this group could also assist by collecting prisoners, holding defiles through which the Tank Brigade was to return, and securing towns and other centers. Although Hobart did not specify what this group was to be, he clearly regarded it as an auxiliary taking little part in the tactical accomplishment of the Tank Brigade's mission.

Lindsay's reply of 17 November outlined a broader concept. While stating his "general agreement" with Hobart's paper, he felt that "having gone as far as we have in the development of the Tank Brigade and the Motorised Infantry Brigade, we must now take a step forward and organize and experiment with a Mobile Division."[20] Such a division was to consist of a motorized cavalry brigade, a tank brigade, a motorized infantry brigade, supporting troops, and aircraft.[21] The motorized cavalry brigade, with its own armored car regiments and motorized machine-guns, would locate the enemy, keep him off balance, and fix him in position for the decisive blow by the tank brigade, which would be based on the existing model but with more modern equipment. The motorized infantry brigade would consist of four small infantry battalions armed with light automatic weapons and antitank guns. Its functions would be to establish supply bases, occupy significant tactical positions, and secure lines of retreat. The supporting elements would include mechanized artillery, engineers, signals, and antiaircraft units. The aircraft group would have to be specially trained to work with the division and include the capacity to deliver supplies by air. In order to test this concept, Lindsay suggested that his brigade be detailed to experiment with the Tank Brigade in 1934 as a prelude to incorporating more elements into the division in 1935.[22]

Hobart's and Lindsay's ideas were similar in many respects. Both saw a tank brigade as the decisive striking arm; both saw the need for a reconnaissance element of armored cars; both saw the need for general security, antiaircraft, and antitank protection of the tank brigade's base; and both saw the need for auxiliary troops to perform tactical missions in its support. They differed fundamentally, however, in their ideas of the scale of auxiliary units that would be required. Hobart felt that these units would be small enough to be made attachments to a tank brigade, while Lindsay realized that the multifarious requirements placed upon these units would dictate a size that could only be incorporated into a division structure. Lindsay was also more acutely aware than Hobart of the need for the ancillary support of artillery, engineers, and signal units. Thus while it would be incorrect to say that Hobart desired the creation of an all-tank army, it was true that Lindsay's Mobile Division Idea provided for a more balanced, comprehensive fighting organization than Hobart's Tank Brigade Idea.[23]

At the end of the 1934 training season the opportunity came to test Lindsay's concept with the amalgamation of his 7th Infantry Brigade and the Tank Brigade into a Mobile Force. In addition to the two principal units, the ad hoc force consisted of two armored car squadrons, a field artillery brigade, an antiaircraft battery, and a mechanized engineer company.[24] Majors R. Bridgeman and J. T. Crocker, the two brigade majors, had conducted a signals exercise earlier in the summer that ensured satisfactory communications between their units.[25] They had not, however, been able to work out the details of a divisional staff. Thus when the decision was made to conduct the Mobile Force exercise in lieu of the projected Southern Command exercises, Lindsay had to improvise a staff to plan and control the operation.[26] This proved to be a critical deficiency, as Lindsay had pointed out earlier to both Hobart and Montgomery-Massingberd. The Mobile Force was opposed by the 1st Division augmented with two armored car companies, a cavalry brigade, and an antiaircraft battery and commanded by Maj. Gen. J. C. Kennedy.[27]

Burnett-Stuart served as the exercise director. Believing the Tank Brigade to have not paid sufficient attention to its logistical organization and desiring to help restore the morale of the infantry, he designed an exercise that deliberately highlighted several of the Tank Brigade's weaknesses.[28] He required the Mobile Force to conduct a raid against a series of objectives, such as headquarters, supply installations, and airfields, on the far side of the Kennet and Avon Canal approximately sixty miles behind the 1st Division's lines.[29] This was similar to the deep penetration mission that had been assigned to the Tank Brigade at a map exercise in May, but in this case the various objectives were grouped more closely together.[30] Burnett-Stuart set the time for the commencement of the force's movement at 2 A.M. on the first day of the exercise, which prevented the Tank Brigade from moving to the canal bank during the hours of darkness. He also required the Mobile Force to be prepared to take part in a major battle immediately following the raid. These stipulations significantly limited Lindsay's flexibility.[31]

Burnett-Stuart's restrictions were exacerbated by Lindsay and Hobart's difficulty in arriving at a mutually agreeable plan. Lindsay's original concept was to advance on the first day along a broad front in three or four columns, with the motorized infantry and armored cars racing forward to secure crossings over the canal. On the second day several tank columns were to pass through the infantry units, conduct their various raids, and return to the near side of the canal by nightfall.[32] Hobart objected that this plan would overtax the Tank Brigade. He said that 20 percent of the obsolete Vickers Medium Mark IIs would be lost to mechanical failure alone, that the brigade did not have sufficient radios to maneuver on a front wider than eight miles, and that the supply echelon could not be divided into three or four units.[33] Lindsay accepted Hobart's objections and worked up a plan calling on the

Mobile Force to make an extended march around the 1st Division's flank; it would move by night and lie up by day to perform maintenance. The main attack would be on the third day of the exercise.[34]

In forwarding the plan to Burnett-Stuart, Lindsay concealed the true motive behind it and stated that he "planned a much longer and more extended operation in order to test out every component of the Mobile Force, and whether success is obtained or not, I consider this method will produce results of far more importance than would a faster and less ambitious operation."[35] Burnett-Stuart replied that he considered the plan too ambitious and told Lindsay not to "run the risk of queering the pitch of armoured force development in trying too much and so risking a spectacular failure!"[36] Although not compelled by Burnett-Stuart to change his plan, Lindsay deferred to his obvious wishes. His third plan called for an advance by the 7th Brigade to the canal crossings on the first day, with the Tank Brigade moving up in a single bound the following night. Details of the final assault were to be worked out as the exercise progressed. This plan had the two-fold disadvantage of indicating the precise direction of the Tank Brigade's attack over twenty-four hours before it made its move and of leaving the details of the decisive phase of the operation completely undefined.

Lindsay's final plan was probably the best that could have been devised in light of the limited time available, the inadequacies of the Mobile Force staff, and Hobart and Burnett-Stuart's objections to the alternatives.[37] It did not, however, prove effective in execution. The infantry elements moved forward and seized the canal crossings on cue, but they were subjected to heavy air attacks while waiting for the Tank Brigade to join them. Lindsay attempted to devise a number of expedients to hasten the intervention of the Tank Brigade, but Hobart felt that the whole exercise had become a farce and refused to cooperate.[38] The element of surprise was thus lost and with it all hope of the Mobile Force's success. On the afternoon of the second day, Burnett-Stuart directed Lindsay to withdraw his force just as Lindsay had decided to request permission to do so. In the meantime General Kennedy had audaciously sent the motorized elements of the 1st Division around behind the Mobile Force to establish roadblocks and sever its line of retreat. This move was abetted by the umpiring staff, which had consistently intervened in favor of the infantry forces throughout the exercise. Despite these difficulties Lindsay and Hobart salvaged their force by dividing it into multiple columns and withdrawing around Kennedy's main obstacles.

In his critique of the exercise Burnett-Stuart attempted to provide some perspective and balance in interpreting the results.[39] He admitted from the outset that he had designed the exercise to correct a natural tendency to exaggerate the Tank Brigade's powers, but he also cautioned against magnifying the significance of the Mobile Forces' failure. He praised General Kennedy for his bold offensive action, but also pointed out that far more road crater-

Armored formation passing reviewing party at Southern Command Review, 1934. (Courtesy of the Burnett-Stuart family.)

ing and mine laying had been allowed by the umpire staff than would have occurred in reality.[40] He reiterated the constraints placed on the Mobile Force and admitted that he had taken advantage of Lindsay's "broad shoulders" in putting him in such a difficult position. Regarding the exercise itself, however, he criticized Lindsay's final plan for its concentration and directness and suggested that a better plan would have been to attack with multiple columns, each composed to accomplish its particular mission. He was obviously unaware that this had been Lindsay's original concept. He then praised Hobart for the intensity, keenness, and progress of the Tank Brigade's training in 1934. He pointed out, however, that the brigade had certain weaknesses: It was in the habit of traveling in a large group, which made it unwieldy and subject to attacks from the air; it was too certain of its invulnerability, which caused it not to think seriously about enemy capabilities; and finally, it was luxurious in its ideas of logistical support, which tied it to a vulnerable supply tail. He concluded his analysis with another warning against arriving at conclusions too hastily.

    The content of the critique as well as Burnett-Stuart's correspondence with Lindsay before and during the exercise directly refute the notion put forward by Liddell Hart and others that Burnett-Stuart deliberately sabotaged the Mobile Force exercise in order to boost the morale of the infantry.[41] While he was obviously concerned with restoring the infantry's self-confidence, which had been somewhat pummeled in the previous three years' exercises, he was just as concerned with making Hobart and other members

General Burnett-Stuart and Brigadier Hobart on the latter's command tank, Salisbury Plain, circa 1935. (Courtesy of the Times Newspapers Limited.)

of the Tank Corps think more seriously about the progress that still had to be made, particularly in the areas of tactical dispersion and logistical support. Viewed in light of Burnett-Stuart's experience in Egypt, this exercise made eminent sense. The importance of tactical trials lay not so much in their results as in the lessons that the participants derived from them. Burnett-Stuart had deliberately placed Pile in far more difficult positions than he had put Lindsay and Hobart, but Pile had derived great benefit from dealing with those situations.

The difference in this situation, however, was that in Egypt Burnett-Stuart had been able to influence the atmosphere in which his exercises were conducted and to establish a rational framework for the analysis of their results. He could not do so in England, where a host of interested military observers and press reporters frequently drew their own conclusions based simply on the obvious outcome. Thus, in the case of the Mobile Force exercise, Burnett-Stuart was unable to offset the notion that an experimental formation consisting of two of the army's most modern units had been bested by a conventional infantry division with some attached motorized transport. While it is not accurate to contend that Burnett-Stuart torpedoed the exercise, he does merit some criticism for failing to take account of this different psychological atmosphere.

The significance of the Mobile Force's failure, however, lies not in its causes but in its consequences. Liddell Hart argues that it was largely responsible for impeding the development of armored warfare at the very time Germany was beginning to expand its armored capability.[42] This interpretation seems somewhat exaggerated. It is doubtful that Britain would have been able to match Germany armored division for armored division even if the Mobile Force exercise had succeeded. Furthermore, Montgomery-Massingberd announced his plans for the creation of a mobile division in October 1934, just a month after the experiment. Nevertheless, as Liddell Hart points out, there was a decreased emphasis on experiments involving deep penetrations. The Tank Brigade was instructed to concentrate in 1935 on tactical missions in conjunction with a major force, and the mobile division was visualized as a modernized cavalry division.

The exercise was equally significant, however, for its effect on the internal debate within the Royal Tank Corps over the future form of armored forces. Lindsay received a great deal of criticism for the Mobile Force's failure.[43] He was subsequently posted to India and almost entirely cut off from any future influence on armored doctrine. Hobart emerged as the dominant personality of the Royal Tank Corps and devoted himself to the perfection and promulgation of the Tank Brigade Idea, as opposed to the Mobile Division Idea.[44] Thus the form of Britain's armored units was confirmed largely along the lines indicated by Charles Broad in *Mechanised and Armoured Formations* in 1929 and the Provisional Tank Brigade exercises held in 1931.

The other major factor in the evolution of mechanization and armored warfare in the mid-1930s was the place they would have in the total structure of the British Army. To examine that question, our focus must shift to the War Office.

III

Following the Mobile Force exercise the army adopted a policy of gradual mechanization. Although Montgomery-Massingberd established the objective of forming a Mobile Division at the end of 1934, this objective was not attained by the end of his tenure in April 1936. Even more significantly, failure to define clearly the role of the tank in battle resulted in the policy of gradual mechanization not being accompanied by a coherent body of principles for either mechanization or armored warfare. This failure was due not only to the lack of political leadership in defining the army's role, but also to financial stringency, the interests of traditional arms, and the relationships among the leading military personalities of the day. These factors become evident as one examines War Office policy regarding mechanization and armored warfare from the aftermath of the Mobile Force exercise to the end of Alfred Duff Cooper's tenure as secretary of state for war in mid-1937.

On 15 October 1934 Montgomery-Massingberd informed the members of the Army Council that he had "reached the provisional conclusion that, instead of having an independent Tank Brigade and a Cavalry Division containing two horsed cavalry brigades, a more suitable organization would be a "Mobile Division" consisting of the Tank Brigade and one *mechanized* cavalry brigade, together with an adequate proportion of reconnaissance and supporting troops."[45] There were no significant objections from members of the Army Council, so the implementing directive for the C.I.G.S.' decision was published in December.[46]

There were two positive features in this directive. First, the proposed organization for the Mobile Division was in many ways similar to Lindsay's balanced composition – the major difference was the substitution of a mechanized cavalry brigade for an infantry brigade. Second, there was some provision for this unit to conduct "independent armoured action," though exactly what such action entailed was nowhere spelled out. These advantages were offset, however, by a number of disadvantages. The amalgamation of possible missions assigned to the unit betrayed the lack of a clear concept of whether it was to be regarded primarily as a cavalry division in modern guise, or if it was to be an independent force capable of making the deep penetrations advocated by Lindsay and Liddell Hart. Furthermore, the substitution of mechanized, or more properly, motorized cavalry for infantry meant that the soldiers whose task it would be to cooperate with the tanks would not be well-versed in the techniques of fighting on foot. And perhaps most significantly, the method of experimentation dictated that the organization of the mechanized cavalry regiment would have to be well in hand before the Mobile Division could be formed.[47]

In November 1934 Col. G. N. Macready, deputy director of staff duties for organization, explained the thinking behind the decision to form a Mobile Division as well as other matters concerning the army's future at an R.U.S.I. lecture chaired by Montgomery-Massingberd.[48] Colonel Macready stated that the primary factor affecting the army's organization was its diversity of functions – garrisoning the Empire, protecting trade routes, dealing with minor military contingencies, and simultaneously being prepared to intervene on the Continent. The essence of the problem therefore was how to develop "the best and most modern field force compatible with the limits imposed by the Cardwell System."[49] Macready also discussed in some detail the limits of modernization imposed by financial stringency.

In his summing-up remarks, Montgomery-Massingberd articulated his rationale for the policy of gradual mechanization:

One of the most important points Colonel Macready brought out was the danger of going too fast in mechanization. The more one goes into that problem, the more one realizes that, unless we go cautiously, we shall land ourselves in difficulties. . . . if we mechanize too quickly, we may find that in a year or two the larger part of the tanks or machine-gun carriers . . . may very probably be out of

A Cruiser Tank, Mark I, the A9. This tank represented one of several attempts to replace the aging Vickers Medium Mark II. The Vickers Medium Mark III, designed in 1928, was a significant advance but was unaffordable. The A9, designed in 1934 by Sir John Carden, was more economical, but it did not go into even limited production until 1937 because of financial stringency. (Courtesy of the Tank Museum.)

date. I am therefore quite convinced in my own mind that what we have to do is to go steadily along, going to production to a limited extent whenever we have found a really good article and whenever we can get the money, and at the same time to experiment as hard as we can . . . so that if war looms on the horizon again we may be in a position to go into production at once with the latest pattern on the stocks. I am quite certain that that is the only way we can possibly carry on with our limited resources.[50]

The Army Estimates for 1935 demonstrated to some extent the economic stringency to which Montgomery-Massingberd referred. The original figure for army expenditure of £43,550,000 represented an increase of 10 percent over 1934, but was still below the £44,500,000 voted in 1929.[51] In response to this increase Aneuran Bevan reminded the House of the statement made by Lord Hailsham in 1933 that the army was one of the most efficient and highly mechanized in the world: Bevan then accused the government of engineering a deliberate scare program.[52] The opposition was not, however, monolithic. A definite Labour sentiment was expressed that the army should be modernized and that the cavalry in particular should be reduced or eliminated, and Clement Attlee asked a number of pointed questions that suggested the army was taking too long in settling upon a definite organization for the Tank Brigade.[53]

The Royal Tank Corps was the major group objecting to Montgomery-Massingberd's policy. Shortly after the experimental mechanization of one squadron of the 3d Hussars was announced, Hobart, Lindsay, Tilly, Hotblack, and others submitted a paper to the director of military training which argued that although cavalrymen were capable of learning to handle armored cars, the requirements of tank driving, maintenance, and gunnery demanded men specially trained in the Tank Corps school system. They further maintained that the army should develop future armored formations by expanding the R.T.C. rather than by converting cavalry units into tank units.[54]

While Burnett-Stuart did not become directly engaged in this dispute between Montgomery-Massingberd and the Tank Corps, his ideas not only on military organization but also on Britain's strategic priorities and the most likely form of a future European war diverged sharply from those of the C.I.G.S. These divergences were exacerbated by differences in personality and temperament and led to an ever-widening gulf between the two men. The most obvious difference between the two lay in their concepts of loyalty and the role of independent thought. To Montgomery-Massingberd loyalty meant unquestioning obedience. To Burnett-Stuart loyalty meant using one's powers of intelligence to best advantage. In his first training conference held at Southern Command, he told his subordinates,

> What I really want is that you should ponder deeply all matters that concern you and your men . . . & that if after that, you have any contribution to make towards the solution of the many difficult problems that confront us, you should say exactly what you think . . . it is not the person with well-thought-out opposite views who makes a decision difficult, it is the pedant, the time-server, & the shallow-thinker who confuses the issue.[55]

Burnett-Stuart also differed with Montgomery-Massingberd over the general outline of a future war in Europe. In 1935 the War Office and Air Ministry conducted a map exercise to test their plans for the mobilization of the field force and its dispatch to the Continent. As head of the German syndicate, Burnett-Stuart was responsible for developing the German concept of operations. Based on what he felt were British and French expectations of an attack on Belgium, the logistical difficulties of a long march through that country, and the low morale of French troops manning the Maginot Line, he proposed

> to attack in a S.W. direction across the frontier between Belgium and the RHINE with the object of breaking through the French defenses on a 50 mile front, exploiting the breakthrough with the mechanized divisions and tank brigades, followed by fresh troops, and so establishing a wide bridgehead in France from which such further operations as may be necessary can be undertaken.[56]

This plan and the analysis that lay behind it were uncannily accurate forecasts of Lt. Gen. Erich von Manstein's thinking in the winter of 1939–1940, which led to the decisive German victory in the Flanders campaign. It was, however, voted down by Montgomery-Massingberd, who predicted a German advance into Belgium à la 1914.[57]

The two men were also poles apart regarding British strategy. Based on his perception of the army's appalling lack of readiness for a European war as well as the needs of the Empire, Burnett-Stuart was an ardent advocate of limited liability.[58] Montgomery-Massingberd, on the other hand, was an equally ardent supporter of the Continental commitment.[59] Given their fundamental divergences on matters of policy, their antipathetic value systems, and distinctly different temperaments, it is little wonder that relations between Burnett-Stuart and Montgomery-Massingberd continued to deteriorate.[60]

In September 1935 Montgomery-Massingberd prepared a comprehensive plan for the organization of the army that he felt would provide a force capable of effective intervention in a European war. This plan was presented to the new secretary of state for war, Viscount Halifax, in September 1935.[61] It envisioned the initial use of the field force as a "strategic reserve . . . to move in support of the Belgians and Dutch where hard pressed or to relieve the pressure by an unexpected counter-stroke," which would require a small, well-trained rapidly moving force capable of "stubborn resistance and possessed of great offensive power."[62] To achieve this capability, Montgomery-Massingberd reiterated his desire for the formation of a Mobile Division consisting of a tank brigade and mechanized cavalry units and informed Halifax of the changes contemplated in the organization of infantry brigades and motorization of divisional transport. He foresaw, however, the need for even greater power for infantry units and suggested that a larger proportion of tanks would have to be made available to the infantry divisions. He also stated the need for a permanent commander and staff to be found for the Mobile Division.

With his plans for the organization of the army thus drafted and perhaps also aware of his failing powers of concentration and vigor, Montgomery-Massingberd began to look seriously for a successor to whom he could entrust the army's future.[63] The most prominent candidates were General Sir John Gathorne-Hardy, G.O.C.-in-C., Aldershot Command; General Sir Cyril Deverell, G.O.C.-in-C., Eastern Command; and Burnett-Stuart. However, when the War Office announced that the 1935 maneuvers, dubbed by many as the "C.I.G.S. Stakes," would be conducted between Aldershot Command and Eastern Command with Burnett-Stuart acting as the chief umpire, it was fairly obvious that he had been excluded from the running.[64] In the course of the maneuvers, Deverell artfully concealed a division on the southern flank of Gathorne-Hardy's corps, and when the latter attacked north on the third day of the exercise, Deverell struck a decisive blow that was adjudged to have been completely successful.[65] On 19 October, just one month after the victory of Eastern Command over Aldershot Command, the king announced the appointment of General Deverell as chief of the Imperial General Staff, effective April 1936.[66]

In the meantime Montgomery-Massingberd continued his policy of gradual mechanization. The War Office decision concerning the organization of the Mobile Division did not reflect clear thinking on the division of functions between cavalry and tanks. As announced in December 1935 the Mobile Division was to consist of the Tank Brigade, two mechanized cavalry regiments, and one cavalry light tank regiment.[67] Henceforth, there would be three types of cavalry regiments: those equipped with armored cars, those equipped with four-wheeled trucks, and those equipped with light tanks. It was also decided in December 1935 to adopt the experimental infantry brigade organization of three rifle battalions and a machine-gun battalion.[68] This completed the reorganization of the army along the lines contemplated by Montgomery-Massingberd and provides a convenient point at which to assess his accomplishments as C.I.G.S.

Taken as a whole, Montgomery-Massingberd's tenure as C.I.G.S. was moderately progressive regarding the development of materiel, but conservative and uncertain regarding the development of doctrine. The mechanization of cavalry was a major accomplishment, and Montgomery-Massingberd was probably one of the few who could have done it. He also accelerated the motorization of the infantry division's transport, put the Tank Brigade on a permanent footing, and directed the formation of the Mobile Division. Under his aegis the 25-pdr. gun-howitzer, Bren gun, Bren gun carrier, and Boys antitank rifle were tested and procured.[69]

Offsetting these gains in materiel was an assumption that the army would fight the next war essentially as it had fought World War I.[70] The primary purpose of the Mobile Division would be to cover the advance of the Expeditionary Force as the Cavalry Division had done in 1914, after which it would perform the other traditional cavalry tasks of screening, reconnaissance, and occasional raids. The infantry divisions were to have mechanized transport for more rapid movement, but they were also to have a large amount of fire support from heavy artillery and slowly moving tanks in order to help them break the foreseen stalemate. This combination of traditional infantry-cavalry-artillery ideas concerning how best to fight in the 1918 pattern was competing with a completely different doctrine – that of independent armored operations deep in the enemy's rear. Montgomery-Massingberd's decision to form the Tank Brigade represented a relatively minor concession to this concept and served mainly to create doubt as to what British armored doctrine really was.

Given the dichotomy between the extent of his material accomplishments and the inadequacy of his concepts, the balance appears to be negative. At a time when Britain was just entering a period of rearmament, ideas were more important than weapons, and Montgomery-Massingberd's outdated and unclear ideas decisively and adversely affected the evolution of British military doctrine in the years before World War II.[71]

This critical juncture in the history of British doctrinal development provides a useful place to examine the reasons Burnett-Stuart was not selected as C.I.G.S. He appears to have been the most intelligent of the candidates, as well as being the most experienced in the techniques of modern warfare.[72] While the major reason for his nonselection appears to have been his clash with Montgomery-Massingberd, one has to look deeper. Neither the national mood nor the political climate favored a head of the army who habitually spoke his mind with little regard for other people's prejudices. Pacifism was still strong, and the National Government had just been confirmed in office with a mandate to muddle its way out of the depression and go slowly on rearmament. In such a climate Deverell probably appeared to be a safer candidate than Burnett-Stuart.[73] Perhaps if Burnett-Stuart had been more circumspect toward his superiors and more sympathetic toward less-competent comtemporaries, he could have attained the position of C.I.G.S. To have done so, however, would have required a change in nature that was probably beyond his capability.[74] Thus Burnett-Stuart's story assumes some of the elements of a tragedy–tragic for him because he would be unable to make the contributions for which a lifetime of experience and reflection had so admirably prepared him, and tragic for the army because it would not have his capable leadership at a time of impending international crisis.

In the event, the army's leadership in the remaining years of de facto peace did not provide firm, competent direction. This was true in part because neither Duff Cooper, the new secretary of state for war, nor Cyril Deverell, the new C.I.G.S., had a clear sense of what had to be done, and throughout 1936 both were attempting to learn their jobs. Duff Cooper's appointment made a great deal of sense.[75] He recognized the need for ideas on military policy from outside the War Office. In December 1935 he approached Liddell Hart for his views. The two worked out an arrangement to hold confidential discussions on military matters, after which Duff Cooper would take care not to reveal the source of any new ideas presented to the Army Council, and Liddell Hart would retain the freedom to criticize War Office policy in the *Times*.[76]

Duff Cooper's conduct of office, however, revealed an inability to move the Army Council in meaningful reform. In early 1936 he suggested to the adjutant general, General Sir Harry Knox, that a committee should be assembled to examine the possibility of scrapping the Cardwell system in favor of a long-service army in India and, by implication, a home army prepared for Continental warfare.[77] General Knox had a draft proposal prepared, but in forwarding it to Sir Herbert Creedy, the permanent under-secretary, he remarked that he saw no alternative to the Cardwell system so long as a large British force was required in India.[78] Creedy concurred. Deverell recommended that any substantive change be put off until 1939, and that in the interim the army should decide on an ideal size and organization of the field force and overseas garrisons as a prelude to a comprehensive study of the British military system.[79] Duff Cooper accepted Deverell's recommendation and with it laid to rest any ideas of significant reform in the immediate future.[80]

The circulating minutes regarding reform of the Cardwell system suggested that Duff Cooper wanted to make basic changes, but that he did not know how to goad the military leaders into action. With his political stock in late 1936 also falling as a result of his bitter Cabinet debates with Chamberlain over reequipping the territorial army, Duff Cooper's days as secretary of state for war were rapidly drawing to a close.

Deverell also wanted to make changes, but was inhibited both by the pressures of rearmament and the attitudes of his military colleagues. He re-established communication between Liddell Hart and the military side of the War Office and took steps to involve the commanding generals of the home commands in War Office decisions.[81] Nevertheless, his concepts for the reorganization of the army were not significantly different from Montgomery-Massingberd's.

Unlike Montgomery-Massingberd, however, he was unable to keep his more conservative colleagues in check. At the end of 1936 there were a number of rumors in circulation that the Army Council, at Knox's instigation, had tentatively decided to remove the Tank Brigade from the Mobile Division. Hobart despairingly interpreted this as a move eventually to disperse the Tank Brigade into a number of infantry support battalions and thus emasculate the Royal Tank Corps.[82] While it is difficult to establish the veracity of Hobart's statements concerning the Army Council's intention, it does appear that Deverell was having a difficult time controlling the Army Council. His difficulties were also evident in the fact that at the end of 1936 no firm decision had been made concerning who would command the Mobile Division.

The state of the British Army in late 1936 was certainly not cause for optimism. The field force had been neglected for years and was just beginning to get modern equipment. Commitments in Palestine and Egypt as well as inadequate recruiting had placed a severe drain on personnel. And perhaps most significantly, no clear-cut ideas had been developed to guide the army in its preparation for a European war.

The 1937 Army Estimates reflect a continuation of the policy of mechanization as opposed to armored warfare, but at a more rapid rate than that of 1934–1936. Including an appropriation of just over £19 million under the Defence Loan Act, the total was slightly more than £82 million. Of this, approximately £7.6 million, or 9.2 percent of the total, was devoted to wheeled and tracked vehicles. This was opposed to approximately 2.6 percent in 1934, 3.9 percent in 1935, and 6.3 percent in 1936. The amount spent on animals was only £205,500, or .25 percent of the total. This represented a distinct drop from the previous figures of 1.15 percent in 1934, 1.05 percent in 1935, and .70 percent in 1936.[83] There was, however, no mention of the Mobile Division in Duff Cooper's Army Estimates speech.

Since there was still no basic decision as to whether it would be designed primarily for use in an imperial emergency or for intervention on the Continent, the vital question of the Tank Brigade's inclusion remained unanswered. Deverell had, however, decided that the motorized cavalry regiments of the Montgomery-Massingberd era were unsuitable, and for 1937 the experimental cavalry brigades each contained two light tank regiments and one mechanized infantry battalion. The tentative nature of the organization was complicated by equipment shortages. Only one of the two experimental cavalry regiments was fully equipped with light tanks, most of which were outdated models. Furthermore, the machine-gun carriers for both the cavalry regiments and the mechanized infantry battalion were unavailable and had to be represented by light trucks.[84]

In the absence of definite guidance from the War Office concerning the role of the Mobile Division, Burnett-Stuart formulated his own. He presented his ideas at a Southern Command exercise in April 1937, defining the role of the Mobile Division as follows:

It is *not* an independent armoured force to be sent careering over the country against long-distance objectives. . . . And it is *not* designed to form part with other Mobile Divisions of a mobile mass of manoeuvre of the continental scale and after the continental model.

It is the mobile component of a force of one or two normal Corps, in exactly the same way as the old cavalry used to be the mobile component – making allowance of course on the one hand for its increased speed and range of action, its armour, and great sensitiveness to ground. Its job is to provide the medium, as opposed to the close, protection of the force when on the move; to engage by offensive action the enemy mobile troops; to remove by fighting all minor centres of resistance or annoyance from the path of the force; and to cooperate with the force in battle.[85]

In short, it was to act as the covering element of a field force dispatched from England to deal with an imperial emergency. It is important to note that Burnett-Stuart did not rule out the possibility of armored divisions being used to conduct independent operations or to form a concentrated mobile arm of decision. He only stipulated that the priority of imperial defense made such roles inappropriate for British formations.

While Burnett-Stuart was discussing the composition of the Mobile Division based on the diverse demands of imperial defense, Duff Cooper was fighting a losing battle in the Cabinet. From December 1936 to May 1937, the Cabinet vehemently debated the role of the army, with Chamberlain the champion of limited liability and Duff Cooper the untiring advocate of the Continental commitment. On 5 May the Cabinet accepted the C.I.D.'s decision to limit funding of the territorial army to £9 million, thus giving it sufficient equipment with which to train but not to deploy rapidly to the Continent in an emergency.[86] When Stanley Baldwin retired as prime minister later that month, Chamberlain became "undisputed master of the field."[87] Chamberlain may have reasoned that Duff Cooper's dismissal from the Cabinet would incur the displeasure of Churchill and others advocating a stronger defense effort and that his abilities could be put to better use elsewhere, but it was clear that he could no longer be tolerated as secretary of state for war. In the event, Duff Cooper was offered and accepted the position of First Lord of the Admiralty.[88]

Duff Cooper admitted in his memoirs that he "acquired little credit during my tenure of the War Office."[89] Although this was due in large part to his spirited disagreement with Chamberlain's policy of limited liability, one must look deeper to assess his effectiveness as war minister. Duff Cooper's ability to debate well in Commons has already been noted. He was probably more knowledgeable about military affairs than any secretary of state during the interwar period. He argued in the Cabinet for the politicians to pay attention to the desperate needs of the army at a time when it was distinctly unpopular to do so. He got on well with the military members of the Army Council, and he wisely established the position of director general of munitions production under Admiral Harold Brown. He had, however, no real vision of the army's future; and at a time when he recognized the imminent approach of war, he was unable to generate any momentum for reform. Although Duff Cooper could rightfully claim to have been a friend to the army, he defined being a friend as giving the army leaders what they wanted rather than, as Haldane had done, asking the hard questions to make sure that what the army *wanted* was what it really *needed*.

IV

Chamberlain's choice to succeed Duff Cooper at the War Office was the ambitious and dynamic young minister of transport, Leslie Hore-Belisha. Hore-Belisha was a striking contrast to Duff Cooper. His father, Jacob Isaac Belisha, an insurance company manager of Sephardic Jewish background, had died when his son was an infant.[90] When his mother remarried, she requested that he couple the surname of his stepfather, Adair Hore, with his own. Hore-Belisha served in the Great War as a Royal Army Service Corps officer, ultimately rose to the rank of major, and served as a supply officer in the British headquarters in Salonika. While working as a journalist after the war, he developed a reputation for colorful writing and close observation of political affairs. After a flamboyant campaign in Devenport, he entered Parliament at the age of twenty-nine as a Liberal. He was one of the few Liberals to survive the election of 1924.

In 1931 he maneuvered a portion of the Liberal Party into the National Government and thereby won himself an appointment as parliamentary secretary to the Board of Trade. In 1932 he was made financial secretary to the Treasury, apparently at the request of Neville Chamberlain. In 1934 he was appointed minister of transport. Here his reforming zeal and his flair for publicity were put to excellent effect. When Hore-Belisha assumed office, motor traffic conditions in Britain were almost entirely unregulated. The new minister enacted provisions for testing new drivers, revised the highway code, and significantly reduced the number of traffic accidents. The black-and-white-striped poles topped with garish orange lights that were used to mark pedestrian crossings soon became known as Belisha Beacons, which did nothing to hurt his political career. He arrived at the War Office with a charter from Chamberlain to make "drastic changes" in an institution in which, according to the prime minister, "the obstinancy of some of the Army heads in sticking to obsolete methods is incredible."[91]

Shortly after leaving the War Office, Duff Cooper arranged a meeting between Hore-Belisha and Liddell Hart.[92] Liddell Hart informed Hore-Belisha that he was preparing a paper for Sir Thomas Inskip, minister for coordination of defense, on how the army might be reorganized to perform better in light of modern conditions. The new secretary of state requested a copy, and upon receipt was so impressed with its content that he had it reproduced and circulated among the General Staff for comment. Thus was born the Hore-Belisha/Liddell Hart "partnership." This combination of dynamic, reforming secretary of state and thoughtful, analytical adviser seemed to offer great promise for the army. Unfortunately, the temperamental blindness of both men, an aversion to outside influence on the part of the High Command, and the imminence of war, which transformed the struggle for reform into an almost naked battle for power and influence, doomed the partnership to eventual defeat.

While Hore-Belisha and Liddell Hart were beginning their reform program at the War Office, Burnett-Stuart was continuing his study of the Mobile Division.[93] He presented his findings at a conference in early September. His major contention was that the Tank Brigade should not be included in what was predominantly lightly armored cavalry formation. Rather, it should be retained as a separate unit that would be employed when its heavy assault characteristics were required. He also felt that the cavalry scouts should be grouped into separate squadrons rather than dispersed into every troop. This would allow them to conduct missions such as temporarily screening the

The "partnership": Leslie Hore-Belisha and B. H. Liddell Hart. (Courtesy of the Liddell Hart Centre for Military Archives.)

withdrawal of tanks and would prevent the tanks from having to rely on the mechanized infantry on such occasions. As a further cure for what he felt to be the misuse of mechanized infantry, he recommended that the cavalry brigade consist of three light tank regiments instead of two and that the infantry battalions be placed under divisional control rather than being part of the cavalry brigade. Burnett-Stuart's detailed comments on training that followed these general observations demonstrated a knowledgeable and sophisticated understanding of armored cavalry and mechanized infantry tactics. His honest effort to educate his subordinates helped create "a great feeling of satisfaction and . . . confidence in the Commander-in-Chief as a man who was leading us out of the 1914–1918 age into what we knew was coming."[94] This was especially true of the "recently dismounted Cavalry [who] looked to him as the one General who could show them the way in their new armoured role."[95]

While Burnett-Stuart was lecturing on armored cavalry tactics at Southern Command, Hobart, who had recently been appointed deputy director of staff duties for A.F.V., was lobbying in the General Staff for the acceptance of armored units.[96] One was to be an Army Reconnaissance Formation composed of two armored cavalry brigades. The other was to be a Tank Division consisting of a tank brigade, an armored cavalry brigade, and a "holding group" containing mechanized infantry, antiaircraft, antitank, artillery, and engineer formations. It is interesting to note that in Hobart's proposal the Army Reconnaissance Formation, which had a role similar to the one Burnett-Stuart prescribed for the Mobile Division, did not contain a tank brigade. The difference, however, was that Hobart was designing his formations for Continental war. Hence he also wanted a tank division that would be capable of conducting independent striking operations and form, along with other such divisions, a force for decisive maneuver.

The controversy over composition of the Mobile Division soon came to a head. The directors of the General Staff recommended that the Tank Brigade not be included in the Mobile Division, which Hobart again interpreted as a thinly veiled attempt to emasculate the Royal Tank Corps. At this juncture Liddell Hart entered the fray.[97] He replied to a letter from Deverell that he was withholding publication of an article on the Mobile Division in the *Times* until he heard further about the Tank Brigade's inclusion. Deverell invited him for lunch on 18 November and argued that the Tank Brigade was "too precious" to be included in the Mobile Division. Liddell Hart countered with the observation that if the Mobile Division without the Tank Brigade met a German armored division it would surely be defeated. On the 19th the War Office announced that the Mobile Division would consist of the 1st and 2d Cavalry Brigades, the Tank Brigade, and other supporting units. This was an anomalous organization. As Burnett-Stuart had pointed out, the Tank Brigade was not required for the traditional covering force mission, particularly in an imperial war. On the other hand, as Liddell Hart had observed in a memorandum to Hore-Belisha on 16 November, for real striking power the division should have two tank brigades and only one armored cavalry brigade. Thus the final organization of the Mobile Division was the product of a compromise between two competing power groups in the army rather than any coherent concept of its role in war.

The selection of a commander for the new division was the product of a similar compromise. This was partly due to the mechanics of the promotion system and partly to the personalities involved. The promotion of officers to the ranks of brigadier and major general and their subsequent appointments were controlled by the War Office Selection Committee. This committee made recommendations to the secretary of state as the final approving authority.[98] Therefore, the question of who was to command the Mobile Division, a major general's position, required a consensus between the mem-

bers of the Selection Committee and the secretary of state. Deverell felt that
since the Mobile Division was composed primarily of cavalry units, the post
should go to a cavalryman. His nominee, approved by the Selection Committee, was Maj. Gen. John Blakiston-Houston, former commander of the
2d Cavalry Brigade and commandant of the Equitation School.[99]

Although Blakiston-Houston had an excellent record as a cavalryman, Lt.
Gen. Lord Gort, Hore-Belisha's new military secretary, referred to him as
one of the "unsound horses" being put forward by the Selection Committee; he told Ironside that Hore-Belisha was "too clever to buy duds."[100]
Liddell Hart argued that since the Mobile Division was primarily an armored
formation, it should be commanded by a man whose experience was with
tanks rather than horses.[101] He advised Hore-Belisha to hold out for the
appointment of Broad, Hobart, or Pile to command the division. The issue
remained deadlocked for several weeks. Deverell refused to nominate anyone
other than Blakiston-Houston, and Hore-Belisha, fortified by repeated conversations with Liddell Hart, insisted upon an R.T.C. officer. A solution
was finally adopted whereby Maj. Gen. Alan Brooke, an excellent gunner
but a man with no experience in training of mobile troops, was appointed to
command the Mobile Division, and Hobart was designated to replace Brooke
at D.M.T. Thus the Mobile Division was destined to begin life with both its
composition and its commander decided by compromise rather than logic.

The prolonged controversy over the command of the Mobile Division
convinced Hore-Belisha that in order to reform the army he would have to
have a new Army Council. He was extremely disappointed in a report he
commissioned on possible reform of the Cardwell system and felt that both
his parliamentary and his military advisers were conspiring against him.[102]
He felt that Hugh Elles, the M.G.O., was "exhausted and full of nerves."[103]
He called General Knox, the A.G., "the chief obstructionist in the War
Office."[104] But his fundamental difference was with Deverell over the size of
the garrison in India. Liddell Hart had convinced Hore-Belisha that the
introduction of airplanes and mechanized transport allowed the size of the
British contingent in India to be drastically reduced. Deverell replied that he
had "been there twelve years and I tell you that you cannot reduce it."[105] In
response to this opposition Hore-Belisha sent a note to Chamberlain in late
October outlining the psychological hindrances that had to be overcome at
the War Office before meaningful reform could be accomplished.

Hore-Belisha was determined to get at the top a much younger man than
the 63-year-old Deverell. The leading candidates appear to have been Maj.
Gen. Archibald Wavell, 54; Lt. Gen. John Dill, 56; General Edmund Ironside,
57; Maj. Gen. Ronald Adam, 52; Maj. Gen. Frederick Pile, 53; and Lt.
Gen. Lord Gort, 51. Wavell was felt by many, including Gort, to be the
most promising man for the job.[106] Hore-Belisha, however, felt that the
C.I.G.S. needed to be outwardly impressive and that Wavell was too taci-

turn.[107] Dill was felt by many to be one of the finest leaders in the army, but was apparently rejected because of rumors of his indecisiveness while commanding in Palestine.[108] Ironside was the most senior of the younger progressive officers, but Liddell Hart felt that he would be better suited for commander-in-chief in India than C.I.G.S.[109] Adam was one of the most intelligent of the candidates, and he had impressed Hore-Belisha enough to have been appointed commandant of the Staff College; but he was also the most junior, having only recently been promoted to temporary major general.[110] Pile was the most dynamic of the lot, and his case was strongly championed by Liddell Hart as the one true reformer; but he too was quite junior and his selection divisive.[111] That left Gort. But Gort was a commander rather than a staff officer, and he did not want the job. He would have preferred to see Wavell as C.I.G.S., with himself appointed inspector general with authority to supervise all training and designation as commander of the expeditionary force in the event of war.[112]

Hore-Belisha felt, however, that Gort's peerage and Victoria Cross would make him a popular choice. He also felt that by appointing Adam as deputy C.I.G.S. there would be enough brain-power at the top for Gort to handle the staff duties.[113] Hore-Belisha acted quickly to obtain approval of these and other moves.[114] On 3 December the War Office announced far-reaching changes in the Army High Command. Deverell was retired as C.I.G.S., with Gort as the designated successor; Knox was replaced as A.G. by Maj. Gen. Clive Liddell; and Elles was eased out as M.G.O., and his job was fused with that of the director general of munitions production.[115] Hore-Belisha also used this opportunity to reveal Wavell's appointment as G.O.C.-in-C., Southern Command, to succeed Burnett-Stuart, who was due to retire the following April.[116] Hore-Belisha's victory over the old guard was thus seemingly complete. It was not, however, without qualifications. Having picked his own team and traumatized the Army Council once, he could not lightly undertake such action again.

The ensuing six months were marked by an almost constant struggle between the Army Council on one side and Liddell Hart on the other, with Hore-Belisha caught in the middle. Liddell Hart felt that the air defense of Great Britain should be the army's number one priority, followed by the defense of the Empire. Gort—strongly supported by Maj. Gen. Henry Pownall, the new director of military operations and intelligence—argued that the absolute commitment to air defense was having an adverse effect on Britain's ability to fight on the Continent. Hore-Belisha temperamentally sided with Liddell Hart but was ultimately forced to reach a modus vivendi with Gort.

This conflict took place in the context of Cabinet decisions affecting the army's strategic priorities. On 8 November Chamberlain convened a meeting with Hore-Belisha, Inskip, and other key Cabinet members at which it was decided that home air defense was to receive absolute priority in the army's expenditure for war material.[117] And on 22 December the Cabinet formally approved "cooperation in the defence of territories of any allies we may have in war" as the armed services' last priority, to be met only after defense of Great Britain, preservation of trade routes, and protection of the Empire had been fully provided.[118] Hore-Belisha fully supported this decision, reasoning that when the French learned that the British would not provide an expeditionary force on the outbreak of war, they would be motivated to extend the Maginot Line to the sea.[119] This put him at complete loggerheads with Gort and Pownall, who reasoned, more accurately, that political pressure from France and the necessity to defend the low countries would compel Britain to provide an expeditionary force in the event of a Continental war, no matter what the cost. The General Staff, however, had no choice but to revise its thinking in accordance with the Cabinet's declaration of priorities.

The first step of this process was the preparation of a comprehensive statement entitled "The Organisation of the Army for Its Role in War." Shortly before Christmas Hore-Belisha gave Gort a preliminary draft, based heavily on Liddell Hart's ideas.[120] Gort's revision included so much military detail that Hore-Belisha found it almost unintelligible.[121] Pownall made the next effort amidst a number of difficult circumstances, but his too fell short of Hore-Belisha's standard.[122] At the end of January Hore-Belisha requested Liddell Hart's assistance. Liddell Hart argued that the Cabinet's proposed "ideal" air defense scheme of approximately 1,200 guns and 4,700 searchlights should be regarded as a minimum scheme, not a maximum. In a paper entitled "The Army-Basic Needs," he argued that since the air defense was provided by the territorial army it would not affect the regular army. Several days later Liddell Hart said that the final memorandum "must make it plain to the Cabinet that the effective reorganisation of the Army depended upon a solution of the Indian difficulty."[123] The paper went through several more drafts, with Hore-Belisha shuttling it back and forth between Gort, Pownall, and Liddell Hart. The final version, presented to the Cabinet on 16 February 1938, did suggest that the British Army in India should be reduced. On the most important issue of air defense, however, the War Office recommended only a total of 640 guns and approximately 3,000 lights.[124] Hore-Belisha was already beginning to lean toward the General Staff and away from Liddell Hart.

This was the result of an intense behind-the-scenes clash of personalities. Although Gort had actively collaborated with Liddell Hart on a wide variety of questions during his tenure as military secretary, he did a complete volte-face upon becoming C.I.G.S. In a meeting with Liddell Hart on 21 January, he said, "We mustn't upset the people in the clubs by going too fast—we must give them time to get over the shock of the Army Council changes."[125] When Liddell Hart produced his "Basic Needs" paper at the end of January,

Gort, Pownall, and Dill scorned it as the work of an amateur.[126] Gort, who had become almost obsessed with eradicating the idea that Liddell Hart was running the army, went through waves of depression and frequently contemplated resignation.[127] These animosities were exacerbated by Hore-Belisha's disingenuousness. In his early months at the War Office, he had conspicuously advertised his association with Liddell Hart, but when he perceived that this was more a liability than an asset, he pretended not to know Liddell Hart at all.[128] This sham did little to fool the military leaders.

In presenting the Army Estimates for 1938, Hore-Belisha put on an impressive performance, demonstrating historical grasp, parliamentary skill, and his sincere concern for the welfare of the private soldier.[129] He cited Cardwell and Haldane's reforms, which had established the form and organization of the army, but argued that modern means of transporting troops overseas and moving them on land once they arrived had created conditions that allowed for adjustment to the number of troops stationed abroad, especially in India. He announced an agreement by Chamberlain to begin discussions between the War Office and the India Office to address this issue.[130] He articulated the rationale for creation of a deputy C.I.G.S. position in order to "abbreviate the hiatus between consideration and decision."[131] He outlined many steps he had taken to improve the soldier's quality of life – more regular promotion, increased allowances for overseas service, better food, vocational training, and increased pensions. His speech was extremely well received. All external appearances indicated that Hore-Belisha was a popular and successful reformer.

Internally the situation was much different. Two days after the Army Estimates were presented, German troops occupied Austria. The General Staff vociferously argued that Hitler's *Anschluss* demonstrated the folly of placing the Continental commitment in last priority. Hore-Belisha, again caught in a tug of war between Gort and Liddell Hart, began moving closer to his military advisers' line of thinking.[132] In May a disagreement flared up between Liddell Hart and Hore-Belisha on the one hand and the Army Council on the other over the reorganization of the army's air-defense assets. When the *Daily Express* criticized Hore-Belisha for not paying enough attention to air defense, Liddell Hart suggested that he appoint a director general of antiaircraft with direct access to the secretary of state. Hore-Belisha broached the idea to the Army Council at once.[133] Gort, however, felt that this was a cheap publicity stunt and recommended instead the creation of another director of the General Staff who would be under his control.[134] Hore-Belisha persisted, but Gort, Adam, and Liddell, the new A.G., unanimously maintained that a major reorganization was unnecessary. At the end of May Hore-Belisha reached a compromise: There would be a director of antiaircraft and an inspector general for antiaircraft, both under the control of the C.I.G.S.[135]

Another fight soon followed over personalities. Liddell Hart wanted Pile to get the inspector general job, but Gort recommended Brooke. Although Pile had more experience in air defense than Brooke, it appeared to Gort that Hore-Belisha was again lobbying for Liddell Hart's favorites.[136] Liddell Hart felt that Hore-Belisha could push the issue to the point of Gort's resignation based on Pile's greater experience, but Pownall more accurately reflected in his diary that "if he [Hore-Belisha] removes the Army Council twice in six months he cannot survive."[137] After several weeks another compromise was reached in which Maj. Gen. James Marshall-Cornwall was appointed as deputy C.I.G.S. with responsibility for air and coast defense, Brooke was made commander of the newly formed antiaircraft corps, and Pile remained an antiaircraft divisional commander.[138] In a conversation on 27 June Liddell Hart told Hore-Belisha that he would criticize these appointments in the press as inadequate. Hore-Belisha replied that that was Liddell Hart's prerogative, but that his responsibility was to take all the advice he could get and make final decisions based on his own judgment. Within a week of this conversation, the Hore-Belisha/Liddell Hart partnership dissolved, each man feeling he had been dropped by the other.[139]

V

The significance of this struggle for reform can best be assessed in light of the development of mechanization and armored warfare in other armies, the issues around which the reform debate raged, and the personalities involved.

From 1930 to 1938 the German Army made great advances in the development of armored doctrine and organization that offset its inferiority in material preparation. In 1930 Heinz Guderian was posted to command the 3d (Prussian) Motor Transport Battalion, where he worked with companies of dummy tanks and wooden antitank guns to develop the tactics of armored warfare.[140] In early 1934 he demonstrated these techniques at Kummersdorf for an admiring Adolf Hitler.[141] Later that year the *Panzertruppe* was formed as a separate branch of the German Army, with Gen. Oswald Lutz as its head and Guderian its chief of staff. In October 1935 the army decided to create three panzer divisions along the model suggested by Guderian in 1929. Each division contained two tank brigades of two regiments each, an infantry brigade, a motorized artillery regiment, an antitank battalion, and signal and engineer units.[142] These divisions had the mission of conducting deep penetrations and active mobile counterattacks. Coming at the beginning of Germany's rearmament program, this organizational decision "gave the German Army the correct doctrinal insight at a crucial moment."[143] In March 1938 Guderian's panzer troops led the march into Vienna. Although 30 percent of his tanks broke down, the experience provided great political

visibility for armored formations as well as an excellent opportunity to remedy logistical deficiencies.[144]

The French policy of mechanization was governed by the concept of attaining superiority along a linear front. In 1930 one horsed cavalry brigade was
replaced by a regiment of Dragons Portes, or truck-mounted dragoons.[145] In
1934 the first Division Légère Mécanique, or light mechanized division, was
formed. Although its organization was similar to the German panzer division, its roles were limited to strategic reconnaissance and security, the traditional cavalry functions. The same year a young French colonel named
Charles de Gaulle published a book entitled *Vers l'Armée de métier* [Toward
the professional army], which argued that France required an army capable
of making mobile counterattacks against German forces that might penetrate
the frontier.[146] Such an army, de Gaulle maintained, would have to consist
of long-term professionals capable of mastering the technological complexities of armored formations. Although de Gaulle's ideas were championed in
the Chamber of Deputies by Paul Reynaud, they were not politically acceptable.[147] In 1935 General Maurice Gamelin signed a circular reminding officers that the High Command alone was capable of defining doctrine and
that individuals should refrain on all occasions from expressing their personal
thoughts on these matters.[148] And a year later a government commission
headed by General Alphonse Georges concluded that all the principles laid
down in the 1921 instructions remained valid in 1936.[149] Thus, even more
than the British, the French continued to look to the experience of 1918 as
the solution to all tactical and operational questions.

From 1930 to 1938 the Soviet Army made great progress in the development of both materiel and doctrine, but these gains were offset by deficiencies of command and technical education and ultimately undermined by
Joseph Stalin's purges. In the early 1930s threats from Japan in Manchuria
and Germany in the west provided impetus for modernization and
reform.[150] Under the second Five-Year Plan, tank production accelerated,
and by 1935 estimates of Soviet tank strength ranged from three thousand
to ten thousand.[151] Soviet tanks were included in motorized forces and in
the strategic reserve and were also used to support the infantry and cavalry.
This multiplicity of purposes reflects a compromise between the modernizing elements in the Red Army associated with Marshal Mikhail Tukhachevsky
and the more cautious infantry commanders of the Civil War. Nevertheless,
the Soviet field service regulations of 1936 bore Tukhachevsky's unmistak-
able imprint. Mechanized forces, it said,

consisting of tanks, self-propelled artillery and lorry-borne infantry, are able to
carry out independent tasks disengaged from other types of troops, or in cooperation with them. . . . The basic form of operation of the mechanised unity in
combat consists of the tank attack, which must be secured by organised artillery

fire. The manoeuvre and shockblow of the mechanised unity must be supported
by aviation.[152]

The Soviet Army, in summary, was attempting to develop through industrial production an army that combined mass, mobility, and firepower. This
was in contrast to the French emphasis on firepower and mass to the virtual
exclusion of mobility, and the German solution in which mobility was provided by the elite panzer and motorized divisions and firepower and mass by
the foot and horse-mobile infantry divisions. All Soviet doctrinal gains, however, were nullified by Stalin's purges of 1937, which decapitated the High
Command and fell especially hard on the mechanized reformers.[153]

The evolution of American armored doctrine from 1930 to 1938 suffered
from the problems of economic exigencies, traditional thinking at the top,
and the power of the infantry and cavalry branches as separate entities in the
army's organizational structure. The Great Depression and Franklin Delano
Roosevelt's New Deal hamstrung the army for funds and directed many of
its energies into social reconstruction.[154] But most of its doctrinal problems
were internal. In 1931 the new chief of staff, Douglas MacArthur, disbanded
the recently formed Mechanized Force at Fort Eustis and proclaimed the
policy, "Every part of the Army will adopt mechanization and motorization
as far as practicable and possible."[155] This decision meant that American
armored development would proceed in two separate and totally uncoordi-
nated areas – the cavalry and the infantry. One cavalry regiment was mechanized in 1932 and dispatched to Fort Knox. The regiment demonstrated its
flexibility and ability to maneuver over wide distances when opposing two
infantry divisions in the 2d Army maneuvers of 1935, but there was a great
deal of resistance to mechanizing another cavalry regiment in 1936.[156]

There was a similar split in the infantry. Maj. Sereno Brett, commander of
the 1st Tank Regiment at Fort Benning, advocated the inclusion of artillery,
antitank, antiaircraft, communications, reconnaissance, and supply units in
the existing tank organization.[157] He was opposed, however, by his associates, who agreed with MacArthur's pronouncement, "The infantry mission
is to close with the enemy. . . . Its success is a prerequisite to army success;
hence its efforts must not be dispersed in the performance of auxiliary and
supporting missions that can be carried out by other arms."[158] In short, neither the cavalry nor the infantry tank units were able to break out of a
doctrinal straitjacket, and at the end of 1938, the U.S. Army was distinctly behind almost all the major world powers in ideas concerning armored
warfare.

Thus by 1938 the British Army's armored doctrine was still well ahead of
the Americans and also the Soviets, though the latter had not been true
prior to Stalin's purges. The British were roughly even with the French and
lagged seriously behind the Germans in concept, organizational design, and

practical experience in the maneuver of large armored formations over extended distances.

In assessing the struggle for reform in Great Britain during the late 1930s, the major issue was obviously the role of the army. Until that was determined, no meaningful decisions could be made concerning either organization or doctrine. With the addition of air defense as a major task, the dilemma between the imperial and Continental commitments that had plagued the army throughout the interwar years became, in effect, a "trilemma." Given the appalling weakness of the army's antiaircraft forces in 1938, it is hard to say that air defense was not a legitimate concern. The army had neither the guns, searchlights, tracking devices, trained men, nor cohesive units to deal effectively with enemy aircraft.[159] And it is difficult not to empathize with Deverell, Gort, and Pownall, who, having been given the lowest position on the defense totem pole, were told to give absolute priority to a task that was effectively controlled by another service.[160]

One must also have some sympathy for the arguments of Chamberlain, Liddell Hart, and Burnett-Stuart, who, realizing the limitations of Britain's economic, industrial, and military power, felt that in Burnett-Stuart's words, "On the ground, we must have a bye in the first round" of the next European war.[161] Looked at from the point of view of what appeared to be affordable, limited liability made a great deal of sense. It had, however, two fatal weaknesses. The first was that it would be impossible to have several million British citizens in civilian clothes while France was fighting for its life. The second was that a successful German invasion of France and Belgium would put hostile land-based aircraft within striking distance of Great Britain. Those weaknesses were significant enough to make it a very short-sighted strategic concept.

Limited mechanization was consistent with a concept of imperial defense and no land commitment to the Continent, but the doctrine of armored warfare was only germane to the European theater or to the Middle East, if war with a European power were conducted there. Given these facts, there were a number of striking inconsistencies. Liddell Hart, the most outspoken advocate of limited liability in the late 1930s, was also the leader in the struggle for armored warfare. And Deverell, Gort, Pownall, and others who argued vehemently for the preservation of the Continental commitment were openly opposed to armored warfare. The only logically consistent positions were those of Burnett-Stuart, who argued for mechanization and a light form of armored warfare in conjunction with imperial defense, and Hobart, who argued for full-scale capacity for armored warfare in conjunction with the Continental commitment. As was pointed out earlier, the organization of the Mobile Division was a compromise between these two positions, though actually the protagonists in the final decision were Liddell Hart and Deverell rather than Hobart and Burnett-Stuart.

Despite the progress made in the evolution of armored cavalry tactics of 1937, the Mobile Division in 1938 was little more than a conglomeration of assorted units.[162] The army had developed no clear concept of its role and therefore no controlling concept of how its role should be carried out. The relationship between the cavalry regiments and the Tank Brigade was only the beginning of uncertainties. The two mechanized infantry battalions had begun to take form, but despite their cooperation with the armored cavalry regiments, they had not had enough opportunity to develop effective tank-infantry tactics. Nor had there been adequate opportunity for the artillery to develop the techniques for supporting rapidly moving armored formations. The delay in deciding on a commander of the force meant that the different units that had been assembled on Salisbury Plain to form the Mobile Division were still controlled by the headquarters at which they were permanently stationed. The division's supply and administrative units were not gathered together, and many of them, including the maintenance and fuel resupply units, had not even been formed.

Understanding the struggle for reform also requires examination of the leading political and military personalities of the day. The dominant personality of the era was Neville Chamberlain. Even before he became prime minister, he was clearly the most powerful figure in Baldwin's Cabinet. Given Britain's ultimate victory in World War II, one could attempt to justify Chamberlain's policy of economic health before military preparedness. The rigidity with which he adhered to it, however, insisting upon Treasury "approval in detail" on each military expenditure, severely impeded the rearmament program. By attempting to prepare Britain for a long war, Chamberlain came perilously close to having it defeated in a short one. Furthermore, his implicit assumption that Hore-Belisha would be able to reform the War Office without requiring any increase in army expenditures proved totally invalid. As stated earlier, his strategic concepts were equally inappropriate.

Hore-Belisha was a war minister with great promise. He had a charter from the prime minister to make drastic changes, and he had the initial sympathy of a number of thoughtful younger soldiers.[163] By the middle of 1938 he had accomplished a great deal. He had ended the "Buggins' turn next" system of promotion, which had impeded progress for almost two decades, and in so doing had placed a number of able men in positions of authority.[164] He had improved conditions of army life for the private soldier; he had bolstered recruiting; and he had begun to deal in a serious way with the central problem of reducing the garrison in India. Nevertheless, his first year in office was not totally successful because he failed to gain the trust and respect of the senior military men with whom he had to work to be effective.

This failure was the result of his impatience, his lack of sympathy with the senior military professionals, his too-transparent political ambition, and his indiscreet use of Liddell Hart as a military adviser. Hore-Belisha attempted to implement his reform program much too quickly. He commissioned the study of the Cardwell system before he had even begun to change the attitudes of the people most affected by it. He revealed his intention to dismiss the first Army Council before he had had time to consider seriously who the new men would be. And although some of his snap judgments proved sound – as in the cases of Adam and Douglas Brownrigg, his new military secretary – the most vital one did not. Gort was simply not suited to be C.I.G.S., which Hore-Belisha himself realized after it was too late.[165]

Hore-Belisha's lack of sympathy for senior military professionals was evident in his technique of calling them in for brief interviews, which were obviously designed to measure their potential for promotion; his quarrels with the Army Council; and his frequent allusions to its military members as "obstructionist" or "reactionary."[166] This lack of sympathy probably stemmed from differences in social background as well as distinct differences in temperament. Hore-Belisha wanted to become the greatest war minister since Haldane, certainly a legitimate political ambition.[167] But his flair for publicity, which did a great deal to improve the army's recruiting, also gave him the appearance of being a man on the make. He thus disregarded Haldane's example of not appearing to make political gain at the expense of the military.[168] Hore-Belisha's practice of circulating Liddell Hart's papers among the General Staff during the first months of his tenure and his subsequent awkward attempts to conceal the partnership also reveal a lack of balance.

Hore-Belisha and Duff Cooper both ultimately failed as reformers, but for much different reasons. Duff Cooper was too cautious; Hore-Belisha too impetuous. Duff Cooper was overly sympathetic with the High Command and dealt with them too gently; Hore-Belisha was overly unsympathetic and dealt with them too brusquely. Duff Cooper consumed his political capital by defending the General Staff; Hore-Belisha appeared to make political capital by attacking it. Duff Cooper used Liddell Hart's advice discreetly; Hore-Belisha used it recklessly. Hore-Belisha's failures, however, must be weighed against his successes. Whatever his shortcomings, he did have the best interests of the army and the nation at heart, and he did breathe some new life into an institution that needed it badly.

Liddell Hart's role in the struggle for reform borders on tragedy. Intelligent, innovative, eager, and public-spirited, he too rushed in where angels fear to tread – perhaps a reflection of his egocentrism. Not only did he proffer advice on all matters of strategy, policy, organization, and training, he also worked to influence directly promotions and appointments at the highest level. Much of his military advice was sound, especially his emphasis on mobility and flexibility, on tactical quality as opposed to quantity, and on the desirability of developing an imperial reserve for use in the Middle East. Frequently, however, he failed to consider the political realities that influenced military decisions. This was particularly true in the case of India. A major reduction of the garrison there was unacceptable to the government of India, and the earmarking of a proportion of that garrison for defense of the Middle East was unacceptable to the Indians, who were paying for it.

Liddell Hart did not realize until 1938 that the defense of India was the key to the reorganization of the army. This demonstrates the limitations of the military critic, no matter how intelligent, who exists outside the machinery of government. Liddell Hart's advice on appointments had much to commend it also. He was intimately familiar with the personalities of the men involved, and he predicted accurately that the Gort/Adam team would lack the drive to continue Hore-Belisha's program of reform.[169] But his constant championing of Hobart, Pile, Martel, and other advocates of armored warfare gave the impression that no matter how qualified these men were – and they were all highly qualified – Liddell Hart was attempting to maneuver his personal favorites into positions of authority.

It was, therefore, the form of Liddell Hart's advice as much as its substance that alienated him from the army.[170] His obsession with gaining the acceptance of identifiable, discrete ideas may explain why Liddell Hart, who always emphasized the indirect approach in theory, was so startlingly direct in the only chance he really got in life to do something.[171] It also led him into a fatal error. Throughout his "partnership" with Hore-Belisha, he failed to realize how vehemently the Army Council resented the fact that a man with no formal responsibility in the army should have the power not only to influence policy but also to determine their professional destinies.[172]

By taking on the Army Council, Liddell Hart alienated himself from many of the young, progressive officers to whom he had grown so close over the past two decades. It is to his credit that he ultimately realized this. At the end of May 1938 he wrote:

> I am coming to feel that, from a long-term point of view, the most damaging step I've ever taken was to go in with him. Previous to that I was in an unassailable position, standing apart, yet on good terms with most of the rising generation of soldiers. I put forward my ideas in print and could keep up the pressure in print until they were adopted.
>
> Now every suggestion which I put up, *through* H-B, is resisted. And the people I have helped to put in power are trying to cut off my influence. Worse still, they know who are the men of whom I had a high opinion, and are trying to keep them out. Thus it is becoming dangerous to be, and to be known to be, a friend of mine.[173]

He was right, but by then it was too late.

The military men of the day do not in retrospect appear to have performed well either. Deverell was an efficient officer; he was not the military cretin that Hore-Belisha and Liddell Hart made him out to be. His remarks at the 1937 Aldershot exercises indicate a flair for aggressive tactics coupled with sound thinking about the use of mobile troops.[174] One gets the impression that if the secretary of state for war had been a man like Haldane, Deverell might have been mildly progressive on some issues and mildly conservative on others. Hore-Belisha's zealousness, however, accentuated Deverell's temperamental conservatism. Still, Deverell was not the man to be C.I.G.S. in the late 1930s. His gradual approach to change was out of tempo with the demands of the times. His long service in India resulted in an exaggerated sense of importance for its place in the scheme of imperial defense. His inability to articulate his thoughts clearly impeded his relations with the politicians. And his sense of personal propriety inhibited him from trying new ideas.[175] He was, in essence, the "safe" candidate that Montgomery-Massingberd had wanted to succeed him. Although the coarseness of Deverell's precipitous dismissal by Hore-Belisha was unjust, events probably would have forced him to retire before completing his full tenure no matter who the secretary of war had been.[176]

Gort is perhaps the greatest enigma. He was industrious, widely read in military subjects, and while an instructor at the Staff College had corresponded extensively with Liddell Hart on infantry tactics.[177] He had demonstrated exemplary courage during the Great War and was felt to be a compassionate and humane officer when appointed Hore-Belisha's military secretary.[178] His metamorphosis upon becoming C.I.G.S. was, however, phenomenal. Gort's biographer justifies his efforts to insulate Liddell Hart from the War Office on the grounds that military advice to the secretary of state had to come from constituted authority.[179] This argument carries a degree of validity, but it seems odd that Gort was not guided by the same precept in 1937. Gort's biographer also attempts to explain away his remark about not wanting to upset the people in the clubs by saying it was probably just the first thing that came into his head to keep Liddell Hart from meddling in the General Staff's affairs.[180] The dynamics of the situation suggest, though, that Gort meant exactly what he said. He appears to have felt that the imminence of war required that the younger, progressive generals of the day wrest control of the army from the last of the old-guard interwar leaders and that, having gained control, it was necessary for them to stabilize the situation in order to gain the confidence of the whole army (including the retired field marshals and generals in the clubs) and to ensure that the revolution did not continue and bring the radicals into power. In short, it was far better for the army to swallow the Tank Corps than for the Tank Corps to swallow the army.[181]

Burnett-Stuart was not in the position to play a major role during this period. Nevertheless, he did a great deal in his comparatively limited sphere to educate the cavalry to its new task of light armored warfare and to shape the development of the Mobile Division. His suggestions that the cavalry brigades have three regiments rather than two and that the infantry be grouped

The war minister and his C.I.G.S.: Leslie Hore-Belisha and General the Viscount Gort. (Courtesy of the Liddell Hart Centre for Military Archives.)

at division level were both adopted. Based largely on recommendations contained in Burnett-Stuart's annual training report for 1937, the War Office reversed its previous decision to divide infantry units into rifle battalions and support battalions.[182] The decision to give the artillery rather than the infantry the primary responsibility for antitank gunnery also stemmed from this report.[183] His final major act at Southern Command was to attempt to regularize the administrative arrangements for the myriad units of the Mobile Division gathered at Salisbury Plain.[184] While his influence on doctrine during this period was not decisive, it was not insignificant. Despite his personal disappointment and his unflagging opposition to Continental warfare, Burnett-Stuart understood the effects of new technological developments and gave a rising generation of young soldiers a sound tactical education.

It is tempting to speculate on how things might have turned out differently if Burnett-Stuart instead of Deverell had been appointed C.I.G.S. in 1936. He certainly would not have objected to a Tank Corps officer commanding the Mobile Division. He would have fully supported the policy of limited liability, and he was strongly in favor of improving conditions of army life for other ranks. It is also interesting to speculate on what might have happened if he had been appointed C.I.G.S. to succeed Deverell in

1937. Although it seems inconceivable, the idea may have had merit. Burnett-Stuart was four months younger than Winston Churchill, and a four-year term as C.I.G.S. beginning in December 1937 would have carried him only to December 1941. And despite the obvious differences in temperament between Hore-Belisha and Burnett-Stuart, the picture of Burnett-Stuart as the wise, mature C.I.G.S. with a reforming instinct patiently balancing the youthful exuberance of a dynamic war minister almost rings true. While Burnett-Stuart probably would have taken Liddell Hart's advice with a grain of salt, he certainly would not have felt threatened by him as Gort did. This would have made for a much healthier relationship at the War Office and may have made possible a meaningful reform program.

Given Hore-Belisha's emphasis on youth, however, Burnett-Stuart's appointment as C.I.G.S. was never a possibility, and he retired as scheduled in April 1938. Gort became C.I.G.S., and relations between him and Hore-Belisha continued to deteriorate even after the dissolution of the Hore-Belisha/Liddell Hart partnership.[185] And so in mid-1938 the army began a fateful drift toward a war that it was sure was coming but felt powerless to prevent, split at the top between a reforming war minister who could no longer reform and a progressive-looking C.I.G.S. who had reverted to traditionalism. This split, coupled with uncertainty in the Cabinet over the army's role in war, resulted in a failure to define adequately either the purpose or the organization of the Mobile Division. Hence both remained in a state of flux, and Britain went to war in 1939 with neither an effective armored division nor a coherent doctrine of armored warfare.

NOTES

1. C.I.G.S. to A.G. and P.U.S., 29 September 1936, W.O. 32/4614, Committee on the Cardwell System: Report.

2. For details of Hitler's internal consolidation see Raymond Sontag, *A Broken World* (New York, 1971), pp. 262–263, and Gordon Craig, *The Politics of the Prussian Army* (New York, 1964), pp. 477–481.

3. For an excellent discussion of French political problems in this era see Gordon Wright, *France in Modern Times: 1760 to Present* (Chicago, 1960), pp. 469–499.

4. An excellent survey of Anglo-French-German-Italian relations is found in Arnold Wolfers, *Britain and France between Two Wars: Conflicting Strategies of Peace since Versailles* (New York, 1940).

5. Charles Mowat, *Britain between the Wars, 1918–1940,* Beacon Paperback ed. (Boston, 1971), p. 479.

6. Baldwin's position on rearmament in the general election of 1935 has long been a matter of controversy. Although he was not consciously attempting to conceal the need for rearmament, it appears that in his desire not to upset the constituency while educating them about the need to improve Britain's security, he muted the need for greater military expenditures. See Mowat, *Britain between the Wars,* pp. 555–556,

and A. J. P. Taylor, *English History, 1914–1945*, Oxford Paperback ed. (New York, 1970), pp. 383, 387.

7. Mowat, *Britain between the Wars*, pp. 433–434.

8. Ibid., pp. 463–465, 480–490.

9. A. A. Milne, *Peace with Honour* (New York, 1934), p. 15.

10. David C. Lukowitz, "British Pacifism and Appeasement: The Peace Pledge Union," *Journal of Contemporary History* 9 (January 1974): 115–127.

11. One of the most notable of the latter was Hankey's military secretary, Maj. Henry Pownall. In January 1936 he observed in his diary that "if war with Germany comes again . . . we shall again be *fighting for our lives*. Our effort *must* be the maximum, by land, sea, and air." Brian Bond, ed., *Chief of Staff: The Diaries of Lieutenant-General Sir Henry Pownall*, 2 vols. (London, 1972–1975), 1:99.

12. Disarmament Conference 1932–Ministerial Committee Meeting of 3 May 1934, DC(M) (32), 41st Concls. Quoted from Michael Howard, *The Continental Commitment: The Dilemma of British Defence Policy in the Era of the Two World Wars* (London, 1972), p. 107. The report itself is C.P. 64 (34) of 28 February 1934. Stephen W. Roskill, *Hankey: Man of Secrets,* 3 vols. (London, 1970–1974), 3:112 n.

13. D.R.C., "Third Report," 21 November 1935, Cab. 24/259.

14. D.P.R.C., "Report on Programmes of the Defence Services," 12 February 1936, C.P. 26 (36), Cab. 24/259.

15. Cabinet meeting, 25 February 1936, Cab. 23/83.

16. Cmd. 5107, *Statement relating to Defence.*

17. Cabinet meeting, 22 December 1937, Cab. 23/90.

18. Hobart to Lindsay, 10 November 1933, Hobart correspondence file, Liddell Hart papers, LHCMA.

19. Lt. Col. Percy Hobart, "Use of Armoured and Mechanised Forces in the Early Stages of a European War," attached to above letter.

20. Lindsay to Hobart, 17 November 1933, Bridgeman papers, LHCMA. This letter was attached as Appendix D to an undated paper by Lindsay entitled "Experimental Mobile Division," which was included in a letter from Lindsay to Montgomery-Massingberd written in February 1934.

21. See Appendix 9 for a schematic representation of Lindsay's proposed division.

22. In his letter of 10 November, Hobart states that Montgomery-Massingberd was anxious to get some experimental work going. Lindsay was suggesting to Hobart that this condition be exploited by conducting an actual exercise rather than limiting the work strictly to map exercises.

23. Hobart's impatience regarding the modernization of other branches is reflected in the words of one of his most loyal and ardent devotees, Col. Eric Offord: "We didn't want an all-tank army, but . . . what could we do? The infantry were in buses, they couldn't come with us. The artillery were . . . obstructive. They never put the rounds where you needed them; and when you called, it always came too late." Offord interview, 8 November 1972.

24. Lt. Col. A. G. Cunningham, "The Training of the Army, 1934," *JRUSI* 79 (November 1934): 729.

25. Interview with Maj. Gen. the Right Honourable Viscount Bridgeman, 27 September 1972.

26. The Southern Command exercises were cancelled because of a summer drought that severely reduced the amount of water available to horses.

27. Cunningham, "The Training of the Army, 1934," *JRUSI* 79 (November 1934): 729.

28. The question of Burnett-Stuart's motives in this exercise is discussed in detail below.

29. Cunningham, "The Training of the Army, 1934," *JRUSI* 79 (November 1934): 729.

30. Liddell Hart contends that the concentration of objectives constituted only one objective. See B. H. Liddell Hart, *The Tanks: The History of the Royal Tank Regiment and Its Predecessors Heavy Branch Machine-Gun Corps, Tank Corps and Royal Tank Corps, 1914–1945*, 2 vols. (New York, 1959), 1:332–333.

31. Ibid.

32. Maj. Gen. George Lindsay, "Notes on Southern Command 'Mobile Force' Exercise, 18–21 Sep. 34," Bridgeman papers, LHCMA. See also Liddell Hart, *The Tanks*, 1:333–334.

33. Lindsay, "Notes on Southern Command 'Mobile Force' Exercise," Bridgeman papers, LHCMA.

34. Ibid.

35. Ibid. Maj. Gen. George Lindsay, "Plan of Commander, Mobile Force," Lindsay papers, LHCMA.

36. Note from Burnett-Stuart to Lindsay, n.d., filed with Lindsay's plans for the Mobile Force exercise, Lindsay papers, LHCMA.

37. One gets the distinct impression from reading Lindsay's post-mortem that he felt harried and frustrated while planning the exercise. Kenneth Macksey cites a Lindsay diary entry indicating that Lindsay had been distracted by his wife's eccentric behavior for several years prior to the exercise. Macksey, *The Tank Pioneers* (London, 1981), p. 131.

38. B. H. Liddell Hart, *The Memoirs of Captain Liddell Hart*, 2 vols. (London, 1965), 1:254. Liddell Hart was reporting on the exercise and was with Lindsay during this critical period.

39. What follows is based on John T. Burnett-Stuart, "Southern Command Exercise. 18th–21st September 1934, Extracts from G.O.C.-in-C's Notes for Final Conference," Burnett-Stuart papers.

40. Regarding the latter, he said, "The C.R.E. [Commander, Royal Engineers] of the 1st Division seemed to be able to lay as many mines as a daddy-long-legs does eggs. This creature's capacity, I believe, is something like 1,000,000 a minute!"

41. Liddell Hart makes this assertion in *The Tanks*, 1:332, and his *Memoirs*, 1:250–252. Kenneth Macksey, Hobart's biographer, pursues the same line of thought in *Armoured Crusader: A Biography of Major-General Sir Percy Hobart* (London, 1968), p. 111.

42. Liddell Hart, *The Tanks*, 1:336.

43. Lindsay to Liddell Hart, 23 October 1934, Lindsay correspondence file, Liddell Hart papers, LHCMA.

44. The reasons behind Lindsay's fall and Hobart's rise remain somewhat obscure. In part it was due to the fact that Lindsay received the public blame for the failure of the exercise, while Hobart emerged unscathed. It was also due to the fact that there were no major general positions in the army for members of the Royal Tank Corps. Liddell Hart asserts that Montgomery-Massingberd considered Lindsay the man most suited to command a proposed Mobile Division even after the Mobile Force's failure. Liddell Hart, *The Tanks*, 1:335. If this was true, however, it seems that the C.I.G.S. would have found a more suitable appointment for him than command of a second-class district in India. Both Hobart and Lindsay had dealt privately with Montgomery-Massingberd concerning the future of armored warfare, and it seems most likely that

Montgomery-Massingberd's judgment of the two men was to some extent colored by the Mobile Force exercise.

45. C.I.G.S. to A.G., Q.M.G., M.G.O., P.U.S., 15 October 1934, W.O. 32/2847, Introduction of a Mobile Division.

46. Memorandum issued with War Office letter 20/Cavalry/831 (S.D.2), 8 December 1934, W.O. 32/2847. The detailed organization of this division is outlined in Appendix 10.

47. By way of contrast, there had already been five years of experimental work with mechanized infantry formations.

48. Col. G. N. Macready, R.U.S.I. lecture, 14 November 1934, "The Trend of Organization in the Army," *JRUSI* 80 (February 1935): 1–20. Macready was head of S.D.2, the portion of the Directorate of Staff Duties that dealt with organization and equipment.

49. Ibid., p. 2.

50. Remarks by Montgomery-Massingberd following ibid., p. 20.

51. Cmd. 5681, *Memorandum of the Secretary of State for War relating to the Army Estimates for 1938*. The figure for the 1935 estimates in Appendix 4 includes a Supplementary Estimate voted in February 1936.

52. *H. C. Deb.*, 5th Ser., 299 (18 March 1935): 950–951.

53. Ibid., col. 1434–1440.

54. Liddell Hart, *The Tanks*, 1:339–340. Hobart prepared the original draft and then consulted with the others to reach an agreed position.

55. John T. Burnett-Stuart, "Notes on Southern Command Training Conference," n.d. (circa early 1935), Burnett-Stuart papers.

56. "Army and R.A.F. Syndicate Germany, Requirement No. 1," War Office and Air Ministry exercise, 1935, Burnett-Stuart papers.

57. Liddell Hart, *Memoirs*, 1:379.

58. Burnett-Stuart, "British Defence Policy," typescript dated April 1935, Burnett-Stuart papers.

59. This sentiment is strongly expressed in Archibald Montgomery-Massingberd, "Handing Over Notes," n.d. (circa April 1936), Montgomery-Massingberd papers, LHCMA.

60. Upon his return from Egypt, Burnett-Stuart had requested permission not to participate in Montgomery-Massingberd's tour of the Aisne battlefield because of his recent convalescence from a heart condition. Montgomery-Massingberd called him to the War Office and requested Burnett-Stuart resign his command based on conditions of ill health. Burnett-Stuart demurred but did attend the battlefield tour. John T. Burnett-Stuart, "Memoir," 2 vols., 2:106–107. Martel subsequently told Liddell Hart that Burnett-Stuart had deliberately provoked an argument with Montgomery-Massingberd during the tour. Liddell Hart, diary note, 9 September 1934, Liddell Hart papers, LHCMA.

61. Halifax was appointed secretary of state for war in June 1935 when Baldwin succeeded MacDonald as prime minister.

62. C.I.G.S. to secretary of state for war, 9 September 1935, "Future Organization of the British Army," W.O. 32/4612, Future Reorganization.

63. In April 1935 after Montgomery-Massingberd had visited the Canal Brigade, Pile wrote to Liddell Hart, "The C.I.G.S. has been in great heart out here; but I thought he was looking rather old and tired. I hope he stays the course." Pile to Liddell Hart, 16 April 1935, Liddell Hart papers, LHCMA. Montgomery-Massingberd's written memoranda in the War Office were comprehensive and well organized, but his speeches were rambling and disconnected.

64. Although both Southern and Eastern Commands included only one infantry division, Southern Command also contained a cavalry brigade and the Tank Brigade. In many respects it was more significant than even Aldershot Command. Thus Montgomery-Massingberd's decision to make Eastern Command a major headquarters in the maneuvers was considered by Burnett-Stuart's staff to be a direct blow at their chief. Brush interview, 17 September 1972. Fergusson maintains that Burnett-Stuart's designation as umpire made it common knowledge that he was out of the running. Bernard E. Fergusson, *Wavell: Portrait of a Soldier* (London, 1961), p. 29.

65. Complete descriptions of the exercise can be found in Lt. Col. A. G. Armstrong, "Army Manoeuvres, 1935," *JRUSI* 80 (November 1935): 805–812, and J. R. Kennedy, *Modern War and Defence Reconstruction* (London, 1936), pp. 298–304. (Reproduced from the *Army, Navy and Air Force Gazette* of 26 September 1935.)

66. *Times*, 19 October 1935.

67. War Office letter, 20/General 5512 (S.D.1), 18 December 1934, W.O. 32/2826, The Mobile Division: Cavalry Mechanization. Since this was the same organization that Montgomery-Massingberd had proposed to Halifax in early September, Burnett-Stuart's report does not appear to have been seriously considered.

68. *Times*, 23 December 1935, and *JRUSI* 81 (February 1936): 201–204.

69. Montgomery-Massingberd, "Autobiography of a Gunner," p. 62, Montgomery-Massingberd papers, LHCMA.

70. Montgomery-Massingberd shared the French view that a future war would be fought in four distinct phases: a brief phase of mobile warfare, stabilization of the front, a long period of static warfare, and a final phase of decisive breakthrough. C.I.G.S. to secretary of state, "Future Organization of the British Army," September 1935, W.O. 32/4612.

71. This evaluation is in direct variance with that of Robert H. Larson, who says, "He accomplished far more in this three years than had been accomplished in the previous fifteen." Larson, *The British Army and the Theory of Armored Warfare, 1918–1940* (Newark, N.J., 1984), p. 186.

72. Liddell Hart says that Burnett-Stuart was "clearly the ablest of the candidates." *Memoirs*, 1:251.

73. As in the case of Montgomery-Massingberd's selection, there is almost no documentary evidence that sheds light on the actual decision. The author is grateful, however, to General Sir James Steele, a protégé of Deverell's, for an extensive analysis of the personality traits of Deverell, Burnett-Stuart, and Gathorne-Hardy that may have contributed to the former's selection. Steele to author, 15 July 1972.

74. Pile wrote Burnett-Stuart that he had heard his name noised about for C.I.G.S. and advised him to be cautious in what he said so as not to upset his chances. Pile interview, 12 October 1972. It was probably too late for this advice to have been any good, and it seems doubtful that Burnett-Stuart would have followed it, even if it had not.

75. Favorable editorial comment on Duff Cooper's appointment is found in the *AQ* 31 (January 1936): 194.

76. Liddell Hart diary note, 14 December 1935, Liddell Hart papers, LHCMA.

77. A.G. to D.R.O. (director of recruiting and organization), 8 April 1936, W.O. 32/4614.

78. A.G. to P.U.S., 30 April 1936, W.O. 32/4614.

79. C.I.G.S. to A.G. and P.U.S., 29 September 1936, W.O. 32/4614.

80. Secretary of state minute, 24 November 1936, W.O. 32/4614.

81. Deverell told Pile that "nobody in the Army will need to be afraid to know Liddell Hart any more." Liddell Hart diary note, 10 June 1936, Liddell Hart papers,

LHCMA. He also consulted frequently with both Burnett-Stuart and Ironside on matters of army policy.

82. Hobart to Liddell Hart, 18 November 1936, 5 December 1936, Liddell Hart papers, LHCMA.

83. For precise figures see Appendix 4. The Defence Loan Act of 1937 allowed the Treasury to borrow £400 million over a five-year period for the purposes of rearmament.

84. Great Britain, War Office, "Army Training Memorandum No. 17, January 1937" (circulated but unpublished War Office memorandum, 7 January 1937), p. 30; Great Britain, War Office, "Army Training Memorandum No. 18, April 1937" (circulated but unpublished War Office memorandum, 24 March 1937), p. 26.

85. "G.O.C.-in-C.'s Opening Remarks at Marlborough, Southern Command Winter Exercise (The Mobile Division) 1936/1937," Burnett-Stuart papers.

86. Cabinet meeting, 5 May 1937, Cab. 23/88. Inskip informed the Cabinet that Chamberlain's concurrence contained the clear stipulation that these totals would be "subject to Treasury approval in detail."

87. Ian Colvin, The Chamberlain Cabinet (New York, 1971), p. 34.

88. Duff Cooper felt sure that he would be dropped from the government and had even dreamed about a confrontation with Chamberlain. He was astonished when he was offered the Admiralty, which was considered a more desirable post. Diana Cooper, The Light of Common Day (London, 1953), p. 193; Alfred Duff Cooper, Old Men Forget (London, 1953), p. 206.

89. Duff Cooper, Old Men Forget, p. 205.

90. This summary of Hore-Belisha's background is based on Liddell Hart, "Hore-Belisha," DNB, 1951–1960, pp. 503–506; R. J. Minney, The Private Papers of Hore-Belisha (London, 1960), pp. 14–15; and Audax, Men in Our Time (New York, 1940), pp. 144–151.

91. Chamberlain to Hore-Belisha, undated, quoted from Keith Feiling, The Life of Neville Chamberlain (London, 1946), p. 317.

92. This paragraph is based on Liddell Hart, Memoirs, 2:2–3.

93. What follows is based upon a typescript in the Burnett-Stuart papers with the notation "Conference 8/9/37 J.B.S." at the top.

94. Interview with Lt. Col. E. J. A. H. Brush, Burnett-Stuart's A.D.C., 17 September 1972.

95. Burnett-Stuart tribute, RBC (1958): 69.

96. What follows is based upon Macksey, Armoured Crusader, pp. 139–147.

97. This paragraph based on Liddell Hart, Memoirs, 2:55–59.

98. Lt. Gen. Sir Douglas Brownrigg, Unexpected (A Book of Memories) (London, 1942), p. 129. Brownrigg was Hore-Belisha's military secretary after Gort became C.I.G.S.

99. Liddell Hart, Memoirs, 2:20. Details on Blakiston-Houston's career from Who Was Who, 1951–1960, p. 111. As commandant of the Equitation School, Blakiston-Houston was also the inspector of cavalry.

100. Roderick Macleod and Dennis Kelly, eds., Time Unguarded: The Ironside Diaries, 1937–1940 (New York, 1963), pp. 33–34.

101. Liddell Hart, Memoirs, 2:20–48.

102. Ibid., 2:54–55. The report is contained in W.O. 33/1488, Report of the Committee on the Cardwell System.

103. Liddell Hart, Memoirs, p. 50.

104. Ibid., p. 10.

105. Ibid., p. 11.

106. On Gort's preference for Wavell, see J. R. Colville, *Man of Valour: Field Marshal Lord Gort, V. C.* (London, 1927), pp. 77–78, and Liddell Hart, *Memoirs*, 2:67.

107. Lt. Gen. Sir Brian Horrocks, who served under Wavell in the 2d Division and admired him greatly, nevertheless refers to his unloquaciousness as an "almost pathological taciturnity." Brian Horrocks, *A Full Life* (London, 1960), p. 72.

108. Dill's intellectual qualifications were evident in his appointments as the army instructor at the Imperial Defence College and commandant of the Staff College. Maj. Gen. Sir John Kennedy, a protégé of Dill's, makes the blanket statement that "the Army felt that Dill should have been chosen." John Kennedy, *The Business of War* (London, 1957), p. 4. Pile, however, had heard disturbing rumors of Dill's tendency to vacillate as the commander of British troops in Palestine. Pile to Liddell Hart, 7 October 1937, Liddell Hart papers, LHCMA. Liddell Hart echoed these reservations in a conversation with Hore-Belisha on 21 November, when the choice seemed to be narrowed to Wavell or Gort. Liddell Hart, *Memoirs*, 2:63.

109. Liddell Hart, *Memoirs*, 2:22, 63.

110. Ibid., pp. 10, 21, 63.

111. Among Pile's most bitter opponents was Maj. Gen. Henry Pownall. In his diary entry for 2 February 1938, Pownall alluded to the possibility of "some 'creature' like Pile" becoming C.I.G.S. if Gort resigned. Brian Bond, ed., *Chief of Staff*, 1:131.

112. Liddell Hart, *Memoirs*, 2:65–66.

113. Ibid., p. 67.

114. Ibid., pp. 66–69; Colville, *Man of Valour*, p. 81.

115. Liddell Hart, *Memoirs*, 2:50.

116. Ibid., p. 69.

117. This conclusion was noted at a C.I.D. meeting of 16 December 1937, Cab. 2/7. Participants of the meeting are listed in Correlli Barnett, *The Collapse of British Power* (New York, 1972), p. 503n.

118. "Defence Expenditure in Future Years," C.P. 316 (37), Cab. 24/273.

119. Cabinet meeting, 22 December 1937, Cab. 23/90.

120. Liddell Hart, *Memoirs*, 2:83; Colville, *Man of Valour*, p. 83. Chamberlain had earlier commended to Hore-Belisha's reading the chapter entitled "The Role of the British Army," in B. H. Liddell Hart's *Europe in Arms* (London, 1937), pp. 116–140.

121. Colville, *Man of Valour*, p. 83.

122. Bond, ed., *Chief of Staff*, 1:125–126. Bond observes that moving into his job, Pownall had not received any clear guidance on what was required, and that the question of the army's organization was more properly in the sphere of the D.S.D. than the D.M.O.&I.

123. Liddell Hart, *Memoirs*, 2:97.

124. Ibid., p. 100.

125. Ibid., p. 88.

126. Colville, *Man of Valour*, p. 86.

127. Bond, ed., *Chief of Staff*, 1:131–132.

128. Liddell Hart, *Memoirs*, 2:109–113. This latter notion was perpetuated by R. J. Minney, whose *Private Papers of Hore-Belisha* barely mentions Liddell Hart's central role in advising Hore-Belisha on army reforms.

129. Ronald Adam, however, attributed much of Hore-Belisha's Army Estimates speech to notes prepared by Liddell Hart. Colville, *Man of Valour*, p. 87.

130. Ibid. Chamberlain had agreed to this when Hore-Belisha presented his "Role of the Army" paper to the Cabinet. Cabinet meeting, 16 February 1928, Cab. 23/92.

131. *H. C. Deb.*, 5th Ser., 332 (10 March 1938): 2141.

132. Hore-Belisha's support of the General Staff position on the need for an expeditionary force is evident in the minutes of the C.I.D. meeting, 17 March 1938, Cab. 2/7.

133. Liddell Hart, *Memoirs*, 2:114.

134. Colville, *Man of Valour*, p. 97.

135. Liddell Hart, *Memoirs*, 2:116.

136. Colville, *Man of Valour*, pp. 95–98. Colville incorrectly asserts that Pile was a colonel at this time. In fact, he was a major general.

137. Bond, ed., *Chief of Staff*, 1:148.

138. Colville, *Man of Valour*, p. 98; Liddell Hart, *Memoirs*, 2:121.

139. Liddell Hart, *Memoirs*, 2:121–124.

140. Heinz Guderian, *Panzer Leader*, Constantine Fitzgibbon, trans., abridged ed. (New York, 1957), pp. 13–14.

141. Kenneth Macksey points out that Hitler did not become an instant convert to armored warfare as a result of the demonstration. Guderian still had to fight to get his ideas accepted by the General Staff. Macksey, *Guderian: Creator of the Blitzkrieg* (New York, 1976), p. 80.

142. Richard M. Ogorkiewicz, *Armor: A History of Mechanized Forces* (New York, 1960), pp. 72–73.

143. Larry Addington, *The Blitzkrieg Era and the German General Staff, 1865–1941* (New Brunswick, N.J., 1971), p. 34.

144. Macksey, *Guderian*, pp. 94–95.

145. Discussion of French armored organization based on Ogorkiewicz, *Armor*, pp. 64–65.

146. Charles de Gaulle, *Vers l'Armée de métier*, 2d ed. (Paris, 1944), pp. 45–76.

147. Martin Alexander argues that de Gaulle's linkage of his armored warfare doctrine to a professional army was the main reason for its rejection. Brian Bond and Martin Alexander, "Liddell Hart and de Gaulle: The Doctrines of Limited Liability and Mobile Defense," *Makers of Modern Strategy from Machiavelli to the Nuclear Age*, Peter Paret, ed. (Princeton, N.J., 1986), pp. 613–616.

148. André Beaufre, "Liddell Hart and the French Army, 1919–1939," *The Theory and Practice of War*, Michael Howard, ed. (New York, 1965), p. 140.

149. Robert J. Young, "Preparations for Defeat: French War Doctrine in the Inter-War Period," *Journal of European Studies* 2 (1972): 170.

150. The history of the Soviet Army in this period is analyzed in detail in Chapter 11, "The Reaction of Threats from East and West," in John Erickson, *The Soviet High Command, 1918–1941* (New York, 1962), pp. 325–365.

151. The former figure was accepted by German intelligence; the latter was an estimate by Guderian. Erickson, *Soviet High Command*, p. 726n. Malcolm Mackintosh, a British officer who visited the Soviet Union during World War II, gives the figure of seven thousand. Malcolm Mackintosh, *Juggernaut: A History of the Soviet Armed Forces* (New York, 1967), p. 77.

152. "Provisional Field Service Regulations of the Red Army," quoted from Erickson's translation in *Soviet High Command*, p. 438. Emphasis in original.

153. Erickson, *Soviet High Command*, pp. 449–473.

154. With the creation of the Civilian Conservation Corps in 1933, the army mobilized 310,000 men into 1,315 camps for over a year and thereby lost the services of 6,000 regular officers and noncommissioned officers. Tactical training came to a virtual standstill. Maurice Matloff, ed., *American Military History* (Washington, D.C., 1969), p. 413.

155. Mildred Gillie, *Forging the Thunderbolt: A History of the Development of the Armored Force* (Harrisburg, Pa., 1947), p. 47. This was an extremely controversial decision. Col. Daniel Van Voorhis, commander of the force, protested vigorously against its dispersal. He proved to be correct in his statement that separate control of armored doctrine by the infantry and cavalry would be inimical to its coherent development. The decision has also been used as a major criticism of MacArthur's tenure as chief of staff. It did reflect his conservative doctrinal philosophy, which separated tactical functions strictly along branch lines. It was engineered, however, by the army's foremost advocate of armored warfare, Adna Chaffee, who feared that the infantry would seize total control of the Mechanized Force, claiming their right under the National Defense Act of 1920 to employ all the army's tanks. Chaffee apparently assumed that giving the cavalry some voice in armored doctrine would in the long run be more beneficial than complete direction by the infantry.

156. Ibid., pp. 98–99.

157. Ibid., pp. 70–71.

158. Ibid., p. 72.

159. For the inadequacies of Britain's air defenses in late 1937 and early 1938 see Frederick Pile, *Ack-Ack: Britain's Defence against Air Attack during the Second World War* (London, 1949), p. 39.

160. The army received the following percentages of the money spent on rearmament: 1935, 20 percent; 1936, 20 percent; 1937, 21 percent; 1938, 25.5 percent; 1939, 26 percent. "Moreover, the additions were largely absorbed by anti-aircraft defences, thus leaving the allocations to the Army proper at a level which relative to that of the other armed forces was even lower than the . . . figures [of total expenditures] suggest." M. M. Postan, *British War Production* (London, 1952), p. 28.

161. John T. Burnett-Stuart, "G.O.C.-in-C.'s Opening Remarks at Marlborough," April 1937, Burnett-Stuart papers.

162. Details on organization of Mobile Division from Appendix A, War Office letter 20/General/5512 (S.D.2), 10 December 1937, W.O. 32/2826. See Appendix 11 for a schematic representation of this division.

163. On 30 May 1937, Ironside said of Hore-Belisha, "He will probably be our saving. He is ambitious and will not be lazy like some of the others were. He starts in when things are at their worst and will have to show results." Macleod and Kelly, eds., *The Ironside Diaries*, p. 24. Even the conservative *Army Quarterly* editorialized, "He is a keen and energetic politician and has served with success in several ministerial appointments. He has yet to prove his capacity as an administrator, but he can rest assured of the loyal cooperation of the Army in the arduous task with which he has been instructed." *AQ* 34 (July 1937): 194–195.

164. The phrase "Buggins' turn next" from W. G. F. Jackson, *Alexander of Tunis as Military Commander* (London, 1971), p. 88. Jackson points out that it was Hore-Belisha's promotion policy that put Alexander in command of the 1st Division and Montgomery in command of the 3d Division.

165. Liddell Hart, *Memoirs*, 2:109.

166. Ironside was particularly critical of Hore-Belisha's brief interview with him on the eve of the Army Council changes. See his diary entry for 29 November 1937 in Macleod and Kelly, eds., *The Ironside Diaries*, pp. 36–37. Wavell objected to Hore-Belisha's technique of pitting the person being interviewed against the Army Council. John Connell, *Wavell: Scholar and Soldier* (London, 1964), pp. 183–184. A slightly different picture emerges from a description of a dinner held with five major generals in October 1937: "Mr. Hore-Belisha made himself extremely pleasant and ordered

champagne. During dinner the conversation ranged over many aspects of soldiering. The Secretary of State, like a benign kennelman, kept throwing bones of contention on the table and retrieving them well gnawed to examine the toothmarks made by the different dogs." Brownrigg, *Unexpected,* p. 126.

167. A bust of Benjamin Disraeli conspicuously displayed in his library may have indicated that Hore-Belisha's ambitions were somewhat more far-reaching than just becoming known as a great secretary of state for war. Colville, *Man of Valour,* p. 74.

168. In a letter to Sir Arthur Halbriton of 27 February 1906, the prime minister, Campbell-Bannerman, said of Haldane, "I never discuss things with him, but I have warned him against talking and speaking in public too much . . . and have advised him whatever he does to give credit of it to the soldiers, and never to seem to be making capital for himself." W. S. Hamer, *The British Army: Civil-Military Relations, 1885–1905* (Oxford, 1970), p. 260.

169. This point, as well as the extent of Liddell Hart's role in the army's affairs, is evident in his notation of 29 January: "I tried to design the right combination—combining men of drive, men of balance, men of originality, and men of comprehensive outlook. H-B put in the selections in whom balance and comprehensiveness predominated, but has allowed them to leave out those in whom drive and originality predominate. The new regime is like a motor car without ignition, carburettor and pistons." Liddell Hart, *Memoirs,* 2:89.

170. This point was made by Maj. Gen. E. K. G. Sixsmith in a fascinating exchange of correspondence between him and Liddell Hart, that began with Sixsmith's review of Luvaas' *The Education of an Army.* The review is in *AQ* 90 (April 1965): 245–247, and the correspondence in *AQ* 91 (October 1965): 4–6. Liddell Hart maintained that "the Secretary of State's constitutional powers have rarely been exercised with as much sense of responsibility, restraint, and strict propriety as they were in Hore-Belisha's time." Sixsmith replied, "My description of Mr. Hore-Belisha's use of unofficial advice as intolerable and irresponsible is based on the degree and manner of it, and on its effect on the Army." Although the argument appears to have been over Hore-Belisha's role in accepting the advice, it was also obviously over Liddell Hart's role in giving it.

171. The observation on the dichotomy between Liddell Hart's theory of indirect approach and his practice of direct approach was made by Raymond Aron to Michael Howard. See Howard's comment in the transcript of Robert Pocock's production "Liddell Hart: The Captain Who Taught Generals," *The Listener* 88 (28 December 1972): 895.

172. Liddell Hart's *Who's Who* entry—which states that he "collaborated with the War Minister, Mr. Hore-Belisha, in the reorganization of the Army, 1937–1938, suggesting a programme of reforms, of which sixty-two were achieved by 1939"—was particularly galling to the military professionals. See *Who's Who,* 1940, p. 1890, and Brownrigg, *Unexpected,* p. 130.

173. Liddell Hart, *Memoirs,* 2:118.

174. See Lt. Col. A. G. Armstrong, "The Aldershot Command Inter-Divisional Exercise, 1937," *JRUSI* 82 (November 1937): 778–791.

175. When Deverell returned from the German maneuvers of 1936, Lieutenant Colonel Steele asked him what he thought of the German paratroop units. Deverell replied, "I don't think there is a great future for this. I wouldn't ask men to do anything that I wouldn't do myself." Interview with General Sir James Steele, 8 November 1972.

176. Montgomery, for example, said that Deverell "had a very raw deal from . . . Hore-Belisha." Bernard Montgomery, *The Memoirs of Field-Marshal the Viscount Mont-*

gomery of Alamein, K. G. (New York, 1958), p. 37. Liddell Hart argued that both Deverell and Knox should be given financial compensation for their early retirement, but Hore-Belisha demurred. Liddell Hart, *Memoirs*, 2:74.

177. Colville, *Man of Valour,* pp. 51–53.

178. Ironside's comment was, "We shall now have one of the best officers we have in the Army, a man of human parts, who is not finished as regards to Service. He will follow Caesar humanly. He will not deal with men as if they were so many pieces of paper with figures on them." Diary entry for 17 September 1937, Macleod and Kelly, eds., *The Ironside Diaries*, p. 26.

179. Colville, *Man of Valour,* pp. 81–82.

180. Ibid., p. 96.

181. This view was explicitly stated in early 1937. "Far less people would be upset by the absorption of the Royal Tank Corps than by the absorption of the remainder of the Army. The former would mean a relatively small upheaval, the latter a colossal one. The importance of avoiding a colossal upheaval would seem to be the deciding factor." Lt. Col. W. E. Maitland-Dougall, "The Future of Land Warfare," *AQ* 33 (January 1937): 267.

182. Extract from Southern Command Annual Report on Training, 1936/1937, November 1937, Burnett-Stuart papers.

183. Ibid. See also Shelford Bidwell, *Gunners at War: A Tactical Study of the Royal Artillery in the Twentieth Century* (London, 1970), pp. 79–80.

184. These arrangements are outlined in a Southern Command letter of 11 March 1938 contained in W.O. 32/2826.

185. John Kennedy says, "Gort's unsuitability for the post soon became apparent to all. In the War Office this fine fighting soldier was like a fish out of water. When I arrived [October 1938], relations were already considerably strained between him and Hore-Belisha; their mutual dislike increased as time went on until, in the end, they were hardly on speaking terms at all." *The Business of War* (London, 1957), p. 5.

8

EPILOGUE AND CONCLUSIONS

> The disciplined acceptance of traditional values and of traditional solutions is the natural product of a military environment, and the problem of combining this attitude with the scientist's scepticism and agnosticism lies at the root of military education and military training at every level.
>
> — *Michael Howard*[1]

As the British Army drifted at home, affairs abroad continued to deteriorate. Hitler's determination to occupy the Sudetenland and the Czech determination to resist him brought Europe to the brink of war in September 1938. The British and French decision not to support Czechoslovakia merely postponed the conflict. The German occupation of Bohemia and Moravia in March 1939 did not produce a Munich-style crisis, but it did result in a British guarantee to defend Poland against German aggression. In April Britain adopted peacetime conscription for the first time in its history, marking the end of limited liability.[2] When Germany invaded Poland in October 1939, a British Expeditionary Force was dispatched to France. Gort was selected to command the B.E.F. and Ironside became C.I.G.S. Two months later Hore-Belisha was forced out of office when bad blood developed between him and Gort over the construction of fortifications along the British front.[3] The expeditionary force, ultimately built up to thirteen infantry divisions, was in no condition to mount an offensive. Its largely untrained and incompletely equipped status, combined with French inaction, led to a prolonged Allied defensive known as the "phony war."

When the Germans invaded France and Belgium in May 1940, the only British armored units, other than the divisional cavalry regiments, were two battalions of the Royal Tank Regiment assigned to the 1st Army Tank Brigade.[4] The 1st Armoured Division, which had evolved from the Mobile Division, was still at Salisbury Plain and, in the words of its Support Group commander, "still more a basis for argument than an instrument of war."[5] The original German plan had been to conduct the primary attack into Belgium. However, when copies of the orders for this operation were captured, General Erich von Manstein convinced Hitler and the General Staff to attack instead through the Ardennes Forest with a concentrated army of seven panzer divisions in order to rupture the Allied lines and encircle the British and French armies in northern France and Flanders.[6] The ensuing campaign was conducted almost exactly as planned.

The attack was launched on 10 May, and by 14 May Guderian's panzer corps was across the Meuse. A British counterattack at Arras by the 1st Tank Brigade caused Rommel's division to pause but did not affect the main issue.[7] Guderian reached the Channel by the 20th. Gort decided to withdraw the B.E.F. to the west rather than to attack to the south in a useless attempt to link up with the French.[8] This decision and a controversial German order to pause on the outskirts of Dunkirk allowed approximately 224,000 men of the B.E.F. and over 100,000 Frenchmen to be miraculously evacuated, albeit without the equipment abandoned on the beach.[9] In the space of twenty days, the British Expeditionary Force had been decisively defeated.

Although the Flanders campaign of May 1940 was in many respects an aberration, it convincingly demonstrated the value of deep penetration using self-contained armored fighting formations closely supported by tactical aircraft. The British Army suffered similar, though not as disastrous, defeats in the western desert of North Africa. It did not begin to experience consistent victories over the Axis forces until late 1942, when it remedied its material deficiencies and developed an effective means of combatting German armored formations.

In light of the importance of armored warfare, it is surprising how little its original advocates were utilized in the war. After his retirement in 1933, Fuller continued his writings on military affairs.[10] His analysis of the Western democracies' failure to check the spread of the Axis powers to Ethiopia and Spain led him to associate himself with Oswald Mosley's British Union of Fascists. This flirtation with fascism alienated him from the mainstream of British political life, and he was never again offered a military position. After the war Fuller produced a number of excellent historical works, including his magnum opus, *A Military History of the Western World*, in three volumes. In 1963 he and Liddell Hart were simultaneously awarded the Royal United Service Institution Chesney Gold Medal for their contributions to military literature. Fuller died in 1966 at the age of 88.

After the dissolution of his partnership with Hore-Belisha, Liddell Hart continued to write critical commentaries of military affairs, the most notable being *The Defence of Britain*, published in 1939.[11] Liddell Hart's pessimistic statements concerning the West's military weaknesses did not win him many friends in Britain, nor did his private estimate that France and Britain could never win a war against Germany. He suffered a heart attack while preparing the book for publication, and when the editors of the *Times* reversed their opposition to the Continental commitment and proved unwilling to publish his assessments of the war, he resigned in November 1939. During the war he eked out a meager and frustrating existence as a writer and occasional ex-officio adviser to Churchill, but he was never given a substantive position. After the war Liddell Hart's reputation as a military theorist and historian was gradually restored with the publication of *The Other Side of the Hill*

(1948), *The Rommel Papers* (1953), *The Tanks* (1959), successive editions of *Strategy* (1954–1967), and his two-volume *Memoirs* (1965).[12] In addition to receiving the Chesney Gold Medal with Fuller in 1963, he received an honorary doctorate of literature from Oxford in 1964; was made an honorary fellow of Corpus Christi College, Cambridge, in 1965; and was knighted the following year. Liddell Hart died in 1970, shortly before the publication of his *History of the Second World War*.[13]

The other advocates of armored warfare were also shunted aside. Lindsay retired in 1939 after four years of service as a district commander in India.[14] He was subsequently recalled to active duty, given command of the 9th Highland Division, and later made deputy regional commissioner for civil defense in southwest England. He delivered the Lees-Knowles lectures in 1942, and from 1944 to 1946 he served as commissioner of the British Red Cross and Order of St. John in northwest Europe. Lindsay did not, however, participate actively in the war against Germany, nor did he have a role in the evolution of armored tactics during the war. He died in 1956.

Martel was given command of the 50th Northumbrian Division in 1939 and directed the attack at Arras in May 1940 in which two of his battalions cooperated with the 1st Tank Brigade.[15] In December 1940 he was appointed commander of the Royal Armoured Corps, but he became involved in a number of disputes with Hobart; while he was absent on a long tour of India, his position was abolished. Martel was later sent to Moscow as the head of the British military mission. He returned to London in 1944 and lost an eye in the bombing of the Army and Navy Club. Martel retired in 1945 and died in 1958.

Broad served as the chief administrative officer at Aldershot from 1937 to 1939; G.O.C.-in-C., Aldershot, from 1939 to 1940; and G.O.C.-in-C., Eastern Army, India, from 1940 to 1942.[16] He then retired and lived quietly in Beaminster until his death in 1976. Pile proved to be an expert organizer and trainer as an antiaircraft division commander. He was eventually promoted to general and appointed G.O.C.-in-C., Anti-Aircraft Command, in 1939, a position he retained for the duration of the war.[17]

Hobart was eased out of the War Office in June 1938 and sent to Egypt to command the newly forming Mobile Division, which later became the 7th Armoured Division.[18] He was relieved, however, in October 1939 over a conflict of personality with his immediate superior and was sent home to England. Several months after his retirement, he enlisted in the Home Guard. An article by Liddell Hart in *The Sunday Pictorial* entitled "We Have Wasted Brains," as well as Pile's lobbying with Churchill, brought Hobart back into employment, first as commander of the 11th Armoured Division and later as commander of the 79th Armoured Division. The latter division was composed of special amphibious landing vehicles, or "funnies," which made a significant contribution to the success of the Allied landing at Normandy. Hobart died of cancer in 1957.

After leaving Southern Command in 1938 Burnett-Stuart returned to Crichie. In retirement he finally broke his public silence on defense matters. When rumors of French demands for the immediate dispatch of an expeditionary force to the Continent surfaced in November 1938, he wrote a letter to the *Times* stating the case for limited liability.[19] He published a similar article in the *Spectator* in January 1939.[20] These expressions were scornfully received by members of the General Staff who were attempting to bring about a return to the Continental commitment.[21] During the war Burnett-Stuart interviewed applicants for commissions in the Rifle Brigade and performed the other duties associated with being colonel commandant of the regiment.[22] He also served as a regional director of the eastern Aberdeenshire Home Guard and conducted a survey of the defenses of the Shetland Islands for the War Office.[23] While these endeavors were no doubt important, they did not utilize his full capacities. In mid-1941 he was offered the position of governor general of Crete, but just as he was preparing to assume the post, the island fell to the Germans.[24] Later in his retirement Burnett-Stuart moved to Winchester, perhaps to be closer to his regimental headquarters. He died there on 6 October 1958.[25]

This study has attempted to answer three questions. First, how did the doctrine and organization of mechanization and armored warfare in the British Army develop between the wars, and what were the major factors that influenced this development? Second, what was Burnett-Stuart's role in this process? Third, what can be learned from the British interwar experience concerning the dynamics of military reform?

It is relatively easy to trace the evolution of British armored doctrine and organization. Between 1919 and 1926 a number of theoretical articles and books demonstrated the desirability for both mechanization and armored warfare. Fuller and later Liddell Hart were the most prolific and widely noticed theorists, but a number of less-well-known officers echoed their sentiments, while others opposed them. During this period limited practical trials were conducted, including the formation of an experimental unit at Aldershot in 1921 and the use of mechanized forces in the 1925 army exercises. Important experiments were conducted in 1927 with the Experimental Mechanised Force and continued with the Experimental Armoured Force in 1928. These trials resulted in some useful ideas concerning the composition and employment of a brigade-sized group that was self-contained and relatively well-balanced among tank, infantry, artillery, reconnaissance, and supporting units. Milne's decision to focus the experimental effort on the infantry and cavalry rather than on the Tank Corps resulted in the dispersal of the Armoured Force at the end of 1928. From 1929 to 1930 experiments were conducted with the mechanization of the traditional branches. Also during this period Charles Broad codified the results of the 1927–1928 trials in *Mechanised and Armoured Formations*, later revised as *Modern Formations*. From 1931 to 1936 Broad, Laird, and Hobart conducted tactical drills that made the Tank Brigade an efficient, though unbalanced, fighting instrument.

The period from 1934 to 1938 can be looked upon as one long attempt to move from the brigade level to the division level of armored formations. The first effort to create a Mobile Division was the Mobile Force exercise of 1934. Its failure retarded somewhat the progress of armored doctrine but more significantly resulted in the eclipse of George Lindsay, almost the only man in the British Army who had at that time a clear vision of a balanced, self-contained armored division capable of making deep penetrations. Montgomery-Massingberd's subsequent decision to form a Mobile Division by motorizing the cavalry brigades and fusing them with the Tank Brigade set the course for armored doctrine for the rest of the interwar period. From 1935 to 1937 the Tank Brigade marked time, waiting for the resolution of the question of what form mechanized cavalry was to take. When Deverell decided to put the cavalry in light tanks, the resulting Mobile Division became an unbalanced formation whose role in war remained a subject of debate. Although the Mobile Division was reduced in size and redesignated as the 1st Armoured Division, no changes of major significance took place in armored doctrine or organization from mid-1938 to the outbreak of war in October 1939.[26]

An examination of the various forces that favored the evolution of mechanized and armored forces, as well as the forces that impeded it, sheds light on why British mechanized and armored forces developed as they did. The most obvious factor that favored change was the march of technology. Improvements in engines, transmissions, and tires made the truck a more reliable and economical vehicle in 1939 than it had been in 1919. This resulted in the gradual disappearance of the horse from British civil life and almost forced the army to adopt a policy of mechanization in the mid-1930s. Progress in engines, transmissions, turrets, tracks, armament, armor, and radios also made the tank a more reliable and effective instrument in 1939 than it had been at the end of the Great War.[27] Unlike the truck, however, the tank could not be used in civil life. Therefore, armored warfare was technologically feasible but not technologically necessary.

The main factor that favored the development of armored warfare in the British Army was the small band of creative men who formulated and espoused its concepts. The writings and remonstrances of J. F. C. Fuller, Basil Liddell Hart, Giffard Martel, Charles Broad, George Lindsay, and Percy Hobart, as well as a number of less-well-known advocates, provided a major impetus for reform. As mentioned in the introduction, the primary factors that impeded mechanization and armored warfare were military conservatism, political and social indifference, and the imperial defense mission. In order to determine the extent to which these factors influenced the development of mechanization and armored warfare, it is necessary to survey the evidence.

Military conservatism, which may be defined as the tendency to preserve existing military institutions and practices, obviously played a role in the evolution of British doctrine. The case is not, however, as clearly defined as Fuller, Liddell Hart, and others have depicted it. Although the Allied victory in the Great War was achieved at tremendous cost, it did not create a psychological necessity for the reexamination of doctrine.[28] Lord Cavan, C.I.G.S. from 1922 to 1926, and other senior military men of the immediate postwar years seem to have been content with the status quo. The charge that Lord Milne, C.I.G.S. from 1926 to 1933, vacillated between reform and conservatism, with the latter tendency dominating, has an element of truth in it. His speech at Tidworth in 1927 and his decision to continue experiments with a provisional Tank Brigade in 1932, despite the financial crisis, represent a commitment to reform. His decisions to disperse the Armoured Force in 1928 and subsequently not to expand the Tank Corps represent a conservative outlook. And the composition of the army when he left office had scarcely changed since the time he had assumed it. Nevertheless, he did encourage the young, creative men in the army to think; he gave them opportunities to publish their thoughts (in Broad's case, in official manuals); and he encouraged the army at large to consider these concepts in its contemplation of future war. On the whole Milne appears to have done a good deal to move the army forward, particularly given the resource limitations of his time.

Liddell Hart and Fuller's accusation is most valid during Field Marshal Montgomery-Massingberd's tenure as C.I.G.S. from 1933 to 1936. Despite the fact that he sponsored increased mechanization in the army and approved the development of new weapons, Montgomery-Massingberd's overall impact was negative. He imposed rigid centralization on the army; he prevented the widespread circulation of the Kirke Committee report on the Great War, which contained many recommendations for fundamental reform; and more than any other C.I.G.S. between 1927 and 1938 he perpetuated the notion that the next European war would be merely an updated version of the experience of 1914–1918.

In Field Marshal Deverell's case the evidence is mixed. On the one hand, he was adamantly opposed to any revision in the Cardwell system or reduction in India's defenses. He also insisted on appointing a cavalryman to command the Mobile Division and had no real vision of this formation's role in war. On the other hand, his remarks concerning the county regimental system indicated that he was not bound to tradition for its own sake, and his decision to mechanize the divisional cavalry demonstrated an appreciation for tactical mobility.

Gort, who was a progressive if not imaginative thinker throughout most of his career, apparently underwent a rather sudden transformation upon assuming the mantle of leadership. As Hore-Belisha's military secretary he supported the sacking of the Army Council and consulted frequently with Liddell Hart. But as the newly appointed C.I.G.S., he emphasized the need for internal solidarity and worked to keep Liddell Hart insulated from the War Office. Taken as a whole, Fuller and Liddell Hart's argument as applied to the chiefs of the Imperial General Staff appears generally valid in the 1930s, but somewhat less so in the 1920s.

The cavalry's attachment to the horse and its determination to control the Mobile Division is another element in the Fuller/Liddell Hart attack on military conservatism. Here again, some evidence substantiates this thesis, but other factors are also involved. A survey of the *Cavalry Journal* between the wars suggests that the cavalry did have a horsey, folksy spirit and also attempted to marshal every scrap of evidence from the Great War and previous military history to demonstrate the continued utility of horsed cavalry. The cavalry manuals of the period, which emphasized the effectiveness of cold steel as late as 1931, reinforce this point. It was also true that the desire to preserve the cavalry branch, albeit in a new form, was the major factor in Montgomery-Massingberd's decision to use cavalry as a nucleus for the Mobile Division. There are, however, several other points that must be taken into account. First, it was not conservatism alone that caused the cavalry to resist mechanization. Until the light tank was perfected in the mid-1930s, a convincing argument could be made that the horse was a much better means of movement for close-in reconnaissance. Second, although the horse and rider were obviously vulnerable to bullets and shrapnel, the tank was also vulnerable to direct fire from artillery pieces and antitank guns. This was not, of course, a major argument upon which the cavalry could rest its case, but in the absence of definitive data concerning tanks versus antitank weapons, obviously unobtainable in peacetime, it created enough uncertainty to cloud the issue.[29]

The imperial defense mission also led Montgomery-Massingberd to mechanize the cavalry rather than to abolish it. Mechanized cavalry units at home could be easily rotated with mechanized cavalry units overseas. And although R.T.C. armored car and light tank units were being used in India to some effect, a far larger number of cavalry units were already there. Finally, it was not the cavalry that provided the major obstacle to the development of several armored divisions, but the 136 infantry battalions that composed the bulk of the British Army. This factor will be discussed in detail below.

The adverse effect of bureaucratic inertia is another offshoot of the military conservatism argument. This position, too, has evidence to support it. The primary factor was the collective decisionmaking characteristic of the Army Council. The C.I.G.S.' role as primus inter pares rather than the military head of the War Office reduced his ability to implement changes. The objections of the quartermaster general over the absence of billeting facilities at Tidworth, for instance, were among the factors responsible for the delay in forming the Experimental Mechanised Force in 1927. The Army Council system also exacerbated the difficulties in coordination between the deputy director of staff duties (organization) on the General Staff, who was responsible for the army's organization in war, and the director of recruiting and organization in the adjutant general's department, who was responsible for its organization in peace. Milne, after his first year in office, and Montgomery-Massingberd, throughout his tenure, were able to attenuate the disadvantages of this system through the force of their own personalities. It was impossible, however, to bring about a fundamental change in this structure without demonstrating a pressing national need for reform. Liddell Hart's charge that the army failed to organize an operational research organ between the wars to examine trends of the future and their doctrinal implications is very much on the mark.[30] Milne did, however, use Broad as a one-man "think tank," and within the confines of the existing organization Broad was quite productive in that capacity.

The numerous articles on mechanization and armored warfare that were published in military journals between the wars also cut against the military conservatism argument. Even if no consensus existed concerning the army's future organization, there was a healthy amount of printed discussion about what it might be. This was due to the availability of the journals themselves, to the annual prize essay contests sponsored by both the *Army Quarterly* and the R.U.S.I. *Journal*, and to the literate tradition of British society. Although publication in these journals was always impeded by the need to obtain War Office sanction, the lively exchange of ideas, particularly in the 1920s, was not the sign of a moribund institution.

To recapitulate, considerable evidence supports Fuller and Liddell Hart's claim that military conservatism was a causal factor in impeding the evolution of mechanization and, more particularly, armored warfare during the interwar years. But there is also evidence that suggests that attempts were made to anticipate the future and to prepare for it. On the whole, the army appears to have done better in this regard in the late 1920s and early 1930s than in the middle and late 1930s.

Evidence is also available to substantiate the thesis that the army's capacity for armored warfare was limited by political and social indifference. But here again the case is not completely one-sided. None of the interwar prime ministers before Neville Chamberlain took an active interest in the army. This is particularly true of Stanley Baldwin, who had little interest in foreign affairs at all; it is also true of Ramsay MacDonald, who viewed the League of Nations as the primary instrument through which Britain should seek its international objectives. And although Chamberlain was interested in the army, his primary purpose was to keep it relegated to third place in the defense establishment—his desire for its reform was secondary. Without sustained political interest at the highest level, it was extremely difficult for the advocates of armored warfare to make substantial progress.[31]

In Parliament there was a curious mixture of attitudes toward mechanization and armored warfare. In the 1920s most Conservatives wished to keep the Army Estimates at a low level in order to prevent imbalances in national expenditures, and a few mirrored the cavalry position that the horse was still superior to the tank. In the 1930s the latter attitude gradually disappeared, but the supporters of the National Government continued to reflect the idea that rapid rearmament would be uneconomical. Only a minority of Conservatives led by Winston Churchill and Leopold Amery argued for greatly increased defense expenditures. Churchill, however, concentrated his attention on the inadequacies of the air force, and although Amery wished to enhance the army's effectiveness and prestige, he was opposed to the Continental commitment.

On the Labour side a dichotomy of attitudes persisted throughout the interwar period. Moderate Labourites, including men such as Clement Attlee and the perennial John Tinker, wanted an army that was in tune with society and reasonably efficient.[32] They spoke against conservative tendencies in the army that they felt were responsible for resistance to both its democratization and its modernization. They did not, however, favor the Continental commitment, nor did they argue for a large capacity for armored warfare. The left wing of the Labour Party was much more hostile. Its members saw the army as a repressive tool of government whose purpose was chiefly to intervene in industrial disputes, and they often introduced motions to reduce its strength as vehicles for expressing this view. Thus political attitudes in Parliament provided moderate sympathy for a policy of mechanization and almost none for the doctrine of armored warfare.

The public mood is more difficult to gauge. The large sales of memoirs of the trenches and other antiwar literature in the late 1920s as well as responses to the Peace Ballot and the Peace Pledge Union in the early 1930s indicate that the army was not highly esteemed between the wars. Low recruiting figures, especially in the late 1930s when the sons of the Great War veterans were reaching military age, reinforce this point.[33]

General attitudes toward the army were important for giving its members a sense of self-worth and social utility. But the most practical implication of the army's place in society appeared in its budget. The assumption that Britain would not be involved in a major war for a period of ten years was adopted by the Cabinet specifically to prevent the armed services from consuming a large percentage of the national expenditure. From 1927 to 1934 the army's budget averaged approximately £40 million, which was just above subsistence level.[34] It allowed the army to conduct limited experiments and to purchase a modicum of new equipment, but it did not provide for a wholesale conversion to armored formations, which would have required a large capital outlay. The system of Treasury control, which required "approval in detail" for each line of the Army Estimates and allowed neither the transfer of funds among categories nor the application of one year's savings to the following year's expenditures, exacerbated this problem. The estimates rose gradually in 1935 and 1936 to approximately £45 million and £55 million respectively, and dramatically in 1937 and 1938 to roughly £82 million and £106 million.

These figures suggest that economic limitations impeded mechanization and armored warfare throughout the 1920s and into the early 1930s. In the late 1930s, however, the army did have a large enough budget, at least theoretically, to have organized several armored divisions. It did not do so for several reasons. The most obvious was that in 1937 Chamberlain ordered the War Office to place absolute priority on antiaircraft defense. The second was that in 1935 Montgomery-Massingberd had decided to mechanize the whole army rather than creating an independent armored striking force on the German model. Although this decision was motivated in part by Montgomery-Massingberd's desire to preserve the cavalry and with it the social fabric of the army, it was also a matter of practical necessity. For if the bulk of the home army had been converted into armored divisions designed for Continental warfare, there would not have remained sufficient infantry units to relieve the forces defending the Empire.

At this point one is driven to an examination of the effect of the imperial defense mission on the army's interwar doctrine and organization. On the whole its impact on the former was less than on the latter. The army was able to conduct experiments and to codify the results of these experiments without seriously disrupting the Cardwell system, as was demonstrated by the experiments on Salisbury Plain in 1927 and 1928, the publication of *Mechanised and Armoured Formations* in 1929, and the trials of a provisional Tank Brigade in 1931 and 1932.

The imperial defense mission did, however, impede the progress of mechanization in the army as a whole. Every change in the peace establishments of the home army had to be reflected in the organization of the army overseas. The chief obstacle in these changes was the British Army in India, which was paid for and controlled by the Indian government. The expense of mechanization was the main issue, but the political feelings behind these expenses were also significant. Since changes in the home army were decided upon by the War Office, it appeared from the Indian perspective that the British Army at home was able to dictate expenses incurred by the government of India.

Money and politics were not, however, the only issues. Men trained for a skill particular to a mechanized unit at home were not useful overseas. Vehicles that worked well on English roads and in English climes frequently did not work well on Indian roads and in Indian climes. And officers serving in India found it difficult to stay abreast of organizational developments at home. Despite these difficulties, there was some potential for mechanization in India, and by 1936 a gradual beginning was made.[35]

The main effect of the imperial defense mission was to rule out, almost entirely, the development of a large organization for armored warfare. The Tank Brigade was, in effect, an appendage to the British Army. It could be retained in the context of the Cardwell system only by maintaining a number of armored car companies overseas that approximately equaled the number of company-sized units in the Tank Brigade. The imperial defense mission of the armored car companies, however, bore absolutely no relationship to the Tank Brigade's training for Continental warfare.[36] The Mobile Division was maintained within the home/imperial balance only because it was made up primarily of mechanized cavalry units that could be balanced with similar units overseas. The salient fact was that while imperial defense could be enhanced by the mechanization of infantry and cavalry, it could not be performed adequately by large armored formations. Therefore, so long as the home army had to mirror the overseas army to provide reliefs, the home army could not consist primarily, or even largely, of armored divisions.

This raises the question of whether the home army had to mirror the overseas army; or, in concrete terms, was there any alternative to the Cardwell system? In theory there was: a short-term army for home service and a corps of long-term volunteers to garrison the Empire. This arrangement would have provided an army for Continental warfare and reserves of trained men to augment it in the event of war as well as an imperial police force. In practice, however, it was not that simple, for neither the government of India nor the senior leaders of the army were willing to take the risk that an adequate pool of long-term volunteers would be forthcoming.

The problems with the Cardwell system were, first, that the dispatch of forces from England to deal with a number of imperial emergencies, particularly in the 1930s, threw the system out of balance; and, second, that a growing division was taking place between the military demands of Continental and imperial warfare. Haldane had prepared the army to fight on the Continent simply by arranging the diffused battalions at home into a regular hierarchy of brigades, divisions, and corps. Since 1914, however, Continental armies had undergone two technological revolutions: an actual one of increased firepower utilizing the machine-gun and rapid-fire artillery, and a potential one of increased mobility utilizing the tank and the truck. Units organized primarily for imperial defense were simply no longer suitable for the demands of modern war on the Continent. Despite these anomalies, the Cardwell system remained the simplest and most effective means of ensuringthat the demands of the Empire were met. Its survival indicates the priority of the imperial defense mission between the wars; so long as it remained the basis of army organization, the development of a large armored warfare capacity was a virtual impossibility. Nevertheless, by judicious juggling the army could have done somewhat more than it did to develop an organization for armored warfare within the Cardwell system. A more vigorous effort to expand the armored units in Egypt in the mid-1930s could have conceivably resulted in two armored divisions by mid-1938 rather than one that was still in a state of unreadiness.

The imperial defense mission and military conservatism influenced the form and doctrine of Britain's armored forces as well as their size. The decision to mechanize the cavalry rather than expand the Tank Corps, which had roots in both factors, resulted in two-thirds of the Mobile Division consisting of cavalry light tank units. Montgomery-Massingberd felt that the Mobile Division's mission would be to cover the advance of the British Expeditionary Force in the opening phase of a future European war, essentially as its predecessor, the Cavalry Division, had done in 1914. As Liddell Hart pointed out, this concept did not take into account the new factors of time and pace that would dominate the next war on the Continent. Burnett-Stuart also felt that the role of the Mobile Division was to act as a covering force, but his analysis was based on the premise that it would only be used to defend the Empire, presumably against a less-sophisticated adversary. Thus military conservatism and imperial defense combined to make the Mobile Division primarily a reconnaissance and security unit, rather than an independent striking force.

Several other factors influenced the composition and role of the Mobile Division. The Tank Brigade was apparently included because Deverell was anxious to avoid adverse commentary from Liddell Hart in the *Times*, which would have certainly resulted from its exclusion. Because the cavalry had no infantry of its own and the Tank Corps had resisted the integration of other arms into the Tank Brigade throughout the 1930s, there was a small proportion of infantry (two infantry battalions as opposed to nine tank battalions) in the Mobile Division. The failure to develop a concept of close tactical cooperation between the Mobile Division and supporting aircraft, however, was not the army's responsibility. Lindsay, Broad, Hobart, and Burnett-Stuart had all advocated intimate cooperation between tanks and aircraft. And although none had definitively described the relationship that subsequently developed between the Luftwaffe and the German panzer divisions, all had witnessed and encouraged demonstrations of the capacity of the Royal

Air Force to provide this type of direct support. The air force, however, wished to retain a strict doctrine of independent airpower and looked upon cooperation with the army as a diversion from its primary mission of bombing industrial and population centers.[37] Group Capt. Trefford Leigh-Mallory and Wing Comdr. J. C. Slessor were exceptions to this rule, but neither one was senior enough at the time to influence air force policy.[38]

In the final analysis, the size, form, and concepts of Britain's armored units were the result of a complex interaction of forces. The technological improvement of the truck and its wide adoption in British society favored mechanization. The progressive development of the tank and the creative ideas of young tank enthusiasts favored armored warfare. The imperial defense mission, military conservatism, organizational inertia and rivalries, technological uncertainty, conflicting personalities, political indifference, occasional social hostility, and, since it was always impossible to predict how these forces would act upon men and events, the element of chance all acted to one degree or another to impede both mechanization and armored warfare. Of these various factors, the imperial defense mission was the single most significant impediment to the development of armored formations. So long as the army's primary mission was to garrison the Empire, armored divisions were of little utility. But neither the British people nor the army's leaders were entirely blameless for the army's lack of armored formations in the opening campaigns of the Second World War. The political leaders reflected the desires of an electorate that did not wish to be reminded of the need for military forces at all. And, with a few notable exceptions, the senior officers of the army neither possessed nor articulated a reasonably accurate vision of the nature of future war. If they had, the initial trauma of World War II would not have been as great, despite the many significant obstacles that hampered the army's progress for twenty years.

Burnett-Stuart was the most striking exception to this generalization. He was able not only to visualize the nature of future war but also to adapt that vision to the circumstances of the British Army and to express clearly both the vision and its adaptation. An assessment of his role in the evolution of British mechanized and armored doctrine requires an analysis of the kind of man he was, the development of his attitudes toward the new doctrine, his actions to influence that doctrine, and the results of those actions. Burnett-Stuart was a man of lucid, creative intelligence; independent, self-confident temperament; complete but balanced professionalism; and honest and unselfish character.

There were few officers in the British Army between the wars whose intelligence was as widely recognized as Burnett-Stuart's. Although they did not always agree with him, Liddell Hart, Fuller, Pile, Lindsay, Martel, and many other interwar personalities attested to Burnett-Stuart's qualities of perception. His mental gifts stemmed from a keen sense of observation that was evident as early as 1900 in his report on the battle of Koodesrand written for the *Rifle Brigade Chronicle*. This ability to look carefully at and think clearly about what was going on around him was a major factor contributing to the value of his analyses of armored warfare written between 1927 and 1938. He was also able to express his thoughts succinctly both verbally and on paper. His lectures, training addresses, exercise critiques, and official reports were all clearly organized, carefully worded, and forcefully presented. It is interesting to note in this regard that each of his published articles was written for a specific purpose in the context of what he was actually doing, not for the sake of publication itself.

He was imaginative as well as intelligent. As a subaltern in India he learned the value of attempting to think in peacetime about what war would actually be like, and he continued to develop this capacity as director of military operations in New Zealand; as G.O.C., 3d Division; as an independent commander in Egypt; and in a somewhat limiting environment as G.O.C.-in-C., Southern Command. This imagination was coupled with a creative spirit. Burnett-Stuart's description of an ideal armored force prepared in 1928 contained not only the units that had participated in the experiments on Salisbury Plain, but also many that had not. It was one of the clearest blueprints of a balanced, self-contained fighting formation drafted by a serving officer between the wars. His imagination and creativity were complemented, however, by a striking sense of realism. Burnett-Stuart's lecture on mechanization given at the University of London in 1928 and his correspondence with Liddell Hart from Egypt demonstrate that his vision of the future was conditioned by a practical appreciation of the effects of the army's imperial police mission and its not wholly favorable position in society. Liddell Hart's assertion that Burnett-Stuart was a man of "long range if variable vision" was accurately refuted by Bernard Fergusson's statement that "he kept vision and realism in touch with each other."[39]

Burnett-Stuart's independence and self-confidence were manifested throughout his career. As commander of the Madras District in India, Lord Rawlinson, the commander-in-chief, gave him complete authority to deal with the Moplah uprising, despite the tension that had been induced by General Dyer's disastrous mishandling of the Punjab rebellion. Burnett-Stuart thrived in this atmosphere of confidence and soon restored order with a judicious mixture of force and lenience. He was equally successful in Egypt, where he ran his command with little interference from the War Office. While at Southern Command, however, he resented his limited ability to influence the army's preparations for war, particularly during Montgomery-Massingberd's tenure as C.I.G.S. Being a man of independent spirit, he gave his subordinates wide latitude. This, too, was evident in Madras, where he allowed Colonel Humphreys to administer martial law in spite of pressure from his immediate superior to take direct control himself. It was also evident in Egypt, where he allowed Brigadier Pile great freedom in working out his training program. Burnett-Stuart did not, however, abdicate responsibility to his subordinates. He insisted that his commands be run according to his general philosophy and was quick to point out when they were not—for instance, in his pointed criticism of cavalry training in Egypt.

Burnett-Stuart's keen sense of humor was most often aimed at his superiors. His inscription of "Four more reasons for mechanization" on the Army Council's 1927 Christmas card and his deprecation of dining with Montgomery-Massingberd brought knowing smiles to the young officers of the 3d Division. Actions of this nature did not, however, endear him to those in authority. His prickly personality and willingness to tilt at conservative windmills were significant factors in his not being selected as C.I.G.S. in 1936. His own unpretentiousness complemented this attitude. He talked to private soldiers man to man rather than as senior to subordinate. He was seldom concerned with his appearance and frequently allowed his uniform to fall into obvious disrepair.[40] And, as Liddell Hart pointed out, he could accept serious criticism as well as dispense it.

In addition to being at times a difficult subordinate, Burnett-Stuart possessed some other rather disagreeable characteristics. He was strongly opinionated and in some areas bordered on prejudice. This was partly due to the elitism of his regiment, but it also accorded with his own temperament. When corresponding with Kenneth Laird concerning the selection of Tank Corps officers to be sent out to Egypt, George Lindsay cautioned, "You know that the general cannot stand anybody who he does not think is efficient at their job. He also likes pleasant people who he can enjoy being with. . . . I can think of one or two . . . who must be near the top of the Foreign Service Roster, who though first class at their job would not go down with the General at all."[41]

And while Burnett-Stuart's aversion to Continental warfare stemmed primarily from his vivid memory of the slaughter of the Great War, his continual insistence upon the superiority of things British almost reflected an attitude that the "Wogs begin at Calais." He distinctly disliked artillery officers, whom he felt to be overly concerned with the techniques of their profession and not enough with its results.[42] Charles Broad considered him to be moody, and although he was not a man of violent temper, one gets the impression from those around him that it was best not to approach him at the wrong moment.[43] These defects, however, did not seriously mar his personality nor impede his effectiveness as a commander or staff officer.

Burnett-Stuart was, in fact, a thoroughly professional soldier. He was foremost a superb tactician and trainer. He demonstrated these qualities in his handling of the Moplah Rebellion, in his comments on the trials of the Experimental Mechanised Force, and most clearly in his command exercises in Egypt. He was also an expert organizer. He developed this capacity as director of operations and intelligence for the New Zealand Military Forces from 1910 to 1912, but it was also evident in his conceptualization of an armored force in 1928 and in his detailed comments on the organization of armored cavalry regiments in 1937. His perceptive comments as head of the German Syndicate in the War Office exercise of 1935 on the likelihood of a German breakthrough in the Ardennes indicate his qualities as a military strategist.

His extensive cooperation with the R.A.F. in both training and operational missions familiarized him with the capabilities and limitations of the air arm. His four years as director of military operations and intelligence on the General Staff gave him a great deal of insight into political-military affairs. According to Field Marshal Festing, Burnett-Stuart's success in training subordinates was the result of much observation and reflection on the nature of war, which he distilled into the form that was most meaningful to persons ranging from the private soldier to the serious military student at the Staff College.[44] Soldiering was not, however, Burnett-Stuart's all-consuming passion. He found great satisfaction in hunting, fishing, reading poetry, and studying heraldry. According to Pile, his fascination with the desert bordered on obsession.[45] Far from detracting from Burnett-Stuart's professionalism, these outside interests gave him a balance and perspective that enhanced his effectiveness.

Nevertheless, his qualities of mind, temperament, and professional competence would have meant little had they not been complemented by a sense of honesty, loyalty, and unselfishness. Burnett-Stuart seems to have been completely straightforward with people he dealt with. His honesty with his subordinates is evident in his training address in Egypt in which he candidly admitted the deficiencies of the command's organization for war. It was also evident in his training address at Southern Command in which he informed his officers of his reservations concerning the General Staff's proposals for the reorganization of infantry battalions. His honesty with his superiors is shown in his correspondence with Montgomery-Massingberd over the plans to withdraw British forces from Cairo.[46] And being honest with himself, he developed honesty in others. He encouraged his subordinates to speak their minds, asking only that they reasoned before they spoke. His honesty provides the key to his concept of loyalty. Montgomery-Massingberd and Pownall's narrow definition of loyalty, which suggested that policy should never be questioned, was anathema to Burnett-Stuart. He believed instead that the highest form of loyalty was to the good of the army and the nation, and that it was disloyal not to make one's best judgment available to one's superiors.

Although he frequently expressed reservations concerning matters of organization and strategy, he accepted War Office policy when it was firmly set. And while he was in uniform he never argued against the Continental commitment in public, even though he thought the General Staff's attachment to it was a serious mistake. Burnett-Stuart's unselfishness did not mean that he was "devoid of ambition."[47] He was deeply disappointed when passed by for C.I.G.S. His ambition, however, was to make a positive contribution and to reverse a number of trends that he felt were leading Britain and its army toward near disaster. He did not seek power for its own sake, and contrary to many other officers of his day, he did not engage in the practice of spreading gossip about his contemporaries to enhance his own chances of success.

Perhaps the most eloquent summary of Burnett-Stuart's character came from his own pen. It is found in a tribute to Wavell written in June 1950. Although its purpose was to eulogize Wavell, it reveals much of Burnett-Stuart's personality and military philosophy.

> Lord Wavell took his soldiering *con amore*; he admired the qualities of mind and body which it demanded and evoked and which he himself possessed and cultivated in so marked a degree; and he enjoyed the contacts and friendships which it engendered. He had, above all, the great gift of a sense of proportion and its by-product, a sense of humour; he knew instinctively what mattered most, and what mattered less or not at all. And behind his soldiering he had the wider intellectual background which kept his activities in perspective.
>
> He was unconventional; he wrote Regulations but seldom read them; he wore strange work-a-day uniforms; he concocted fanciful schemes for the training of his troops; he indulged in long but never gloomy silences; and he had the proper ideas as to the relative importance of work and leave. All this made him the most delightful and refreshing person to work with; and helped rather than hindered to lead him on his balanced way to advancement and high command. Of all the partnerships in which my own soldiering involved me, those of the years of close association and friendship with Archie Wavell are those which I treasure most.[48]

While these qualities of mind, professional competence, and character made Burnett-Stuart an admirable human being and soldier, they do not entirely explain the development of his attitudes toward mechanization and armored warfare. The early evidence on this point is sketchy. Fuller and Liddell Hart suggested that during the Great War he was at best skeptical concerning the use of tanks. While in command of the 3d Division before the experiments of 1927, he did not appear to be enthusiastic, but he was at least able to ask the War Office the right questions about the purposes of the experiments and to see the need for someone blessed with "a touch of the divine fire" to command the experimental force.[49] The experience of watching the Experimental Mechanised Force in action for several months and, more significantly, of having his division chased by it all over Salisbury Plain made him a convinced believer in the potential of armored warfare. Unlike Milne he did not vacillate after his conversion. And unlike many younger officers, he was not blinded to the limitations of the mechanized force. He was fully aware of "its great sensitiveness to ground, its pre-occupation with defiles, its insatiable thirst for fuel, its delicate mechanism."[50] With all these weaknesses, however, he recognized it as a force of great strength that would revolutionize the future of war. His report at the end of the 1928 trials indicates that in contrast to Montgomery-Massingberd and Milne he was eager to continue the experiments for at least another year. And the armored force that he recommended in 1928 shows he understood the significance of integrating all arms, including infantry, artillery, and aircraft, into armored formations.

Burnett-Stuart's correspondence with Lindsay before assuming command in Egypt depicts his desire to adapt mechanized concepts to the demands of desert warfare. The extensive maneuvers carried out in the western desert during his tenure demonstrate his ability to achieve that objective. Although there were few tanks in Egypt, his pressure for the expansion of armored units at the expense of cavalry and his remarks at Lindsay's third battle of Gaza staff exercise indicate his wish to bring armored warfare to the desert as well. His direction of the Mobile Force exercise in 1934 reveals a desire to correct what he felt were deficiencies in the Tank Brigade, particularly its tendency to fight concentrated rather than dispersed and its dependence upon a too large and vulnerable supply echelon. This was misinterpreted by Hobart and Liddell Hart as a reversion to military conservatism. His analysis of German capabilities in the 1935 War Office exercise indicates a keen appreciation of the potential of Continental armored forces for maneuver at the operational level. But his guidance to the armored cavalry in 1937 shows that he felt such missions were inappropriate for British armored formations, which in his opinion should be primarily concerned with imperial defense. Thus Burnett-Stuart remained an advocate of armored warfare, but his thoughts on British strategy led him to a different conclusion from that of the tank advocates concerning the form that Britain's armored forces should take.

From 1927 to 1938 Burnett-Stuart made a number of substantial contributions to mechanization and armored warfare. His most significant contribution was to encourage the young officers who were actually handling the armored formations. He praised Pile's audacity in moving twenty-five miles beyond his limit to make contact with the enemy force when many other commanders would have chastised Pile for not acting in accordance with the rules. He and Wavell kept the 1928 trials moving as productively as possible despite Brigadier Collins' paramount concern with administrative matters. In Egypt he demonstrated to many young officers, including Bernard Montgomery, that mechanized operations were practical. He also grounded these officers in the principles of realistic training, especially in night operations.

While G.O.C.-in-C., Southern Command, he encouraged Hobart to develop more flexibility in the Tank Brigade and to reduce its logistical tail. And finally he provided a tactical education to a rising generation of young officers in the armored cavalry.

There are, however, two incidents that offset these accomplishments. Burnett-Stuart's letter to Fuller in February 1927 admonishing him for attempting to dictate conditions for command of the experimental brigade contributed to Fuller's decision to submit his resignation. Although his resignation was subsequently withdrawn, Fuller did not get command of the experimental force, and this was an irreparable loss to the army. Burnett-Stuart's letter may have been partially justified by Fuller's high-handed attitude, but he seems to have written it in a moment of pique. It was certainly inconsistent with his previously stated desire to have appointed a man with "a touch of the divine fire."

Burnett-Stuart's second miscalculation was the way in which he directed the Mobile Force exercise in 1934. The stringent limitations placed on the Mobile Force and the freedom given to the 1st Division contributed to the defeat of the former at the hands of the latter. This defeat impeded the development of an armored division and, more significantly, brought about George Lindsay's eclipse as the primary spokesman for the Royal Tank Corps. When Hobart subsequently emerged as the Tank Corps' leading light, the Tank Brigade became a thing unto itself rather than the nucleus of a balanced armored formation. Since the element of chance placed a major role in the outcome of this exercise and since the results were grossly misinterpreted, Burnett-Stuart is not wholly to blame. Greater prudence on his part, however, as well as an awareness of the psychological climate that surrounded the home army maneuvers, could have perhaps prevented the exercise from turning out as badly as it did.

Taken as a whole, however, his record as a reformer was remarkable. This was particularly evident in the reaction of conservative officers against him. They were implacably hostile not only because of his personality but also because his vision of the future and attitudes toward the development of armored warfare revealed the fallacies of their own positions. Burnett-Stuart's contribution was as an intelligent interpreter of his own times. He carefully analyzed the implications of the new military technology and showed how it could be adapted to meet the demands of the British Army. He also painted a clear and convincing picture of the nature of future war to a rising generation of professional soldiers. These were major accomplishments that entitle him to a significant place in the history of the British Army between the wars.[51]

The final question to be addressed is, What can one learn from the British Army's experience between the wars that illuminates the general problem of military reform? Several answers seem to emerge. There is a close and dynamic relationship between the purposes of military institutions and the forms those institutions take. There is a continuous requirement for senior military leaders to articulate a vision of the nature of future war. This vision requires intellectual mastery of the nature of war in many different forms, a product of which should be sound ideas concerning how future war should be waged, i.e., doctrine. Doctrine requires actual field testing both for its own validation and refinement and for specific decisions concerning how it is to be implemented in terms of organization, weapons and equipment, and methods of training. These decisions require high-level support and consensus building in order to overcome ingrained habits and branch parochialism. And finally, reformers must be able to combine original thought with traditional temperaments that prevent them from being isolated from the mainstream of the institutions they serve.

The primacy of the strategic requirements in influencing the doctrine and organization of a peacetime army should not be surprising to anyone who extrapolates a bit from Clausewitz's dictum that war is a continuation of policy. It imposes, however, stringent demands on both political and military leaders. If politicians want an instrument that is capable of executing their will, they must maintain a continuous dialogue with military leaders to keep them intimately informed of what the political requirements are and are likely to become. Likewise, senior military leaders have a continuing obligation to discuss with their political masters the institutional implications of their policies and the capabilities and limitations of existing and proposed organizational forms and doctrines. These areas are often neglected in political-military consultations that tend to focus strictly on the resource implications of policy and strategy.

Senior military leaders also have the responsibility to articulate to their subordinates a reasonably accurate vision of the nature of future war. This vision must be informed by strategic requirements, emerging technologies, the nature of one's likely adversaries, and one's own historical and cultural operational styles. Frequently the ability to articulate such a vision is inhibited by multiple strategic requirements. That was true for the British Army between the wars. It is even more true for the U.S. Army in the late twentieth century.

The complexity of this task places great demands on military leaders. It dictates intellectual mastery of the nature of war in general as well as the various forms that war assumes in a given era. Such mastery requires firm grounding in the theory of war, informed historical study, close analysis of contemporary developments, and an ability to project trends into the future in order to anticipate requirements. Such intellectual mastery also demands an institutional ethos of argument and analysis in which the best ideas about how to fight ultimately win out based on logical examination of objective evidence. Some formal mechanism is required to produce these "best ideas," which form the basis for sound doctrine. Doctrine must then be tested in actual field trials. These trials serve first to validate, refine, or invalidate the basic concepts. They also serve to reach specific judgments concerning organizational forms, weapons and equipment, and methods of training.

This marks the rub point. So long as ideas per se are all that are at issue, relatively little objection is encountered in the reform process. Changes in organization, equipment, and training, however, carry with them specific and frequently adverse consequences for various groups of the military organization. The desire of the threatened groups not to lose influence and a genuine conviction that these groups make a significant contribution to victory in combat act to impede change. Overcoming this resistance requires three things: support at the top of the organization, a mechanism for building consensus that change is necessary, and the habit of rational analysis of tactical and operational ideas mentioned above.

Of all the requirements, the last seems to be the most significant and also the hardest to produce. As Michael Howard has so eloquently observed, there is an inherent tension between the disciplined acceptance of authority required for reliable battlefield performance and the questioning attitude of the skeptic required for successful adaptation to new demands. The implications for the erstwhile military reformer are that he who will be most successful is he who harbors a radical intellect in a traditional temperament. The implications for armed forces are that those which adapt most successfully will be those which systematically nurture the development of such soldiers.

NOTES

1. Michael Howard, "Military Science in an Age of Peace," *JRUSI* 119 (March 1974): 6.
2. For a lucid analysis of this decision that illuminates the close connection between the Continental commitment and conscription see Peter Dennis, *Decision by Default: Peacetime Conscription and British Defence, 1919–1939* (Durham, N.C., 1972).
3. The reasons for Hore-Belisha's wartime resignation were purposely obscured for reasons of national solidarity, and he was unable to respond to unfounded allegations, which were simultaneously published, that he had been involved in financial scandals in the 1920s. The proximate reason for his resignation was the "pill-box" controversy. When the war began Hore-Belisha was concerned about the inadequacy of fortifications from the Maginot Line to the Channel and urged the construction of a large number of concrete and steel emplacements along the British front to remedy that deficiency. Gort resented Hore-Belisha's urgings and misinterpreted them as a lack of confidence in him on the part of the secretary of state. Gort's resentment, coupled with Hore-Belisha's desire to make the army a more democratic institution and perhaps a subtle streak of anti-Semitism in the upper echelons of the officer corps, again forced Chamberlain to choose between his secretary of state and the

military leadership. Unlike December 1937, when he had backed Hore-Belisha against the Army Council, the demands of the war seem to have forced him to side with the military, and he asked Hore-Belisha to leave the War Office for the Board of Trade. Hore-Belisha demurred, submitted his resignation, and spent the remainder of the war in relative obscurity. He served as minister of national insurance from May to June 1945, was elevated to the peerage in 1954, and died of a heart attack in France in 1957. R. J. Minney, *The Private Papers of Hore-Belisha* (London, 1960), pp. 250–309; J. R. Colville, *Man of Valour: Field Marshal Lord Gort, V.C.* (London, 1972), pp. 157–167; B. H. Liddell Hart, *The Memoirs of Captain Liddell Hart*, 2 vols. (London, 1965), 2: 266–274.

4. B. H. Liddell Hart, *The Tanks: The History of the Royal Tank Regiment and Its Predecessors Heavy Branch Machine-Gun Corps, Tank Corps and Royal Tank Corps, 1914–1945*, 2 vols. (New York, 1959) 2: 6–7.

5. Frederick E. Morgan, *Peace and War: A Soldier's Life* (London, 1961), p. 134.

6. For a description of the effort required to win the General Staff's and Hitler's approval for this plan see Field Marshal Erich von Manstein, *Lost Victories*, Anthony G. Powell, trans. and ed. (Chicago, 1958), pp. 94–126.

7. The British side of the action is recounted in Liddell Hart, *The Tanks*, 2:9–16; the German side is told in B. H. Liddell Hart, ed., *The Rommel Papers* (New York, 1953), pp. 29–34.

8. The story behind this key decision, which earned for Gort the accolade "Savior of the B.E.F.," is told in Colville, *Man of Valour*, pp. 206–217, and C. N. Barclay, *On Their Shoulders: British Generalship in the Lean Years, 1939–1942* (London, 1964), pp. 36–49. F. W. Winterbotham's *The Ultra Secret* (New York, 1974) has revealed that interception of a German radio message ordering the continuation of an encircling movement was a significant element in Gort's decision.

9. B. H. Liddell Hart, *History of the Second World War* (London, 1970), pp. 79–80.

10. What follows is based primarily on David H. Zook, "John Frederick Charles Fuller: Military Historian," *Military Affairs* 23 (Winter 1959–1960): 185–193. See also Anthony J. Trythall, *"Boney" Fuller: The Intellectual General* (London, 1977), pp. 180–275. Fuller's tendency toward authoritarianism is especially evident in his *Towards Armageddon: The Defence Problem and Its Solution* (London, 1937).

11. What follows is based primarily on Liddell Hart, *Memoirs*, 2:186–259, and Martin Blumenson and James Stokesbury's essay on Liddell Hart in *Masters of the Art of Command* (Boston, 1975), pp. 220–229. Liddell Hart is included in this essay as one of the "Masters of Mobile Warfare," which in a theoretical sense is a legitimate claim. Given his reluctance to accept Burnett-Stuart's offer for him to command a desert column in Egypt, however, it seems somewhat ironic that he is included in a work of this title. For biographical details see *Who Was Who*, 1961–1970, p. 676.

12. In a soon to be published study, *Liddell Hart and the Weight of History*, John Mearsheimer argues with substantial documentation that Liddell Hart's efforts to restore his reputation included the manipulation of evidence to enhance interpretations of his influence on the evolution of armored doctrine, particularly among the German generals of World War II.

13. Michael Howard summarizes Liddell Hart's contribution to military thought as follows: "I would not say that it was his doctrine of armored war. I wouldn't say it was his doctrine of the indirect approach. I certainly wouldn't say it was his doctrine about the British way in warfare. I would say that it was the habit of mind which he brought to thinking about war: a humanity, a compassion, a scholarship, and a determination that military thinking should serve the cause of peace. He coined a phrase which may long outlive the rest of his works. It is quite untrue, he said, that

if one wishes peace one should prepare for war: but if one wishes peace one should understand war." Michael Howard in Robert Pocock, "Liddell Hart: The Captain Who Taught Generals," *The Listener* 88 (28 December 1972): 896.

14. B. H. Liddell Hart, "Lindsay," *DNB*, 1951–1960, pp. 644–645.

15. B. H. Liddell Hart, "Martel," *DNB*, 1951–1960, pp. 699–701. See also Giffard Martel, *An Outspoken Soldier: His Views and Memoirs* (London, 1949).

16. Information on Broad from *Who's Who*, 1975, p. 379, and author's personal knowledge.

17. On Frederick Pile's role in World War II, see his memoirs, *Ack-Ack: Britain's Defence against Air Attack during the Second World War* (London, 1949).

18. On Hobart in World War II see Kenneth Macksey, *Armoured Crusader: A Biography of Major-General Sir Percy Hobart* (London, 1968), pp. 155–321.

19. *Times*, 28 November 1938.

20. *The Spectator*, 27 January 1939. A copy of this article is in the Burnett-Stuart papers.

21. Pownall was especially incensed. On 28 November he recorded in his diary, "Jock Burnett-Stuart writes to *The Times* and does us no good. It is thoroughly evil of him. He has no responsibility now and would be wise to keep his hands out of other people's business. When he had he did *not* take that line at all. And all because he got up against Montgomery-Massingberd." Brian Bond, ed., *Chief of Staff: The Diaries of Lieutenant-General Sir Henry Pownall*, 2 vols. (London, 1972–1975), 1:138. Pownall's statement not only reveals an uncharitable interpretation of Burnett-Stuart's motives, it also reveals an ignorance of the fact that Burnett-Stuart was privately expressing his thoughts on limited liability well before his retirement.

22. Nigel R. Blockley (N. R. B.) to the *Times*, 15 October 1958.

23. Correspondence relating to this survey is in the Burnett-Stuart papers.

24. Based on conversations with Burnett-Stuart's grandson, J. G. S. Burnett-Stuart, and with his housekeeper, who was at Crichie when he received the call from the War Office. His deep disappointment was reflected in the fact that after he hung up the phone, he went out to the garden and sat in a chair for several hours with a crestfallen look on his face, muttering under his breath about those "– –Germans."

25. Burnett-Stuart's obituary, *Times*, 8 October 1958.

26. The 1st Armoured Division consisted of a Light Armoured Brigade (one of the two former Mechanised Cavalry Brigades), a Heavy Armoured Brigade (formerly the Tank Brigade), and a Support Group that contained one motorized rifle battalion, a motorized artillery regiment, and an engineer company. Its smaller size made it much less cumbersome than the Mobile Division, but the ratio of infantry battalions to tank battalions was actually lower, 1:6 in lieu of 2:9. Richard M. Ogorkiewicz, *Armor: A History of Mechanized Forces* (New York, 1960), p. 59.

27. The best survey of technical improvements in tanks and trucks is found in Maj. Gen. S. C. Peck, "The Early Days of Mechanization," *JRUSI* 91 (August 1946): 387–395, and Lt. Gen. Sir Giffard Martel, "The Development of Mechanization, 1933–1939," *JRUSI* 91 (November 1946): 577–583.

28. What Peter Paret said when discussing the effect of the Prussian defeat at Jena in 1806 demonstrates the psychological impetus to change that the British Army did not have in the wake of the Great War: "Not only does the shock of failure weaken preconceptions, demonstrate the fallibility of certain traditional methods, but the confidence of the established order in the rightness of its own procedures and personnel may also be weakened, and ideas and institutions are more ready to change." Paret, *Innovation and Reform in Warfare: The Harmon Memorial Lectures in Military History*, no. 8 (United States Air Force Academy, Colorado, 1966), p. 8.

29. These points are made in Edward L. Katzenbach, "The Horse Cavalry in the Twentieth Century: A Study in Policy Response," *Public Policy* 8 (1958): 120–149.

30. On Liddell Hart's desire for an operational research organ see his *Memoirs*, 2:12–13.

31. Theodore Ropp makes this point in his review of the second volume of Liddell Hart's *Memoirs*, *Air University Review* 18 (March–April 1967): 105–109.

32. Tinker was the Labour member for Leigh who rose almost every year during the presentation of the Army Estimates to denounce the cavalry.

33. The magnitude of the recruiting problem was evident in the 10,000-man deficit in the army's strength in 1937 and a projected deficit of 20,000 men in 1938. Report by the Committee on Recruiting for the Army, 14 January 1937, Cab. 24/267.

34. See Appendix 4 for figures on the Army Estimates.

35. The mechanization of the Indian Army was very difficult. It did not really begin until the British government provided a grant of £600,000. See *Times*, 19 November 1937, 29 November 1937, 3 December 1937, and 17 December 1937, for the evolution of the Indian Army mechanization policy.

36. For a description of armored car and light tank operations in India see Maj. E. W. Sheppard et al., "The Royal Tank Corps in India between the Wars," in Liddell Hart, *The Tanks*, 1:405–416, and John Connell, *Auchinleck: A Biography of Field-Marshal Sir Claude Auchinleck* (London, 1959), pp. 59–62.

37. On R.A.F. policy between the wars see Basil Collier, *A History of Air Power* (London, 1974), pp. 108–115.

38. Leigh-Mallory was commandant of the School of Army Cooperation from 1927 to 1930 and instructor in air subjects at the Staff College, Camberley, from 1930 to 1931. W. B. Callaway, "Leigh-Mallory," *DNB*, 1941–1950, pp. 498–500; *Who Was Who*, 1941–1950, p. 676. Slessor commanded the No. 4 Army Cooperation Squadron at Farnborough, which trained with the 2d Division, from 1925 to 1928 and succeeded Leigh-Mallory as the air instructor at the Staff College. Sir John Slessor, *The Central Blue: An Autobiography of Sir John Slessor, Marshal of the R.A.F.* (New York, 1957), pp. 42–44, 76–100. His book *Air Power and Armies* (London, 1936) is a detailed exposition of the techniques of Army Cooperation in light of the experience of the Great War.

39. First quotation on Burnett-Stuart's vision from his obituary in the *Times*, 8 October 1958, p. 13. Liddell Hart's authorship attributed by the almost identical wording of his assessment of Burnett-Stuart in the *DNB*, 1951–1960. The second quotation is from Bernard E. Fergusson (B. E. F.) to the Times, headlined "Sir J. Burnett-Stuart: A Soldier of Vision," 13 October 1958.

40. Remarks on Burnett-Stuart's uniform habits from Brush interview, 17 September 1972.

41. Lindsay to Laird, 21 May 1932, Lindsay papers, LHCMA.

42. Brush interview, 17 September 1972.

43. Broad said, "Jock Stuart . . . was a most curious character, he was almost like a woman in his changes of mood." Broad interview, 10 November 1972.

44. Festing interview, 24 September 1972.

45. Pile interview, 12 October 1972.

46. During the negotiations between the Foreign Office and the government of Egypt in 1934, Montgomery-Massingberd argued for preservation of a military presence in Cairo even after the political basis for such a presence had been withdrawn. Burnett-Stuart, on the other hand, felt that it would be best to bow to the inevitable and "transfer ourselves intact and unencumbered to the Canal Zone, where our only legitimate post-treaty military responsibilities will presumably lie, and whence we can

more effectively watch our interests and prepare for a return of the tide." Burnett-Stuart to Montgomery-Massingberd, 20 February 1934, Burnett-Stuart papers.

47. Bernard Fergusson made the statement in his letter to the *Times*, 13 October 1958. The tribute to Burnett-Stuart in the *RBC* (1958; pp. 67–70) qualifies it.

48. Burnett-Stuart to the *Times*, 1 June 1950.

49. Burnett-Stuart to D.S.D., August 1926, quoted from Liddell Hart, *The Tanks*, 1:244.

50. John T. Burnett-Stuart, "The Progress of Mechanization," *AQ* 16 (April 1928): 50.

51. According to Bernard Fergusson, "Lord Wavell always maintained that Jock Stuart was far and away the greatest military personality in this country between the wars." Bernard Fergusson to the *Times*, 13 October 1958.

APPENDIX 1
SYNOPSIS OF BURNETT-STUART'S
MILITARY CAREER

Commissioned 2d Lieutenant, Rifle Brigade	1895
3d Battalion, Rifle Brigade (India)	1895–1899
Lieutenant	26 July 1897
Division Signalling Officer, 6th Division (South Africa)	1899–1901
Captain	20 Feb. 1901
4th Battalion, Rifle Brigade (Egypt)	1902
Student, Staff College, Camberley	1903-1904
Staff Captain, GSO3, GSO2, War Office	1905–1909
Director of Military Operations, New Zealand Military Forces	1910–1912
Brevet Major	29 July 1911
Directing Staff, Staff College, Camberley	1913–1914
Temporary Lieutenant Colonel	21 Sept. 1913
Major (substantive)	4 Oct. 1913
GSO2, 6th Division, B.E.F.	1914–1915
GSO1, 15th (Scottish) Division, New Armies	1915
Lieutenant Colonel (substantive)	11 Nov. 1915
B.G.G.S., G.H.Q. (Staff Duties)	1916–1917
Brevet Colonel	3 June 1916
B.G.G.S., VII Corps	1917
D.A.G., G.H.Q.	1917–1919
Temporary Major General	26 Dec. 1917
Major General (substantive)	3 June 1919
G.O.C., Madras District	1920–1922
Director of Military Operations and Intelligence, War Office	1922–1926
G.O.C., 3d Division	1926–1930
Lieutenant General	18 Feb. 1930
G.O.C., British Troops in Egypt	1931–1934
General	10 Feb. 1934
G.O.C.-in-C., Southern Command	1934–1938

Source: Based on B. H. Liddell Hart, "Burnett-Stuart, Sir John Theodosius," *DNB,* 1951–1960, pp. 160–161, and Great Britain, War Office, "Gradation List of Officers of the British Army," *The Army List, July 1937* (London, 1937), p. 11.

APPENDIX 2
MEMBERS OF THE ARMY COUNCIL, 1927–1938

Secretary of State for War

Laming Worthington-Evans	7 Nov. 1924
Thomas Shaw	8 June 1929
The Marquess of Crewe	26 Aug. 1931
Viscount Hailsham	9 Nov. 1931
Viscount Halifax	7 June 1935
A. Duff Cooper	27 Nov. 1935
Leslie Hore-Belisha	28 May 1937

Parliamentary Under-Secretary

The Earl of Onslow	12 Nov. 1924
The Duke of Sutherland	4 Dec. 1928
The Earl de la Warr	10 June 1929
Lord Marley	13 June 1930
Earl Stanhope	11 Nov. 1931
Lord Strathcona and Mount Royal	3 Feb. 1934

Financial Secretary

H. D. King	12 Nov. 1924
A. Duff Cooper	14 Jan. 1928
E. Shinwell	10 June 1929
W. S. Sanders	6 June 1930
A. Duff Cooper	1 Sept. 1931
H. G. A. Warrender	29 Nov. 1935

Permanent Under-Secretary

Herbert Creedy	3 Mar. 1924

Chief of the Imperial General Staff

General George Milne	19 Feb. 1926
General Archibald Montgomery-Massingberd	19 Feb. 1933
General Cyril Deverell	7 Apr. 1936
General the Viscount Gort	6 Dec. 1937

Adjutant General to the Forces

Lieutenant General Robert Whigham	1 Mar. 1923
General Walter Braithwaite	1 Mar. 1927
General Archibald Montgomery-Massingberd	1 Mar. 1931
General Cecil Romer	19 Feb. 1933
Lieutenant General Harry Knox	1 Mar. 1935
Major General Clive Liddell	13 Dec. 1937

	Date Appointed

Master General of the Ordnance

Lieutenant General J. F. Noel Birch	1 Oct. 1923
Lieutenant General Webb Gillman	1 Oct. 1927
Major General James Charles	1 Mar. 1931
Lieutenant General Hugh Elles	5 May 1934

Quartermaster General

Lieutenant General Walter Campbell	16 Mar. 1923
Lieutenant General Warren Anderson	16 Mar. 1927
Lieutenant General Felix Ready	2 Feb. 1931
Lieutenant General Reginald May	2 Feb. 1935

Director General of Munitions Production[1]

Vice Admiral Harold A. Brown	14 Sept. 1936

Director General of the Territorial Army[2]

Lieutenant General Walter M. Kirke	1 Apr. 1936

Source: Based on *The War Office List and Administrative Directory, 1927–1938* (London, 1907–1938) and David Butler and Jennie Freeman, *British Political Facts, 1900–1960* (New York, 1960). Ranks for military officers are as of date appointed.
[1]Established as member of the Army Council by Order in Council of 26 September 1936.
[2]Established as member of the Army Council by Order in Council of 22 October 1937.

APPENDIX 3
BURNETT-STUART'S LETTER TO
J. F. C. FULLER, 18 FEBRUARY 1927

Dear Boney:

I found your letters of the 15th and 16th on my return this evening—but I understand that you have had a talk with my G.O.C. in C. [General Godley] since you wrote them.

If I didnt know you as well as I think I do, I should be annoyed—also I should be afraid that you were losing your sense of proportion which I couldn't bear. But I know that your obvious anxiety is due to diffidence lest you should not be able to live up to what you think is expected of you, rather than to fear of honest work.

The conditions under which you are being called on to function are far from ideal, but they are the best that the authorities are able to give us, so we can only play up & do our best. Incidentally you have been appointed to certainly the pleasantest Bde. Command in England, & to one which bids fair, despite difficulties, to be the most interesting. There are many first-rate fellows who would give their eyes to have it, so dont think you are conferring a boon on society by accepting it. With what may have been said in the House, the Press or at the Imperial Conference about this mechanised force I have nothing to do, nor have you. The facts are as I have given them to you: viz. that certain mechanised units and appliances of war are incorporated in this Division to be tried out, the 7th inf. Bde. being the nodal point for combined experiment. That is all there is to it. You are not being invited to tie a wet towel round your head & evolve a new military heaven & new earth. On the contrary, you are being invited to come as one of my Bde. commanders. I confess I am looking forward very much to having you to work with me; and incidentally I applaud a system which ensures that individuals containing a spark of the divine fire should take their places among the fighting troops & help to vitalise the organisation from within. It may be a less spectacular role, but it is infinitely more useful than fulminating from above.

Finally, I dont think it is right to bother the C.I.G.S. with all sorts of difficulties. I think I know what he wants & he is quite certain to give us all that is in his power to provide towards the desired results. So dont worry, & dont try & reorganize my own division for me. I have a weakness for running my own show. And when you come to this pleasant place, come with a light heart, a reali[z]ation of your good luck, your sense of humour intact, & an appreciation of the privilege of commanding troops—even infantry!

All this is rather like a sermon (not usual with me) & I would apologise for it if I didn't really think it was rather good of me to write it.

Yrs. ever J.B.S.

Source: Fuller papers, Rutgers University, New Brunswick, New Jersey.

APPENDIX 4

PROVISION OF ARMY ESTIMATES FOR PURCHASE AND MAINTENANCE OF ANIMALS AND VEHICLES, 1927–1938[1] (IN £)

Year	Forage[2]	Petrol, Oil, and Lubricants[3]	Remounts[4]	Wheeled Vehicles		Tracked Vehicles	Total Estimate	Total Vehicles		Total Animals	
				Transport[5]	Combat[6]			Amount	% of Total Estimate	Amount	% of Total Estimate
1927	603,800	78,900	124,500	238,790	190,250	520,000	41,565,000	1,027,940	2.48	728,330	1.75
1928	576,500	70,600	156,100	288,550	171,000	555,000	41,050,000	1,085,150	2.65	732,600	1.78
1929	527,500	86,750	161,700	353,020	254,000	540,000	40,545,000	1,233,770	3.04	689,200	1.70
1930	511,000	110,300	157,500	345,320	178,000	319,000	40,500,000	952,620	2.35	668,500	1.65
1931	437,500	93,900	151,000	272,500	221,000	357,000	39,930,000	944,400	2.36	588,500	1.47
1932	361,800	97,000	114,000	187,000	226,000	309,000	36,488,000	819,700	2.24	480,300	1.32
1933	363,800	108,200	114,000	270,500	158,000	348,500	37,950,000	885,200	2.34	477,800	1.26
1934	326,000	117,200	128,000	231,700	193,000	501,500	39,600,000	1,043,400	2.64	454,000	1.15
1935[7]	367,000	131,000	106,000	461,400	407,000	772,000	44,900,000	1,771,400	3.95	473,000	1.05
1936[8]	288,000	171,000	84,000	767,130	1,729,000	842,000	55,881,000	3,509,130	6.29	392,000	0.70
1937	196,500	464,000	9,000	757,570	2,747,000	3,625,000	82,174,000[9]	7,593,570	9.24	205,500	0.25
1938	139,000	1,735,000	31,000[10]	1,313,238		7,870,000[11]	106,500,000[12]	10,918,238	10.35	170,000	0.16

[1]The intention of this chart is to analyze policy; therefore, the Army Estimates that are policy documents were selected rather than statements of actual expenditure. The amounts estimated and actually spent on vehicles remained nearly equal until 1937, when monies allocated under the Defence Loan Act were not completely expended due to lack of plant space.

[2]These figures include forage purchased minus receipts for forage sold.

[3]These figures include petrol, oil, and lubricants purchased minus receipts for the sale of same.

4These figures include the purchase of horses and mules, subsidies paid under the light-horse breeding scheme, and wages of civilian personnel at remount establishments minus receipts from the sale of animals and officers' payments for hire of chargers.

5These figures include the purchase of wheeled motor vehicles operated by the R.A.S.C., spare parts, hire of civilian motor transport, subsidies paid to civilian owners of military-type vehicles, and wages of civilian personnel at R.A.S.C. workshops.

6These figures include the purchase of all wheeled motor vehicles other than those operated by the R.A.S.C.

7Includes Supplementary Estimate of 12 February 1936.

8Includes Supplementary Estimate of 6 July 1936.

9The estimate for 1937 was actually £63,120,000, with an additional issue of £19,054,000 under the Defence Loan Act.

10This increase was primarily due to a decrease in estimated revenues from the sale of horses.

11There was no distinction made between expenses for wheeled and tracked combat vehicles in 1938. This may have reflected an increased concern for security.

12The estimate for 1938 was actually £85,357,000, with an additional issue of £21,143,000 under the Defence Loan Act.

APPENDIX 5

J. F. C. FULLER'S NEW MODEL DIVISION, 1919

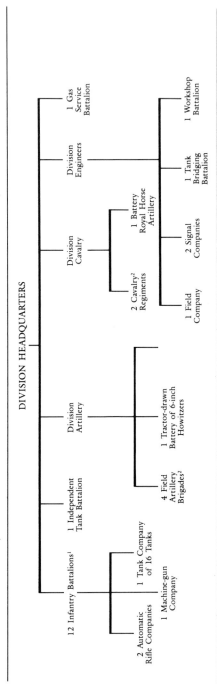

DIVISION HEADQUARTERS

12 Infantry Battalions[1]
- 2 Automatic Rifle Companies
- 1 Machine-gun Company
- 1 Tank Company of 16 Tanks

1 Independent Tank Battalion

Division Artillery
- 4 Field Artillery Brigades[2]
- 1 Tractor-drawn Battery of 6-inch Howitzers

Division Cavalry
- 2 Cavalry[2] Regiments
- 1 Battery Royal Horse Artillery

Division Engineers
- 1 Field Company
- 2 Signal Companies
- 1 Tank Bridging Battalion
- 1 Workshop Battalion

1 Gas Service Battalion

Source: Based on J. F. C. Fuller, "Gold Medal (Military) Prize Essay for 1919: The Application of Recent Developments in Mechanics and Other Scientific Knowledge to Preparation and Training for Future War on Land," *JRUSI* 65 (May 1920): 263. This was a transitional configuration between the 1919 army and Fuller's future army consisting of tanks.

[1] Although he did not specifically say so, Fuller intimated that these battalions would be organized into three brigades of four battalions each.

[2] Artillery brigades and cavalry regiments are the approximate equivalent of infantry battalions.

APPENDIX 6

B. H. LIDDELL HART'S NEW MODEL DIVISION, 1922

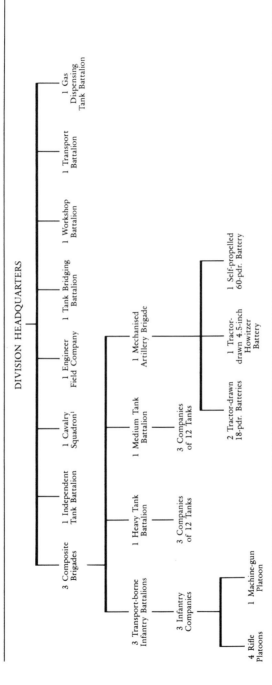

Source: Based on B. H. Liddell Hart, "The Development of the 'New Model' Army: Suggestions on a Progressive but Gradual Mechanicalisation," *AQ* 9 (October 1924): 43 (written originally in 1922). This was a transitional configuration between the 1922 army and Liddell Hart's future army consisting mostly of tanks.

[1]A cavalry squadron is the approximate equivalent of an infantry company.

APPENDIX 7

COMPOSITION OF THE EXPERIMENTAL MECHANISED FORCE, 1927

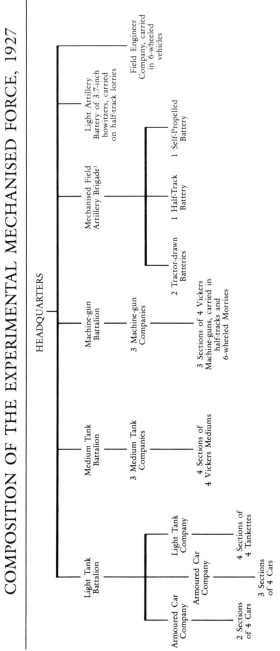

HEADQUARTERS

Light Tank Battalion
— Armoured Car Company
— Armoured Car Company
— Light Tank Company
— 2 Sections of 4 Cars
— 3 Sections of 4 Cars
— 4 Sections of 4 Tankettes

Medium Tank Battalion
— 3 Medium Tank Companies
— 4 Sections of 4 Vickers Mediums

Machine-gun Battalion
— 3 Machine-gun Companies
— 3 Sections of 4 Vickers Machine-guns, carried in half-tracks and 6-wheeled Morrises

Mechanised Field Artillery Brigade[1]
— 2 Tractor-drawn Batteries
— 1 Half-Track Battery
— 1 Self-Propelled Battery

Light Artillery Battery of 3.7-inch howitzers, carried on half-track lorries

Field Engineer Company, carried in 6-wheeled vehicles

Source: Based on B. H. Liddell Hart, *The Tanks*, 2 vols. (New York, 1959), 1:247.

[1]Liddell Hart does not mention what types of guns were in this brigade, but it was most likely two batteries of 18-pdrs. and one battery of 4.5-inch howitzers in addition to the battery of self-propelled 60-pdr. "Birch guns" that were standard to the mechanized field artillery brigade.

APPENDIX 8

BURNETT-STUART'S RECOMMENDED ARMOURED FORCE, 1928

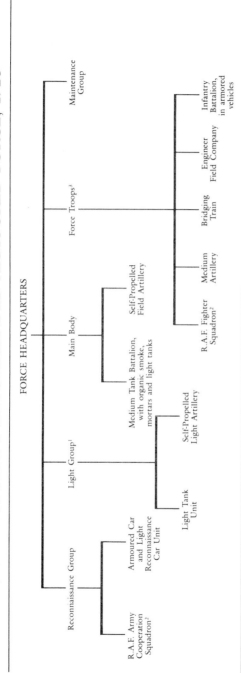

FORCE HEADQUARTERS

Reconnaissance Group
- R.A.F. Army Cooperation Squadron[2]
- Armoured Car and Light Reconnaissance Car Unit

Light Group[1]
- Light Tank Unit
- Self-Propelled Light Artillery
- Medium Tank Battalion, with organic smoke, mortars and light tanks

Main Body
- Self-Propelled Field Artillery

Force Troops[3]
- R.A.F. Fighter Squadron[2]
- Medium Artillery
- Bridging Train
- Engineer Field Company
- Infantry Battalion, in armored vehicles

Maintenance Group

Source: Based on Maj.-Gen. J. T. Burnett-Stuart, "Armoured Force Training Report—1928," November 1928, W.O. 32/2828.

[1]Although not stipulated, this was probably a light tank battalion with a battery of supporting artillery.

[2]It is not clear what command arrangements Burnett-Stuart envisioned between the R.A.F. and the army units, but he did feel that these two squadrons needed to constitute part of the force. The Army Cooperation Squadron was for reconnaissance, while the fighter squadron was for close support of ground forces.

[3]The Force Troops were actually part of a Headquarters Group; other units were to be attached as required.

LINDSAY'S PROPOSED MOBILE DIVISION, FEBRUARY 1934

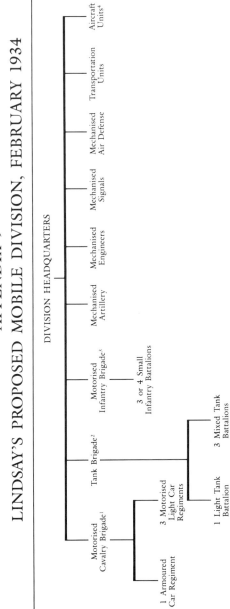

DIVISION HEADQUARTERS

- Motorised Cavalry Brigade[1]
  - 1 Armoured Car Regiment
  - 3 Motorised Light Car Regiments
- Tank Brigade[2]
  - 1 Light Tank Battalion
  - 3 Mixed Tank Battalions
- Motorised Infantry Brigade[3]
  - 3 or 4 Small Infantry Battalions
- Mechanised Artillery
- Mechanised Engineers
- Mechanised Signals
- Mechanised Air Defense
- Transportation Units
- Aircraft Units[4]

Source: Based on Appendix A, "Suggested Composition of the Mobile Division," to paper drafted by Brig. George Lindsay and his brigade major, Maj. the Honourable Robert Bridgeman, entitled "Experimental Mobile Division," enclosed with letter from Lindsay to the C.I.G.S., General Sir Archibald Montgomery-Massingberd, February 1934, Bridgeman papers, LHCMA.

[1]The function of the Cavalry Brigade was to "locate the enemy, worry him by guerrilla tactics, keep him under observation, perhaps pin him to the ground while the Tank Brigade manoeuvres for its decisive blow, and after the decisive blow has been struck to 'mop up' the localities captured." Lindsay felt that this unit could consist of either mechanized cavalry units or mechanized light infantry units resuming "their traditional role of operations ahead of the main force."

[2]This was the existing organization for the Tank Brigade.

[3]The Infantry Brigade was to be "heavily armed with light automatics, machineguns and anti-tank weapons." Its purpose was "to follow up in rear of the other two echelons [the Cavalry Brigade and Tank Brigade] and establish bases from which they can operate. Also to hold defiles, e.g. river crossings, the possession of which is vital to the Tank Brigade. To protect bases to which supplies can be delivered and at which the division can refill."

[4]The aircraft were to be "specially trained to work with the division, capable if need be of transporting supplies by air."

APPENDIX 10

MONTGOMERY-MASSINGBERD'S PROPOSED MOBILE DIVISION, DECEMBER 1934

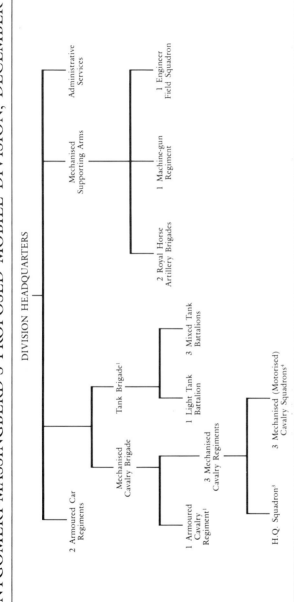

DIVISION HEADQUARTERS

- 2 Armoured Car Regiments
- Mechanised Cavalry Brigade
  - 1 Armoured Cavalry Regiment[1]
  - 3 Mechanised Cavalry Regiments
    - H.Q. Squadron[3]
    - 3 Mechanised (Motorised) Cavalry Squadrons[4]
- Tank Brigade[1]
  - 1 Light Tank Battalion
  - 3 Mixed Tank Battalions
- Mechanised Supporting Arms
  - 2 Royal Horse Artillery Brigades
  - 1 Machine-gun Regiment
  - 1 Engineer Field Squadron
- Administrative Services

Source: Based on "Organisation of Mobile Troops," a memorandum issued with War Office letter 20/Cavalry/831 (S.D.2) dated 8 December 1934, W.O. 32/2847, Introduction of a Mobile Division.

[1]This was the existing organization of the Tank Brigade.

[2]The Armoured Cavalry Regiment would "probably resemble a light tank battalion of the Royal Tank Corps."

[3]The Headquarters Squadron of the Mechanised Cavalry Regiment was to contain signal units, mortars, and scouts in light cars.

[4]The Mechanised Cavalry Squadron was the key element in Montgomery-Massingberd's proposal. Its particular function was to "co-operate with armoured cavalry or with the tank brigade; it may also operate independently." Its tactics were to generally "follow the principles laid down in Cavalry Training, Volume II." The basic unit was the section that consisted of a driver, section commander, and six men mounted in a light truck and "equipped for alternative employment as a rifle section or a light machine gun section." The purpose of the 1935 tests was to determine the optimal organization for the Mechanised Cavalry Squadron.

THE MOBILE DIVISION, DECEMBER 1937

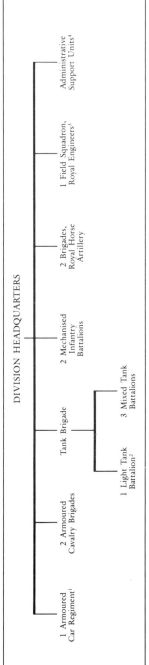

DIVISION HEADQUARTERS

| 1 Armoured Car Regiment[1] | 2 Armoured Cavalry Brigades | Tank Brigade | 2 Mechanised Infantry Battalions | 2 Brigades, Royal Horse Artillery | 1 Field Squadron, Royal Engineers[3] | Administrative Support Units[4] |

Tank Brigade:
- 1 Light Tank Battalion[2]
- 3 Mixed Tank Battalions

Source: Based on Appendix A to War Office letter 20/General/5512 (S.D.2), 10 December 1937, W.O. 32/2826, The Mobile Division: Cavalry Mechanisation.

[1] This regiment was only attached to the Mobile Division for training.

[2] This light tank battalion of the Tank Brigade was sent to Egypt in March 1938.

[3] There was also an as-yet unformed Royal Engineer Field Park Troop.

[4] These consisted of R.A.S.C. companies for the cavalry brigades and Tank Brigade at cadre strength and the following units that were not yet formed: the R.A.S.C. companies for division headquarters and division troops; and the division R.A.O.C. Petrol Park, Reserve Supply Park, Workshop, and Field Park Section.

BIBLIOGRAPHY

PRIMARY MATERIALS

Unpublished Sources

War Office Papers
W.O. 32/2820, Initiation of Experimental Mechanical Force.
W.O. 32/2821, Proposed Establishment of an Experimental Mechanical Force.
W.O. 32/2823, Distribution and Strength of the British Army in Relation to Its Duties.
W.O. 32/2824, Disarmament: Views of Marshal Foch on Mechanization.
W.O. 32/2825, Experimental Formations for 1929.
W.O. 32/2826, The Mobile Division: Cavalry Mechanization.
W.O. 32/2828, Experimental Armoured Force, 1928: Report.
W.O. 32/2841, Cavalry Committee: Interim Report.
W.O. 32/2842, Cavalry Committee: Final Report.
W.O. 32/2847, Introduction of a Mobile Division.
W.O. 32/2852, General Situation of Tank Units at Home and in Egypt: Resulting Reorganization.
W.O. 32/3115, Lessons of the 1914–1918 War.
W.O. 32/3548, Army Council Instructions for the General Officer Commanding, British Forces in Egypt.
W.O. 32/4612, Future Reorganization.
W.O. 32/4614, Committee on the Cardwell System: Report.
W.O. 33/1297, Report of the Committee on Certain Lessons of the Great War.
W.O. 33/1305, Notes on Certain Lessons of the Great War.

Cabinet Papers
Cabinet 2, Committee of Imperial Defence Minutes.
Cabinet 23, Cabinet Minutes.
Cabinet 24, Cabinet Papers.
Cabinet 53, Chiefs of Staff Sub-Committee of the Committee of Imperial Defence Minutes and Papers.

Private Papers
Bridgeman papers, Liddell Hart Centre for Military Archives, King's College, University of London.
Burnett-Stuart papers, Crichie, Stuartfield, Aberdeenshire.
Cavan papers, Churchill College, Cambridge.
Fuller papers, Rutgers University, New Brunswick, New Jersey.
Kiggell papers, Liddell Hart Centre for Military Archives, King's College, University of London.
Liddell Hart, papers, Liddell Hart Centre for Military Archives, King's College, University of London.

Lindsay papers, Liddell Hart Centre for Military Archives, King's College, University of London.
Lindsay papers, Royal Armoured Corps Museum, Bovington Camp, Dorset.
Montgomery-Massingberd papers, Liddell Hart Centre for Military Archives, King's College, University of London.

Other Manuscript Sources
Great Britain, War Office. "Army Training Memorandum No. 17, January 1937." Ministry of Defence Library (Central and Army).
Great Britain, War Office. "Army Training Memorandum No. 18, April 1937." Ministry of Defence Library (Central and Army).

Interviews
Lt. Col. Sir Rory Baynes, Bt., 11 November 1972.
Maj. Gen. the Right Honourable Viscount Bridgeman, 27 September 1972.
Lt. Gen. Sir Charles Broad, 10 November 1972.
Lt. Col. E. J. A. H. Brush, 17 September 1972.
J. G. S. Burnett-Stuart, 14 September 1972.
Field Marshal Sir Francis Festing, 19 September 1972.
Lt. Gen. Sir Alexander Galloway, 15 September 1972.
Maj. Gen. F. E. Hotblack, 24 October 1972.
J. H. Leslie, 6 November 1972.
Col. Eric Offord, 8 November 1972.
General Sir Frederick Pile, 12 October 1972.
General Sir James Steele, 8 November 1972.
Brig. George Taylor, 3 October 1972.

Correspondence
Lt. Gen. Sir Charles Broad, 15 July 1972.
J. G. S. Burnett-Stuart, 11 February 1973.
Maj. Gen. Sir Francis De Guingand, 3 October 1972.
W. B. Downing, 12 October 1972.
Lt. Gen. Sir John Evetts, 5 October 1972.
Brig. W. A. F. Kerrich, 20 September 1972.
Brig. A. C. Stanley-Clarke, 3 September 1972.
General Sir James Steele, 15 July 1972.
J. W. Taylor, 26 August 1972.
K. M. White, 7 March 1972.
Maj. Gen. Douglas Wimberley, 10 November 1972.

PUBLISHED SOURCES

War Office Publications
Great Britain, War Office. *The Army List.* London: H.M.S.O., 1865–1939.
_____, *Army Training Memorandum No. 1 (Collective Training Period, 1930).* London: H.M.S.O., 1930.
_____, *Army Training Memorandum No. 2 (Collective Training Period, 1930, Supplementary).* London, H.M.S.O., 1931.
_____, *Army Training Memorandum No. 4 (Collective Training Period, 1931).* London: H.M.S.O., 1931.
_____, *Field Service Regulations, Vol. II (Operations), 1924.* London: H.M.S.O., 1924.
_____, *Infantry Training, Vol. II (War), 1926.* London: H.M.S.O., 1926.

_____, *Mechanised and Armoured Formations (Instructions for Guidance when Consider-ing Their Action), 1929 (Provisional)*. London: War Office, 1929.

_____, *Modern Formations, 1931 (Provisional)*. London: H.M.S.O., 1931.

_____, *Report on Army Manoeuvres, 1925*. London: H.M.S.O., 1926.

_____, *Report on the Staff Conference Held at the Staff College, Camberley, 16th to 19th January 1928*. London: H.M.S.O., 1928.

_____, *Report on the Staff Conference Held at the Staff College, Camberley, 14th to 17th January 1929*. London: H.M.S.O., 1929.

_____, *Signalling Instructions, 1896*. London: H.M.S.O., 1896.

_____, *Supplementary Memorandum on Army Training (Collective Training Period, 1928)*. London: H.M.S.O., 1929.

_____, *Supplementary Memorandum on Army Training (Collective Training Period, 1929)*. London: H.M.S.O., 1930.

_____, *The War Office List and Administrative Directory*. London: H.M.S.O., 1907–1938.

Parliamentary Papers and Debates

Cmd. 1552, *Telegraphic Information, etc., regarding the Moplah Rebellion, 24th August to 6th December* (1921).

Cmd. 1581, *First Interim Report of the Committee on National Expenditure.*

Cmd. 2528, *Memorandum of the Secretary of State for War relating to the Army Estimates for 1926.*

Cmd. 2810, *Memorandum of the Secretary of State for War relating to the Army Estimates for 1927.*

Cmd. 3036, *Statement of the Secretary of State for War relating to the Army Estimates for 1928.*

Cmd. 5107, *Statement relating to Defence.*

Cmd. 5681, *Memorandum of the Secretary of State for War relating to the Army Estimates for 1938.*

House of Commons Debates, 4th Series, 1906.

House of Commons Debates, 5th Series, 1919–1938.

House of Lords Debates, 5th Series, 1923.

Other Published Documents

Medlicott, W. N.; Dakin, Douglas; and Lambert, M. E., eds. *Documents on British Foreign Policy, 1919–1939*. Series IA, vol. 1: *The Aftermath of Locarno, 1925–1926*. London: H.M.S.O., 1966.

Contemporary Books

Aston, George, ed. *The Study of War for Statesmen and Citizens: Lectures Delivered at the University of London during the Years 1925–1926*. London: Longmans Green & Co., 1927.

Cole, D. H. *Imperial Military Geography*. 7th ed. London: Sifton Praed, 1934.

de Gaulle, Charles. *Vers l'Armée de métier*. 2d ed. Paris: Berger-Levrault, 1944.

Dening, B. C. *The Future of the British Army: The Problems of Its Duties, Cost and Composition*. London: H&G Witherby, 1928.

Elles, Hugh J. Introduction to *The Tank Corps*, by Clough Williams-Ellis and A. Williams-Ellis. New York: George H. Doran, 1919.

France, Ministère de la Guerre, Etat-Major de l'Armée. *Instruction provisoire sur l'emploi tactique des grandes unitées*. Paris: Charles-Lavauzelle, 1922.

Fuller, J. F. C. *Generalship: Its Diseases and Their Cure*. Harrisburg, Pa.: Military Service Publishing Co., 1936.

————. *Lectures on F.S.R. II.* London: Sifton Praed, 1931.

————. *Lectures on F.S.R. III (Operations between Mechanized Forces).* London: Sifton Praed, 1932.

————. *On Future War.* London: Sifton Praed, 1928.

————. *The Reformation of War.* New York: E. P. Dutton, 1923.

————. *Sir John Moore's System of Training.* London: Hutchinson, [1925].

————. *Towards Armageddon: The Defence Problem and Its Solution.* London: Lovat Dickson, 1937.

————. *Watchwords.* London: Skeffington & Son, 1944.

General Service Schools. *The Employment of Tanks in Combat.* Fort Leavenworth, Kans.: Command and General Staff College, 1925.

Harding-Newman, J. C. *Modern Military Administration, Organization and Transportation.* Aldershot: Gale and Polden, 1933.

Kennedy, J. R. *Modern War and Defence Reconstruction.* London: Hutchinson, 1936.

Liddell Hart, B. H. *The British Way in Warfare.* London: Faber & Faber, 1932.

————. *Europe in Arms.* London: Faber & Faber, 1937.

————. *The Future of Infantry.* London: Faber & Faber, 1933.

————. *The Ghost of Napoleon.* London: Faber & Faber, 1933.

————. *Great Captains Unveiled.* London: Blackwood, 1927.

————. *Paris: or the Future of War.* New York: E. P. Dutton, 1925.

————. *A Science of Infantry Tactics Simplified.* 3d ed. London: William Clowes, 1926.

————. *When Britain Goes to War.* London: Faber & Faber, 1935.

Lindsell, W. G. *Military Organization and Administration.* 12th ed. Aldershot: Gale & Polden, 1932.

Martel, G. LeQ. *In the Wake of the Tank: The First Fifteen Years of Mechanization in the British Army.* London: Sifton Praed, 1931; 2d ed., 1935.

Milne, A. A. *Peace with Honour.* New York: E. P. Dutton, 1934.

Montgomery [-Massingberd], Archibald. *The Story of the Fourth Army in the Battles of the Hundred Days, August 8th to November 11th, 1918.* London: Hodder and Stoughton, 1920.

New Zealand, Military Forces. *Regulations (Provisional) for the Military Forces of the Dominion of New Zealand, 1911.* Wellington: John Mackay, 1911.

Psomades, Jean. *The Military Organization of France and Formation of the French Army, and Modern French-English Military Terms.* Paris: Libraire Hachette, 1926.

Rowan-Robinson, H. *The Infantry Experiment.* London: Clowes, 1934.

Slessor, John. *Air Power and Armies.* London: Humphrey Milford, 1936.

Swinton, Ernest D. [Backsight Forethought]. *The Defence of Duffer's Drift.* London: William Clowes, 1904.

Wavell, A. P. *The Palestine Campaigns.* London: Constable, 1928.

Memoirs and Diaries

Bond, Brian, ed. *Chief of Staff: The Diaries of Lieutenant-General Sir Henry Pownall.* 2 vols. London: Leo Cooper, 1972–1975.

Boraston, J. H., ed. *Sir Douglas Haig's Despatches (December 1915–April 1919).* 2 vols. London: J. M. Dent, 1919.

Brownrigg, Douglas. *Unexpected (A Book of Memories).* London: Hutchinson, 1942.

Churchill, Winston S. *My Early Life: A Roving Commission.* London: Thornton Butterworth, 1930.

Cooper, Diana. *The Light of Common Day.* London: Rupert Hart-Davis, 1953.

De Guingand, Francis. *Operation Victory.* London: Hodder & Stoughton, 1947.

Duff Cooper, Alfred. *Old Men Forget.* London: Rupert Hart-Davis, 1953.

Fuller, J. F. C. *Memoirs of an Unconventional Soldier.* London: I. Nicholson & Watson, 1936.

Gough, Hubert. *Soldiering On.* New York: Robert Speller, [1957].

Guderian, Heinz. *Panzer Leader.* Translated by Constantine Fitzgibbon. Abridged ed. New York: Ballantine, 1957.

Harington, Charles. *Tim Harington Looks Back.* London: John Murray, 1940.

Horrocks, Brian. *A Full Life.* London: Collins, 1960.

Kennedy, John. *The Business of War.* London: Hutchinson, 1957.

Liddell Hart, B. H. *The Memoirs of Captain Liddell Hart.* 2 vols. London: Cassell, 1965.

_____, ed. *The Rommel Papers.* New York: Harcourt, Brace, 1953.

Lyttleton, Neville. *Eighty Years: Soldiering, Politics, Games.* London: Hodder & Stoughton, [1927].

Macleod, Roderick, and Kelly, Dennis, eds. *Time Unguarded: The Ironside Diaries, 1937–1940.* New York: David McKay, 1963.

MacMunn, George. *Behind the Scenes in Many Wars.* London: John Murray, [1930].

Macready, Nevil. *Annals of an Active Life.* 2 vols. New York: George H. Doran, 1925.

Manstein, Erich von. *Lost Victories.* Translated and edited by Anthony G. Powell. Chicago: H. Regnery, 1958.

Martel, Giffard. *An Outspoken Soldier: His Views and Memoirs.* London: Sifton Praed, 1949.

Montgomery, Bernard. *The Memoirs of Field-Marshal the Viscount Montgomery of Alamein, K.G.* New York: World, 1958.

Morgan, Frederick E. *Peace and War: A Soldier's Life.* London: Hodder & Stoughton, 1961.

Pile, Frederick. *Ack-Ack: Britain's Defence against Air Attack during the Second World War.* London: Harrap, 1949.

Robertson, William. *From Private to Field-Marshal.* Boston: Houghton Mifflin, 1921.

_____. *Soldiers and Statesmen, 1914–1918.* 2 vols. New York: Charles Scribner's, 1926.

Seeckt, Hans von. *Thoughts of a Soldier.* Translated by Gilbert Waterhouse. London: Benn, 1930.

Slessor, John. *The Central Blue: An Autobiography of Sir John Slessor, Marshal of the R.A.F.* New York: Praeger, 1957.

Slim, William. *Defeat into Victory.* 2d ed. London: Cassell, 1956.

Swinton, Ernest D. *Eyewitness: Being Personal Reminiscences of Certain Phases of the Great War, including the Genesis of the Tank.* London: Hodder & Stoughton, 1932.

Newspapers
Daily Telegraph
The Spectator
Times (London)

Articles, Essays, Lectures, and Correspondence

Altham, A. E. "The Cardwell System." *Journal of the Royal United Service Institution* 73 (February 1928): 108–114.

Appleton, G. L. "The Cardwell System: A Criticism." *Journal of the Royal United Service Institution* 72 (August 1927): 591–599.

Armstrong, A. G. "The Aldershot Command Inter-Divisional Exercise, 1937." *Journal of the Royal United Service Institution* 82 (November 1937): 778–791.

————. "Army Manoeuvres, 1935." *Journal of the Royal United Service Institution* 80 (November 1935): 805–812.

"The Army France Requires." *Journal of the Royal United Service Institution* 72 (May 1927): 284–294. (Translation and summary of article published in *Revue des Deux Mondes* [November 1926].)

"Army Notes." *Journal of the Royal United Service Institution* 72 (February 1927): 206–221.

Ashmore, E. B. "Anti-Aircraft Defence." *Journal of the Royal United Service Institution* 72 (February 1927): 1–15.

Baird Smith, A. G. "The Theory and Practice of Mechanization." *Journal of the Royal United Service Institution* 75 (May 1930): 302–309.

Bate, T. R. F. "Horse Mobilisation." *Journal of the Royal United Service Institution* 67 (February 1922): 16–25.

Birch, Noel. "Artillery Development in the Great War." *Army Quarterly* 1 (October 1920): 79–89.

Bisson, T. A. "The Military Problem in India." *Foreign Policy Reports* 7 (October 1931): 299–308.

Boileau, D. W. "Gold Medal Essay (Military), 1930: With the increase of mechanization the mobility of land forces over large areas will become increasingly dependent upon adequate supply systems. Discuss the advantages to be gained by increased speed and range of manoeuvre of mechanized forces in view of the limitations imposed by the necessity of organizing elaborate supply systems particularly in regard to their operation in semi-civilized countries." *Journal of the Royal United Service Institution* 76 (May 1931): 335–354.

Broad, Charles. "The Development of Artillery Tactics, 1914–1918." *Journal of the Royal Artillery* 49 (1922–1923): 62–81, 127–148.

————. "A Mechanized Formation." *Journal of the Royal United Service Institution* 73 (February 1928): 1–16.

————. "Tactics of Armoured Fighting Vehicles." *Journal of the Royal Artillery* 55 (January 1929): 415–437.

Burnett-Stuart, John T. "Address on Training Given at Cairo, October 1931." *The Fighting Forces* 9 (April 1932): 28–40.

————. "Elementary Principles of Training for Territorial Regimental Officers." *New Zealand Military Journal* 1 (January 1912): 5–12.

————. "In India Sixty Years Ago." *Rifle Brigade Chronicle* (1954): 55–59.

————. "Modder River to Bloemfontein with the Sixth Division." *Rifle Brigade Chronicle* (1900): 129–142.

————. "The Progress of Mechanization." *Army Quarterly* 16 (April 1928): 30–51.

Chevinex Trench, R. "Gold Medal (Military) Prize Essay for 1922: Discuss the manner in which scientific inventions and science in general may affect, both strategically and tactically, the next great European war in which the British Empire may be engaged. Indicate the organisation and training required to secure the views which you may have formed as regards the imperial military forces." *Journal of the Royal United Service Institution* 68 (May 1923): 199–227.

Collins, R. J. "The Experimental Mechanised Force." *Journal of the Royal Artillery* 55 (April 1928): 12–26.

Correspondence. *Ca Ira: The Journal of the West Yorkshire Regiment* 5 (September 1932): 5–6.

Correspondence. *Ca Ira: The Journal of the West Yorkshire Regiment* 5 (December 1932): 64.

Correspondence. *Journal of the Northhamptonshire Regiment* 4 (October 1932).

Croft, W. D. "Second Military Prize Essay for 1919: The Application of Recent Developments in Mechanics and Other Scientific Knowledge to Preparation and Training for Future War on Land." *Journal of the Royal United Service Institution* 65 (August 1920): 443–476.

Cunningham, A.G. "The Training of the Army, 1934." *Journal of the Royal United Service Institution* 79 (November 1934): 723–732.

Deedes, C. P. "The Influence of Ground on Modern Military Operations." *Journal of the Royal United Service Institution* 74 (February 1929): 38–48.

Dening, B. C. "Military Prize Essay, 1924: No Great Power will voluntarily submit to position warfare in the next war, with all its attendant evils of great length, excessive cost, enormous casualties and possibly indecisive results. Consequently, the armies of the future must be more mobile, deploy more quickly and hit harder than is the case at present. What is the ideal composition (a) of a division, (b) of a corps of two divisions for future wars, making use of all modern inventions and improvements in weapons both on land and in the air?" *Army Quarterly* 8 (July 1924): 236–260.

Drayson, H. P. "The War Office Experimental Convoy, 1933." *Royal Engineers' Journal* 48 (March 1934): 60–72.

Drummond, Algeron. "Old Days in the Rifle Brigade." *The National Review* 98 (April 1932): 501–506.

"Editorial." *Army Quarterly* 1 (October 1920): 1–10.

"Editorial." *Army Quarterly* 21 (January 1931): 239–240.

Edwards, J. Keith. "Second (Military) Prize Essay for 1927: Prior to 1914, the centre of gravity of military affairs was unmistakably in Europe. We still have military commitments in Europe imposed on us by treaty or pact, but the centre of gravity is now not so closely defined. Discuss the organization and training of our military forces, having regard to the situation of to-day." *Journal of the Royal United Service Institution* 73 (August 1928): 458–473.

Edwards, T. J. "Cavalry Battle Honours." *Cavalry Journal* 22 (January 1932): 95–105.

Elles, H. J. "Some Notes on Tank Development during the War." *Army Quarterly* 2 (July 1921): 267–281.

"Extracts from the Memorandum of the Secretary of State for War relating to the Army Estimates for 1933." *Journal of the Royal United Service Institution* 78 (May 1933): 425–428.

Firth, O. T. "Mechanical Draught and Field Artillery." *Army Quarterly* 11 (October 1925): 142–146.

Fisher, B. D. "The Training of the Regimental Officer." *Journal of the Royal United Service Institution* 74 (May 1929): 241–261.

Franklyn, Harold. "1914," in "Four Generations of Staff College Students." *Army Quarterly* 65 (October 1952): 46–49.

Fuller, J. F. C. "The Development of Sea Warfare on Land and Its Influence on Future Naval Operations." *Journal of the Royal United Service Institution* 65 (May 1920): 281–298.

_____. "Gold Medal (Military) Prize Essay for 1919: The Application of Recent Developments in Mechanics and Other Scientific Knowledge to Preparation and Training for Future War on Land." *Journal of the Royal United Service Institution* 65 (May 1920): 239–274.

_____. "One Hundred Problems on Mechanization." *Army Quarterly* 19 (October 1929): 14–25; 19 (January 1930): 256–259.

_____. "Progress in the Mechanicalisation of Modern Armies." *Journal of the Royal United Service Institution* 70 (February 1925): 73–89.

Germains, Victor Wallace. "The Limitations of the Tank." *Journal of the Royal United Service Institution* 75 (February 1930): 124–129.

Haldane, Viscount. Discussion following "National Cadets," by W. R. Ludlow. *Journal of the Royal United Service Institution* 68 (February 1923): 45–60.

Hambro, Percy. "The Horse and the Machine in War." *Journal of the Royal United Service Institution* 72 (February 1927): 85–100.

Howard, T. N. S. M. "The Impatience of an Infantryman." *Journal of Royal Artillery* 54 (January 1928): 536–542.

Hume, E. H. "Mechanization from a Cavalry Point of View." *Journal of the Royal United Service Institution* 72 (November 1927): 808–811.

Ironside, Edmund. "A Division in Future War and Its Problems." *Journal of the Royal Artillery* 55 (April 1928): 1–11.

Johnson, P. "The Use of Tanks in Undeveloped Country." *Journal of the Royal United Service Institution* 66 (May 1921): 191–204.

Kaye, G. L. "The Evolution of Anti-Tank Defence." *Journal of the Royal United Service Institution* 70 (May 1925): 320–333.

Lachlan, L. A. W. B. "Mechanized-Mindedness." *Journal of the Royal United Service Institution* 78 (August 1933): 554–558.

Liddell Hart, B. H. "Armoured Forces in 1928." *Journal of the Royal United Service Institution* 73 (November 1928): 720–729.

_____. "Army Exercises in 1929." *Journal of the Royal United Service Institution* 74 (November 1929): 789–797.

_____. "The Army Exercises of 1930." *Journal of the Royal United Service Institution* 75 (November 1930): 681–690.

_____. "Army Manoeuvres, 1925." *Journal of the Royal United Service Institution* 70 (November 1925): 647–655.

_____. "Contrasts of 1931: Mobility or Stagnation?" *Army Quarterly* 23 (January 1932): 235–250.

_____. Correspondence. *Army Quarterly* 8 (April 1924): 8.

_____. "The Development of the 'New Model' Army: Suggestions on a Progressive but Gradual Mechanicalisation." *Army Quarterly* 9 (October 1924): 37–50.

_____. "Economic Pressure or Continental Victories." *Journal of the Royal United Service Institution* 76 (August 1931): 486–510.

_____. "The Grave Deficiencies of the Army." *English Review* 56 (February 1933): 147–151.

_____. "The 'Man-in-the-Dark' Theory of Infantry Tactics and the 'Expanding Torrent' System of Attack." *Journal of the Royal United Service Institution* 66 (February 1921): 1–22.

_____. "Military Critics and the Military Hierarchy: A Historical Examination as to whether Superior Rank and Number Promise Superior Wisdom." *Army Quarterly* 22 (April 1931): 41–56.

_____. "Mind and Machine: Part II–Tank Brigade Training, 1932." *Army Quarterly* 26 (April 1933): 51–58.

_____. "Seven Years: The Regime of Field-Marshal Lord Milne." *English Review* 56 (April 1933): 376–386.

_____. [Bardell]. "Study and Reflection *v.* Practical Experience: A Critical Examination of the Claims of Age, the Professional and the 'Practical' Soldier to Unique Authority on War." *Army Quarterly* 6 (July 1923): 318–331.

_____. "Suggestions for the Future Development of the Combat Unit: The Tank as a Weapon of Infantry." *Journal of the Royal United Service Institution* 64 (November 1919): 666–669.

_____. "The Tale of the Tank." Review of *Eyewitness*, by Ernest Swinton. *The Nineteenth Century and After* (November 1932): 595–607.

Lindsay, James. "Chairman's Address." *Journal of the Royal United Service Institution* 1 (1858): 1–7.

Macready, G. N. "The Trend of Organization in the Army." *Journal of the Royal United Service Institution* 80 (February 1935): 1–20.

Maitland-Dougall, W. E. "The Future of Land Warfare." *Army Quarterly* 33 (January 1937): 261–269.

Martel, Giffard. "The Development of Mechanization, 1933–1939." *Journal of the Royal United Service Institution* 91 (November 1946): 577–583.

"Military Notes." *Journal of the Royal United Service Institution* 67 (November 1922): 753.

"Military Notes." *Journal of the Royal United Service Institution* 68 (August 1923): 530.

Montanaro, C. A. H. "The Mechanized Unit in the Field." *Journal of the Royal Artillery* 57 (October 1931): 302–321.

Montgomery, Bernard. "21st (British) Army Group in the Campaign in North-West Europe, 1944–1945." *Journal of the Royal United Service Institution* 90 (November 1945): 431–454.

Oakley, Richard. "My Horse (An Equestrian Odyssey)." *Cavalry Journal* 22 (January 1932): 46–66.

Paine, J. "Exploits of the Eighth Hussars." *Cavalry Journal* 22 (January 1932): 1–8.

Peck, S. C. "The Early Days of Mechanization." *Journal of the Royal United Service Institution* 91 (August 1946): 387–395.

_____. "The Evolution of Armoured Fighting Vehicles." *Journal of the Royal Artillery* 56 (July 1930): 143–161.

Pile, Frederick. "Liddell Hart and the British Army, 1919–1939." In *The Theory and Practice of War*, edited by Michael Howard. New York: Praeger, 1965.

Polson Newman, E. W. "The Defence of the Suez Canal." *Journal of the Royal United Service Institution* 75 (February 1930): 159–162.

Redway, G. W. "The Elimination of Infantry." *Journal of the Royal United Service Institution* 74 (February 1929): 144–147.

Review of *In the Wake of the Tank*, by G. LeQ. Martel. *Army Quarterly* 23 (October 1931): 189.

Review of *Lectures on F.S.R. III*, by J. F. C. Fuller. *Journal of the Royal United Service Institution* 77 (August 1932): 682.

Richmond, Herbert W. "The Service Mind." *The Nineteenth Century and After* (January 1933): 90–97.

Ross, G. MacLeod. "The Utility of the Tank." *Journal of the Royal United Service Institution* 76 (November 1931): 786–794.

Scarlett, P. G. "Developments in Army Organization." *Journal of the Royal United Service Institution* 75 (August 1930): 503–515.

Shaw, G. C. "Spares and Repairs." *Army Quarterly* 24 (July 1932): 349–357.

"A Thinking Bayonet." Correspondence. *Journal of the Royal United Service Institution* 74 (May 1929): 398–401.

"The Tochi Valley Expedition." *Rifle Brigade Chronicle* (1897): 113–135, 220–227.

Wade, D. A. L. "The Future of Mechanization." *Journal of the Royal United Service Institution* 74 (November 1929): 695–704.

Wavell, A. P. "The Army and the Prophets." *Journal of the Royal United Service Institution* 75 (November 1930): 665–675.

SECONDARY MATERIAL

UNPUBLISHED SOURCES

Hacker, Barton C. "The Military and the Machine: An Analysis of the Controversy over Mechanization–the British Army, 1919–1939." Ph.D. dissertation. University of Chicago, 1967.
Nenninger, Timothy K. "The Development of American Armor, 1917–1940." M.A. thesis. University of Wisconsin, 1968.

PUBLISHED SOURCES

General Histories
Aldcroft, Derek H. *The Inter-War Economy: Britain, 1919–1939*. London: B. T. Batsford, 1970.
Barnett, Corelli. *The Collapse of British Power*. New York: Morrow, 1972.
Butler, David, and Freeman, Jennie. *British Political Facts, 1900–1960*. New York: St. Martin's, 1960.
Cole, G. D. H. *A History of the Labour Party from 1914*. New York: A. M. Kelly, 1969.
Colvin, Ian. *The Chamberlain Cabinet*. New York: Taplinger Publishing Company, 1971.
Eyck, Erich. *A History of the Weimar Republic*. Translated by Harlow P. Hanson and Robert G. L. Waite. 2 vols. Cambridge, Mass.: Harvard University Press, 1963.
Louis, William. *British Strategy in the Far East, 1919–1939*. Oxford: The Clarendon Press, 1971.
Marwick, Arthur. *Britain in the Century of Total War: War, Peace and Social Change, 1900–1967*. London: The Bodley Head, 1968.
Mowat, Charles. *Britain between the Wars, 1918–1940*. Beacon Paperback ed. Boston: Beacon Press, 1971.
Peden, G. C. *British Rearmament and the Treasury, 1932–1939*. Edinburgh: Scottish Academic Press, 1979.
Seaman, L. C. B. *Life in Britain between the Wars*. London: B. T. Batsford, 1970.
Skidelsky, Robert. *Politicians and the Slump: The Labour Government of 1929–1931*. London: Macmillan, 1967.
Sontag, Raymond. *A Broken World*. New York: Harper & Row, 1971.
Taylor, A. J. P. *English History, 1914–1945*. Oxford Paperback ed. New York: Oxford University Press, 1970.
Tucker, W. R. *The Attitude of the British Labour Party to European and Collective Security Problems, 1920–1939*. Geneva: Imprimerie du Journal de Genève, 1950.
Walder, David. *The Chanak Affair*. New York: Macmillan, 1969.
Webster, F. A. M. *Our Great Public Schools: Their Traditions, Customs, and Games*. London: Ward, Lock, 1937.
Wolfers, Arnold. *Britain and France between Two Wars: Conflicting Strategies of Peace since Versailles*. New York: Harcourt, Brace, 1940.
Wright, Gordon. *France in Modern Times: 1760 to Present*. Chicago: Rand McNally, 1960.

Military Histories
Addington, Larry. *The Blitzkrieg Era and the German General Staff, 1865–1941*. New Brunswick, N.J.: Rutgers University Press, 1971.

Barclay, C. N. *On Their Shoulders: British Generalship in the Lean Years, 1939–1942.* London: Faber & Faber, 1964.

Barnett, Correlli. *Britain and Her Army, 1509–1970: A Military, Political and Social Survey.* New York: William Morrow, 1970.

_____. *The Desert Generals.* New York: Ballantine, 1972.

Biddulph, Robert. *Lord Cardwell at the War Office: A History of His Administration.* London: John Murray, 1904.

Bidwell, Shelford. *Gunners at War: A Tactical Study of the Royal Artillery in the Twentieth Century.* London: Arms & Armour Press, 1970.

_____, and Graham, Dominick. *Fire-Power: British Army Weapons and Theories of War, 1904–1945.* London: George Allen & Unwin, 1982.

Blumenson, Martin, and Stokesbury, James. *Masters of the Art of Command.* Boston: Houghton Mifflin, 1975.

Bond, Brian. *British Military Policy between the Two World Wars.* Oxford: Clarendon Press, 1980.

_____. *The Victorian Army and the Staff College, 1854–1914.* London: Eyre & Methven, 1972.

Bryant, Arthur. *Jackets of Green: A Study of the History, Philosophy, and Character of the Rifle Brigade.* London: Collins, 1972.

Collier, Basil. *A History of Air Power.* London: Weidenfeld & Nicolson, 1974.

Craig, Gordon. *The Politics of the Prussian Army.* Oxford Paperback ed. New York: Oxford University Press, 1964.

Crow, Duncan, ed. *AFVs in Profile.* Vol. 4: *American AFVs of World War II.* New York: Doubleday, 1972.

_____, ed. *Armoured Fighting Vehicles of the World.* Vol. 1: *AFVs of World War One.* Windsor, Berkshire: Profile Publications, 1970.

Curtis, W. P. S. *A Short Account of 3rd Green Jackets, the Rifle Brigade.* 3d rev. ed. Aldershot: Gale & Polden, 1959.

Dennis, Peter. *Decision by Default: Peacetime Conscription and British Defence, 1919–1939.* Durham, N.C.: Duke University Press, 1972.

Doughty, Robert A. *The Seeds of Disaster: The Development of French Army Doctrine, 1919–1939.* Hamden, Conn.: Archon Books, 1985.

Dunlop, John K. *The Development of the British Army, 1899–1914.* London: Methuen, 1938.

Erickson, John. *The Soviet High Command, 1918–1941.* New York: St. Martin's, 1962.

Fortescue, John W. *A History of the British Army.* Vol. 13. London: Macmillan, 1930.

Gillie, Mildred. *Forging the Thunderbolt: A History of the Development of the Armored Force.* Harrisburg, Penn.: Military Service Publishing Company, 1947.

Godwin-Austen, A. R. *The Staff and the Staff College.* London: Constable, 1927.

Gordon, D. C. *The Dominions Partnership in Imperial Defence, 1870–1914.* Baltimore: Johns Hopkins University Press, 1965.

Great Britain, War Office. *Military Operations France and Belgium, 1914: Antwerp, La Bassee, Armentières, Messines, and Ypres October–November 1914.* London: Macmillan, 1925.

_____. *Military Operations France and Belgium, 1914: Mons, the Retreat to the Seine, the Marne, and the Aisne August–October 1914.* London: Macmillan, 1922.

_____. *Military Operations France and Belgium, 1915: Battles of Aubers Ridge, Festubert, and Loos.* London: Macmillan, 1928.

_____. *Military Operations France and Belgium, 1917: The Battle of Cambrai.* London: H.M.S.O., 1948.

————. *Military Operations France and Belgium, 1917: The German Retreat to the Hindenburg Line and the Battle of Arras.* London: Macmillan, 1940.

————. *Military Operations France and Belgium, 1918: 8th August–26th September, the Franco-British Offensive.* London: H.M.S.O., 1947.

Gwynn, Charles. *Imperial Policing.* 2d ed. London: Macmillan, 1939.

Hamer, W. S. *The British Army: Civil-Military Relations, 1885–1905.* Oxford: The Clarendon Press, 1970.

Higham, Robin. *Armed Forces in Peacetime: Britain, 1918–1940, a Case Study.* London: G. T. Foulis, 1962.

————. *The Military Intellectuals in Britain, 1918–1939.* New Brunswick, N.J.: Rutgers University Press, 1966.

Howard, Michael. *The Continental Commitment: The Dilemma of British Defence Policy in the Era of the Two World Wars.* London: Maurice Temple Smith, 1972.

Hughes, Judith. *To the Maginot Line: The Politics of French Military Preparation in the 1920s.* Cambridge, Mass.: Harvard University Press, 1971.

Kirby, S. W. *Singapore: The Chain of Disaster.* London: Cassell, 1971.

Kolkowicz, Raymond. *The Soviet Army and the Communist Party: Institutions in Conflict.* Santa Monica, Calif.: The Rand Corporation, 1966.

Larson, Robert H. *The British Army and the Theory of Armored Warfare, 1918–1940.* Newark, N.J.: University of Delaware Press, 1984.

Liddell Hart, B. H. *History of the First World War.* London: Cassell, 1970.

————. *History of the Second World War.* London: Cassell, 1970.

————. *The Other Side of the Hill.* Rev. ed. London: Cassell, 1951.

————. *The Tanks: The History of the Royal Tank Regiment and Its Predecessors Heavy Branch Machine-Gun Corps, Tank Corps and Royal Tank Corps, 1914–1945.* 2 vols. New York: Praeger, 1959.

Lupfer, Timothy T. *The Dynamics of Doctrine: The Changes in German Tactical Doctrine during the First World War.* Fort Leavenworth, Kans.: U.S. Army Command and General Staff College, 1981.

Luvaas, Jay. *The Education of an Army: British Military Thought, 1815–1940.* Chicago: University of Chicago Press, 1964.

Mackintosh, Malcolm. *Juggernaut: A History of the Soviet Armed Forces.* New York: Macmillan, 1967.

Macksey, Kenneth. *Panzer Division.* New York: Ballantine, 1968.

————. *The Tank Pioneers.* London: Janes, 1981.

————. *Tank Warfare: A History of Tanks in Battle.* New York: Stein & Day, 1972.

Matloff, Maurice, ed. *American Military History.* Washington, D.C.: Office of the Chief of Military History, Department of the Army, 1969.

Miksche, F. O. *Attack: A Study of Blitzkrieg Tactics.* New York: Random House, 1942; reprint ed., Carlisle Barracks, Penn.: U.S. Army War College, 1983.

Nalder, R. F. H. *The Royal Corps of Signals: A History of Its Antecedents and Development (circa 1800–1955).* London: Royal Signals Institution, 1958.

Ogorkiewicz, Richard M. *Armor: A History of Mechanized Forces.* New York: Praeger, 1960.

Postan, M. M. *British War Production.* London: H. M. S. O., 1952.

Royal Armoured Corps Tank Museum. *The Inter War Period, 1919–1939.* Bovington, Dorset: Royal Armoured Corps Centre, 1970.

Sixsmith, E. K. G. *British Generalship in the Twentieth Century.* London: Arms & Armour Press, 1970.

Smyth, John. *Sandhurst.* London: Weidenfeld & Nicholson, 1961.

Watt, D. C. *Too Serious Business: European Armed Forces and the Approach to the*

Second World War. Berkeley, Calif.: University of California Press, 1975.

Wavell, A. P. Foreword to *The Black Watch and the King's Enemies,* by Bernard E. Fergusson. London: Collins, 1950.

White, Brian T. *German Tanks and Armored Vehicles.* New York: Arco Publishing Company, 1968.

Williamson, Samuel R. *The Politics of Grand Strategy: Britain and France Prepare for War, 1904–1914.* Cambridge, Mass.: Harvard University Press, 1969.

Winterbotham, F. W. *The Ultra Secret.* New York: Harper & Row, 1974.

Woolcombe, Robert. *The First Tank Battle: Cambrai, 1917.* London: Arthur Barker, 1967.

General Biographies

Bonham-Carter, Victor. *In a Liberal Tradition: A Social Biography, 1700–1950.* London: Constable, 1960.

Feiling, Keith. *The Life of Neville Chamberlain.* London: Macmillan, 1946.

Maurice, Frederick. *Haldane: The Life of Viscount Haldane of Cloan.* 2 vols. London: Faber & Faber, 1937–1939.

Minney, R. J. *The Private Papers of Hore-Belisha.* London: Collins, 1960.

Roskill, Stephen W. *Hankey: Man of Secrets.* 3 vols. London: Collins, 1970–1974.

Military Biographies

Bond, Brian. *Liddell Hart: A Study of His Military Thought.* New Brunswick, N.J.: Rutgers University Press, 1977.

Collins, R. J. *Lord Wavell (1883–1914): A Military Biography.* London: Hodder & Stoughton, 1948.

Colville, J. R. *Man of Valour: Field Marshal Lord Gort, V.C.* London: Collins, 1972.

Connell, John. *Auchinleck: A Biography of Field-Marshal Sir Claude Auchinleck.* London: Cassell, 1959.

———. *Wavell: Scholar and Soldier.* London: Collins, 1964.

Evans, Geoffrey. *Slim as Military Commander.* London: B. T. Batsford, 1969.

Fergusson, Bernard E. *Wavell: Portrait of a Soldier.* London: Collins, 1961.

Hamilton, Nigel. *Monty: The Making of a General, 1887–1942.* New York: McGraw-Hill, 1981.

Harington, Charles. *Plumer of Messines.* London: John Murray, 1935.

Jackson, W. G. F. *Alexander of Tunis as Military Commander.* London: B. T. Batsford, 1971.

Macksey, Kenneth. *Armoured Crusader: A Biography of Major-General Sir Percy Hobart.* London: Hutchinson, 1968.

———. *Guderian: Creator of the Blitzkrieg.* New York: Stein & Day, 1976.

Maurice, Frederick. *The Life of General Lord Rawlinson of Trent.* London: Cassell, 1928.

Montgomery, Brian. *A Field-Marshal in the Family.* London: Constable, 1973.

Morehead, Alan. *Montgomery: A Biography.* London: Hamilton, 1946.

Terraine, John. *Douglas Haig: The Educated Soldier.* London: Hutchinson, 1963.

Thornton, L. H., and Fraser, Pamela. *The Congreves Father and Son: General Sir Walter Norris Congreve, V.C., Bt.-Major William La Toche Congreve, V.C.* London: John Murray, 1930.

Trythall, Anthony J. *"Boney" Fuller: The Intellectual General.* London: Cassell, 1977.

Biographical Reference

Audax. *Men in Our Time.* New York: R. M. McBride, 1940.

Burke's Landed Gentry. 8th ed. 2 vols. London: Burke's Peerage, Ltd., 1894.

Burke's Landed Gentry. 18th ed. 3 vols. London: Burke's Peerage, Ltd., 1965–1972.
Dictionary of National Biography.
Times (London) Obituaries.
Who's Who.
Who Was Who.

Articles, Essays, Lectures, and Correspondence

Beaufre, André. "Liddell Hart and the French Army, 1919–1939." In *The Theory and Practice of War,* edited by Michael Howard. New York: Praeger, 1965.

Blake, Robert. "Great Britain: From Crimea to the First World War." In *Soldiers and Governments: Nine Studies in Civil-Military Relations,* edited by Michael Howard. London: Eyre & Spottiswoode, 1957.

Bond, Brian. "The Effects of the Cardwell Reforms on Army Organization, 1878–1904." *Journal of the Royal United Service Institution* 105 (November 1960): 515–524.

———. "Prelude to the Cardwell Reforms, 1856–1868." *Journal of the Royal United Services Institute for Defense Studies* 106 (May 1961): 229–236.

———. "The Retirement of the Duke of Cambridge." *Journal of the Royal United Service Institution* 106 (November 1961): 544–553.

———, and Alexander, Martin. "Liddell Hart and de Gaulle: The Doctrines of Limited Liability and Mobile Defense." In *Makers of Modern Strategy from Machiavelli to the Nuclear Age,* edited by Peter Paret. Princeton, N.J.: Princeton University Press, 1986.

Carver, Michael. Review of *Jackets of Green,* by Arthur Bryant. *Journal of the Royal United Service Institute for Defense Studies* 118 (March 1973): 92–93.

Festing, Francis; Blockley, Nigell; Fulford, "Tony"; and Brush, "Peter." [F. W. F., N. R. B., F. E. A. F., E. J. A. H. B.] "The Late General Sir John Burnett-Stuart." *Rifle Brigade Chronicle* (1958): 67–70.

Gooch, John. "The Creation of the British General Staff, 1904–1914." *Journal of the Royal United Services Institute for Defense Studies* 116 (June 1971): 50–53.

Hallgarten, George W. "General Hans von Seeckt and Russia, 1920–1922." *Journal of Modern History* 21 (March 1949): 28–34.

Holley, I. B., Jr. "The Doctrinal Process: Some Suggested Steps." *Military Review* 59 (April 1979): 2–13.

Howard, Michael. "The Armed Forces." *The New Cambridge Modern History.* Vol. 12: *Material Progress and World-Wide Problems, 1870–1898.* Cambridge: Cambridge University Press, 1962.

———. "The Liddell Hart Memoirs." *Journal of the Royal United Services Institute for Defence Studies* III (February 1966): 58–61.

———. "Lord Haldane and the Territorial Army." In *Studies in War and Peace,* edited by Michael Howard. New York: The Viking Press, 1971.

———. "Military Science in an Age of Peace." *Journal of the Royal United Service Institute for Defence Studies* 119 (March 1974): 3–9.

Katzenbach, Edward L. "The Horse Cavalry in the Twentieth Century: A Study in Policy Response." *Public Policy* 8 (1958): 120–149.

Liddell Hart, B. H. "Armies." *The New Cambridge Modern History.* Vol. 11: *The Zenith of European Power, 1830–1870.* Cambridge: Cambridge University Press, 1960.

Lukowitz, David C. "British Pacifism and Appeasement: The Peace Pledge Union." *Journal of Contemporary History* 9 (January 1974): 115–127.

Ogorkiewicz, Richard. "Soviet Tanks." In *The Red Army,* edited by B. H. Liddell Hart. Gloucester, Mass.: Harcourt, Brace & World, 1968.

Paret, Peter. "Clausewitz and the Nineteenth Century." In *The Theory and Practice of War*, edited by Michael Howard. New York: Praeger, 1965.

———. *Innovation and Reform in Warfare: The Harmon Memorial Lectures in Military History*, no. 8. United States Air Force Academy, Colorado, 1966.

Pocock, Robert, producer. "Liddell Hart: The Captain Who Taught Generals." *The Listener* 88 (28 December 1972): 892–896.

Ropp, Theodore. "A Theorist in Power." Review of *The Memoirs of Captain Liddell Hart*, vol. 2, by B. H. Liddell Hart. *Air University Review* 18 (March–April 1967): 105–109.

Silverman, Peter. "The Ten Year Rule." *Journal of the Royal United Service Institution* 116 (March 1971): 42–44.

Sixsmith, E. K. G. Review of *The Education of an Army*, by Jay Luvaas. *Army Quarterly and Defence Journal* 90 (April 1965): 245–247.

Starry, Donn A. "To Change an Army." *Military Review* 63 (March 1983): 20–27.

Tucker, Albert V. "Army and Society in England, 1870–1900: A Reassessment of the Cardwell Reforms." *Journal of British Studies* 2 (May 1963): 110–141.

Tunstall, W. C. B. "Imperial Defence, 1874–1914." *The Cambridge History of the British Empire*. Vol. 3: *The Empire Commonwealth, 1870–1919*. Cambridge: Cambridge University Press, 1959.

Underhill, Garrett. "The Story of Soviet Armor." *Armored-Cavalry Journal* 53 (January–February 1949): 22–30.

Wass de Czege, Huba. "Preparing for War: Defining the Problem." Fort Leavenworth, Kans.: School of Advanced Military Studies, 1984.

Young, Robert J. "Preparations for Defeat: French War Doctrine in the Inter-War Period." *Journal of European Studies* 2 (1972): 155–172.

Zook, David H. "John Frederick Charles Fuller: Military Historian." *Military Affairs* 23 (Winter 1959–1960: 185–193.

INDEX